Taking care

Understanding and encouraging self-protective behavior

Edited by

NEIL D. WEINSTEIN

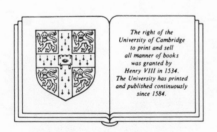

The right of the
University of Cambridge
to print and sell
all manner of books
was granted by
Henry VIII in 1534.
The University has printed
and published continuously
since 1584.

CAMBRIDGE UNIVERSITY PRESS

Cambridge
New York   New Rochelle
Melbourne   Sydney

Published by the Press Syndicate of the University of Cambridge
The Pitt Building, Trumpington Street, Cambridge CB2 1RP
32 East 57th Street, New York, NY 10022, USA
10 Stamford Road, Oakleigh, Melbourne 3166, Australia

First published 1987

Printed in the United States of America

Library of Congress Cataloging-in-Publication Data
Taking care.
Outgrowth of a conference held in June 1984 at Rutgers.
Includes index.
1. Self-protective behavior–Congresses. 2. Health
behavior–Congresses. I. Weinstein, Neil D.
[DNLM: 1. Health Promotion–congresses. 2. Primary
Prevention–congresses. WA 108 T136 1984]
BF697.5.S45T35   1987   155.9   87-6354

ISBN 0 521 32435 1

British Library Cataloging-in-Publication applied for

To Carol, Rachel, and Laura

Contents

Contributors

Professor James R. Averill, Department of Psychology, University of Massachusetts, Amherst, Massachusetts

Professor Paul D. Cleary, Department of Social Medicine and Health Policy, Harvard Medical School, Cambridge, Massachusetts

Dr. Alexander Cohen, Program in Applied Psychology and Ergonomics, National Institute for Occupational Safety and Health, Cincinnati, Ohio

Dr. Robert Crawford, Amanda Park, Washington

Dr. Baruch Fischhoff, Decision Research, a branch of Perceptronics, Inc., Eugene, Oregon

Professor Russell E. Glasgow, Department of Psychology, North Dakota State University, Fargo, North Dakota

Dr. Stephanie W. Greenberg, Department of Research and Statistics, Mountain States Telephone and Telegraph Co., Denver, Colorado

Dr. Fred Heinzelmann, Office of Crime Prevention and Criminal Justice Research, National Institute of Justice, Washington, D.C.

Dr. Sarah Lichtenstein, Decision Research, a branch of Perceptronics, Inc., Eugene, Oregon

Professor Alfred McAlister, Center for Health Promotion Research and Development, University of Texas, Austin, Texas

Dr. Kevin D. McCaul, Oregon Research Institute, Eugene, Oregon

Professor Dennis S. Mileti, Department of Sociology, Colorado State University, Fort Collins, Colorado

Dr. Leon S. Robertson, Nanlee Research, Branford, Connecticut

Professor Everett M. Rodgers, Annenbery School of Communications, University of Southern California, Los Angeles, California

Dr. Paul Slovic, Decision Research, a branch of Perceptronics, Inc., Eugene, Oregon

Dr. John H. Sorensen, Energy Division, Oak Ridge National Laboratory, Oak Ridge, Tennessee

Professor Neil D. Weinstein, Departments of Human Ecology and Psychology, Rutgers–The State University of New Jersey, New Brunswick, New Jersey

Acknowledgments

This book is an outgrowth of a conference on self-protective behavior held at Rutgers–The State University of New Jersey. I would like to thank Alexander Cohen for his encouragement during the planning of this conference and the National Institute for Occupational Safety and Health, which provided major funding. Additional funding from Cook College of Rutgers University and from the Rutgers Research Council is gratefully acknowledged. Finally, I wish to thank my wife Carol for her indispensable support and sound advice through all stages of this project.

Introduction: studying self-protective behavior

Neil D. Weinstein

Recent decades have seen an explosion of information about the hazards we face from natural and human-made sources and from our own life-styles. Some of these hazards, such as acid rain, toxic shock syndrome, autoimmune deficiency syndrome (AIDS), and nuclear winter, are new discoveries. Other potential dangers, such as pesticides in food, can be detected at lower levels than ever before. Masses of data and vivid media images impress us with the magnitude of the losses caused by hazards. On the individual level, risk factor analyses make us wonder whether we are the ones particularly susceptible to harm. At the same time, new counter-measures are available to reduce these risks, including the installation of smoke detectors and automobile air bags and the use of anti-cholesterol drugs.

The information we receive about the hazards in our environment is certainly a mixed blessing. Some problems, like the small amounts of carcinogens found in drinking water, are so difficult to avoid that warn-ings may just create feelings of frustration and futility. And individuals acting alone can do little to reduce the risk of nuclear war. Most prob-lems, however, are not so intractable. Hazard information often suggests ways of decreasing our vulnerability. The recognition of a link between asbestos and lung disease, for example, has led people to reduce the amount of asbestos in their environment and has diminished the risk of asbestos-caused illness.

The growing hazard awareness in our society has contributed to an unprecedented interest in prevention. Messages urging us to take pre-cautions in order to protect ourselves from harm have become more and more frequent. Nevertheless, people often fail to take this advice. They suffer illness, injury, financial loss, and emotional trauma that could have been avoided. It seems that well-intentioned suggestions seldom lead to the adoption of preventive behaviors. Even programs that are specifically designed to increase protective action frequently fall short of

1

their goals. The investment of money, time, and effort is no guarantee that a program will have any effect at all. The apparent explanation – a half-truth – is that people are not nearly so interested in self-protection as we thought.

The topic of this volume is "self-protective behavior," actions people can take to reduce their own vulnerability to harm or the vulnerability of groups to which they belong. "Preventive behavior" is another, equivalent term for the types of actions we shall consider.

Case studies in prevention[1]

The three case studies that follow illustrate some of the surprising outcomes of actual prevention programs.

Case I. Increasing the preparedness of urban flood plain residents (Waterstone, 1978)

Hazard problem. In spite of dams and other engineering works, annual losses to flooding in the United States continue to increase. Particularly in urban areas, where land costs are high, housing developments and other structures are often built in recognized flood plains. Unless a flood has occurred recently, people who live in these areas frequently have no idea that they are at risk and have neither floodproofed their homes nor made any plans for escaping from a serious flood.

Approach. The jurisdiction of the Denver Urban Drainage and Flood Control District includes many communities that have a high potential for flood damage but low flood awareness. Brochures were prepared to alert residents to the fact that they live near a creek subject to flooding. The brochures contained a map depicting the limits of the 100-year flood plain, a definition of the term "100-year flood plain," and the suggestion that residents buy flood insurance and plan an escape route. The brochures were mailed to all households in the flood plain and its fringe.

Evaluation. Residents were interviewed either before or after the brochures were distributed, and the responses of these two groups were compared. People who had received the brochures were more likely to know what the term "100-year flood plain" meant (the error rate was still

75%) and could more accurately describe where they lived in relation to the boundaries of the flood plain. Brochure recipients, however, were somewhat *less* likely to know that the creek near them had flooded in the past and were *less* concerned about the risk of flooding. Although more people who were sent the brochure claimed to have established an escape plan, there was no noticeable impact on the purchase of flood insurance. Most of these between-group differences were not statistically significant. Overall, the program seemed to have made very little difference. One-third of the people who had been sent the brochures could not even remember seeing them.

Case II. Monetary incentives for automobile seat belt use
(Robertson, 1984)

Hazard problem. The deaths and serious injuries caused by automobile accidents would be sharply reduced if seat belts were used more often. Nevertheless, educational campaigns to motivate seat belt use have been consistently unsuccessful. The public agrees that seat belts are worthwhile; they just do not use them. Lotteries and prizes can increase the number of seat belt wearers, but the effects of these incentives fade quickly when they are withdrawn.

Approach. The Nationwide Insurance Company offers an unusual financial incentive. Since 1963, this company has provided a 50% increase in compensation to policyholders injured in car crashes who were wearing seat belts at the time of their accident. Early in 1983, this extra payment was increased to 100% of the standard compensation, and an extra $10,000 was offered to heirs of anyone insured by the company who was killed while wearing a seat belt. The opportunity to receive these extra payments was automatic; it was not an extra-charge option. During 1983, Nationwide mailed notices announcing this new policy to every policyholder and placed advertisements in local media.

Evaluation. In early 1984, the seat belt use of 1,049 drivers was observed unobtrusively at sites in New Haven and Hartford, Connecticut. The insurers of the cars observed were determined from license plate numbers and state records. Just 9% of the Nationwide drivers were found to be using their seat belts, a figure no greater than that of drivers whose insurance companies did not offer monetary incentives.

Case III. Smoking prevention in junior high school (McAlister, Perry, Killen, Slinkard, & Maccoby, 1980)

Hazard problem. A major change in smoking behavior occurs between the seventh and ninth grades. In those years, many youngsters change from occasional, experimental smoking to habitual use. Because smoking is often so difficult to stop, it has become accepted that antismoking information must reach children early, before they have a chance to start.

Approach. One antismoking approach, the School Health Curriculum Project, is an intensive health education program that begins in the third grade and continues through the seventh grade. It uses sophisticated, active learning exercises to teach students about health risks and about the physiological effects of smoking. An apparatus with glass bottle lungs and sponges to collect and display the tar in cigarette smoke is an example of the materials used in this widely praised curriculum. Students enrolled in this program show a dramatic improvement on tests covering the effects of smoking, physiological mechanisms, and health statistics. The curriculum includes at least 30 hours related to smoking.

A second program flaunts conventional wisdom by waiting until the seventh grade to start. Furthermore, it teaches nothing about the effects of cigarette smoking on health. Its goals are to strengthen norms against smoking and to help students develop social skills for resisting pressures to start smoking. All sessions are led by a socially attractive high school student. Told "You're likely to become a smoker whether you want to or not," students learn to anticipate situations in which they might be encouraged to smoke, and they practice responses that allow them to decline without losing face. The program totals seven class hours over a two-year period.

Evaluation. The social skills program was introduced into the seventh grade of a school that, according to its administrators, had significant smoking and alcohol problems. In earlier grades, the students had received only a limited, traditional curriculum of health textbooks and occasional teacher lectures. The seventh-grade class of the comparison school had gone through the full School Health Curriculum Project. The two seventh-grade cohorts started at the same, very low level of smoking, but thereafter the percentages of students who smoked steadily diverged. By the end of the ninth grade, 20% of students in the health-information-oriented program were smokers; the proportion of smokers in the social-skills-oriented program was half as great, only 10%.

The multihazard approach to self-protective behavior

The case studies just described contain some unexpected results. In the flood plain and seat belt programs, for example, information and incentives that sponsors expected to be quite persuasive had little impact on their intended audiences. Yet such results are not unusual. To those who have broad experience with hazards, these outcomes are entirely predictable. The trouble is that such breadth of experience is rare, particularly among those who plan and carry out prevention programs. Experts who concentrate on only one aspect of a hazard – for example, its medical, geophysical, or engineering dimensions – are much more common. Furthermore, although all the fields included in this volume – health promotion and disease prevention, consumer safety, natural hazards preparedness, community crime prevention, and occupational safety and health – are quite active, each has developed on its own. Neither theoretical knowledge about what motivates and sustains protective behavior nor practical knowledge about the kinds of programs that are most effective is exchanged. Disciplinary boundaries and a focus on the hazard rather than on hazard behavior have kept the fields apart.

Current hazard categories – illness, crime, safety, and so on – reflect similarities in the physical or institutional characteristics of the problems: Health issues concern the human body; all crimes involve the violation of law; all natural hazards arise in the geophysical environment. This set of categories is reinforced by the organization of our governments. Responsibility for different hazards is assigned to different government agencies, and these are the primary source of funds for research and intervention programs. Nevertheless, the hazard categories are not homogeneous with respect to the behavioral issues they pose. The problem of encouraging people to protect themselves against burglary, for example, has more in common with the issue of reducing workshop injuries than it does with rape prevention.

The aim of this book is to bring together knowledge about a range of hazards so that we can better understand why people adopt or fail to adopt precautions. In a sense, this volume is an attempt to create a new field, the study of protective behavior. The chapters present major theories of protective behavior and critical analyses of the programs that attempt to increase protective actions. A basic assumption behind this book is that there is much to gain by a multihazard approach to the study of protective behavior because there are many similarities in the ways people respond to risk situations. Health researchers unaware of work on consumer safety and occupational health have been missing data and theoretical insights that could enlighten their own efforts. Those who develop programs to increase readiness for natural hazards could learn a great deal from community crime prevention activities.

It is unrealistic, however, to expect everyone involved in prevention activities or research to become an expert in all hazard areas. The task is too great. Most of the natural hazards and crime prevention reports, for example, are government documents or working papers and are very difficult to locate. Reviews, when they exist, are usually addressed to readers who are already experts in the field. The chapters in this volume have a different intent. Their primary goal is not to present new theories or describe new intervention programs but to make information about a wide range of hazards available to everyone interested in prevention.

In addition to facilitating the exchange of information across hazards, this book aims to stimulate a more sophisticated view of protective behavior than presently prevails. Even if we pool our knowledge about reactions to illness, crime, natural hazards, and safety issues, major gaps in our understanding remain. Consider, for example, the following questions:

- Can information about low-probability, high-cost risks be presented in a way that leads people to act?
- Are appeals to motives like status, well-being, and financial savings more effective than appeals to self-protection?
- How important are social pressure and imitation in the adoption of new precautions?
- Should more emphasis be placed on group and community approaches to hazard response and less effort be directed toward the delivery of risk information to individuals?
- Is there a consistent tendency to deny or underestimate risk?
- Under what conditions are educational approaches that are unlinked to fear arousal or to positive incentives worthwhile?
- Are people such prisoners of their past experience that they will not act until they themselves have become victims?
- Is individual behavior so difficult to change that we should stop trying to get people to protect themselves and instead attempt to reduce the riskiness of the environment in which they live and work?

These questions are fundamental for all hazard reduction efforts. Yet most prevention programs are not even aware that they ought to be considered. Even though the answers to these questions are not settled, the knowledge we do have is often sufficient to improve the prevention effort significantly.

.As we continue to study these questions, we are likely to find that some answers remain the same for all kinds of hazard settings. The answers to other questions, however, may be quite situation specific. If we can reach this point, we will have achieved a more sophisticated view of protective behavior than we had in the past. The range of topics in this volume provides an opportunity to search for empirical findings and theoretical principles that apply to a wide range of hazards. This breadth may also reveal that a conclusion presented as if it were a general principle of risk behavior actually has a very limited domain. The fact that a "principle" rests on specific hazard features will remain hidden until the principle is tested in a variety of situations.

Another aspect of our attempt to encourage a more sophisticated view of hazard response is the inclusion of chapters presenting five different theoretical perspectives on risk behavior. Although each point of view offers new and valuable insights, most hazard programs take no more than one or two of these perspectives into account.

Assigning responsibility for prevention

In asking Why do people take precautions? or How can we encourage people to act? we are limiting ourselves implicitly to hazard situations in which risk-reducing actions by individuals or groups of individuals are possible. This is not to say, however, that society should always expect individuals to take every possible precaution. A worker should not be expected to wear burdensome protective clothing when a better factory ventilation system would achieve the same result. Nor should a rape victim be blamed merely because she failed to stay indoors after dark. Deciding how much responsibility individuals bear for reducing their own risks and how much responsibility government or employers should take for maintaining a safe environment is a difficult and important task, but a task beyond the scope of this book.

Nevertheless, it is important to point out potential biases in the perspectives of professionals and officials that may create unrealistic expectations about the ease of change and shift too much responsibility for prevention onto individuals. If protective actions seem easy, inaction will tend to be viewed as laziness, denial, lack of interest in self-protection, or purposeful risk taking, and those who suffer harm will be blamed for their inaction.

A first source of bias concerns the types of preventive behaviors that become the subject of organized programs. These programs necessarily focus on actions people have *not* taken. Precautions that were adopted quickly and easily are no longer problems. Thus, without realizing it, we tend to center our attention on behaviors that have proved resistant to change. If hazard experts believe that certain precautions make good sense but the public has not accepted their recommendations, there may be unrecognized difficulties in adopting these measures. A focus on such a biased set of problems can result in excessively pessimistic conclusions about the public's willingness to change its behavior.

A second source of bias concerns the amount of risk that is acceptable. A public health official naturally wants to reduce illness as much as possible. Any illness morbidity is unacceptable if the amount could be reduced. Yet the risk at an individual level may already be very low. Given this low level of risk, an individual may consider it absurd to spend time or money to decrease the risk still further. Cost–benefit analyses are often performed when society must pay for risk reduction. The value of government flood insurance, for instance, has been subjected to intense scrutiny. Similarly, manufacturers do not hesitate to protest when they believe that the costs of government-mandated safety features outweigh the expected benefits. But when the action must be carried out by individual citizens, the costs in time, energy, and money are often overlooked. Although individuals rarely engage in a formal cost–benefit analysis, they often compare the costs and benefits in a more informal manner. From the individual's point of view, following a recommendation may not be worth the trouble.

A final factor that may lead to unrealistic expectations is the tendency of experts to focus on a single hazard. The American Heart Association, naturally, thinks mainly about heart disease; a flood control specialist is preoccupied with floods; fire safety officials are responsible for reducing fire losses. The public, however, must try to respond to all these hazards and to other life demands as well. An action that seems desirable when viewed in isolation may reflect an inappropriate use of resources when all hazards and potential precautions are considered together. Furthermore, a narrow focus can obscure the fact that risk-relevant behaviors often serve many functions. For example, maintaining good health is only one of a multitude of factors governing eating behavior. Behaviors that satisfy many different needs are likely to be resistant to change.

The preceding argument suggests that people sometimes have good reasons for not following the advice of experts. If hazard professionals are aware of the potential biases in their perspectives, they will be able to set behavioral goals that are more realistic, and individuals will not have to shoulder as much of the blame for failing to act.

Organization of the volume

This volume is divided into two main parts. The five chapters in the first section present theoretical perspectives that are particularly useful for analyzing hazard behavior. The second section contains reviews of hazard research and evaluations of programs designed to increase preventive behavior. Each of the fields of health promotion, crime prevention, and natural hazards is represented by several chapters, one attempting to answer the question Why do people take precautions against this hazard? and another (two more in the case of health promotion) examining the types of programs that have increased or failed to increase protective behavior. The topics of consumer safety and occupational safety and health are each represented by a single chapter. A concluding chapter returns to the eight questions posed earlier in this introduction and discusses recurring themes in the study of protective behavior.

Note

1 I am indebted to Fred Heinzelmann, Alfred McAlister, Leon Robertson, and John Sorensen for suggesting the case studies included in this chapter.

References

McAlister, A., Perry, C., Killen, J., Slinkard, L. A., & Maccoby, N. 1980. Pilot study of smoking, alcohol and drug abuse prevention. *American Journal of Public Health, 70:* 719–21.
Robertson, L. 1984. Insurance incentives and seat belt use. *American Journal of Public Health, 74:* 1157–8.
Waterstone, M. 1978. *Hazard mitigation behavior of urban flood plain residents.* Natural Hazards Research Working Paper No. 35. Institute of Behavioral Science, University of Colorado, Boulder.

Part I

Theoretical perspectives

There is no single starting point in prevention, for any significant hazard involves an impressive number of actors and issues. To reduce flood losses, for example, we must consider the meteorologist's accuracy in predicting storms, the engineer's ability to construct flood works, the city council's success in discouraging construction on the flood plain, the civil defense warning and rescue system, and the government's willingness to pay for all of these. We must not overlook the mass media's depiction of the flood threat, not just during an emergency but at all other times. Finally, we cannot ignore the flood plain occupants, those who could lose their lives and property, and must ask whether they have purchased insurance, floodproofed their homes, and devised evacuation plans or whether they even realize that the flood warnings apply to them.

Because the focus of this book is on protective behavior – actions individuals can take to reduce their vulnerability to harm – our focus here would be on the responses of the flood plain dwellers. Yet even with this restriction, there are many perspectives to consider. Each behavioral scientist tends to emphasize a different aspect of human nature: cognitive processes, emotions, social interaction, history, and others. No one of these perspectives is sufficient to explain how people react to hazards. The greater our awareness of these different facets of human nature, the better will be our understanding of the adaptive and sometimes maladaptive behaviors we see.

In the past, most research on prevention has been tied to specific hazards, and researchers have seldom been well-informed about the many different theoretical perspectives that could assist their own work. Links between specific hazards and specific social science disciplines narrow the range of ideas considered still further. For example, people involved in health promotion tend to come from public health, health education, or, more recently, psychology. Reactions to the threat of crime tend to be studied by individuals with backgrounds in criminal justice or sociology.

11

Most natural hazards researchers are geographers. Though geographers are unusually willing to look across disciplinary boundaries, they sometimes end up with a superficial understanding of behavioral concepts.

The chapters in this section of the book were chosen to introduce the reader to five perspectives on human behavior that are particularly relevant to hazard situations. The perspectives should be seen as complementing one another, not as competitors. Together they help us to recognize the variety of motives, cognitive processes, and cultural influences that combine to shape protective behavior. These perspectives were not developed to explain particular hazards. Instead, they concern aspects of human nature that are relevant to every situation in which people face threats to their well-being.

The first chapter, by Paul Slovic, Baruch Fischhoff, and Sarah Lichtenstein, represents a decision-making view of protective behavior. It emphasizes the cognitive processes involved as people weigh the costs and benefits of various courses of action. The authors describe how perceptions of risk are formed and why the risk perceptions of the public differ from those of experts. They also point out limitations in people's ability to process information that may affect protective behavior and suggest ways of presenting information that may minimize decision-making errors.

Alfred McAlister, in his presentation of social learning theory, brings several aspects of human nature to our attention. This model of individual behavior emphasizes social motivation, modeling, imitation, and self-reinforcement. McAlister describes the main features of social learning theory and then uses them to analyze three hazard-relevant behaviors: smoking, seat belt use, and voting. In each case he draws on the social learning perspective to suggest strategies that would enhance the effectiveness of prevention campaigns.

The idea that people take precautions because they are afraid of being harmed is an ancient and familiar one. But what do we mean by fear? Is it really fear that motivates us to act? How are emotions different from other cognitive processes that guide our actions? What is added to our understanding of protective behavior if we take the time to examine the nature of emotions? These are the kinds of difficult questions James Averill confronts in his chapter. He combines a discussion of the conceptual issues underlying the meaning of "fear," a much misused term, with specific suggestions for encouraging preventive action.

The first three chapters of this section adopt an individual level of analysis. But people are not isolated. They interact with one another. They receive information and recommendations from a variety of communications media. Not only must we understand how beliefs affect people's behavior; we must understand where these beliefs come from. Can they be changed? How can they be changed? A model of individual behavior might allow us to predict how a person will act in a particular situation, but what will happen next? Will the action be greeted with ridicule or applause? Is the precaution – a dietary change, for example – part of a vigorous cultural trend, a "movement" reinforced by ideologies of self-improvement, individual responsibility, and chemical suspicion. Or is the precaution inconsistent with prevailing wisdom? Are the personal attributes that lead an individual to act distributed at random throughout the population or are they confined to certain groups?

These questions imply that no model of individual human behavior, however complete, will suffice to tell us how to encourage appropriate risk-protective action. We need to know about the social and, sometimes, physical environment in which an action will occur. We have to understand how that action is related to deeper values held by the culture and whether these values are changing. We must know something about the structure of the society if we are to predict the rate of adoption and the groups within the society that are most and least likely to act.

A precaution is not adopted by society at random. Someone must be first and someone must be last, and the structure of the society and the channels of communication will govern the flow of this new idea. The spread of a new preventive measure is determined by a number of factors carefully outlined in the chapter by Everett Rogers, a pioneer in the study of the "diffusion of innovations." He explains why it is particularly difficult to promote "preventive innovations" and describes the strategies that have increased the acceptance of preventive measures – birth control, energy conservation, heart disease prevention – in both Western and Third World countries.

Robert Crawford, in the final theoretical chapter, confronts an even larger question, the reasons for the greatly increased interest in prevention in the United States. Crawford asks why our society – mainly the middle and upper classes, he suggests – has become preoccupied with hazards, self-protection, and self-improvement. His answer takes us into economics, history, politics, the environment, and deep-seated cultural values. He suggests that there is much more to prevention than reducing harm and that issues of individual versus public and corporate responsibility, the profit motive, diminished job opportunities, and competing conceptions of health all play important roles in this powerful social movement.

1 Behavioral decision theory perspectives on protective behavior

Paul Slovic, Baruch Fischhoff, and Sarah Lichtenstein

Introduction

What determines whether people will protect themselves against the severe losses that might arise from some rare hazard? What factors underlie the perception and acceptability of risks associated with technology? The answers to questions such as these are vital for understanding how people cope with threats from accidents, diseases, and natural hazards and for helping them manage their lives more effectively in the face of such risks. The role that the study of judgment and decision processes can play in providing answers to these questions will be explored in this chapter. Experiments concerning insurance decisions, risk perception, and evaluation of technological risks will be described, and the implications of this research for matters of public safety and health will be discussed.

Overview

This paper is divided into five sections. It begins with a brief description of the leading normative theory of protective decision making, which proposes that a rational decision maker acts so as to maximize expected utility.

The second section contrasts this idealized view with research on human intellectual limitations showing that people are, at best, "boundedly rational." In this section, we focus on the problems that occur when people seek to make sense of a probabilistic environment and attempt to resolve the value conflicts arising from decisions about beneficial but hazardous activities. We point out the difficulties people have in thinking intuitively about risk and uncertainty. We argue that people's perceptions of the world are sometimes distorted and that their preferences can be unstable, vague, or inconsistent. The results of this research run counter

Work on this chapter was supported in part by the National Science Foundation under Grant PRA-8419168.

14

to the traditional presumptions of knowledge and rationality that underlie economic approaches to decision making under risk.

The third section shows how some of the findings of the second section can be applied to two specific policy problems dealing with protective behavior: purchasing flood insurance and wearing seat belts. We argue that, to be effective, policies must be based on knowledge regarding the determinants of people's protective behavior. Empirical research can play an important role in providing such knowledge.

The fourth section describes research on the perception of risk. This research explores what people mean when they say that an activity or a technology is "risky." We find that many attributes other than death rates determine judgments of riskiness. Such attributes include catastrophic potential, risk to future generations, and dread. In contrast to the first section, the tone of this section is optimistic. We find that laypeople have strong, consistent, and reasonable views about risk. In fact, their model of what constitutes risk appears to be much richer than that held by most technical experts.

The final section is a discussion of the problems encountered in trying to inform people about risk. A common reaction of industry and government officials to evidence of ignorance, misinformation, or faulty thinking has been to call for educational programs to correct these shortcomings. Although we applaud such efforts and do believe that people can be educated, our emphasis is on the obstacles educational programs must overcome in order to be effective.

A rational model for making protective decisions

Decision theory provides a model, based on the maximization of expected utility, that serves as a normative or "rational" basis for making protective decisions. It is rational in the sense that it attempts to prescribe a course of action that is consistent with the decision maker's goals, expectations, and values.

In this model, decisions made in the face of risk are typically represented by a payoff matrix in which the rows correspond to alternative acts the decision maker can select and the columns correspond to possible states of nature. In the cells of the payoff matrix are a set of consequences contingent on the joint occurrence of a decision and a state of nature. A simple illustration for a traveler is given in Table 1.1.

Since it is impossible to make a decision that will turn out best in every eventuality, decision theorists view choice alternatives as gambles and try

Table 1.1. *Example of a payoff matrix*

		State of nature	
Alternative act		Sun (E_1)	Rain (E_2)
A_1	Carry umbrella	(+1) Stay dry carrying umbrella	(+1) Stay dry carrying umbrella
A_2	Leave umbrella	(+2) Dry and unburdened	(0) Wet and unburdened

to choose according to the "best bet." In 1738, Bernouli defined the notion of best bet as one that maximizes the quantity

$$EU(A) = \sum_{i=1}^{n} P(E_i)U(X_i)$$

where $EU(A)$ represents the expected utility of a course of action that has consequences $X_1, X_2, \ldots, X_n$ depending on events $E_1, E_2, \ldots, E_n$; $P(E_i)$ represents the probability of the ith outcome of that action; and $U(X_i)$ represents the subjective value or utility of that outcome. If we assume that the values in parentheses in the cells of Table 1.1 represent the traveler's utilities for the various consequences and if the probability of sun and rain are taken to be 0.6 and 0.4, respectively, we can compute the expected utility for each action as follows:

$$EU(A_1) = 0.6(+1) + 0.4(+1) = 1.0$$
$$EU(A_2) = 0.6(+2) + 0.4(0) = 1.2$$

In this situation, leaving the umbrella has greater expected utility than taking it along. The same form of analysis can be applied to computing the expected utility of heeding a flood warning, getting vaccinated against the flu, or buying insurance. Such analyses consider the probability of harm if the precaution is taken and if it is not, the amount of harm that would be experienced with and without taking the precaution, and the cost of the precaution.

A major advance in decision theory came when von Neumann and Morgenstern (1947) developed a formal justification for the expected utility criterion. They showed that, if an individual's preferences satisfied certain basic axioms of rational behavior, then his or her decisions could be described as the maximization of expected utility. Savage (1954) later generalized the theory to allow the $P(E_i)$ values to represent subjective or personal probabilities.

Maximization of expected utility commands respect as a guideline for wise behavior because it can be deduced from axiomatic principles that presumably would be accepted by any rational person. One such principle, that of *transitivity,* asserts that, if a decision maker prefers outcome A to outcome B and outcome B to outcome C, then he or she should prefer outcome A to outcome C. Any individuals who are deliberately and systematically intransitive can be turned into "money pumps." Let us assume that some people prefer A to B, B to C, and C to A. You can say to them, "I'll give you C. Now, for a penny, I'll take back C and give you B." Since they prefer B to C, they accept. Next you offer to replace B with A for another penny and again they accept. You complete the cycle by offering to replace A by C for another penny; the person accepts and is three cents poorer, back where he or she started, and ready for another round.

A second important tenet of rationality, known as the *extended sure-thing principle,* states that, if an outcome X_i is the same for two risky actions, then one should disregard the value of X_i in choosing between the two options. Another way to state this principle is that outcomes that are not affected by one's choice should not influence one's decision.

These two principles, combined with several others of technical importance, imply a rather powerful conclusion – namely, that the wise decision maker chooses that act with the highest expected utility. To do otherwise would violate one or more basic tenets of rationality.

Applied decision theory assumes that rational decision makers wish to select actions that are logically consistent with their basic preferences for outcomes and their feelings about the likelihoods of the events on which those outcomes depend. Given this assumption, the practical problem becomes one of listing the alternatives and scaling the subjective values of outcomes and their likelihoods so that subjective expected utility can be calculated for each alternative. Another problem in application arises from the fact that the range of theoretically possible alternatives is often quite large. In addition to carrying an umbrella, the risk-taking traveler in our earlier example may have the options of carrying a raincoat, getting a ride, waiting for the rain to stop, or many others. Likewise, the outcomes are considerably more complex than in our simple example. For example, the consequences of building a dam are multiple, involving effects on flood potential, hydroelectric power, recreation, and local ecology. Some specific approaches that have been developed for dealing with the additional complexities of any real decision situation are discussed in the decision theory literature (see, e.g., Keeney & Raiffa, 1976).

Confronting human limitations

Bounded rationality

The traditional view of human mental processes assumes that we are intellectually gifted creatures. Shakespeare referred to humans as "noble in reason, infinite in faculties . . . the beauty of the world, the paragon of animals." The rational model described above, with its presumption of well-informed, utility-maximizing decision makers, has echoed this theme. As economist Frank Knight put it, "We are so built that what seems reasonable to us is likely to be confirmed by experience or we could not live in the world at all" (1921, p. 227).

An important early critic of the economic model's descriptive adequacy was Herbert Simon, who drew on psychological research to challenge traditional assumptions about the motivation, omniscience, and computational capacities of decision makers. As an alternative to utility maximization, Simon (1957) introduced the notion of "bounded rationality," which asserts that cognitive limitations force people to construct simplified models of the world in order to cope with it. To predict behavior "we must understand the way in which this simplified model is constructed, and its construction will certainly be related to 'man's' psychological properties as a perceiving, thinking, and learning animal" (p. 198).

During the past twenty years, the skeleton theory of bounded rationality has been fleshed out. We have learned much about human cognitive limitations and their implications for behavior – particularly with regard to making decisions in the face of uncertainty and risk. Numerous studies show that people (including experts) have great difficulty in judging probabilities, making predictions, and otherwise attempting to cope with uncertainty. Frequently these difficulties can be traced to the use of judgmental heuristics, which serve as general strategies for simplifying complex tasks. In many circumstances these heuristics are valid, but in others they lead to large and persistent biases with serious implications for decision making. Much of this work has been summarized by Kahneman, Slovic, and Tversky (1982), Nisbett and Ross (1980), Slovic, Fischhoff, and Lichtenstein (1977), and Tversky and Kahneman (1974). In the remainder of this section we shall discuss two general manifestations of bounded rationality that are particularly relevant to the regulation of risk. These topics are judgmental biases and unstable preferences.

Judgmental biases in risk perception

If people are to respond optimally to the risks they face, they must have reasonably accurate perceptions of the magnitude of those risks. Yet the formal education of most laypeople rarely includes any serious instruction in the assessment of risks. Their subsequent learning is typically restricted to unsystematic personal experience and news media reports. It should not be surprising that people are often misinformed, rely on suboptimal risk assessment strategies, and fail to understand the limits of their own knowledge.

Availability. One inferential strategy that has special relevance to risk perception is the availability heuristic (Tversky & Kahneman, 1973). People using this heuristic judge an event to be likely or frequent if instances of it are easy to imagine or recall. Because frequently occurring events are generally easier to imagine or recall than are rare events, availability is often an appropriate cue. However, availability is also affected by factors unrelated to frequency of occurrence. For example, a recent disaster or a vivid film could seriously bias risk judgments.

Availability bias is illustrated by several studies in which people judged the frequency of 41 causes of death (Lichtenstein, Slovic, Fischhoff, Layman, & Combs, 1978). In one study, these people were first told the annual death toll in the United States for one cause (50,000 deaths from motor vehicle accidents) and then asked to estimate the frequency of the other 40 causes. Figure 1.1 compares the judged number of deaths per year with the number reported in public health statistics. If the frequency judgments equaled the statistical rates, all data points would fall on the identity line. Although more likely hazards generally evoked higher estimates, the points were scattered about a curved line that lay sometimes above and sometimes below the line representing accurate judgment. In general, rare causes of death were overestimated and common causes of death were underestimated. In addition to this general bias, sizable specific biases are evident in Figure 1.1. For example, accidents were judged to cause as many deaths as diseases, whereas diseases actually take about 16 times as many lives. Homicides were incorrectly judged to be more frequent than deaths from diabetes and stomach cancer. Pregnancies, births, and abortions were judged to take about as many lives as diabetes,

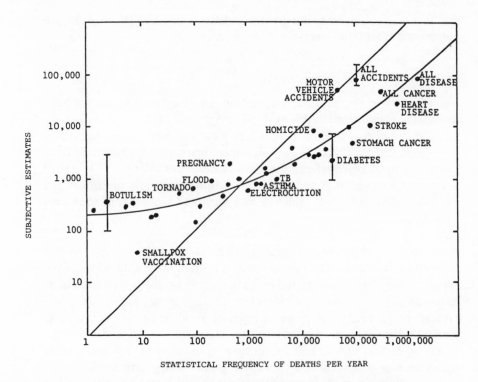

Figure 1.1. Relation between judged and statistical frequencies for 41 causes of death. *Source:* Lichtenstein, Slovic, Fischhoff, Layman, & Combs (1978).

though diabetes actually causes about 80 times more deaths. In keeping with availability considerations, causes of death that were overestimated (relative to the curved line) tended to be dramatic and sensational (accidents, natural disasters, fires, homicides), whereas underestimated causes tended to be unspectacular events that claim one victim at a time and are common in nonfatal form (e.g., smallpox vaccinations, stroke, diabetes, emphysema).

The availability heuristic highlights the vital role of experience as a determinant of perceived risk. If one's experiences are misleading, one's perceptions are likely to be inaccurate. Unfortunately, much of the information to which people are exposed provides a distorted picture of the world of hazards. One result of this is that people tend to view themselves as personally immune to certain kinds of hazards. Research shows that the great majority of individuals believe themselves to be better than average drivers (Svenson, 1981), more likely than average to live past the age of 80 years (Weinstein, 1980), less likely than average to be harmed

by products they use (Rethans, 1979), and so on. Although such perceptions are obviously unrealistic, the risks may seem very small from the
perspective of each individual's experience. Consider automobile driving:
Despite driving too fast, following other cars too closely, and so on, poor
drivers make trip after trip without mishap. This personal experience
demonstrates to them their exceptional skill and safety. Moreover, their
indirect experience via the news media shows that, when accidents happen, they happen to others. Given such misleading experiences, people
may feel quite justified in refusing to take protective actions such as
wearing seat belts (Slovic, Fischhoff, & Lichtenstein, 1978).

In some situations, failure to appreciate the limits of available data may
lull people into complacency. For example, we asked people to evaluate
the completeness of a fault tree showing the problems that could prevent
a car from starting when the ignition key was turned (Fischhoff, Slovic, &
Lichtenstein, 1978). The respondents' judgments of completeness were
about the same when they looked at the full tree as when they looked at a
tree in which half of the causes of starting failure were deleted. In keeping with the availability heuristic, what was out of sight was also out of
mind. The only antidote to availability-induced biases is to recognize the
limitations in the samples of information received from the world and
produced by one's own mind. Doing so requires a knowledge of the world
and of mental processes that few people can be expected to have. Even
scientists often have difficulty in identifying systematic biases in their
data.

Overconfidence. A particularly pernicious aspect of heuristics is that
people typically have too much confidence in judgments based on them.
In a follow-up of the study on causes of death, people were asked to
indicate the odds that they were correct in choosing the more frequent of
two lethal events (Fischhoff, Slovic, & Lichtenstein, 1977). Odds of
100 : 1 or greater were given often (25% of the time). However, about
one of every eight answers associated with such extreme confidence was
wrong (fewer than 1 in 100 would have been wrong had the odds been
appropriate). At odds of 10,000 : 1, people were wrong about 10% of the
time. The psychological basis for this unwarranted certainty seems to be
an insensitivity to the tenuousness of the assumptions on which one's
judgments are based. For example, extreme confidence in the incorrect
assertion that homicides are more frequent than suicides may occur because people fail to appreciate that the greater ease of recalling instances
of homicides is an imperfect basis for inference.

Overconfidence manifests in other ways as well. A typical task in estimating uncertain quantities such as failure rates is to set upper and lower bounds so that there is a certain fixed probability that the true value lies between them. Experiments with diverse groups of people making many different kinds of judgments have revealed that true values tend to lie outside the confidence boundaries much too often. Results with 98% bounds are typical. Rather than 2% of the true values falling outside such bounds, 20% to 50% usually do so (Lichtenstein, Fischhoff, & Phillips, 1982). Thus, people think that they can estimate uncertain quantities with much greater precision than they actually can.

Unfortunately, once experts are forced to go beyond their data and rely on judgment, they may be as prone to overconfidence as laypeople. Fischhoff, Slovic, and Lichtenstein (1978) repeated their fault-tree study with professional automobile mechanics (averaging about 15 years of experience) and found them to be about as insensitive as laypeople to deletions from the tree. Hynes and Vanmarcke (1976) asked seven "internationally known" geotechnical engineers to predict the height of an embankment that would cause a clay foundation to fail and to specify confidence bounds around this estimate that were wide enough to have a 50% chance of enclosing the true failure height. None of the bounds specified by those individuals actually enclosed the true failure height.

Unstable preferences: difficulties in evaluating risk

The process of evaluation is the heart of decision making. Evaluating the (good and bad) outcomes associated with hazardous activities might seem to be relatively straightforward. Certainly people know what they like and dislike. Research has shown, however, the assessment of values to be as troublesome as the assessment of facts. Evidence is mounting in support of the view that our values are often not clearly apparent, even to ourselves; that methods for measuring values are intrusive and biased; and that the structure of any decision problem is psychologically unstable, leading to inconsistencies in choice.

Labile values. When one is considering simple, familiar events with which people have direct experience, it may be reasonable to assume that they have well-articulated preferences. But that may not be so in the case of the novel, unfamiliar consequences potentially associated with outcomes of such events as surgery, automobile accidents, carbon dioxide–induced climatic changes, nuclear meltdowns, or genetic engineering. In these and other circumstances, our values may be incoherent, not sufficiently thought out (Fischhoff, Slovic, & Lichtenstein, 1980a,b). When we think about risk management policies, for example, we may be unfamiliar with the terms involved (e.g., social discount rates, minuscule probabilities, megadeaths). We may have contradictory values (e.g., a strong aversion to catastrophic losses of life but an awareness that we are no more moved by a plane crash with 500 fatalities than by one with 300). We may occupy different roles in life (parents, workers, children), each of which produces clear-cut but inconsistent values. We may vacillate between incompatible but strongly held positions (e.g., freedom of speech is inviolate, but it should be denied to authoritarian movements). We may not even know how to begin thinking about some issues (e.g., the appropriate trade-offs between the outcomes of surgery for cancer versus the very different outcomes from radiation therapy). Our views may change so much over time (say, as we near the hour of decision or of experiencing the consequences) that we are disoriented as to what we really think.

Competent decision analysts may tell us what primary, secondary, and tertiary consequences to expect, but not what these consequences really entail. To some extent we are all prisoners of our past experiences, unable to imagine drastic changes in our world, our health, or our relationships with others.

Unstable decision frames. In addition to the uncertainties that sometimes surround our values, our perceptions of the basic structure of a decision problem are also unstable. The acts or options available, the possible outcomes or consequences of those acts, and the contingencies or conditional probabilities relating outcomes to acts make up what Tversky and Kahneman (1981) have called the "decision frame." Much as changes in vantage point induce alternative perspectives on a visual scene, the same decision problem can be subject to many alternative frames (Figure 1.2). Which frame is adopted is determined in part by the external formulation of the problem and in part by the structure spontaneously imposed by the decision maker. Tversky and Kahneman have demonstrated that normatively inconsequential changes in the framing of decision problems significantly affect preferences. These effects are noteworthy because they are sizable (often complete reversals of preference), because they violate important consistency and coherence requirements of economic theories of choice, and because they influence not only behavior, but how the consequences of behavior are experienced.

Tversky and Kahneman (1981) have presented numerous illustrations of framing effects, one of which involves the following pair of problems, given to separate groups of respondents:

1. Problem 1. Imagine that the United States is preparing for the outbreak of an unusual Asian disease, which is expected to kill 600 people. Two

A civil defense committee in a large metropolitan area met
recently to discuss contingency plans in the event of various
emergencies. One emergency threat under discussion posed two
options, both involving some loss of life.

Option A: Carries with it a .5 probability of containing the
threat with a loss of 40 lives and a .5 probability of losing
60 lives. It is like taking the gamble:

.5 lose 40 lives
.5 lose 60 lives

Option B: Would result in the loss of 50 lives:

lose 50 lives

The options can be presented under three different frames:

I. This is a choice between a 50-50 gamble (lose 40 or lose
60 lives) and a sure thing (the loss of 50 lives).

II. Whatever is done at least 40 lives will be lost. This
is a choice between a gamble with a 50-50 chance of either losing
no additional lives or losing 20 additional lives (A) and the sure
loss of 10 additional lives (B).

III. Option B produces a loss of 50 lives. Taking Option A
would mean accepting a gamble with a .5 chance to save 10 lives
and a .5 chance to lose 10 additional lives.

Figure 1.2. Decision framing: three perspectives on a civil defense problem.
Source: Fischhoff (1983).

alternative programs to combat the disease have been proposed. Assume
that the consequences of the programs are as follows. If Program A is
adopted, 200 people will be saved. If Program B is adopted, there is ⅓
probability that 600 people will be saved and ⅔ probability that no
people will be saved. Which of the two programs would you favor?

2. Problem 2 (same cover story as Problem 1). If Program C is adopted,
400 people will die. If Program D is adopted, there is ⅓ probability that
no one will die and ⅔ probability that 600 people will die. Which of the
two programs would you favor?

The preference patterns tend to be quite different for the two problems. In a study of college students, 72% of the respondents chose Program A over Program B and 78% chose Program D over Program C.
Another study, surveying physicians, obtained very similar results. On
closer examination, we can see that the two problems are essentially
identical. The only difference between them is that the outcomes are
described by the number of lives saved in Problem 1 and the number of
lives lost in Problem 2.

One important class of framing effects deals with a phenomenon that Tversky and Kahneman (1981) have called "pseudocertainty." It involves altering the representations of protective actions so as to vary the apparent certainty with which they prevent harm. For example, an insurance policy that covers fire but not flood could be presented either as full protection against the specific risk of fire or as a reduction in the overall probability of property loss. Because outcomes that are merely probable are undervalued in comparison with outcomes that are obtained with certainty, Tversky and Kahneman hypothesized that this insurance policy should appear more attractive in the first context (pseudocertainty), which offers unconditional protection against a restricted set of problems. We have tested this conjecture in the context of one kind of protection: vaccination. Two forms of a "vaccination questionnaire" were created. Form I (probabilistic protection) described a disease expected to afflict 20% of the population and asked people whether they would volunteer to receive a vaccine that protects half of the people receiving it. According to Form II (pseudocertainty), there were two mutually exclusive and equiprobable strains of the disease, each likely to afflict 10% of the population; the vaccination was said to give complete protection against one strain and no protection against the other.

The participants in this study were college students, half of whom received each form. After reading the description, they rated the likelihood that they would get vaccinated in such a situation. Although both forms indicated that vaccination reduced one's overall risk from 20% to 10%, we expected that vaccination would be more attractive to those who received Form II (pseudocertainty) than to those who received Form I (probabilistic protection). The results confirmed this prediction: 57% of those who received Form II indicated they would get vaccinated compared with 40% of those who received Form I.

The pseudocertainty effect highlights the contrast between the reduction and the elimination of risk. As Tversky and Kahneman have indicated, this distinction is difficult to justify on any normative grounds. Moreover, manipulations of certainty would seem to have important implications for the design and description of other forms of protection (e.g., medical treatments, insurance, flood-proofing and earthquake-proofing activities).

Studies of protective behavior

In this section we shall describe studies of two kinds of protective behavior: insurance purchases and the use of seat belts. This research, which was designed to provide basic knowledge relevant to regulatory decisions, illustrates the complex interplay between cognitive limitations and public policy.

National Flood Insurance Program

Although few residents of flood and earthquake areas voluntarily insure themselves against the consequences of such disasters, many turn to the federal government for aid after suffering losses. Policy makers have argued that both the government and the property owners at risk would be better off financially under a federal insurance program. Such a program would shift the burden of disasters from the general taxpayer to individuals living in hazardous areas and would thus promote wiser decisions regarding the use of flood plains (Kunreuther et al., 1978).

Without a firm understanding of how people perceive and react to risks, however, there is no way of knowing what sort of disaster insurance programs would be most effective. For example, the National Flood Insurance Program took the seemingly reasonable step of lowering the cost of insurance in order to stimulate purchases. However, despite heavily subsidized rates, relatively few policies were bought (Kunreuther, 1974).

An integrated program of laboratory experiments and field surveys by Kunreuther et al. (1978) and Slovic, Fischhoff, Lichtenstein, Corrigan, and Combs (1977) was designed to determine the critical factors influencing the voluntary purchase of insurance against such natural hazards as floods and earthquakes. Analysis of the survey data revealed widespread ignorance and misinformation regarding the availability and terms of insurance and the probabilities of damage from a future disaster. The laboratory experiments showed that people preferred to insure against relatively high-probability, low-loss hazards and tended to reject insurance in situations where the probability of loss was low and the potential losses were high. These results suggest that people's natural predispositions run counter to economic theory (e.g., Friedman & Savage, 1948), which assumes that individuals are risk averse and should desire a mechanism that protects them from rare catastrophic losses.

When asked about their insurance decisions, the subjects in both the laboratory and survey studies indicated a disinclination to worry about low-probability hazards. Such a strategy is understandable. Given the limitations on their time, energy, and attentional capacities, people have a finite reservoir of concern. Unless they ignored many low-probability threats, they would become so burdened that productive life would be impossible. Another insight gleaned from the experiments and the survey is that people think of insurance as an investment. Receiving payment on a claim seems to be viewed as a return on the premium – one that is received more often with more probable losses. The popularity of low-deductible insurance plans (Fuchs, 1976; Pashigian, Schkade, & Menefee, 1966) provides confirmation from outside the laboratory that people prefer to insure against relatively probable events with small consequences.

One surprising survey result was that homeowners' lack of interest in disaster insurance did not seem to be due to the expectation that the federal government would bail them out in an emergency. The majority of individuals interviewed said they anticipated no aid at all from the government in the event of a disaster. Most appeared not to have considered how they would recover from flood or earthquake damage.

If insurance is to be marketed on a voluntary basis, consumers' attitudes and information-processing limitations must be taken into account. Policy makers and insurance providers must find ways to communicate the risks and arouse concern for the hazards. One method found to work in the laboratory experiments is to increase the perceived probability of disaster by lengthening the individual's time horizon. For example, considering the risk of experiencing a 100-year flood at least once during a 25-year period, instead of considering the risk in 1 year, raises the probability from .01 to .22 and may thus cast flood insurance in a more favorable light. Another step would be to give insurance agents an active role in educating homeowners about the proper use of insurance as a protective mechanism and providing information about the availability of insurance, rate schedules, deductible values, and so on. If such actions were not effective, it might be necessary to institute some form of mandatory coverage. Recognizing the difficulty of inducing voluntary coverage, the National Flood Insurance Program now requires insurance as a condition for obtaining federal funds for building in flood-prone areas.

Seat belts

Another form of protection that people do not often make use of is the automobile seat belt. Promotional efforts to get motorists to wear seat belts have failed dismally (Robertson, 1976). Despite expensive advertising campaigns and buzzer systems, fewer than 20% of motorists "buckled up for safety" prior to laws requiring seat-belt use. Policy makers have criticized the public for failing to appreciate the risks of driving and the benefits of using seat belts. However, results of risk perception research provide an alternative perspective that seems at once more respectful of drivers' reasoning and more likely to increase seat belt use.

As noted above, people's insurance decisions reflect a disinclination to worry about very small probabilities. Reluctance to wear seat belts might therefore be due to the extremely small probability of incurring a fatal accident on a single automobile trip. Because a fatal accident occurs only about once in every 3.5 million person-trips and a disabling injury only once in about every 100,000 person-trips, refusing to buckle up one's seat belt may seem quite reasonable. It may seem less reasonable, however, if one frames the problem within a multiple-trip perspective. This is, of course, the perspective of traffic safety planners, who see the thousands of lives that might be saved annually if belts were used regularly. For the individual, during 50 years of auto travel (about 40,000 trips), the probability of being killed is .01 and the probability of experiencing at least one disabling injury is .33. In laboratory experiments, we found that people induced to consider this lifetime perspective responded more favorably toward the use of seat belts (and air bags) than did people asked to consider a trip-by-trip perspective (Slovic, Fischhoff, & Lichtenstein, 1978). More recent studies suggest that television and radio messages based on this lifetime-cumulative-risk theme can increase actual seat belt use (Schwalm & Slovic, 1982).

Understanding perceived risk

If it is to aid hazard management, a theory of perceived risk must explain people's extreme aversion to some hazards, their indifference to others, and the discrepancies between these reactions and experts' recommendations. Why, for example, do some people react vigorously to the location of a liquid natural gas terminal in their vicinity, despite the assurances of experts that it is safe? Why, in contrast, do people living below great dams generally show little concern for experts' warnings? Over the past few years researchers have been attempting to answer such questions as these by examining the opinions that people express when they are asked, in a variety of ways, to characterize and evaluate hazardous activities and technologies. The goals of this descriptive research are (a) to develop a taxonomy of risk characteristics that can be used to understand and predict societal responses to hazards and (b) to develop methods for assessing public opinions about risk in a way that could be useful for making policy decisions.

The psychometric paradigm

Psychometric scaling methods and multivariate analysis techniques have been used to produce quantitative representations of risk attitudes and perceptions (Brown & Green, 1980; Fischhoff, Slovic, Lichtenstein, Read, & Combs, 1978; Gardner et al., 1982; Green, 1980a,b; Green & Brown, 1980; Johnson & Tversky, 1984; Renn, 1981; Slovic, Fischhoff, & Lichtenstein, 1979, 1980a, 1985; Vlek & Stallen, 1981; von Winterfeldt, John, & Borcherding, 1981). Researchers employing the psychometric paradigm have typically asked people to judge the current and desired riskiness (or safety) of diverse sets of hazardous activities, substances, and technologies and to indicate their desires for risk reduction and regulation of these hazards. These global judgments have then been related to judgments about the following:

1. The hazard's status in relation to characteristics that have been hypothesized to account for risk perceptions and attitudes (e.g., voluntariness, dread, knowledge, controllability)
2. The benefits each hazardous activity provides to society
3. The number of deaths caused by the hazard in an average year
4. The number of deaths caused by the hazard in a disastrous year
5. The perceived seriousness of a death from various causes

Among the generalizations that have been drawn from the results of psychometric studies are the following:

1. Perceived risk is quantifiable and predictable. Psychometric techniques seem well suited for identifying similarities and differences among groups with regard to risk perceptions and attitudes (see, e.g., Table 1.2).
2. "Risk" means different things to different people. When experts judge risk, their responses correlate highly with technical estimates of annual fatalities (Figure 1.3, top). Laypeople can assess annual fatalities if they are asked to (and produce estimates somewhat similar to the technical estimates). However, their judgments of risk are sensitive to other factors as well (e.g., catastrophic potential, threat to future generations) and, as a result, are not closely related to their own (or experts') estimates of annual fatalities (Figure 1.3, bottom).
3. Even when groups disagree about the overall riskiness of specific hazards, they show remarkable agreement when rating those hazards on such characteristics of risk as knowledge, controllability, dread, and catastrophic potential.
4. Many of these risk characteristics are highly correlated with one another across a wide domain of hazards. For example, voluntary hazards tend also to be controllable and well known; hazards that threaten future generations tend also to be seen as having catastrophic potential. Analysis of these interrelations shows that the broader domain of characteristics can be condensed to three higher-order characteristics or factors. These factors reflect the degree to which a risk is understood, the degree to which it evokes a feeling of dread, and the number of people exposed to the risk (Figure 1.4). This factor structure has been found to be similar across groups of laypeople and experts judging large and diverse sets of hazards. Making a set of hazards more specific (e.g., partitioning nuclear power into radioactive waste transport, uranium mining, nuclear

Table 1.2. *Ordering of perceived risk for 30 activities and technologies*

Activity or technology	League of Women Voters	College students	Active club members	Experts
Nuclear power	1	1	8	20
Motor vehicles	2	5	3	1
Handguns	3	2	1	4
Smoking	4	3	4	2
Motorcycles	5	6	2	6
Alcoholic beverages	6	7	5	3
General (private) aviation	7	15	11	12
Police work	8	8	7	17
Pesticides	9	4	15	8
Surgery	10	11	9	5
Firefighting	11	10	6	18
Large construction	12	14	13	13
Hunting	13	18	10	23
Spray cans	14	13	23	26
Mountain climbing	15	22	12	29
Bicycles	16	24	14	15
Commercial aviation	17	16	18	16
Electric power (nonnuclear)	18	19	19	9
Swimming	19	30	17	10
Contraceptives	20	9	22	11
Skiing	21	25	16	30
X rays	22	17	24	7
High School and college football	23	26	21	27
Railroads	24	23	20	19
Food preservatives	25	12	28	14
Food coloring	26	20	30	21
Power mowers	27	28	25	28
Prescription antibiotics	28	21	26	24
Home appliances	29	27	27	22
Vaccinations	30	29	29	25

Note: The ordering is based on the geometric mean risk ratings within each group. Rank 1 represents the most risky activity or technology.
Source: Slovic, Fischhoff, & Lichtenstein (1981).

reactor accidents, etc.) appears to have little effect on the factor structure or its relation to risk perceptions (Slovic, Fischhoff, & Lichtenstein, 1985).

5. Many of the characteristics, particularly those associated with the factor Dread Risk, correlate highly with laypeople's perceptions of risk. The higher an activity's score on the Dread Risk factor, the higher its perceived risk, the more people want its risks reduced, and the more they want to see strict regulation employed to achieve the desired reductions in risk (Figure 1.5). The factor Unknown Risk tends not to correlate

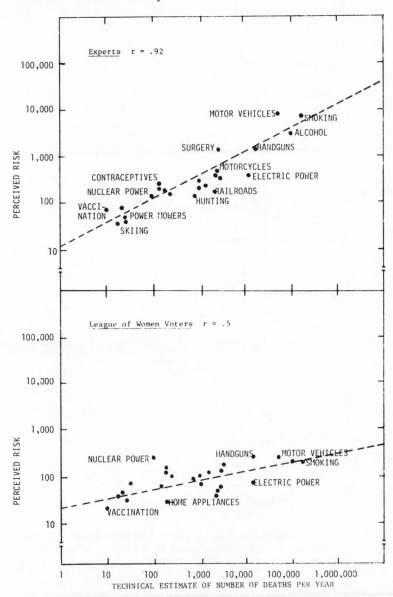

Figure 1.3. Judgments of perceived risk by experts (top) and laypeople (bottom) plotted against the best technical estimates of annual fatalities for 25 technologies and activities. Each point represents the average responses of the participants. The dashed lines are the straight lines that best fit the points. The experts' risk judgments are seen to be more closely associated with annual fatality rates than are the lay judgments. *Source:* Slovic, Fischhoff, & Lichtenstein (1979).

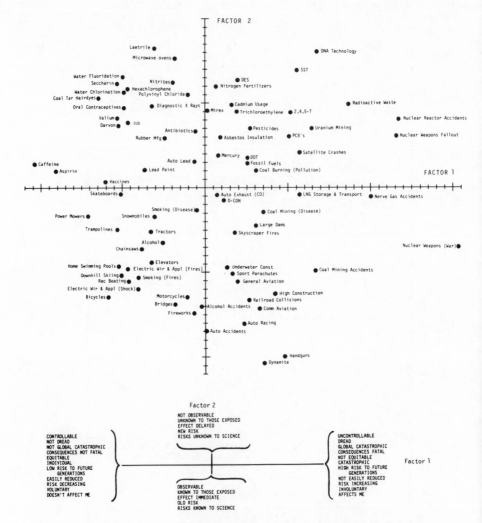

Figure 1.4. Hazard locations on Factors 1 and 2 of the three-dimensional structure derived from the interrelationships among 18 risk characteristics. Factor 3
(not shown) reflects the number of people exposed to the hazard and the degree
of one's personal exposure. The diagram beneath the figure illustrates the characteristics that comprise the two factors. *Source:* Slovic, Fischhoff, & Lichtenstein
(1985).

highly with risk perception. Factor 3, Exposure, is moderately related to lay
perceptions of risk. In contrast, experts' perceptions of risk are *not* related
to any of these risk characteristics or factors derived from them. As noted
above, experts' risk perceptions seem determined by annual fatalities.

6.   The perceived seriousness of an accident is systematically related to its

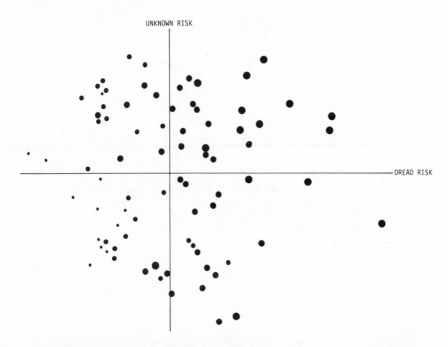

Figure 1.5. Attitudes toward regulation of the hazards in Figure 1.4. The larger the point, the greater the desire for strict regulation to reduce risk. *Source:* Slovic, Lichtenstein, & Fischhoff (in press).

"signal potential," the degree to which that accident serves as a warning signal, providing information about the probability that similar or more destructive mishaps might occur. Signal potential and perceived seriousness are systematically related to both Dread Risk and Unknown Risk factors (Figure 1.6).

7. In agreement with hypotheses originally put forth by Starr (1969), people's acceptance of risk appears to be related to their perception of benefit. All other things being equal, greater perceived benefit is associated with a greater acceptance of risk. Moreover, acceptability depends on various qualitative aspects of risk, including its voluntariness, familiarity, catastrophic potential, and perceived uncertainty. In sharp contrast to Starr's views, however, our respondents did not believe that society has managed hazards so well that optimal trade-offs among these characteristics have already been achieved.

Implications of risk perception research

In the results of the psychometric studies, we have the beginnings of a perceptual or psychological classification system for hazards. Ultimately, we need not only a better psychological taxonomy but one that also

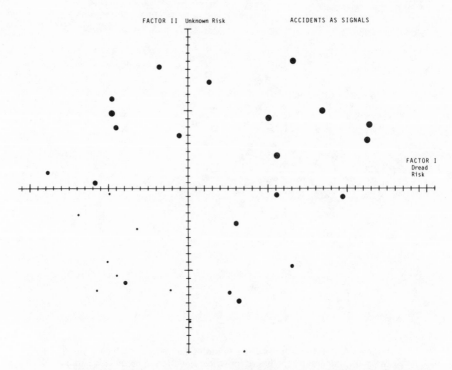

Figure 1.6. Relation between signal potential and risk characterization for 30 hazards in Figure 1.4. The larger the point, the greater the degree to which an accident involving the hazard was judged to "serve as a warning signal for society, providing new information about the probability that similar or even more destructive mishaps might occur within this type of activity." *Source:* Slovic, Lichtenstein, & Fischhoff (1984).

reflects physical, biological, and social or managerial elements of hazards. Such a taxonomy would be a potent device for understanding and guiding social regulation of risk. We are far from achieving this goal, though a start toward an expanded taxonomy has been made (Hohenemser, Kates, & Slovic, 1983). For the present, more modest insights and applications must suffice.

Forecasting public response. Despite the lack of a complete understanding of public attitudes and perceptions, we have attempted to use the results from risk perception studies to explain and forecast reactions to specific technologies. Nuclear power has been the principal object of such analysis because of the obvious role of social factors governing this important technology. Weinberg (1976), reflecting on the future of nuclear power, observed that "the public perception and acceptance of nuclear energy . . . has emerged as the most critical question." The reasonableness of these perceptions has been the topic of an extensive public debate, filled with charges and countercharges. For example, one industry source has argued that public reaction to Three Mile Island has cost "as much as $500 billion . . . and is one measure of the price being paid as a consequence of fear arising out of an accident that according to the most thorough estimates may not have physiologically hurt even one member of the public" ("Assessment," 1980, p. 30).

Risk perception research offers some promise of clarifying the concerns of opponents of nuclear power (Fischhoff, Slovic, & Lichtenstein, 1983; Slovic, Fischhoff, & Lichtenstein, 1980c; Slovic, Lichtenstein, & Fischhoff, 1979). In particular, psychometric studies show that these people judge its benefits to be quite low and its risks to be unacceptably great. On the benefit side, most opponents do not see nuclear power as a vital link in meeting basic energy needs; rather, they view it as a supplement to other sources of energy that are themselves adequate. On the risk side, nuclear power occupies a unique position in the factor space, reflecting people's views that its risks are unknown, dread, uncontrollable, inequitable, catastrophic, and likely to affect future generations (see Figure 1.4). Opponents recognize that few people have died to date as a result of nuclear power. However, they have great concern over the potential for catastrophic accidents. Nuclear hazards are particularly memorable and imaginable, yet hardly amenable to empirical verification. These special qualities blur the distinction between the possible and the probable and produce an immense gap between the views of most technical experts and those of a significant portion of the public. Because much of the opposition to nuclear power can be understood in terms of basic psychological principles of perception and cognition or traced to deep-seated differences in values, this opposition is not likely to be reduced by information campaigns that focus on safety. What might improve the industry's status is convincing information about its benefits, perhaps in conjunction with energy shortages. A superb safety record might, over time, reduce opposition, but because nuclear risks are perceived to be unknown and potentially catastrophic, even small accidents will be judged to be quite serious (see Figure 1.6), will be highly publicized, and will have immense social costs. This fact has direct implications for the setting of safety standards (Slovic, Fischhoff, & Lichtenstein, 1980c).

This type of research may also forecast the response to technologies that have yet to catch the public's eye. For example, our studies indicate that recombinant DNA technology shares several of the characteristics that make nuclear power so difficult to manage (Slovic, Fischhoff, & Lichtenstein, 1985). If it somehow seizes public attention, this new technology could face some of the same problems and opposition now confronting the nuclear industry.

Informing people about risk

One consequence of the growing concern about hazards has been pressure on the promoters and regulators of hazardous enterprises to inform citizens, patients, and workers about the risks they face from their daily activities, their medical treatments, and their jobs (see Cohen, Chapter 14, this volume). Attempts to implement information programs depend on a variety of political, economic, and legal forces (e.g., Gibson, 1985; Sales, 1982). The success of such efforts depends, in part, on how clearly the information is presented (Fischhoff, 1985; Slovic, Fischhoff, & Lichtenstein, 1980a, 1981).

One thing that past research demonstrates clearly is the difficulty of creating effective risk information programs. Doing an adequate job means finding cogent ways of presenting complex technical material that is often clouded by uncertainty. Reactions to the material may be distorted by the listeners' preconceptions (and possibly the presenter's misrepresentations) of the hazard and its consequences. Difficulties in putting risks into perspective or resolving the conflicts posed by life's gambles may cause risk information to frighten and frustrate people rather than aid their decision making.

If an individual has formed strong initial impressions about a hazard, results from cognitive social psychology suggest that those beliefs may structure the way subsequent evidence is interpreted. New evidence will appear to be reliable and informative if it is consistent with one's initial beliefs; contrary evidence may be dismissed as unreliable, erroneous, or unrepresentative. As a result, strongly held views will be extraordinarily difficult to change by informational presentations (Nisbett & Ross, 1980).

When people lack strong prior opinions about a hazard, the opposite situation exists – they are at the mercy of the way the information is presented. Subtle changes in the way risks are expressed can have a major impact on perceptions and decisions. One dramatic example of this comes from a study by McNeil, Pauker, Sox, and Tversky (1982), who asked people to imagine that they had lung cancer and had to choose between two therapies: surgery or radiation. The two therapies were described in some detail. Then, some subjects were presented with the cumulative probabilities of surviving for various lengths of time after the treatment.

Other subjects received the same cumulative probabilities framed in terms of dying rather than surviving (e.g., instead of being told that 68% of those having surgery will have survived after one year, they were told that 32% will have died). Framing the statistics in terms of dying reduced the percentage of subjects choosing radiation therapy over surgery from 44% to 18%. The effect was as strong for physicians as for laypeople.

Numerous other examples of framing effects have been demonstrated by Tversky and Kahneman (1981). Some of these effects can be explained in terms of the nonlinear probability and value functions proposed by Kahneman and Tversky (1979) in their theory of risky choice. Others can be explained in terms of other information-processing considerations such as compatibility effects, anchoring processes, and choice heuristics (Slovic, Fischhoff, & Lichtenstein, 1982). Whatever the causes, the fact that subtle differences in the presentation of risks can have such marked effects suggests that those responsible for information programs have considerable ability to manipulate perceptions and behavior. Indeed, since these effects are not widely known, people may inadvertently be manipulating their own perceptions by casual decisions they make about how to organize their knowledge.

Behavioral research can make a number of contributions to the process of informing people about risk. Research can alert people to potential biases so that the parties involved can defend their own interests. It can also assess the feasibility of informational programs by determining how well people can be informed. Fortunately, despite the difficulties that have been discovered, there is evidence that properly designed information programs can be beneficial. Research indicates that people can understand some aspects of risk quite well and that they do learn from experience. In situations in which misperception of risks is widespread, people's errors can often be traced to inadequate information and biased experiences, which educational programs may be able to counter. Finally, research can determine how interested people are in being given information at all. Despite occasional claims to the contrary by creators of risk, people seem to want information (Fischhoff, 1983; Slovic, Fischhoff, & Lichtenstein, 1980a), even when the nature of that information is threatening (Weinstein, 1979; 1985).

Comparing risks

One common approach to deepening people's perspectives is presenting quantified risk estimates for a variety of hazards. These presentations typically involve elaborate tables and even "catalogues of risks" in which diverse indices of death or disability are displayed for a broad spectrum of life's hazards. Some of these provide extensive data on risks per hour of exposure, showing, for example, that an hour of riding a motorcycle is as risky as an hour of being 75 years old. One analyst developed lists of activities, each of which is estimated to increase one's chances of death (in any year) by 1 in one million. Other analysts have ranked hazards in terms of their expected impact on life expectancy. Those who compile such data typically assume that they will be useful for decision making.

The research on perceived risk described earlier implies that comparisons such as these will not, by themselves, be adequate guides to personal or public decision policies. Risk perceptions and risk-taking behaviors appear to be determined not only by accident probabilities, annual mortality figures, or the mean losses of life expectancy, but also by numerous other characteristics of hazards such as uncertainty, controllability, catastrophic potential, equity, and threat to future generations. Within the perceptual space defined by these and other characteristics, each hazard is unique. To many persons, statements such as "The annual risk from living near a nuclear power plant is equivalent to the risk from riding an extra three miles in an automobile" are ludicrous because they fail to give adequate consideration to the important differences in the nature of the risks from these two technologies. However, comparisons within the same hazard domain may be useful. For example, one may gain some perspective on the amount of radiation absorbed from a medical X ray by comparing it with radiation received on a transcontinental flight or from living in Denver for a year. Unfortunately, we need considerably more research to determine how best to compare risks and how to present risk statistics.

Recognizing the difficulties

The development of programs to inform patients, workers, and consumers about risk is an admirable goal. However, as the discussion above indicates, it is important to recognize the difficulties confronting such programs. Since every decision about the content and format of an information statement is likely to influence perception and behavior (and ultimately product viability, jobs, electricity costs, compliance with medical treatments, and other important consequences), extreme care must be taken in the selection of knowledgeable and trustworthy designers and program coordinators. Finally, it is important to recognize that informing people, whether by warning labels, package inserts, or extensive media presentations, is but part of the larger problem of helping them to cope with the risks and uncertainties of modern life. We believe that much of the responsibility lies with the schools, whose curricula should include material designed to teach people that the world in which they live is probabilistic, not deterministic, and to help them learn judgment and decision strategies for dealing with that world. These strategies are as necessary for navigating in a world of uncertain information as geometry and trigonometry are to navigating among physical objects.

References

Assessment: The impact and influence of TMI. (1980). *Electric Power Research Institute Journal, 5*(5), 24–33.

Brown, R. A., & Green, C. H. (1980). Precepts of safety assessments. *Journal of the Operational Research Society, 11,* 563–71.

Fischhoff, B. (1983). Informed consent for transient nuclear workers. In R. Kasperson & R. W. Kates (Eds.), *Equity issues in radioactive waste management.* Cambridge, MA: Oelgeschlager, Gunn & Hain.

Fischhoff, B. (1985). Cognitive and institutional barriers to "informed consent." In M. Gibson (Ed.), *To breathe freely: Risk, consent, and air* (pp. 169–85). Totowa, NJ: Rowman & Allanheld.

Fischhoff, B., Slovic, P., & Lichtenstein, S. (1977). Knowing with certainty: The appropriateness of extreme confidence. *Journal of Experimental Psychology: Human Perception and Performance, 3,* 552–64.

Fischhoff, B., Slovic, P., & Lichtenstein, S. (1978). Fault trees: Sensitivity of estimated failure probabilities to problem representation. *Journal of Experimental Psychology: Human Perception and Performance, 4,* 330–44.

Fischhoff, B., Slovic, P., & Lichtenstein, S. (1980a). Knowing what you want: Measuring labile values. In T. Wallsten (Ed.), *Cognitive processes in choice and decision behavior* (pp. 117–41). Hillsdale, NJ: Erlbaum.

Fischhoff, B., Slovic, P. & Lichtenstein, S. (1980b). Labile values: A challenge for risk assessment. In J. Conrad (Ed.), *Society, technology, and risk assessment* (pp. 57–66). New York: Academic Press.

Fischhoff, B., Slovic, P., & Lichtenstein, S. (1983). The "public" vs. the "experts": Perceived vs. actual disagreement about the risks of nuclear power. In V. Covello, G. Flamm, J. Rodericks, & R. Tardiff (Eds.), *Analysis of actual vs. perceived risks* (pp. 235–49). New York: Plenum.

Fischhoff, B., Slovic, P., Lichtenstein, S., Read, S., & Combs, B. (1978). How safe is safe enough? A psychometric study of attitudes towards technological risks and benefits. *Policy Sciences, 8,* 127–52.

Friedman, M., & Savage, L. J. (1948). The utility analysis of choices involving risk. *Journal of Political Economy, 56,* 279–304.

Fuchs, V. R. (1976). From Bismarck to Woodcock: The irrational pursuit of national health insurance. *Journal of Law and Public Policy, 19,* 347–59.

Gardner, G. T., Tiemann, A. R., Gould, L. C., DeLuca, D. R., Doob, L. W., & Stolwijk, J. A. J. (1982). Risk and benefit perceptions, acceptability judgments, and self-reported actions toward nuclear power. *Journal of Social Psychology, 116,* 179–97.

Gibson, M. (Ed.). (1985). *Risk, consent, and air.* Totowa, NJ: Rowman & Allanheld.

Green, C. H. (1980a). Risk: Attitudes and beliefs. In D. V. Canter (Ed.), *Behavior in fires.* New York: Wiley.

Green, C. H. (1980b). Revealed preference theory: Assumptions and presumptions. In J.

Conrad (Ed.), *Society, technology and risk assessment* (pp. 49–56). New York: Academic Press.

Green, C. H., & Brown, R. A. (1980). *Through a glass darkly: Perceiving perceived risks to health and safety.* Research paper, School of Architecture, Duncan of Jordanstone College of Art/University of Dundee, Scotland.

Hohenemser, C., Kates, R. W., & Slovic, P. (1983). The nature of technological hazard. *Science, 220,* 378–84.

Hynes, M., & Vanmarcke, E. (1976). Reliability of embankment performance prediction. In *Proceedings of the ASCE Engineering Mechanics Division Specialty Conference.* Waterloo, Ontario, Canada: University of Waterloo Press.

Johnson, E. J. & Tversky, A. (1984). Representations of perceptions of risks. *Journal of Experimental Psychology: General, 113,* 55–70.

Kahneman, D., & Tversky, A. (1979). Prospect theory. *Econometrica, 47,* 263–92.

Kahneman, D., Slovic, P., & Tversky, A. (Eds.). (1982). *Judgment under uncertainty: Heuristics and biases.* Cambridge University Press.

Keeney, R. L., & Raiffa, H. (1976). *Decisions with multiple objectives.* New York: Wiley.

Knight, F. H. (1921). *Risk, uncertainty, and profit.* Boston: Houghton-Mifflin.

Kunreuther, H. (1974). Disaster insurance: A tool for hazard mitigation. *Journal of Risk and Insurance, 41,* 287–303.

Kunreuther, H., Ginsberg, R., Miller, L., Sagi, P., Slovic, P., Borkan, B., & Katz, N. (1978). *Disaster insurance protection: Public policy lessons.* New York: Wiley.

Lichtenstein, S., Fischhoff, B., & Phillips, L. D. (1982). Calibration of probabilities: The state of the art to 1980. In D. Kahneman, P. Slovic, & A. Tversky (Eds.), *Judgment under uncertainty: Heuristics and biases* (pp. 306–34). Cambridge University Press.

Lichtenstein, S., Slovic, P., Fischhoff, B., Layman, M. & Combs, B. (1978). Judged frequency of lethal events. *Journal of Experimental Psychology: Human Learning and Memory, 4,* 551–78.

McNeil, B. J., Pauker, S. G., Sox, H. C., Jr., & Tversky, A. (1982). On the elicitation of preferences for alternative therapies. *New England Journal of Medicine, 306,* 1259–62.

Nisbett, R., & Ross, L. (1980). *Human inference: Strategies and shortcomings of social judgment.* Englewood Cliffs, NJ: Prentice-Hall.

Pashigian, B. P., Schkade, L., & Menefee, G. H. (1966). The selection of an optimal deductible for a given insurance policy. *Journal of Business, 39,* 35–44.

Renn, O. (1981). *Man, technology and risk: A study on intuitive risk assessment and attitudes towards nuclear power* (Report Jul-Spez 115). Julich, Federal Republic of Germany: Nuclear Research Center.

Rethans, A. (1979). *An investigation of consumer perceptions of product hazards.* Unpublished doctoral dissertation, University of Oregon, Eugene.

Robertson, L. S. (1976). The great seat belt campaign flop. *Journal of Communication, 26,* 41–45.

Sales, J. B. (1982). The duty to warn and instruct for safe use in strict tort liability. *St. Mary's Law Journal, 13,* 521–86.

Savage, L. J. (1954). *The foundations of statistics.* New York: Wiley.

Schwalm, N. D., & Slovic, P. (1982). *Development and test of a motivational approach and materials for increasing use of restraints* (Final Technical Report PFTR-1100-82-3). Woodland Hills, CA: Perceptronics, Inc.

Simon, H. A. (1957). *Models of man: Social and rational.* New York: Wiley.

Slovic, P., Fischhoff, B., & Lichtenstein, S. (1977). Behavioral decision theory. *Annual Review of Psychology, 28,* 1–39.

Slovic, P., Fischhoff, B., & Lichtenstein, S. (1978). Accident probabilities and seat belt usage: A psychological perspective. *Accident Analysis and Prevention, 10,* 281–5.

Slovic, P., Fischhoff, B., & Lichtenstein, S. (1979). Rating the risks. *Environment, 21*(3), 14–20, 36–9.

Slovic, P., Fischhoff, B., & Lichtenstein, S. (1980a). Facts and fears: Understanding perceived risk. In R. Schwing & W. A. Albers, Jr. (Eds.), *Societal risk assessment: How safe is safe enough?* (pp. 181–214). New York: Plenum.

Slovic, P., Fischhoff, B., & Lichtenstein, S. (1980b). Informing people about risk. In L. Morris, M. Mazis, & I. Barofsky (Eds.), *Product labeling and health risks* (Banbury Report 6, pp. 165–181). Cold Spring Harbor, New York: Cold Spring Laboratory.

Slovic, P., Fischhoff, B., & Lichtenstein, S. (1980c). Perceived risk and quantitative safety goals for nuclear power. *Transactions of the American Nuclear Society, 35,* 400–1.

Slovic, P., Fischhoff, B., & Lichtenstein, S. (1981). Informing the public about the risks of ionizing radiation. *Health Physics, 41,* 589–98.

Slovic, P., Fischhoff, B., & Lichtenstein, S. (1982). Response mode, framing, and information-processing effects in risk assessment. In R. Hogarth (Ed.), *New directions for methodology of social and behavioral science: Question framing and response consistency* (pp. 21–36). San Francisco, CA: Jossey-Bass.

Slovic, P., Fischhoff, B., & Lichtenstein, S. (1985). Characterizing perceived risk. In R. W. Kates, C. Hohenemser, & J. Kasperson (Eds.), *Perilous progress: Managing the hazards of technology* (pp. 91–125). Boulder, CO: Westview.

Slovic, P., Fischhoff, B., Lichtenstein, S., Corrigan, B., & Combs, B. (1977). Preference for insuring against probable small losses: Implications for the theory and practice of insurance. *Journal of Risk and Insurance, 44,* 237–58.

Slovic, P., Lichtenstein, S., & Fischhoff, B. (1979). Images of disaster: Perception and acceptance of risks from nuclear power. In G. Goodman & W. Rowe (Eds.), *Energy risk management* (pp. 223–45). New York: Academic Press.

Slovic, P., Lichtenstein, S., & Fischhoff, B. (1984). Modeling the societal impact of fatal accidents. *Management Science, 30,* 464–74.

Starr, C. (1969). Social benefit versus technological risk. *Science, 165,* 1232–8.

Svenson, O. (1981). Are we all less risky and more skillful than our fellow drivers? *Acta Psychologica, 47,* 143–8.

Tversky, A., & Kahneman, D. (1973). Availability: A heuristic for judging frequency and probability. *Cognitive Psychology, 5,* 207–32.

Tversky, A., & Kahneman, D. (1974). Judgment under uncertainty: Heuristics and biases. *Science, 185,* 1124–31.

Tversky, A., & Kahneman, D. (1981). The framing of decisions and the psychology of choice. *Science, 211,* 1453–8.

Vlek, C. A. J., & Stallen, P. J. M. (1981). Judging risks and benefits in the small and in the large. *Organizational Behavior and Human Performance, 28,* 235–71.

von Neumann, J., & Morgenstern, O. (1947). *Theory of games and economic behavior,* 2nd Ed. Princeton, NJ: Princeton University Press.

von Winterfeldt, D., John, R. S., & Borcherding, K. (1981). Cognitive components of risk ratings. *Risk Analysis, 1,* 277–87.

Weinberg, A. M. (1976). The maturity and future of nuclear energy. *American Scientist, 64,* 16–21.

Weinstein, N. D. (1979). Seeking reassuring or threatening information about environmental cancer. *Journal of Behavioral Medicine, 2,* 125–39.

Weinstein, N. D. (1980). Unrealistic optimism about future life events. *Journal of Personality and Social Psychology, 39,* 806–20.

Weinstein, N. D. (1985). Reactions to life-style warnings: Coffee and cancer. *Health Education Quarterly, 12,* 129–34.

2 Social learning theory and preventive behavior

Alfred McAlister

Introduction

Behavioral science has come to the forefront of public efforts to reduce rates of disease and injury. However, students of human behavior have lacked the unifying theories that have facilitated progress in the so-called hard sciences. Without a sound theoretical foundation, behavioral scientists may find it difficult to meet increasing demands for solutions to societal problems.

Human behavior has resisted scientific study, and comprehensive theories capable of explaining diverse behavioral phenomena have been slow to appear. Significant progress has occurred with the development of Albert Bandura's (1969, 1977a) social learning theory. As the name implies, it is a merging of two distinct theoretical perspectives in academic psychology. Traditionally, proponents of behaviorism, or learning theory, have studied such phenomena as conditioning or reinforcement in the laboratory. They have emphasized the use of quantifiable, physical stimuli and have examined responses by animals and humans in controlled learning situations. In contrast, social psychologists have accumulated a body of theoretical and empirical information on more natural, social influences on behavior, studying such subjective phenomena as values, attitudes, and personality. Albert Bandura synthesized these two traditions by advancing a theory in which behaviorist principles operate in social learning situations through the mediation of simple symbolic and cognitive processes.

Several of the most important concepts of social learning theory are described briefly in the following section. The purpose is to acquaint the reader with the basic features of the theory and with its vocabulary for describing behavioral phenomena. Following this overview, three examples will be presented to show how social learning concepts can be applied to the promotion of health- and safety-related behaviors: (a) avoidance of cigarette smoking or alcohol abuse; (b) use of seat belts and restraining devices for children in automobiles; and (c) voting behavior, as related to the prevention of nuclear war.

Basic concepts in social learning theory

Cognitive processes in conditioning

Conditioning has been one focus of attention in traditional learning theory. Beginning with Pavlov's (1927) classic experiment, a long line of research has established the fact that various stimuli (observable events or sensations) can be made to elicit various responses (observable behaviors) by systematically and repeatedly pairing or otherwise connecting them. With dogs, a bell rung before each feeding begins to elicit salivation in a process termed "classical conditioning." With humans, much more complex responses result from this basic form of learning by temporal association. Theories of classical conditioning tend to take a mechanistic view of this process and to avoid conjecture about the thought processes that might accompany it. A mechanistic perspective is probably adequate for describing the behavior of simple organisms, but studies of conditioning in humans reveal that more complex cognitive processes are almost always involved.

In social learning theory, these cognitive processes are considered to mediate virtually all natural learning in social settings. Stimuli are conceptualized as sources of information that a person can use to predict upcoming events, not as mechanistic forces. The most important such cognitive process is the generation of hypotheses about the cause-and-effect relations between associated events. Thus, a man who hears a dinner bell might salivate because he *thinks* he will be fed. The possibility of conditioning without thinking is not denied, but the social learning paradigm considers involuntary or unconscious learning to be a phenomenon of secondary importance in human behavior. Actions that may be viewed by strict behaviorists as "conditioned" are seen in social learning theory as caused by the beliefs and expectations that arise in a particular situation. This is a significant unifying notion because it links one of the major branches of learning theory to the area of social psychology that examines the formation of beliefs and the development of attributions for causality (Bem, 1970; Zimbardo, Ebbesen, & Maslach, 1969; Ross, 1977).

Incentives and reinforcers

In another traditional strand of learning theory, emphasis is given to the process of reinforcement. Rats were found to press levers and perform other tasks in order to receive food, avoid punishment, and so on (Skinner, 1953). Variations in the frequency, intensity, and duration of responses could be produced by manipulating the quantity and timing of the reinforcement. Among most behaviorists there was a tendency to discount the role of thought in the reinforcement process. Social learning theory, in contrast, sees reinforcement phenomena as wholly dependent on cognition. Reinforcement is considered to be a motivating factor, with decisions about actions reflecting the individual's beliefs about the *incentives* available for different responses. This perspective links learning theory to the related body of research and theory on decision making.

In this view of motivation, behavior is a function of the ways incentives are perceived and understood by the individual. Priorities among competing incentives can be explained in terms of a hierarchy of needs, such as the hierarchy proposed by Maslow (1959). The motivating powers of basic physiological needs are obvious, but in social learning theory emphasis is placed on social reinforcement. Social approval is seen as an extremely powerful motivator, even leading people to endure physical discomfort if they believe that their actions will be approved by significant others. For example, the first use of cigarettes is physically aversive, but children are often willing to continue smoking if they believe that it will win the approval of their peers.

Different kinds of incentives exert unique influences on behavior, effects that can be predicted by social learning theory. Generally, positive reinforcement is more effective than punishment in developing and controlling complex new patterns of behavior. This is because punishment acts more to inhibit existing behavior than to elicit new actions. Punishment may also arouse autonomic responses, such as anxiety, that interfere with learning. In some circumstances, however, punishment may be effective in the elimination of previously learned behavior patterns.

The phenomenon of self-reinforcement (Mahoney & Thoreson, 1974) receives special attention in social learning theory. When immediate social or material rewards are not present, it is considered possible to reinforce *oneself* through positive thoughts. Self-reinforcement is seen as central to self-control and the delay of gratification. It is particularly relevant to the understanding of behaviors that require effort and that persist in spite of immediate negative consequences. Many apparently irrational and self-destructive behaviors become understandable once the underlying patterns of self-reinforcement are recognized. For example, a person may drive recklessly on a crowded freeway because he or she is reinforced by a feeling of domination over other commuters. The gratification derived from this sense of power may outweigh the perceived threat of punishment in the form of a speeding ticket or automobile accident.

Modeling

According to social learning theory, patterns of self-reinforcement as well as most other patterns of thought and behavior are learned through social modeling (Bandura, 1977a). "Social modeling" is a term that refers to the process of observational or imitative learning when the thoughts and behaviors of others are reproduced or approximated by observers. A number of psychological studies have examined the attributes that determine the capacity of social models to influence changes in attitudes and beliefs, decision making, and the acquisition of new patterns of behavior. Such factors as attractiveness, perceived social competence, perceived expertise, and perceived trustworthiness determine the power of specific models. Individuals appearing on television or in other mass media as symbols of desired characteristics (power, sex appeal, courage) may be particularly influential (Bandura, 1973). However, powerful influences are also found when the observers perceive similarities between the models and themselves. Thus, peers are often the most influential models in day-to-day social learning.

The actual learning of skilled behaviors and complex behavioral sequences is not just a matter of simple observation. The most important factor in skill acquisition is the model's demonstration of complex sequences in a gradual, step-by-step manner. Different parts of the action sequence must be explicitly identified and repeated before the learner attempts to aggregate these components into the whole behavior pattern. Complex motor tasks are typically learned in this fashion. For example, to play golf a person must learn the grip, the stance, and a number of other discrete elements before they can be pulled together into an effective performance. Printed reminders and simple procedures for recording progress may be useful during the early stages of learning a complex behavior. Research also shows that learning is facilitated when models are shown coping realistically with problems that arise. For example, models who fail occasionally are more influential than those who seem to master difficult tasks too easily (Meichenbaum, 1971).

Social learning theory's description of the modeling process includes a fundamental distinction between the acquisition and the performance of new behaviors (Bandura, 1977a). A celebrity appearing in the mass media can model new behaviors and they may be learned (acquired) on a cognitive level (i.e., the observer *knows how* to perform the behavior). But direct social reinforcement or the expectation of reinforcement is usually needed for behavioral learning (i.e., *actually performing* the new behavior). The importance of social reinforcement is also apparent in training situations in which people are being taught to perform complex new behaviors through the use of models appearing on film. Numerous studies find that effectiveness is sharply enhanced when supplementary personal contact is also available to provide encouragement, feedback, and reinforcement.

Self-efficacy

The concept of self-efficacy is emphasized in advances in the articulation of social learning theory (Bandura, 1977b). This term is roughly equivalent to "self-confidence." It is also related to the notion that people differ in their perceptions of whether events are under "internal" control (the individual's control) or "external" control (determined by chance or by forces outside the individual) (Rotter, 1966). Research shows that active efforts to learn new responses depend on a person's expectations about the likelihood that he or she can achieve a successful performance in a reasonable period of time. Factors that support positive performance expectations have been systematically analyzed. Realistic goal setting is particularly important and may depend on previous social modeling or on the social expectations evoked in a particular situation. The individual's actual learning experiences are very important, but initially unfavorable experiences can be overcome by social reinforcement or self-reinforcement.

Efficacy expectations are usually specific to particular situations and behaviors, but stress and lack of social support can have detrimental effects on self-confidence in general. According to social learning theory, the competence to cope with the challenges of human existence depends ultimately on the quality of the social models and social relationships that guide learning. Individuals with phobias, addictive behaviors, and other habits that are difficult to change can be helped by therapists who provide appropriate modeling, guided practice, and social reinforcement, with the development of efficacy expectations playing a key role in behavior therapy. Similar processes may also occur naturally in the course of human interactions. In social learning theory, a "therapist" is simply a skilled source of guidance and reinforcement (Bandura, 1969).

Applications to the promotion of health and safety

As a system of explaining and modifying human behavior, social learning theory offers many suggestions for promoting self-protective behaviors. To illustrate how concepts in this field can be applied, three different types of behavior will be considered.

Cigarette smoking

Cigarette smoking is understandable from the concepts of conditioning and reinforcement. Among habitual smokers, the consumption of tobacco is supported by the positive situations with which it has been associated or by the reinforcing feelings of stress reduction and efficacy enhancement that have been demonstrated in psychopharmacological studies (Levanthal & Cleary, 1980). Social reinforcement and perceived pressures to conform have been found to be important in initial experimentation with cigarettes (Leventhal & Cleary, 1980). The physical experience of first-time users may be negative, but the new behavior may be encouraged by important peer models who make social reinforcement contingent on emulation of their smoking behavior. This may occur, for example, when a smoking teenager tells friends that they are "chicken" if they do not smoke cigarettes.

The positive psychoactive properties of nicotine may also be a function of modeling in the young smoker's learning experiences (McAlister, Krosnick, & Milburn, 1984). Fear of long-term health consequences is, for many young people, a much less salient motivator than the expectation of social approval from smoking peers or the discovery of a way in which social anxiety can be managed. Later in life, when health consequences become more important, the habit is maintained by positive associations and feelings of reduced stress and increased efficacy. From the social learning perspective, the persistence of addictive habits involving nicotine, alcohol, and other fast-acting, psychoactive substances is easy to understand.

Efforts to promote smoking cessation can be guided by principles of social learning theory. The decision to stop smoking can be elicited by altering a person's perceptions of the relative balance between the consequences of cessation and the consequences of continued smoking (decisional balance approach). Taxes and insurance incentives can encourage attempts to stop smoking (Harris, 1980). Evidence about the effects of cigarette smoke on children can provide a new incentive for parents to

Table 2.1. *Self-reported behavior changes in two study areas*

Behavior change	North Karelia (%)	Kuopio (%)
Tried to quit smoking (of smokers)	7.1	7.0
Succeeded in quitting (of smokers)	6.4	4.4[a]
Lost weight (of total)	10.7	10.6
Lost 5 kg (of total)	3.5	2.2[b]
Significantly increased physical activity[c] (of all)	3.0	3.2
Reduced intake of fat (of total)	29.6	31.2
Reduced intake of salt (of total)	29.6	28.7
Increased intake of vegetables (of all)	33.6	31.4
N (total)	1,600	1,605
N (smokers)	405	502

[a] $\chi^2 = 4.7$, $p \leq .05$.
[b] $\chi^2 = 4.6$, $p \leq .05$.
[c] By two or more occasions of at least 30 minutes' duration.
Source: A. McAlister, P. Puska, A. Smolander, & J. Pekkola (unpublished data).

stop. The introduction of direct social reinforcement can also influence smoking behavior, but systematic social punishment may not have the desired effects because it elicits negative emotional states that increase the salience of the psychopharmacological reinforcement offered by nicotine. Because they reduce self-efficacy expectations, most forms of "nagging" are not recommended by social learning theory.

Social modeling can also be employed effectively to reduce smoking. In a number of mass media programs the process of overcoming tobacco dependency has been demonstrated by attractive social models. In Finland a 15-part, four-month television series followed a group of seven selected Finns as they learned to become nonsmokers (Puska, McAlister, Pekkola, & Koskela, 1981). Smokers in the viewing audience were urged to emulate the self-directed chance process modeled by the television group. To stimulate cessation efforts, volunteer opinion leaders were recruited from communities in the Finnish state of Karelia and trained to provide social reinforcement by praising friends and neighbors who attempted to stop smoking along with the television models. The results are displayed in Table 2.1.

Modeling can also contribute to the prevention of smoking among teenagers. Peer models can influence the perceived social desirability of cigarette smoking and, to some extent, the perceived enjoyment of the psychoactive effects of tobacco. A number of studies have shown that modeling and guided practice can also be used to teach assertiveness and other "life skills" that help deter the initiation of smoking. For example, role playing can be used in combination with reinforcement from attractive, older peers to teach a young person how to say no when feeling pressured to smoke cigarettes. Research has demonstrated the effectiveness of these and related prevention methods. An illustration of this approach can be found in McAlister, Perry, Killen, Slinkard, and Maccoby (1980).

Seat belt use

The difficulty of promoting seat belt use can also be analyzed according to social learning theory. Conditions for learning the use of seat belts are not particularly favorable for the acquisition or maintenance of this simple behavior. The use of seat belts has no immediately evident reinforcing consequences. Modeling of seat belt use and reinforcements contingent on their use may be introduced by some parents, but rarely with the consistency necessary for a persistent habit to be learned. When a person drives alone, social reinforcement cannot be easily provided. From the perspective of traditional learning theory, even modest rates of seat belt use are somewhat difficult to explain.

The mediating phenomenon in the use of seat belts, according to social learning theory, is self-reinforcement for the avoidance of imagined consequences. Such self-reinforcement can be learned through any of a number of social modeling displays, but this self-reinforcement can be easily undermined. New beliefs may be acquired that contradict the expectation that seat belts will reduce the risk of injury. A person who is told by a trusted friend that seat belts actually increase risk may discard the seat belt habit quite easily. Furthermore, long-term consequences are easily discounted when use is inconvenient, as when a person who is late for work decides not to give up the time needed to fasten a seat belt. Patterns of self-reinforcement can also be disturbed under stress when long-term or less probable risks may be discounted in the face of immediately threatening circumstances.

Principles of social learning theory are quite applicable to efforts to increase rates of seat belt use. One obvious recommendation is the provision of external incentives – for example, laws or policies requiring the use of seat belts. This approach is possible for some occupations and in some political jurisdictions. But the threat of punishment must be real. Enforcement can be an expensive burden for police officers or plant safety officials, a responsibility not accepted with enthusiasm. In some areas, political opposition to legal sanctions rules out this approach. However, if sanctions are accepted by enough of the population, such a strategy can be quite effective.

An alternative form of external reinforcement is social approval. When attractive media models recommend seat belt use, the perceived social desirability of the behavior is enhanced. Desired patterns of self-reinforcement can be encouraged by models who praise themselves as they fasten their seat belts. Attractive models from the mass media might also help to develop norms in which occupants of motor vehicles encourage and praise fellow travelers who use their seat belts. Concepts like this lie behind some public service announcements that promote seat belt use, but the effort could probably be improved by more systematic application of social learning principles.

The schools might be a particularly appropriate setting for such efforts. For example, participant modeling procedures can be adapted to driver training programs in secondary schools. As in the successful smoking prevention programs, peer leaders might be trained to guide learning experiences (e.g., to model the process of self-reinforcement when fastening seat belts and the encouragement of seat belt use by other vehicle occupants), increasing the perceived social desirability of the behavior.

Of course, it is crucial that the actual performance environment favor the desired action. Like any safety device, seat belts must be designed so that they can be used with as little effort or difficulty as possible. Some new passive restraint devices seem particularly promising in this regard, and their effectiveness deserves careful monitoring. Legislative sanctions and media campaigns are only partial solutions to the problem of automobile injuries. Motor vehicles and roadways must also be designed for maximum safety.

Voting behavior

Voting is a potentially self-protective action. Voters are asked to make judgments that bear on a variety of hazard issues – judgments about politicians whose policies might increase or decrease the risk of nuclear war, referenda on land-use plans that could influence the danger of flooding, bond issues to clean up toxic waste dumps, and many others. Voting has several interesting features from the perspective of social learning theory. The behavior itself has two distinct elements: (a) the act of getting out to vote and (b) the selection of a preference from among the choices on the ballot. Like seat belt use, voting behavior has no immediately reinforcing consequences. Some people may be exposed to early parental or peer modeling and receive guided practice to promote voting behavior. At the ballot place, social reinforcement may be provided. Positive early learning experiences are not provided for everyone, however, and in polarized societies minority groups or disadvantaged segments of the population may even be discouraged from voting.

Once an individual is at the ballot place, the voting decision is determined by a variety of factors. Complex decisions about major candidates or referenda may be guided by expectations concerning the effects of different election outcomes on important issues like employment, inflation, and the risk of war. However, making a choice among what a person perceives to be minor candidates may not be personally involving, with selection based not on reasoning but on simple decision rules or mere familiarity with candidates' names. Such a behavior pattern is particularly common when incentives to vote are provided but choices among the options are not believed to be significant. If voting is to be more than a social occasion or an unthinking patriotic gesture, the decisions involving issues or candidates must be perceived to have meaningful consequences. Low self-efficacy expectation – the belief that voting will not make a difference – is the basis of voter apathy.

The preceding analysis suggests strategies for inducing people to vote. Several examples can be drawn from the voter registration drives conducted in connection with the 1984 general election. In many areas, external conditions have been found to inhibit voting among the less educated segments of the population. For example, registration forms may include questions that require the applicant to have a very good vocabulary. The warning that giving an incorrect answer can be punishable as a criminal felony may be boldly printed on voting forms. Such practices have been the subject of civil lawsuits. The importance given to such barriers to registration and voting by those working to increase voter registration is wholly consistent with the significance given them in social learning theory. The notion of providing free transportation to polling places may be too obvious a recommendation to be considered "theoretical."

Of course, there will always be some inconvenience in voting. Social reinforcements must be provided to initiate and maintain the behavior. Perceived social reinforcement at the polling place may significantly influence the decision to vote. Perhaps one way to promote minority voting is to include representatives of different minority groups among the polling officials. This is easier to recommend than it would be to implement, however. We know from history that legal or civil protest action may be required to change polling practices. Methods using the mass media or the public school system to promote citizenship can also be derived from social learning theory. Systematic peer reinforcement could be combined with guided practice in schools for those approaching the age to vote.

In the long run, voting behavior should be maintained by a person's perception that the vote makes a difference. It is well known that candidates challenging incumbents need to take the initiative and convince the electorate that favorable changes would follow their assumption of public office. If people believe that nuclear war is inevitable, they may fail to vote even when politicians have widely different policies regarding the use of military power and may even feel a general sense of helplessness that inhibits all political activity.

General issues

It is interesting to consider how social learning theory might shed light on some general questions related to the promotion of the self-protecting behaviors examined in this volume. One question concerns the relative usefulness of legal, administrative sanctions versus that of voluntary approaches such as education, modeling, and guided learning. To answer this question one must consider the different learning patterns that are evoked by rewards and punishments. Social learning theory supports the recommendation that educational efforts take priority because they instill self-reinforcement practices that can be maintained without expensive legal and bureaucratic machinery. One could argue, however, that legislative sanctions are more important because they can alter important environmental conditions, such as those affecting tobacco advertising, the design of seat belts, or the ease of voter registration. Obviously, there is a place for both approaches in any comprehensive attempt to increase preventive behaviors.

Another general question asks whether particular social programs have a broad impact on a number of superficially diverse health-promoting or self-protective behaviors. There is intriguing evidence that education may have such an effect, but the mechanism is not clear. Self-esteem or generalized self-efficacy may be involved, but this mechanism is not strongly supported by social learning theory. Research shows that efficacy expectations tend to be highly specific, varying greatly across behaviors and situations. However, several factors may have a general, nonspecific impact on learning. For example, social isolation can weaken self-efficacy by reducing opportunities for modeling and reinforcement. Autonomic states associated with stressful events and cognitions can also have far-ranging effects. Preoccupation with frequent short-term threats may lead a person to discount the probabilistic or long-term dangers associated with a whole range of unsafe or unhealthy behaviors. Particularly because such effects could be so far reaching, such phenomena deserve careful examination.

References

Bandura, A. 1969. *Principals of Behavior Modification.* New York: Holt, Reinhart & Winston.

Bandura, A. 1973. *Aggression: A Social Learning Analysis.* Englewood Cliffs, N.J.: Prentice-Hall.

Bandura, A. 1977a. *Social Learning Theory.* Englewood Cliffs, N.J.: Prentice-Hall.

Bandura, A. 1977b. Self-efficacy: Toward a unifying theory of behavior change. *Psychological Review, 84:* 191–215.

Bem, D. 1970. *Beliefs, Attitudes and Human Affairs.* Monterey, Calif.: Brooks/Cole.

Harris, J. 1980. Taxing tar and nicotine. *American Economic Review, 70:* 300–11.

Leventhal, H., and Cleary, P. 1980. The smoking problem: A review of the research and theory in behavior risk modification. *Psychological Bulletin, 88:* 370–405.

Mahoney, M., and Thoreson, C. 1974. *Self Control: Power to the Person.* Monterey, Calif.: Brooks/Cole.

Maslow, A. 1959. Psychological data and value theory. In *New Knowledge in Human Values,* ed. A. H. Maslow. New York: Harper & Row.

McAlister, A., Krosnick, J., and Milburn, M. 1984. Causes of adolescent cigarette smoking: Tests of a structural equation model. *Social Psychology Quarterly, 47*(1): 24–36.

McAlister, A., Perry, C., Killen, J., Slinkard, L., and Maccoby, N. 1980. Pilot study of smoking, alcohol and drug abuse prevention. *American Journal of Public Health, 70:* 719–21.

Meichenbaum, D. 1971. Examination of model characteristics in reducing avoidance behavior. *Journal of Personality and Social Psychology, 17:* 298–307.

Pavlov, I. 1927. *Conditioned Reflexes: An Investigation of the Physiological Activity of the Cerebral Cortex,* trans. F. C. Anrep. New York: Oxford University Press.

Puska, P., McAlister, A., Pekkola, J., and Koskela, K. 1981. Television in health promotion: Evaluation of a national programme in Finland. *International Journal of Health Education, 2*(4): 2–14.

Ross, L. 1977. The intuitive psychologist and his shortcomings: Distortions in the attribution process. In *Advances in Experimental Social Psychology,* ed. L. Berkowitz. New York: Academic Press, *10:* 174–220.

Rotter, J. 1966. Generalized expectancies for internal versus external control of reinforcement. *Psychological Monographs, 89*(1): Whole No. 609.

Skinner, B. F. 1953. *Science and Human Behavior.* New York: Macmillan.

Zimbardo, P., Ebbesen, E., and Maslach, C. 1969. *Influencing Attitudes and Changing Behavior.* Reading, Mass.: Addison-Wesley.

3 The role of emotion and psychological defense in self-protective behavior

James R. Averill

Early and provident fear is the mother of safety.
Edmund Burke

Introduction

As a young woman was driving to work one wintry morning, her car hit a patch of ice and veered into oncoming traffic. What might the young woman have experienced as she felt her car go out of control and head for a possibly fatal accident? Fear, most likely. But what is fear? Perhaps the young woman felt her heart pound and a sinking feeling in the pit of the stomach; her thoughts may have raced, but without coherence; and perhaps she engaged in frantic maneuvers, or simply froze at the wheel. These are all typical manifestations of fear. But it is also possible (and commonly reported in such instances) that the young woman's attention was so riveted on controlling the vehicle and taking evasive action that none of these symptoms of fear was evident. Was she then lacking in fear?

Assume the evasive actions were successful, and the young woman's car reached the other side of the road without a collision. Also assume, for the sake of argument, that the car overturned on an embankment and was totally wrecked. The young woman fortunately escaped injury because she was wearing a seat belt. Only after the car had come to rest did she lose her composure, start to tremble, and break out in a cold sweat. Was she then experiencing fear, even though she knew the danger had passed?

Going back in time before the accident, what motivated the young woman to fasten her seat belt in the first place? Was that also fear? And if at a later date she wanted to convince a friend to wear a seat belt, could she frighten him into doing so, for example, by graphically describing her own harrowing experience? Let us suppose that her friend has a self-image of not being easily frightened, and the more graphic the woman becomes, the more he dismisses her arguments as hysterical. He has been in similar situations and has been able to control the car. He would never be involved in a fatal collision, and, besides, seat belts are for sissies.

The purpose of this chapter is to examine how emotions and psychological defenses influence the way a person interprets and responds to potential hazards. To lend some coherence to the discussion, I shall refer frequently to the anecdote of the young woman in an automobile accident and to the questions it raises. This means that the discussion will be limited primarily to the emotion of fear and related psychological defenses (e.g., denial). This limitation is worth mentioning, because many of the hazards people face in everyday life elicit emotions other than fear. For example, the threat of crime may elicit more anger than fear, and a fatal disease that threatens oneself or a loved one may occasion depression and anticipatory grief. Needless to say, people may do very different things depending on whether they are fearful, angry, or depressed, and these differences can be ignored only at a loss of considerable precision. Still, for reasons of economy, this discussion will be limited to fear and (on a more abstract level) to features common to most emotions.

Within these limitations, the chapter could take either of two approaches (space does not allow both). One approach would be to review empirical research on the relation between fear and self-protective behavior. Unfortunately, it is difficult to make many firm generalizations in this area. It is not that there are so many exceptions to the rules; rather, the exceptions seem to be the rule. When such a state of affairs exists, the problem can typically be traced more to conceptual confusion than to inadequacies in the empirical research. Emotional concepts are inherently ambiguous, and there is no assurance that two researchers mean the same thing simply because they use the same term (e.g., "fear"). This suggests that a conceptual analysis might be the most fruitful approach this chapter could take. Therefore, without ignoring empirical research, I shall examine critically what we mean by fear and the ways that fear can be–and often is–used to cajole people into action (before the fact) or to explain their behavior (after the fact).

Some preliminary observations

Identifying responses that are uniquely emotional is somewhat like hunting a snark. The quest is hotly pursued, but no one seems to agree when the quarry has been captured–or that it even exists. The range of responses – behavioral, physiological, and cognitive – that may be exhibited during emotion is almost unlimited (recall the description of the young woman in an automobile accident). A common strategy among theorists is to select some subset of responses, such as physiological arousal or a certain mode of information processing, as definitive of emotion. Such a strategy has the advantage of simplicity, but when a part is made to stand for the whole, the study of emotion is thrown out of perspective.[1] A better approach is to treat emotions as complex syndromes. The concept of a syndrome is familiar from its use in medicine. However, unlike many disease syndromes (such as polio), emotional syndromes are polythetic (Averill, 1980a). That is, no single response or kind of response (e.g., physiological arousal) is essential to the whole. This observation might seem relatively uncontroversial. Actually, however, it is a point of considerable dispute, and one about which I shall have more to say later in the chapter.

Another point of dispute is whether emotional syndromes are primarily biological or social in origin. Some theorists argue that emotions are biologically based ("instinctive") patterns of behavior. By contrast, I have argued that emotions might better be conceived of as socially constituted syndromes or transitory social roles (Averill, 1980a,b). Stated somewhat differently, emotions are more a product of social than of biological evolution. Of course, some elements of an emotional syndrome may be little more than biological reflexes (e.g., the goose flesh characteristic of acute fear). I believe, however, that such elementary responses have been given undue prominence in theories of emotion. Biologically based responses are not specific to emotions (one may have goose flesh when one is cold as well as when one is frightened), nor are they always present during emotion (one can be fearful without having goose flesh).

When emotions are conceptualized as syndromes, the focus of attention shifts from specific responses to the way responses are organized. Thus, when I say that emotional syndromes are socially constituted, I mean not only that some of the elements of emotion are acquired during socialization, but also that the various elements are formed into a coherent whole by socially based principles of organization (rules of emotion), as opposed to genetically based principles. (For a more detailed discussion of rules of emotion, see Hochschild, 1979, and Averill, 1984.)

Psychological defense

Before we examine the nature of emotional syndromes in greater detail, a few words should be said about psychological defenses, particularly denial. When a person is confronted with potential harm and shows few of the usual signs of fear, it is sometimes inferred that that person is engaging in denial or some other psychological defense. The denial presumably represents a kind of protective barrier that must be overcome before the person can be motivated to take effective action.

This description of denial contains a number of assumptions that require critical examination. Perhaps the most important assumption is the implied antithesis between denial and fear: If a person engages in denial, fear will be, to a greater or lesser extent, short-circuited. But there is another way of interpreting the relation between fear and denial. In the anecdote of the young woman in an automobile accident, we noted some of the diverse ways that fear can be manifested. Many of the manifestations of fear are incompatible with one another. For example, the young woman might have frozen at the wheel, or she might have taken evasive action – but not both at the same time. These are common, albeit incompatible behavioral manifestations of fear. Other common manifestations of fear are primarily cognitive. Worrying is one example; denial is another. Denial is a way of cognitively avoiding a threatening event; as such, it may be incompatible with worry and also with certain behavioral and physiological manifestations of fear. In other words, denial is not antithetical to fear as a syndrome; it is an element of the syndrome. The antithesis, when it exists, is with other elements of the syndrome. (Needless to say, denial is not linked exclusively to fear; it can be associated with a wide variety of emotional syndromes. For a detailed and wide-ranging discussion, see Breznitz, 1983.)

Within the psychoanalytic tradition, defense mechanisms have been viewed as means of avoiding the anxiety generated by one's own impulses (e.g., unacceptable sexual desires) while at the same time allowing a surreptitious expression of those impulses in modulated form. This way of conceptualizing defense mechanisms appears to contradict the notion that psychological defenses are part of the emotional syndrome itself. The apparent contradiction disappears, however, once it is recognized that people respond to their own thoughts, feelings, and actions, just as they respond to external events. For example, if I suffer from stage fright, I may literally fear how I might react when I step before an audience. ("The only thing we have to fear is fear itself.") In order to avoid the unpleasant consequences of my own fear, I may in fact deny its existence and inhibit its more obvious manifestations. In such instances, denial may be considered a manifestation of a "second-order" fear syndrome.

More commonly, denial is part of a "first-order" syndrome; that is, it is a direct response to a fearful stimulus. If, for example, I am told that I

have terminal cancer, I cannot simply run away, as though threatened by
a robber. I can, however, attempt to avoid the threat in a variety of other
ways, one of which is to deny the accuracy of the diagnosis. There is no
need in such an instance to say that I am defending myself against fear.
The denial is a manifestation of my fear.

Of course, the denial of a fearful event may not be a particularly
adaptive way of avoiding the potential harm – but the same could be said
about breaking out in a cold sweat or visiting a faith healer. To the extent
that denial interferes with other necessary or desirable behaviors, the
"defensive barrier" must indeed be overcome. But the issue of adaptive-
ness should not be prejudged. In many situations, denial may be the most
reasonable and appropriate response that a person could make.

To summarize, in the remainder of this chapter, I will not treat psychological defenses as a separate category, as though the considerations that
apply to other manifestations of an emotional syndrome do not apply to
defense mechanisms. Rather, I shall treat psychological defenses simply
as one of a wide variety of potential manifestations of emotion. Exactly
what is being defended against (the original threat or one's own potential
reactions to the threat) and the adaptive value of the defense are issues
that cannot be decided in the abstract, for they may vary from one emotional episode to another, depending on the circumstances.

Emotions as causes

In both popular and scientific discourse, emotions are often invoked to
explain why a person did – or did not – take protective measures. "The
young woman took evasive action because of her fear." In what sense did
she act *because* of her fear? Or, stated more formally, in what sense can
fear *cause* behavior?

Aristotle (*Physics,* Bk. II) described four ways in which a person might
answer the question Why? These ways refer to efficient, formal, final,
and material causation. This fourfold distinction among types of causes
remains useful today as a starting point for analysis. Due to the exigencies
of space, the present discussion is limited to a brief consideration of how
emotions can be conceptualized as efficient and formal causes.

Emotions as efficient causes

When most people think of causation today, they have in mind an efficient cause – some event antecedent to another event (the effect), such
that the occurrence of the former leads to the occurrence of the latter,

provided that other conditions are favorable. Emotions have often been conceived of in this way, that is, as events (mental or physiological) that impel, prod, or stimulate a person to action.

A relevant example of an efficient-cause type of formulation is the drive model of fear. Janis (1967) has used a variation of this model to explain the effects of fear appeals on compliance with a persuasive message. Very briefly, when fear increases from low to intermediate levels (induced, say, by a vivid depiction of what might happen if the recommended self-protective measures are not adopted), compliance presumably increases. Beyond an optimal level, however, further increases in fear tend to reduce compliance, ostensibly because the fear is so aversive that psychological defenses are activated.

Leventhal (1970) has questioned the adequacy of a drive model to account for the relation between fear and self-protective behavior. In its stead, he has proposed a "parallel response" model, in which fear is viewed as only one of a variety of responses that might be activated by a persuasive message. The various responses (fear, instrumental coping behavior, psychological defenses) may interact with one another, depending on the circumstances, but for the most part they occur in parallel, each subject to its own regulatory principles. More recently, Leventhal (1980; Leventhal & Mosbach, 1983) has expanded this formulation into a more general information-processing model of emotion. According to this latest version of the theory, emotions are like metering or "readout" devices that reflect moment-by-moment changes in the state of the individual. The output of these readout devices (feelings of fear, anger, etc.) is one source of information on which an individual may act.

My purpose is not to criticize the formulations of Janis or Leventhal. Their research is among the best in this area. I do, however, wish to question an assumption they share with numerous other theorists of diverse persuasion – namely, that emotions represent specific events within the organism (drive stimuli, a unique kind of information, or whatever) that can cause the individual to act, in an efficient-cause sense. I shall return to this issue shortly.

Emotions as formal causes

Formal causes are conceptually quite different from efficient causes, and their meaning is not so easily explicated. In one sense, a formal cause can be conceived of as a pattern of prototypic features that guide the formation of an event (or, in the case of an already formed event, that allow it to be classified as a certain type). In another sense, a formal cause is the capacity or disposition to act in a particular way. I shall expand briefly on both senses and note the relation between them.

With respect to the first sense, to say that a person acted because of fear is simply to say that the actions in question conform – more or less – to our prototype of fear or, stated somewhat differently, that the actions are intelligible as members of the class of actions that comprise the category of fear.

When conceived of in this way, fear is an abstraction, a blueprint for guiding and interpreting behavior. In order for that blueprint to become actualized in any given episode of fear, a person must have the capacity or disposition to respond in the appropriate manner. Such a disposition can also be considered a formal cause, but in the second sense noted above.[2]

To illustrate this dispositional sense of formal cause, consider the following questions and answers: Why did the young woman take evasive action? Because she was in a fearful state. Why did the chemical burst into flames? Because it was in a combustible state. Note that, in these explanations, neither fear nor combustibility refers to specific events. The efficient cause of the young woman's evasive action may have been the sight of an oncoming car; it was not her fear. Similarly, the event that caused the fire (in an efficient-cause sense) may have been a spark; it was not the combustibility of the chemical.

The conception of emotion as a syndrome outlined in the previous section is consistent with the notion of a formal cause, in both the senses just described (i.e., as a prototype and as a disposition to respond). Specifically, *to say that a person is in an emotional state implies that the person is disposed to respond in a fashion that conforms to the prototypic features of the syndrome* (cf. Ryle, 1949).

To summarize briefly, there are two common ways in which fear can be said to cause behavior: (a) Some component reactions during fear, and even the belief that one is in a fearful state, may serve as stimuli for the behavior in question (efficient cause); and (b) fear may refer to a syndrome or disposition, of which the behavior in question is one possible manifestation (formal cause). Each type of explanation can be valid and informative under appropriate circumstances; but of the two, the second is the more common and, I believe, the more generally useful. Therefore, I shall expand on it, with special reference to the psychological mechanisms that mediate emotional dispositions.

Psychological mediating mechanisms

To say that emotions are formal causes, in a dispositional sense,[3] does not take us very far. In the physical sciences, dispositional variables (com-

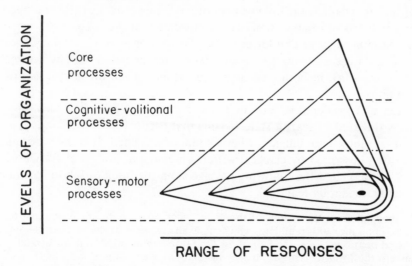

Figure 3.1. Schematic representation of the hierarchical organization of emotional syndromes. Each "cone" represents the set of responses an individual is disposed to make when in a fearful state, and associated mediating mechanisms. The dot to the right of the center of the base of the cones signifies the appraised object of the emotion.

bustibility, elasticity, solubility, and the like) are often explained in terms of processes that occur at a different level of analysis (e.g., molecular structure and activity). Behavioral dispositions, too, must ultimately be explicable in terms of processes defined at other levels of analysis – neurological, psychological, or social, depending on the type of theory being developed. In this section I shall focus on psychological processes. At present, such processes can be described in only the crudest, most hypothetical form. Nevertheless, some important distinctions can be made.

Let us begin with the observation that emotional syndromes not only are variable in time and response, but also are hierarchically organized, lower-order processes being coordinated and informed by higher-order processes. For present purposes, we distinguish three levels of hierarchically organized mediating mechanisms, recognizing that the divisions between levels are inherently arbitrary and that subdivisions could easily be made. These three levels are depicted along the vertical axis of Figure 3.1. The scope or range of responses encompassed by an emotional syndrome is also depicted in Figure 3.1, along the horizontal axis.

More specifically, three classes of emotional syndromes are illustrated in Figure 3.1, each represented by a cone-shaped structure. The area encompassed by the base of each "cone" represents the set of responses the individual is disposed to make while in the emotional state; the height of the cone depicts the involvement of mediating processes at increasingly higher levels of organization. The arrangement of the cones in a concentric fashion suggests that lower levels of organization (e.g., sensory-motor processes) are influenced by higher levels; the direction of influence can, however, work in both directions (i.e., from bottom up as well as from top down).

Let us consider first the innermost "cone" in Figure 3.1. This represents the kind of fearful state (fright) that occurs when a person is faced with an immediate danger, whether real or imagined. It is the syndrome so often described by classical writers on emotion. For example, Darwin (1872/1965) cited the following passage from the Book of Job to illustrate what he meant by fear:

In thoughts from the visions of the night, when deep sleep falleth on men, fear came upon me, and trembling, which made all my bones to shake. Then the spirit passed before my face; the hair of my flesh stood up. It stood still, but I could not discern the form thereof: an image was before my eyes, there was silence, and I heard a voice saying, Shall mortal man be more just than God? Shall a man be more pure than his Maker? (Job 4:13)

During acute fear, many responses (e.g., trembling, goose flesh) tend to be automatic and reflexive; that is, they are mediated by simple sensory–motor processes. Even during acute episodes, however, instrumental responses may be the primary manifestations of fear. This fact is not apparent from the description of Job, but recall the anecdote of the young woman in the automobile accident: She took evasive action to avoid a head-on collision and did not "break down," trembling, until after the danger had passed. Evasive actions are instrumental responses that require at least minimal involvement of higher-order (cognitive–volitional) processes.

The passage taken from the Book of Job is also of interest for what it says about the appraised object of fear (the spirit that passed before Job's face). The appraised object cannot be identified in any simple way with the events that actually initiate an episode (in an efficient-cause sense). The appraised object is an evaluation, a meaning imposed on events; it is part of the syndrome itself. The actual events that trigger the syndrome (e.g., that caused Job to "see" a spirit and to "hear" voices) may not be known or recognized as such. To capture this feature of emotional objects, as well as the fact that the symptoms of fear do not necessarily cease when the appraised danger has passed, I have drawn the bases of the cones in Figure 3.1 so that they encompass the appraised object.[4]

The middle cone in Figure 3.1 represents syndromes intermediate in scope. Consider again the young woman in our anecdote. Because of the bad weather conditions, she might have been afraid of an accident from the time she left for work in the morning, not just from the time her car started to skid on the ice. Hence, she drove especially carefully, took unusual safety precautions, and so forth. In other words, her fear was mediated largely by cognitive–volitional processes. The intensity of fear in such instances is judged not by the amount of physiological arousal, say, that the person exhibits, but by the range of behavior that can be explained by reference to the fear.

Let us turn now to long-standing fears, represented by the outermost cone in Figure 3.1, and to the highest levels of mediation. Job, it may be assumed, did not fear God only on the nights that he experienced apparitions. Rather, the apparitions, trembling, goose flesh, and other signs of acute fear were just some of the manifestations of a long-standing fear of God. Stated differently, fear of God lay at the core of Job's personality and helped to define the kind of person he was. But what sort of processes constitute the core of one's personality?

A number of psychologists have proposed that individual behavior is guided by implicit "theories" (e.g., Epstein, 1973, 1980; Guidano & Liotti, 1983) about oneself and the world. The basic argument can be summarized as follows. Implicit theories that constitute the self share with more formal scientific theories what Lakatos (1974) has called a "metaphysical hard core." In the case of scientific theories, the metaphysical hard core is a set of tacit assumptions and rules that determine the kinds of questions that are asked, the research procedures that are employed, and even what will count as data or empirical facts. Similarly, individual theories about the self presume a set of core assumptions and rules that are poorly articulated ("unconscious," in a sense) but that determine much of a person's conscious experience and behavior, emotional as well as deliberate. For example, a person whose core assumptions include a strong sense of duty and personal responsibility may not be able to experience anger in certain situations (e.g., orders from a superior that are perceived as legitimate), but instead may manifest frustration in other ways, such as depression or even somatic illness. Colloquially speaking, it is not "in that person" to become angry in such situations. Similarly, the agoraphobic who cannot leave the house for fear of being alone among strangers is suffering from faulty assumptions and rules that lie at the core of his or her personality (Guidano & Liotti, 1983).

At this point, the question arises, Of the three cones depicted in Figure 3.1, which represents "true" fear? The answer is that they all do. Most psychological theories have focused on the acute fears represented by the innermost cone (for an exception, see Leeper's, 1970, motivational theory of emotion). However, as other chapters in this volume indicate, the concept of fear is often – even usually – used in a broader sense, roughly equivalent to the intermediate cone. Thus, when Greenberg (Chapter 11) discusses the relation between fear of crime and self-protective behavior, she is not referring to the acute reactions a person might experience during an actual armed robbery, but rather to more extended dispositions to respond. Such dispositions may last for months or even years, and they may encompass a broad range of behavior, depending on the personality (core constructs) of the individual and on uniformities in the environment.

But if the various kinds of fear I have been discussing are equally real (and imperceptibly shade into one another), it does not follow that the same considerations apply to each, any more than the same considerations apply to the acute and chronic manifestations of a disease (such as malaria). One of the greatest sources of confusion in this area is undoubtedly the tendency to conflate emotional syndromes that are of different scope and that involve different mediating mechanisms.

The relation of emotion to cognition and physiological arousal

In the preceding sections, I have argued for the following two propositions: (a) To say that a person acts because of fear is usually (and most properly) to offer a dispositional explanation, as opposed to an explanation in terms of efficient causes; and (b) emotional dispositions are mediated by hierarchically organized mechanisms or processes. I shall now add a third proposition: (c) the relevant mediating mechanisms are not unique to emotion, but involve the same processes that mediate other forms of behavior. Like most propositions concerning the emotions, this one is subject to considerable controversy. I do not wish to enter into the controversy here. However, no discussion of emotion would be complete without some reference to the possible relations between emotion and cognition, on the one hand, and between emotion and physiological arousal, on the other.

Emotion and cognition

Theorists who argue that there is something unique about the emotions (i.e., in terms of underlying processes) can find support in the distinction between emotion and cognition that is inherent in ordinary language. *Webster's Third New International Dictionary* defines "cognition" as "the act or process of knowing in the broadest sense; *specif:* an intellectual process by which knowledge is gained about perception or ideas – distinguished from *affection* and *conation.*" Even cognitive psychologists, who tend to extend the concept of cognition to cover the full range of psychological phenomena, draw a distinction between "hot" (emotional) and "cold" (rational) cognitions.

Some speculations by Simon (1983), a leading cognitive theorist as well as economist, illustrate what is meant by a "hot" cognition. Referring to Rachel Carson's book, *Silent Spring,* Simon asks why this work had such an impact when the problems it depicted were already known to ecologists and biologists. Answering his own question, Simon asserts that Carson described the problems in a way that aroused emotion; and the emotion, once aroused, "wouldn't let us go off and worry about other problems until something had been done about this one" (p. 30). Simon makes similar observations about works of art and the humanities in general – for example, *War and Peace* versus a treatise on military sociology, Proust and Chekov versus a textbook on personality, and so forth. Simon further suggests that

most human beings are able to attend to issues longer, to think harder about them, to receive deeper impressions that last longer, if information is presented in a context of emotion – a sort of hot dressing – than if it is presented wholly without affect. (p. 32)

Simon's main concern in the work cited (1983) is with human reasoning or rationality; his remarks on emotion are therefore rather cursory, and I do not want to read more into them than he intended.[5] Nevertheless, his remarks are indicative of a common argument among cognitive theorists. That argument goes somewhat as follows. When a person reads a book like *Silent Spring* or *War and Peace,* two kinds of processes occur – a "cold" cognition (rationality), which mediates comprehension of the factual material, and a "hot" cognition (emotion), which guides a person's attention and goads that person into action.

The difficulty with this line of argument becomes apparent if we return for a moment to our earlier distinction between efficient and formal causes. Because people respond differently when emotionally involved in a topic than when in a more disinterested or dispassionate state, it is tempting to postulate some inner efficient cause to account for the difference. However, emotion is not something added – "a sort of hot dressing" – that makes us think harder and longer about an issue. Rather, "emotional" is one of the ways we describe an issue about which we think long and hard (i.e., that is personally involving). Stated in dispositional (formal-cause) terms, emotional concepts are shorthand ways of indicating the kinds of reactions a person is disposed to make in situations that are personally involving.

I do not deny that there may be a variety of ways in which information can be conveyed and processed. For example, the type of analogical, holistic thought manifested in imagery may involve different processes than the more linear, analytic thought characteristic of verbal reasoning. It should go without saying, however, that imagery and related processes cannot be equated with emotionality: For one thing, imagery plays an important role in many nonemotional activities; for another thing, analytic thought processes can profoundly influence emotional reactions.

What is true of imagery is also true of other modes of information processing that might be postulated as uniquely emotional. Almost 100 years ago, Dewey (1895) made the following observation:

We take a certain phase which *serves a certain end,* namely, giving us information, and call that intellectual; we take another phase, having another end or value, that of excitement, and call that emotional. But does any one suppose that, *apart from our interpretation of values,* there is one process in itself intellectual, and another process in itself emotional? I cannot even frame an idea of what is meant. (p. 21)

If Dewey were alive today, I suspect he would have equal difficulty in trying to frame an idea of what is meant by "hot" as opposed to "cold" cognition.

Emotion and physiological arousal

It might be objected that emotional states are distinguished, not by unique cognitive processes, but rather by the involvement of physiological arousal or the central neural mechanisms that mediate such arousal (see Schachter, 1971). Without going into detail on this issue, I shall simply make the following points:

1. The tendency to associate emotions with physiological activity has a long history within Western intellectual tradition. It is, however, a history marked by prejudicial assumptions and symbolic associations that have little basis in reality (Averill, 1974).
2. In some non-Western societies, physiological arousal seems to have little or no bearing on the attribution of emotion, either to oneself or another (Lutz, 1982).
3. Even within Western tradition, the novelist (not to mention the proverbial person-in-the-street) focuses more on the instigating conditions and on how the world is perceived than on physiological arousal when describing emotions (Benson, 1967).
4. The *belief* that one is aroused may be more important in determining the experience of emotion than is a person's actual state of physiological arousal (Valins, 1967).
5. At best, any close relation between physiological arousal and emotional

experience is limited to rather short term, acute episodes (e.g., those represented by the innermost cone in Figure 3.1) and to some emotions but not others (e.g., fear as opposed to hope).

6. Even limiting consideration to short-term fear reactions, there is no simple relation between the emotion and physiological arousal. A person who flees is in a different state of arousal than a person who freezes or who faints. Patterns of physiological arousal are no less variable than patterns of overt activity.

7. These considerations indicate that physiological arousal is not a necessary condition for emotions. Even more obvious is the fact that physiological arousal is not a sufficient condition. That is, states of high arousal may occur without any corresponding emotional experience, (e.g., after strenuous exercise).

8. What is true of physiological arousal is also true, mutatis mutandis, of other reactions (facial expressions, gestures, etc.) often associated with emotional states.

In short, physiological arousal may be an important and common component of some emotional syndromes. However, any attempt to link emotions too closely with arousal is liable to confuse rather than clarify the problems that face us.

The art of persuasion

Thus far, I have been dealing with issues that are rather abstract and perhaps a bit removed from the concerns of those whose task it is to encourage self-protective behavior. In this section, therefore, I shall try to relate some of the above considerations to one applied area, namely, the use of emotional appeals as an aid to persuasion. Let me begin by examining briefly some of the criteria for classifying an appeal as emotional.

Just as there is nothing unique about the emotions (at the level of part processes or internal mediating mechanisms), neither is there anything unique about emotionally arousing stimuli. Indeed, as described earlier, the appraised object of an emotion is a meaning imposed on events, a part of the emotional syndrome itself. Nevertheless, we can say something about the characteristics of appeals that are commonly classified as emotional:

1. Perhaps the most important criterion for classifying an appeal as emotional is its factual content; that is, does the appeal describe or portend a situation that is socially recognized as emotional, for example, because it connotes danger (fear), loss (grief), insult (anger), and so forth? This criterion might seem blatantly obvious. However, as the warning on cigarette packages indicates, not all descriptions of danger or other adverse situations are particularly emotional–or persuasive.

2. An emotional appeal relates the situation (danger, loss, etc.) to the self in an immediate and personal way. This is the criterion emphasized by

Simon (1983) when he said of Rachel Carson's book, *Silent Spring*, that it "wouldn't let us go off and worry about other problems until something had been done about this one."
3. The third major criterion for classifying an appeal as emotional has to do with the contrast, discussed earlier, between emotion and cognition (rationality). Appeals that are either *non*rational or *ir*rational may be classified as emotional, almost by default.

Let me expand on this third criterion briefly. A *non*rational appeal is one to which the concept of rationality simply does not apply. For example, a work of art, such as a painting or symphony, is not judged by the rules of logic. Extending this example, an appeal that makes prominent use of imagery, vivid scenes, or other "artistic" techniques to increase the impact of the message is often regarded as emotional.

An *ir*rational appeal is one that involves a fallacious or unreasonable argument. Unfortunately, people tend to regard as irrational any argument with which they strongly disagree. Even when they cannot find anything wrong with the underlying logic, they can always question the basic assumptions. Hence, it is not uncommon for a person to label an appeal as emotional simply because it does not conform to his or her prior convictions.

These three criteria for classifying an appeal as emotional (factual content, personal relevance, and contrast with the rational) can be illustrated by reference to the television movie *The Day After*. Although ostensibly politically neutral, the implicit intent of the film was to promote nuclear disarmament, and its showing was highly publicized by the nuclear freeze movement. The film depicted the devastation, suffering, and breakdown in social order that would occur after even a limited nuclear war between the United States and the Soviet Union. This information was made highly personal through the focus on events in a prototypical American city and through viewer identification with the major characters in the film (an ordinary family). The information was conveyed almost exclusively by nonrational means. The movie did not indicate how the war started, nor did it contain any explicit recommendations for averting such a war. Rather, the focus was on the horribleness of the event, graphically portrayed by visual imagery and symbolism. Most viewers agreed that the film had a highly emotional appeal.

In anticipation of future arguments, let us consider briefly the effectiveness of *The Day After* as a persuasive film. In a poll conducted for *Time* magazine (Kelly, 1983) by Abt Associates of Cambridge, Massachusetts, viewers were questioned before and after the film. The number of people (unspecified) who thought that war is unlikely by the year 2000 rose slightly from 32 to 35%; also, the percentage of people who approved present defense policies increased from 54 to 58%. At least in the short run, the film evidently did not achieve the effects hoped for by the nuclear freeze movement.

Why was *The Day After* seemingly so ineffective? If the analysis of the preceding sections has any validity, one would anticipate that the arousal of fear per se would simply increase the probability that people would make whatever coping responses they are already disposed to make. Hardly anyone doubts the horribleness of a nuclear holocaust; there is, however, little agreement on the best strategy to prevent such an event. Thus, after seeing a movie such as *The Day After,* people who believed beforehand that a strong defense is the best deterrence should have been strengthened in their conviction; similarly, people who believed that disarmament is the appropriate course should have been strengthened in their opinion. And each group would most likely accuse the other of engaging in mass denial or simplistic thinking – of responding to emotion rather than to reason.[6]

Let me turn now to the results of controlled laboratory and field research. In a typical study of this genre, a message designed to encourage the use of seat belts, say, might be presented under conditions of low, intermediate, and high levels of fear. At the lowest level of fear, the risks of not wearing a seat belt might be presented in a straightforward, factual manner, with visual aids innocuously displayed. At an intermediate level, the visual presentations might be made more prominent, thus dramatizing potential injuries. At the highest level of fear, the "blood and guts" of an automobile accident might be shown in close-up, highlighting the suffering of the victim. In all conditions, the factual information is supposedly held constant. (However, as will be discussed more fully below, that is not really possible. Inevitably, the fear manipulation alters the focus of attention, personalizes events, makes some features of the message salient, distracts from other features, provokes prior associations, and so forth. Thus, the factual information may remain constant, but only in a technical sense – i.e., in the mind of the experimenter, not in the mind of the subject.)

Many variations on the above design can be imagined: The detail and logic of the factual argument could be varied; the effects of different subject variables (social class, sex, driving experience, etc.) might be investigated; alternative coping strategies could be recommended and assessed; and so forth.

After reviewing a large number of studies of this type, Rogers (1983) concluded that a fear appeal increases the persuasiveness of a message only if it alters (a) the appraisal of the potential harm caused by the hazard, (b) the subjective probability that the hazard will occur if self-protective measures are not taken, and/or (c) the judged effectiveness of any self-protective measures that are recommended. These three factors, it might be noted, are the same factors emphasized in the health belief model, as described by Cleary (Chapter 6), as well as in other, more rationalistic models of behavior change (e.g., Ajzen & Fischbein's, 1980, theory of reasoned action).

The question then becomes, Under what conditions does a fear appeal influence one or another of these three variables? Perhaps the easiest way to address this question is to ask a series of more specific questions.

Does the fear appeal focus attention on salient features of the persuasive message, leading a person to think about and elaborate on its content? As noted earlier, one of the typical features of an emotional appeal is that it "captures" a person's attention and "demands" active involvement. Of course, a high level of fear can either direct attention toward or draw attention away from the content of the message. Let us consider only the former case (since the latter simply leads to the converse conclusions). Whether attention and involvement increase the persuasiveness of a message depends, in part, on the strength of the argument (or the extent to which it is convincing). When a message is weak, at least from the standpoint of the recipient, or elicits strong counterarguments, greater persuasion can sometimes be achieved under conditions of low involvement (see Eagly & Chaiken, 1984, for a discussion of relevant research). To take a concrete example, if the arguments presented in Rachel Carson's book, *Silent Spring,* had been weak, the emotional appeal of the book might have been counterproductive; but the arguments were not weak, and hence the book was quite persuasive.

Does the fear appeal alter the believability of the persuasive message? One of the greatest impediments to the adoption of preventive measures is a belief in personal invulnerability. Others may suffer disaster, but I do not. (See Weinstein, 1984, for a discussion of some of the factors that lead to such an attitude.) A major rationale for the use of fear appeals is that they have the potential to eliminate this sense of invulnerability. By fostering identification with the victims ("people just like you") and through dramatic imagery that cannot be ignored, the fear appeal is designed to change a person's attitude from "It can't happen to me" to "It could easily happen to me." There are, however, two potential difficulties with this approach. First, unless clear and reasonable protective measures are available, the fear appeal may simply encourage an attitude of resignation: "Whatever will be will be, so why worry about it." Second, when the probability of a hazard actually occurring is low–as is usually the case–the fear appeal may be dismissed as a "scare tactic," thus reducing the credibility of the message as a whole. In this respect, instructive parallels can be drawn between fear appeals and warning signals. The latter lose their credibility if the predicted hazard does not materialize, and the loss of credibility is a function of the amount of prior fear induced by the warning (Breznitz, 1984).

Does the fear appeal alter the content or meaning of the persuasive message? As discussed earlier, emotions do not simply arise; they are meaningful and often purposeful patterns of response, even if we do not always recognize them as such. To experience the appropriate emotion at the appropriate time and in the appropriate manner is a goal avidly sought by many persons. This may not be as true of fear as of many other emotions (e.g., love). Still, there is an excitement about fear that is intrinsically motivating to many persons (Zuckerman, 1979); and under certain circumstances, extrinsic motives may be associated with the manifestations of fear. Job's fear of God, described earlier, illustrates this point. On a more mundane level, people who do not show fear when danger is real may be regarded–by themselves as well as others–as fools rather than heroes. The important point is that a fear appeal almost always has implications for an individual's own motives and goals, sense of self (core processes), and broader cultural values. These implications can alter the meaning of the persuasive message, sometimes radically–for example, by changing a threat into a dare.

Does the fear appeal trigger preestablished ways of thinking that lead people to process information in a "mindless" fashion? In everyday affairs, decisions are often made on the basis of simple decision rules or heuristics (rules of thumb). In the case of a persuasive message, a decision may be based on such superficial cues as the length of the message, the number of arguments, and the likability of the source (Chaiken, 1980; Slovic, Fischhoff, & Lichtenstein, Chapter 1). In a sense, psychological defense mechanisms can also be conceptualized as simple and relatively automatic decision rules that are triggered by early warnings of danger. I have already discussed denial as a defense (a cognitive avoidance response). It goes without saying that if denial and related defenses are triggered, the persuasiveness of a message may be short-circuited. But there is another class of defense mechanisms, generally grouped under the rubric of sensitization (a kind of hypervigilance), that may have the opposite effect. A person prone to sensitizing modes of defense has a low threshold for the perception of threat and hence may be *too* prone to adopting preventive measures. The hypochondriac is a good example. For people predisposed to either denial or sensitization, a fear appeal may be counterproductive.

Does the fear appeal increase the probability of behavioral responses being incompatible with the recommended response? A prototypic feature of fear is avoidance behavior; yet many preventive measures require that a person approach or confront a potential danger. In such instances, a fear appeal may arouse incompatible response tendencies. This phenomenon is well illustrated by a study by Leventhal and Watts (1966). Visitors at a state fair viewed motion pictures dealing with smoking and lung cancer. The films were designed to elicit high, medium, or low levels of fear. Two types of preventive behavior were assessed: Immediately after the films, the subjects had the opportunity to obtain a chest X ray, and five months later, a questionnaire was sent to all the subjects to determine whether they had reduced their smoking. The number of smokers who had obtained X rays actually *decreased* as fear arousal increased. However the follow-up questionnaire revealed that smokers in the high-fear condition now smoked less than the other groups. Evidently, subjects who saw the film eliciting a high level of fear avoided the X ray because it might reveal the very condition they feared. A reduction in smoking, by contrast, was more consistent with a normal avoidance response.

I could continue with similar questions, but by now the major point should be clear. Fear is not a simple event – a special cognitive process or mode of response – that directly influences the persuasiveness of a message and hence the adoption of preventive measures. Rather, "fear" is a shorthand term for a complex and highly variable syndrome. The way that fear is manifested on any given occasion is a function of a host of personal (predisposing) and situational variables. Does an appeal to fear facilitate persuasion? Sometimes it does (probably more often than not), and sometimes it does not. In the final analysis, persuasiveness depends on the factual content of a message, both with regard to the nature of the danger (its harmfulness and probability) and the potential effectiveness of any recommended coping responses. The usefulness of a fear appeal in increasing persuasiveness depends on whether attention is directed toward or away from the factual content, whether comprehension is facilitated or inhibited, and whether compatible or competing coping responses are elicited.

At present, persuasion is more an art than a science, and perhaps it will always be so. If that is the case, the role of the social sciences in this area may have to be reevaluated. Specifically, social scientists can contribute to the art of persuasion in three main ways. First, populations most at risk must be identified and characterized (e.g., in terms of their motives, goals, and values). Second, through systematic research, conceptual tools should be honed and analytic skills developed, so that those responsible for the design of programs do not overlook potentially confounding variables. Third, social scientists can play a role analogous to that of art critics in the evaluation of programs. As Robertson (Chapter 13) has illustrated with respect to education programs related to driving and drug abuse, intuitive appeal and face validity offer no assurance that a program will be successful.

Emotion: when is a snark not a snark?

At the onset of this chapter, I said that trying to find responses or processes that are uniquely emotional is like hunting a snark. In fact, during the course of the chapter it might seem that I have eliminated any need for considering emotions as a separate class of phenomena. In a sense, that is true. There is no thread, no essence, that is common even to all fears (no less to all emotions) and that is not shared by at least some other, nonemotional phenomena. But this does not mean that emotional concepts are meaningless, or that they could be easily dispensed with. Before concluding this chapter, therefore, let me illustrate briefly by analogy where I believe the meaning and significance of emotional concepts are to be found.

In the nineteenth century, some "radical" physiologists proposed that disease concepts could be eliminated from medicine (Temkin, 1968). After all, they pointed out, the same physiological processes are operative during both health and disease. When a person comes down with the measles, say, a new "measles process" need not be invoked. What happens is that the ordinary physiological process becomes exaggerated in response to the pathogen or, if not exaggerated, then organized in a fashion that interferes with other processes vital to the well-being of the individual. If the interference is sufficient to be recognized by society, we may speak of an illness or disease. "Disease," however, has no special status as a physiological concept.

In response to these arguments, it may be said that the way a disease is recognized and categorized is of utmost importance, both for the individual and for society. Any attempt to eliminate disease concepts would have wide-ranging and largely negative consequences. But the radical physiologists were nevertheless correct in one important respect. The strong tendency to reify diseases as though they involve unique and fundamentally different physiological processes is a theoretical dead end.

From time to time, some psychological theorists (e.g., Duffy, 1941) have suggested that emotional concepts can – and should – be eliminated from scientific discourse, since emotions do not involve processes that are different from those that mediate nonemotional behavior. Other theorists, recognizing that emotional concepts are too useful to be abandoned, have concluded that emotions *must* somehow involve unique processes.

If this chapter were devoted to theories of emotion, I would try to demonstrate how emotional concepts can be theoretically significant and yet not refer to processes that are in themselves "emotional." The direction that such a demonstration would take is perhaps evident by now. If emotions cannot be reduced to unique psychological or physiological processes, their meaning and significance must be sought on another level of analysis.

Elsewhere (e.g., Averill, 1976b, 1980a,b, 1982, 1984), I have attempted to show how emotions are *socially* constituted or institutionalized ways of responding. That kind of theoretical analysis is not of particular relevance to our present concerns, except in one important respect. If we better understand the social norms and rules that help constitute various emotional syndromes, we would be in a better position to design programs that would enlist emotions in the service of preventive behavior. Unfortunately, most research on the emotions has tended to be reductionistic and to focus almost exclusively on short-term emergency reactions. This is particularly true in the case of fear. As a result, we are in the position of a person who can speak a language fluently (i.e., we all know what it is to fear something) but who cannot articulate the grammatical (social) rules that make speech (fear) meaningful.

Conclusions and implications

Emotions are hierarchically organized dispositions to appraise situations in particular ways and to respond accordingly. A common misconception is to interpret emotions as efficient causes (i.e., events within the individual), thus deflecting attention from the personal, situational, and social variables that actually control behavior.

It follows that studying the effects of fear is not at all like studying the effects, say, of a new drug. Fear is not an unknown quantity that somehow promotes self-protective behavior, as a drug might promote healing. A major goal of psychological research on emotion should be to make explicit what we already know implicitly (i.e., the social norms and rules that in part constitute emotional syndromes), so that we do not distort, obscure, or ignore important variables in our attempt to understand and influence behavior.

The manifestations of fear are quite varied. To say anything meaningful, much greater precision is needed than is typically found in the literature. It is not sufficient to say, for example, that a person fears cancer and that is why the person did (or did not) adopt a certain protective measure. What is it about cancer that this person most fears – pain and suffering, financial hardship, possible death, loss of contact with family and friends? And how does the person perceive that a particular coping response will help protect against the feared outcomes? Finally, how does the person regard his or her fear in relation to sense of self and broader social values? Without such specificity, reference to fear may be more misleading than informative.

In the case of broad-based programs designed to encourage self-protective behavior, it is not possible to tailor an appeal to fit the idiosyncracies of each individual. However, if we had a better understanding of the general cultural and subcultural norms regarding fear, we would be in a better position to encourage self-protective behavior. Fear has a different meaning in different contexts and for different subgroups of the population.

If a program to encourage self-protective behavior is to have lasting effects, it must touch on higher mediating processes, especially those related to an individual's sense of self. This requires a mix of strategies. An appeal that evokes only short-term, low-level fear responses may have correspondingly short-term effects, or perhaps even effects contrary to those intended.

It is sometimes easier to shame people into action than to frighten them into action; many people will do things out of affection for others that they would not do out of fear for themselves; and if their pride is at stake, some people may face almost any danger. Anger can be a particularly effective emotion in getting people to take corrective action against unwarranted or avoidable dangers (Averill, 1982). (Witness the success of MADD – Mothers Against Drunk Driving – in mobilizing public opinion and legislative action.) Unfortunately, such emotions as shame, affection, pride, and anger have been little investigated in the context of persuasion or preventive behavior. I do not wish to reinforce the oversight by the focus of this chapter on fear.

Ideally, evaluation should be an integral part of any program to encourage self-protective behavior. Emotional appeals, in particular, may have a face validity that does not translate into practical results.

Notes

1 An amusing example of identifying an emotion with one of its aspects is provided by a Grimm's fairy tale, "The Story of the Youth Who Went Forth to Learn What Fear Was." The hero of the story is a young man of lowly birth and limited intelligence who had never experienced fear, which he equated with shuddering. Because of his lack of fear, he embarked on many dangerous undertakings, surviving by dumb luck. His feats eventually won him a treasure and the hand of a princess in marriage. He was still discontented, however, because he wanted to know what it was like to experience fear. One morning while he was asleep, his wife doused him with cold water. He awoke with a shudder, immensely pleased. At last, he thought he knew what fear was. (I thank Randy Cornelius of Vassar College for bringing this tale to my attention.)

2 The notions of formal cause as prototype and as disposition correspond roughly to the conceptions of Plato and Aristotle, respectively. For additional details, see Averill (1976a: Chs. 3, 5).

3 In order to avoid confusion, emotional states must be distinguished from personality traits, such as timidity and hostility. Emotional states are episodic dispositions; that is, they are focused on a specific event and are relatively time limited, reversible, and sometimes coterminous with their expression. In contrast, personality traits are relatively enduring predispositions to enter into emotional states under appropriate circumstances.

4 If the frightening event is sufficiently severe, signs of emotional upset may be manifested even after an extended lapse of time, as in the post-traumatic stress syndrome.

5 See Simon (1967, 1982) for more extended discussions of his views on emotion.

6 Schofield and Pavelchak (1985) have published a detailed review of the impact of *The Day After*. They present evidence that the film may have been more influential than the surveys (such as that by Abt Associates, reported above) indicate. But Schofield and Pavelchak attribute the impact not to the film per se, but rather to the publicity and political controversy that surrounded it. For the most part, their analysis is consistent with that presented in this section.

References

Ajzen, I., & Fishbein, M. 1980. *Understanding attitudes and predicting social behavior.* Englewood-Cliffs, N.J.: Prentice-Hall.

Averill, J. R. 1974. An analysis of psychophysiological symbolism and its influence on theories of emotion. *Journal for the Theory of Social Behavior 4:* 147–90.

Averill, J. R., ed. 1976a. *Patterns of psychological thought: Readings in classical and contemporary texts.* Washington, D.C.: Hemisphere.

Averill, J. R. 1976b. Emotion and anxiety: Sociocultural, biological, and psychological determinants. In *Emotion and anxiety: New concepts, methods and applications,* ed. M. Zuckerman & C. C. Speilberger, pp. 87–130. New York: LEA-Wiley.

Averill, J. R. 1980a. A constructivist view of emotion. In *Theories of emotion,* ed. R. Plutchik & H. Kellerman, pp. 305–39. New York: Academic Press.

Averill, J. R. 1980b. On the paucity of positive emotions. In *Assessment and modification of emotional behaviors,* ed. K. R. Blankstein, P. Pliner, & J. Polivy, pp. 7–45. New York: Plenum.

Averill, J. R. 1982. *Anger and Aggression: An essay on emotion.* New York: Springer-Verlag.

Averill, J. R. 1984. The acquisition of emotions during adulthood. In *Affective processes in adult development,* ed. C. Z. Malatesta & C. Izard, pp. 23–43. Beverly Hills, Calif.: Sage.

Benson, J. 1967. Emotion and expression. *Philosophical Review 76:* 335–57.

Breznitz, S. 1983. *The denial of stress.* New York: International Universities Press.

Breznitz, S. 1984. *Cry wolf: The psychology of false alarms.* Hillsdale, N.J.: Erlbaum.

Chaiken, S. 1980. Heuristic versus systematic information processing and the use of source versus message cues in persuasion. *Journal of Personality and Social Psychology 39:* 752–66.

Darwin, C. 1965. *The expression of the emotions in man and animals.* University of Chicago Press. (Original work published 1872.)

Dewey, J. 1985. The theory of emotion. II. The significance of emotions. *Psychological Review 2:* 13–32.

Duffy, E. 1941. An explanation of "emotional" phenomena without the use of the concept "emotion." *Journal of General Psychology 25:* 283–93.

Eagly, A. H., & Chaiken, S. 1984. Psychological theories of persuasion. In *Advances in experimental social psychology,* vol. 17, ed. L. Berkowitz, pp. 267–359. New York: Academic Press.

Epstein, S. 1973. The self-concept revisited, or a theory of a theory. *American Psychologist 28:* 404–16.

Epstein, S. 1980. The self-concept: A review and the proposal of an integrated theory of personality. In *Personality: Basic aspects and current research,* ed. E. Staub, pp. 82–132. Englewood Cliffs, N.J.: Prentice-Hall.

Guidano, V. F., & Liotti, G. 1983. *Cognitive processes and emotional disorders.* New York: Guilford.

Hochschild, A. R. 1979. Emotion work, feeling rules, and social structure. *American Journal of Sociology 85:* 551–75.

Janis, I. L. 1967. Effects of fear arousal on attitude change: Recent developments in theory and experimental research. In *Advances in experimental social psychology,* vol. 3, ed. L. Berkowitz, pp. 166–224. New York: Academic Press.

Kelly, J. 1983, December 5. Fallout from a TV attack. *Time,* pp. 38–40.

Lakatos, I. 1974. Falsification and the methodology of scientific research programs. In *Criticism and the growth of knowledge,* ed. I. Latkatos & A. Musgrave, pp. 91–195. Cambridge University Press.

Leeper, R. W. 1970. The motivational and perceptual properties of emotions as indicating their fundamental character and role. In *Feelings and emotions: The Loyola Symposium,* ed. M. B. Arnold, pp. 151–85. New York: Academic Press.

Leventhal, H. 1970. Findings and theory in the study of fear communications. In *Advances in experimental social psychology,* vol. 5, ed. L. Berkowitz, pp. 119–86. New York: Academic Press.

Leventhal, H. 1980. Toward a comprehensive theory of emotion. In *Advances in experimental social psychology,* vol. 13, ed. L. Berkowitz, pp. 140–207. New York: Academic Press.

Leventhal, H., & Mosbach, P. A. 1983. The perceptual–motor theory of emotion. In *Social psychophysiology,* ed. J. T. Caciappo & R. E. Petty, pp. 353–88. New York: Guilford.

Leventhal, H., & Watts, J. 1966. Sources of resistance to fear arousing communications on smoking and lung cancer. *Journal of Personality 34:* 155–75.

Lutz, C. 1982. The domain of emotion words on Ifaluk. *American Ethnologist 9:* 113–28.

Rogers, R. W. 1983. Cognitive and physiological processes in fear appeals and attitude change: A revised theory of protection motivation. In *Social psychophysiology,* ed. J. T. Cacioppo & R. E. Petty, pp. 153–76. New York: Guilford Press.

Ryle, G. 1949. *The concept of mind.* London: Hutchinson.

Schachter, S. 1971. *Emotion, obesity, and crime.* New York: Academic Press.

Schofield, J., & Pavelchak, M. 1985. *The Day After:* The impact of a media event. *American Psychologist 40:* 542–8.

Simon, H. A. 1967. Motivational and emotional controls of cognition. *Psychological Review 74:* 29–39.

78   JAMES R. AVERILL

Simon, H. A. 1982. Affect and cognition: Comments. In *Affect and Cognition: The 17th Annual Carnegie Symposium on Cognition,* ed. M. S. Clark & S. T. Fiske, pp. 333–42. Hillsdale, N.J.: Erlbaum.

Simon, H. A. 1983. *Reason in human affairs.* Stanford, Calif.: Stanford University Press.

Temkin, O. 1968. The history of classification in the medical sciences. In *The role and methodology of classification in psychiatry and psychopathology* (Public Health Service Publication No. 1584), ed. M. M. Katz, J. O. Cole, & W. E. Barton, pp. 11–20. Washington, D.C.: U.S. Government Printing Office.

Valins, S. 1967. Emotionality and information concerning internal reactions. *Journal of Personality and Social Psychology 6:* 458–63.

Weinstein, N. 1984. Why it won't happen to me: Perceptions of risk factors and susceptibility. *Health Psychology 3:* 431–57.

Zuckerman, M. 1979. *Sensation seeking: Beyond the optimal level of arousal.* New York: Wiley.

4　　The diffusion of innovations perspective

Everett M. Rogers

This chapter reviews the main lesson learned to date about the diffusion of preventive innovations. It discusses the application of these lessons to such issues as preventive health behavior (especially heart disease prevention), family planning, and energy conservation. I shall argue here that preventive behaviors are particularly difficult to bring about, whether they entail going on a low-salt diet, installing a burglar alarm system in one's home, or purchasing flood insurance. Prevention campaigns that have adopted strategies drawn from diffusion theory have tended to be more effective than other preventive efforts.

Preventive innovations

Diffusion is the process by which an innovation is communicated through certain channels over a period of time among the members of a social system (Rogers, 1983: 5). Thus, diffusion is a type of communication – the communication of messages about new ideas. *Communication* is a process in which participants create and share information with one another in order to reach a mutual understanding (Rogers & Kinkaid, 1981). Although early definitions of communication implied a one-way process, we now think of communication as a two-way process of convergence. Such convergence (or divergence) occurs as two or more individuals move toward one another (or farther apart) in the meanings they ascribe to events.

One important type of message deals with innovations. An *innovation* is an idea, practice, or object that is perceived to be new by an individual or other unit of adoption (Rogers, 1983: 35). Many innovations offer an immediate increase in some desired quantity. For example, a farmer may adopt a new fertilizer in order to increase crop yields; a medical doctor may prescribe a new drug to cure an ailing patient. Most of the approximately 3,500 past studies of the diffusion of innovations concern innovations of this type.

79

However, a few studies in the diffusion tradition have looked at *preventive innovations*. Here the individual or organization adopts an innovation now (at time t_1) in order to avoid an unwanted event at some future time (t_2). Examples are the use of contraceptives to prevent pregnancy and the use of automobile seat belts to reduce the risk of injury. A distinctive aspect of preventive innovations is that their beneficial effects are (a) delayed in time and (b) difficult to assess because, even without the precaution, the harm might never have occurred. A certain degree of uncertainty is always involved in the decision to adopt an innovation, because innovations represent new ideas. The uncertainty is especially great when the innovation is preventive.

Diffusion of innovations research[1]

Diffusion research began in the United States, and this is where a general theoretical model of diffusion was first formulated. Beginning about 1960, this diffusion model was applied to Third World nations, initially without adequate questioning of its legitimacy in this new context. Only in the 1970s did scholars begin to assess the distinctiveness of Third World conditions. The diffusion model has been incorporated into development programs in Latin America, Africa, and Asia. It fits well with the desire of national governments to convey new ideas in agriculture, health, family planning, and education to their people.

A tremendous body of research has accumulated since the mid-1940s on the diffusion of innovations. From these investigations has come a series of generalizations (Rogers, 1983) about such issues as the characteristics of innovations that influence the rate of adoption and the characteristics of individuals who are likely to adopt an innovation first. We summarize the findings under the four main elements of the diffusion model: the innovation, communication channels, time, and the social system.

The innovation

It should not be assumed, as has sometimes been the case, that the characteristics of all innovations are basically the same in terms of their effect on the rate of diffusion. To do so is to make a gross oversimplification. Figure 4.1 shows that the rate of adoption of innovations differs widely. The rate of adoption is positively related to several characteristics of the innovation as they are perceived by the members of the system in which the innovation is diffusing: (a) relative advantage, the degree to

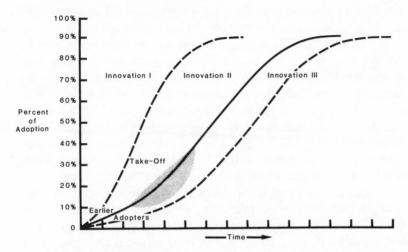

Figure 4.1. Diffusion is the process by which an innovation is communicated through certain channels over time among the members of a social system.

which the innovation is perceived to be superior to the idea that it is intended to replace; (b) compatibility, the degree to which an innovation is perceived to be consistent with the existing values, past experiences, and needs of potential adopters; (c) complexity, the degree to which an innovation is perceived to be difficult to understand and use; (d) trialability, the degree to which an innovation can be experimented with on a limited basis; and (e) observability, the degree to which the results of an innovation are visible to others.

These factors help us to understand why most preventive innovations are characterized by a relatively low rate of adoption: Adopters have difficulty in determining the preventive innovation's relative advantage; preventive innovations often are not very compatible with individuals' values, attitudes, or lifestyles; the cause-and-effect relations involved are complex; trial is difficult or impossible; and the innovation's results are not easily observed, because they are delayed. Decreasing the proportion of fat in one's diet to reduce the risk of cancer and heart disease is a preventive innovation that illustrates these obstacles.

Communication Channels

Communication is the means by which messages get from one individual to another. Mass media communication channels are more effective in creating knowledge of innovations, whereas interpersonal channels are more effective in forming and changing attitudes toward an innovation and thus in influencing an individual's decision to adopt or reject the innovation. Most individuals evaluate an innovation, not on the basis of scientific research by experts, but on the basis of the subjective evaluations of near peers who have already adopted the innovation. These peers serve as models whose behavior is imitated by others in the social system (see McAlister, Chapter 2). Thus, imitation and social modeling are essential elements of the diffusion process (Bandura, 1977).

An illustration of the role of modeling in a preventive campaign is provided by the experience of the Stanford Heart Disease Prevention Project. In 1984 this project selected and trained about 500 "health promoters" in the two California communities where the program was implemented. These people had made important changes in their own heart disease preventive behavior by stopping smoking, changing their diet, exercising regularly, or reducing their stress, but in their socioeconomic and other characteristics they were not particularly different from the rest of the community. Each health promoter was paired with an average of 10 "followers," individuals who were thought to have a relatively high risk of developing heart disease. These 5,000 individuals, who represented about 5% of the total population of the two communities, then passed along the preventive health information to the rest of the community.

Interpersonal networks play a crucial role in the diffusion of both precautions and coping behaviors. Morgan (1983), for example, found that information exchanged in network relationships helps individuals foresee and minimize potential sources of stress in such events as a heart attack or death of a spouse. Gourash (1978), on the basis of her review of the research literature on help seeking, concluded that more than half of adults in the United States who experience troublesome life events seek help initially from friends, relatives, and neighbors. Only later might they look for professional aid. Even then, their network relationships often determine which professional they visit.

Getting professional assistance for preventive purposes is least likely for low-income high-risk populations, and the dropout rates of these groups from treatment programs are highest as well. Bickel and Repucci (1983) show that this relative lack of preventive behavior by people who seem to need it most is due in part to the nature of their social networks. The network partners of low-income high-risk individuals are less likely to encourage preventive acts or to reinforce such decisions once made.

It is the activation of peer communication networks that leads to the "take-off" in the rate of adoption shown in Figure 4.1. The first adopters of an innovation, called innovators, are usually perceived to be atypical members of their local community, and their example is not immediately followed. The innovators tend to be of high socioeconomic status, have considerable mass media exposure, and travel over a wide area. The next category of individuals to adopt the innovation consists of "early adopters." They are people who occupy a key position in the community's communication network and are seen to embody the norms of the social system. The early adopters are treated with respect, and their behavior is followed by many others in the local system.

Certain individuals in a social system play an especially important role in the interpersonal diffusion of innovations. They are called opinion leaders. *Opinion leadership* is the degree to which an individual is able to influence informally other individuals' attitudes or overt behavior. Diffusion programs have often sought to identify the opinion leaders in a community and to obtain their assistance in diffusing innovations to others in the system. Once the adoption of an innovation has reached 10 or 20% (i.e., when the opinion leaders have adopted the innovation), it is usually impossible to prevent further diffusion of the innovation.

The mass media also have an important role in prevention campaigns. The media are unique in being able to reach a mass audience quickly with a standard message. The media can thus create awareness or knowledge of an innovation and may be able to provide how-to information. But it is usually unrealistic to expect the mass media to persuade individuals to adopt an innovation. At best, the media can bring about behavior change indirectly, when mass communication influences opinion leaders, whose decisions then affect others in the social network.

Time

The element of time is important in several ways: (a) in the innovation decision process by which individuals move from first awareness to adoption or rejection; (b) in the innovativeness of an individual or other unit of adoption (i.e., the length of time that elapses before a person adopts the innovation); and (c) in an innovation's rate of adoption (measured as the number of members of a system who adopt an innovation in a given time period).

The innovation decision process. There are five main steps in the innovation decision process: (a) acquisition of knowledge, which occurs when an individual or some other decision-making unit is exposed to the innovation and gains some understanding of the way it functions; (b) persuasion, which occurs when the individual forms a favorable or unfavorable attitude toward the innovation; (c) decision making, which occurs when the individual engages in activities that lead to a choice to adopt or reject the innovation; (d) implementation, which occurs when the individual puts the innovation to use; and (e) confirmation, which occurs when the individual seeks reinforcement of an innovation decision already made (although he or she may reverse this decision if exposed later to different messages about the innovation).[2]

Innovativeness. Innovativeness is the degree to which an individual or other unit of adoption is willing to adopt new ideas before other members of a social system do so. Innovativeness is often broken up into five adopter categories: (a) innovators, the first to adopt; (b) early adopters; (c) early majority; (d) late majority; and (e) laggards. Some characteristics of the innovators and early adopters were mentioned previously. The late majority and laggards are of lower socioeconomic status than the others and are the most parochial and traditional in their perspectives.

Rate of adoption. Rate of adoption is the relative speed with which an innovation is adopted by members of a social system. When the cumulative number of individuals adopting a new idea is plotted over time, the resulting distribution is an S-shaped curve (Figure 4.1). As stated previously, preventive innovations generally have a lower rate of adoption than other new ideas whose relative advantage is more apparent.

The social system

A social system is a set of interrelated units engaged in joint problem solving to accomplish some goal. The structure of a social system affects an innovation's diffusion in several ways.

Norms are the established behavior patterns of the members of a social system. They define the range of tolerable behavior and serve as a guide or standard. Some norms, such as religious or cultural norms that affect food habits or contraceptive behavior, can be a barrier to diffusion. Norms can also facilitate diffusion.

Another way in which the social system influences diffusion behavior concerns consequences, the changes that affect the individual or social system as a result of adoption or rejection. Obviously, an innovation has little effect until it is put to use. Neither researchers nor officials in charge of diffusion campaigns have paid much attention to the consequences of a innovation for the social system; they have usually assumed that it will have only beneficial results. Often, this has not been so. For example, medical doctors and health educators strongly encourage people to stop smoking cigarettes in order to lower their risk of heart disease and lung cancer. However, many individuals fear an additional consequence – that their body weight will increase if they stop smoking. Similarly, some people refuse to adopt contraceptives because they believe that their sexual satisfaction during intercourse will be reduced. And some individuals do not buckle their automobile seat belts out of concern for wrinkling their clothes. There are many other examples of professionals' failure to recognize fully the consequences of a preventive innovation that are considered to be negative by their clients.

Consequences are not unidimensional; they can be classified along at least three dimensions: desirable versus undesirable, direct versus indirect, and anticipated versus unanticipated.[3]

Desirable consequences are the functional effects of an innovation on an individual or social system. Undesirable effects are dysfunctional. Understandably, people want to reap the functional consequences (e.g., increased effectiveness, efficiency, or convenience) and to avoid dysfunctional effects (e.g., disruptive changes in social values and institutions). Not all consequences are equally important. Every system has certain qualities that should not be destroyed if the welfare of the system is to be maintained: respect for human life and property, maintenance of individual dignity, and appreciation of others. Many other sociocultural elements can be modified, discontinued, or supplanted with little effect. Most innovations have both desirable and undesirable consequences.

Consequences can also be classified as direct and indirect. Direct consequences are the changes that occur in immediate response to an innovation. Indirect consequences are the changes that occur as a result of the direct consequences. For example, the direct results of computer chips include energy savings when they are used in "smart appliances" like water heaters and clothes dryers and labor savings when they are built into sophisticated cash registers at checkout stands in grocery markets. These direct consequences are likely to be accompanied by many indirect consequences of the microelectronics revolution, such as lower oil prices and unemployment (Rogers & Larsen, 1984).

The indirect consequences of an innovation are often unanticipated. Anticipated consequences are changes caused by an innovation that are recognized and intended by the members of the social system. Unanticipated consequences are neither intended nor expected. A system is like a bowl of marbles; if any one of its elements is moved, the position of all the others are changed. Usually, the anticipated consequences are also direct and desirable; the unanticipated consequences are usually undesirable and indirect.

Weaknesses of the diffusion approach

Despite its popularity as a framework for research, for our present purposes the diffusion paradigm has certain shortcomings. One might criticize diffusion research for its proinnovation bias, the implication that an innovation should be diffused and adopted by all members of a social system and that it should be diffused rapidly. Diffusion research can also be criticized for fostering an individual blame bias, a tendency to hold the members of the social system responsible for their problems (because they have not adopted the innovations offered) rather than the social system of which individuals are a part. Furthermore, because relatively little diffusion research has focused on preventive innovations, we are better able to facilitate other types of innovations, although preventive innovations usually present more difficult problems.

Awareness of such possible shortcomings is, of course, the first step toward overcoming the criticisms. For example, scholars and practitioners could keep an open mind toward matters of individual blame, at least until more data are available about the causes of a social problem. Furthermore, potential adopters – not just agency officials and others who may represent the establishment view – should be involved in identifying the diffusion problem and planning the diffusion program.

Lessons from family planning diffusion

In order to draw certain general conclusions, we now turn to several situations in which preventive innovations have been diffused. We begin with the case of family planning.

Relatively small family planning programs were mounted in the United States and other Western nations before 1960 (mainly by private organizations like Planned Parenthood). But family planning diffusion programs became a priority of national governments about 25 years ago when Third World nations realized that their economic development was being slowed by unchecked population growth. These programs appeared first in Asia, then in Latin America, and finally in Africa. United Nations agencies and the U.S. Agency for International Development offered technical and financial assistance.

These preventive-type programs were launched in Third World nations about the time that the new contraceptive technologies – the intrauterine device (IUD), the contraceptive pill, and sterilization–were becoming available. The national family planning programs were based rather directly on the diffusion model. It was about "the only wheel in town" and had already been used in agricultural development programs in many Third World countries. Despite the strong political support accorded these family planning programs and the substantial resources that were poured into them, the results of the early programs were not very impressive. Birth rates did not drop in India and Pakistan, two countries that pioneered family planning. The difficulties of diffusing preventive innovations had been severely underestimated.

This early lack of success led officials and scholars (including the author) to study the impact of family planning diffusion programs and to consider how such programs could be improved. As a result, in the 1970s the classical diffusion model was modified in three important ways (Rogers, 1973):

1. Extensive use was made of paraprofessional aides, less than fully professional change agents who had intensive contact with clients in order to influence their innovation decisions. It was necessary to utilize aides in family planning programs because there were not enough health professionals involved. Furthermore, the aides were closer in social status to the typical clients (rural peasants or urban poor), hence more effective in communicating the idea of family planning. The aides were often asked by their clients what type of contraceptives *they* used and to what effect. Physicians and nurses were almost never asked such questions. Thus, the aides provided a social model for their clients' preventive behavior.
2. Cash or in-kind incentives were often paid to adopters or diffusers of family planning innovations, which had some success in raising the rate of adoption. Incentives tend to increase the perceived relative advantage of an innovation.
3. Local networks of peers were activated to influence individuals and families to adopt contraceptives and decrease family size. Examples are the *banjar* system on the Indonesian island of Bali and the group planning of births in the People's Republic of China. Strong peer pressure to have children was exerted. In recent years in China, a family size limit of one child has been rather strongly encouraged. The experience of Bali and China suggests that local groups have a potential for increasing the adoption of preventive innovations.

During the late 1970s and early 1980s, a number of national family planning programs succeeded in reducing the rates of population growth (those in Korea, Taiwan, Indonesia, and China are examples). Part of this success can be attributed to appropriate diffusion strategies, but an even greater part is probably due to rapid socioeconomic development, which has changed the context of family planning decisions in these countries. For example, in urban environments there are fewer economic reasons for having many children. In areas like India's Punjab, where rapid rural development has occurred, parents realize that having many sons is no longer an economic benefit. Birth rates have fallen, but not only because of the impact of the family planning program.

Particularly ineffective in inducing the adoption of contraceptives in the Third World were government exhortations to have fewer children. For instance, the Indian government told its citizens via the mass media "to have two or three children, then stop." They did not.

Energy conservation

Beginning with the 1973 Yom Kippur War in the Middle East, the United States and many other Western nations began to face the problem of energy conservation. A second severe crisis occurred in 1979 with the Iranian revolution, and further energy crunches undoubtedly lie ahead. The sharply increased price of fuel in the 1970s was accompanied in the United States by the creation of the U.S. Department of Energy and by President Carter's call for a program of conservation that would be "the moral equivalent to war."

The considerable efforts by public and private organizations to diffuse the preventive innovation of energy conservation produced only a minor decrease in energy consumption in the United States. Most of this decrease was probably due to the higher fuel prices that prevailed. In 1983–1984, when fuel prices stopped increasing and actually decreased somewhat, energy conservation behavior also slackened. The Reagan administration cut back sharply on energy conservation programs (including solar power initiatives) in the 1980s, and the issue of energy conservation dropped from public attention.

As with family planning in the Third World, patriotic appeals through the mass media were ineffective. Individuals plan their families and conserve energy in light of the perceived costs and benefits to themselves, not to their nation.

Many energy conservation diffusion programs were carried out by public power utilities and by private oil companies. The mass media campaigns of such sponsors were not given much credibility by the public, who perceived that energy conservation was not in the interest of organizations that sold petroleum and electrical power. In fact, the sponsors of the energy conservation campaigns of the 1970s had been urging the public to use *more* energy for many years. This paradoxical situation puzzled the public and helped negate the energy conservation diffusion campaigns conducted by power and oil companies.

Nevertheless, there were some bright spots. One occurred in Davis, California, where a tremendously effective energy conservation program was mounted by city officials and community members in the 1970s. Davis was already a very ecology-minded university city of 35,000 before the first energy crisis. A no-growth political movement took over the city's government in the "revolution of 1972" and began implementing municipal ordinances to require solar heating in all homes and to promote other forms of energy conservation. The nation's mass media began to feature Davis as the "energy conservation capital of America," and guests began to throng to Davis (about 5,000 per year). Davis received little or no federal government assistance for its energy conservation program, nor was the diffusion of the Davis approach to hundreds of other American cities sponsored by Washington.

The Davis program of energy conservation is an example of decentralized diffusion in that power and control were widely shared by the members of the diffusion system (Rogers, 1983: 335). Many of the Davis municipal ordinances, solar designs, and other innovations came from local experimentation by nonexperts rather than from formal research and development. The "invented here" nature of the Davis program was a major cause of pride and an important factor in its success.

The Davis experience suggests that institutional arrangements can be an important force for successful preventive innovation diffusion. These arrangements may consist of banning certain products, taxing their use, restricting their sales, or legislating the use of alternatives. In other diffusion situations, such as preventing obesity and promoting exercise, an approach directed toward individual action may be more appropriate. Both individual and institutional strategies may contribute to smoking cessation and the control of alcohol abuse (McGuire, 1984).

Heart disease prevention

Since 1973, a two-phased field experiment to reduce the risk of heart disease has been carried out by Stanford University in several California communities. This project, the Stanford Heart Disease Prevention Program (SHDPP), is funded by the National Institutes of Health and conducted by a multidisciplinary team of researchers from the Stanford Medical School and the Institute for Communication Research.

The SHDPP was first carried out in three small California communities during the 1970s by means of a mass media campaign coupled with small-group instruction to teach the behavioral skills required for smoking cessation, weight reduction through exercise and dietary change, and stress management. The Phase I results showed an encouraging reduction in the risk of heart disease in the two treatment communities compared with the control community (Maccoby & Solomon, 1981).[4]

Accordingly, during the 1980s we launched a Phase II field experiment in five medium-sized California communities. A heart disease prevention effort was mounted in two of these cities with the other three as reference points. The goal of this campaign is also smoking cessation, weight reduction, and stress management. Again the mass media – television, radio, and newspapers – are being utilized to inform people of the risk of heart disease and to recruit them to small groups for behavior skills instruction. Formative evaluation[5] is used to create effective media messages, and annual surveys are conducted to evaluate the impact of the program. Considerable effort is made to involve the local communities, their formal organizations, and their leaders in carrying out the campaign.

Phase II of the SHDPP differs somewhat from the previous three-community study in that we are gradually turning over major responsibility for the project to the two treatment communities. Our goal is to ensure that heart disease prevention activities will not cease when Stanford University's research involvement ends. There are important ethical reasons for such a transfer of responsibility, as well as considerable efficiencies. If, in the future, every community to mount a similar heart disease prevention campaign needed the assistance of a university, the impact of the SHDPP would indeed be very limited.

Results from the first several years of the SHDPP in the two experimental sites indicate that, as in Phase I, the preventive heart disease campaign is producing a measurable decrease in risk. A number of lessons have been learned that may apply to the diffusion of other preventive innovations.

1. The mass media, when used appropriately (such as when coupled with formative evaluation) can play an important role in creating awareness of a preventive innovation, in conveying information about the innovation, and in recruiting individuals to small-group instructional classes. However, the mass media should not be expected to change strongly held behaviors, such as those associated with well-established habits. The objective of the SHDPP is to achieve a 20% reduction in overall risk in the two experimental communities through a 9% reduction in cigarettes smoked per day, a 2% weight reduction, a 7% reduction in systolic blood pressure, and a 4% reduction in total plasma cholesterol. These changes might seem small, but because smoking, exercise, and dietary patterns are so tenacious, we believe they represent

significant accomplishments, especially when one remembers that the changes refer to the entire community.

Thus, the SHDPP utilizes the mass media primarily to activate existing interpersonal communication networks by providing social models for desired behavior change in the media messages and by recruiting individuals to small-group classes. For example, SHDPP television spots show average citizens (a teacher, a policeman, etc.) who have lost weight through dieting and exercise. The SHDPP depends mainly on these near-peer networks for actual changes in behavior. Reinforcement from friends and acquaintances, not television messages, helps convince cigarette smokers to stop and not to backslide.

An obvious way of maximizing interpersonal communication in a diffusion campaign is to utilize opinion leaders. How can one identify them and reach them with messages they can pass along to their "followers"? The SHDPP identified opinion leaders with the help of knowledgeable informants who knew the communities well. These nonprofessional leaders have been trained to contact high risk audience members with information about heart disease prevention. The results are very encouraging, with 500 trained lay leaders contacting 5,000 "followers" in our two California communities.

2. Audience segmentation strategies play an important role in targeting specific messages about preventive behavior change to particular audiences. For example, we identified teenagers as a target for the SHDPP smoking prevention materials. The main advantage of audience segmentation is that more effective messages can be delivered to each of the more homogeneous subaudiences. An alternative to segmentation would be to "drop messages from airplanes" so as to cover everyone in the audience. This approach would obviously be much less efficient.

3. Formative research can produce messages that are more effective in bringing about specific types of preventive behavior change. We discovered early in the SHDPP that it was very difficult to convince people to run for exercise during the winter rainy season. Through formative evaluation, we learned that it was better to encourage brisk walking (Maccoby & Solomon, 1981: 120).

We gathered considerable "feedforward" data about our intended audiences before beginning the prevention campaign. We also pretested our messages, so that they were improved gradually before they were communicated. The information provided by formative evaluation comes at a cost, but it is very valuable, especially when communicators are not entirely certain about their audiences' preexisting behavior.

4. Some of the preventive health behavior changes we are promoting occur in response to "trigger events" in the lives of individuals. For example, one SHDPP respondent initiated drastic lifestyle changes when his younger brother had a heart attack. Another person was ordered by his medical doctor to stop smoking and lose weight, and he did so. Such trigger events transform intentions to change behavior (intentions that may have been created by our mass media campaign) into action. The SHDPP campaign seeks to capitalize on the trigger events that occur naturally in the lives of our audience. For example, we have found that some women are especially interested in stopping cigarette smoking during pregnancy.

5. Accessible and timely messages have maximum effects. We once mailed a heart-shaped educational message about heart disease prevention to each of our target households on Valentine's Day. Also, we learned through formative research that refrigerator doors are an important locus of communication about nutritional topics. So we created a series of messages about smoking, weight control, and nutrition that are placed on the refrigerator door under a red, heart-shaped magnet. The strategy here is similar to point-of-sale advertising in marketing a commercial product.

Additional obstacles to diffusing preventive innovations

At the beginning of this chapter, a number of characteristics of preventive innovations that inhibit their diffusion were described. There are several other obstacles that prevention programs face.

The adoption of preventive innovations is seldom motivated by profit, either by the adopters or by the organizations promoting adoption (some exceptions are the sale of earthquake insurance, contraceptive products, and exercise equipment). Instead, there is usually much greater financial benefit for those opposing the behavior change. Examples include the profits made from the advertising and sales of cigarettes and highly salted and sugared convenience foods. The financial rewards of advertising health-enhancing products, like running shoes and special dietary products, are small by comparison.

The training, rewards, and professional values in many fields discourage prevention. For example, in the medical profession much greater value is placed on curing patients than on preventing disease, even though a preventive approach is much less costly for society.

Members of the public often feel a stigma attached to admitting that they need help. An example is a smoker who is embarrassed at her inability to stop and delays seeking professional help until a serious health problem appears.

Conclusions

A number of general lessons can be learned from program experiences and research on the diffusion of preventive innovations.

1. Interpersonal communication through peer networks is very important for the adoption of preventive innovations. One of the most important functions of the mass media in prevention campaigns is to activate near-peer networks. Most individuals evaluate innovations and decide whether to adopt them on the basis of the subjective experiences of their friends and other peers.
2. Changing the context of preventive innovations can sometimes encourage their adoption if program officials capitalize on such change. An illustration is provided by Third World countries in which rapid socio-economic development has motivated couples to have smaller families and facilitated the diffusion of contraception. Likewise, heightened public interest in personal health and fitness in the United States assists preventive health campaigns like the SHDPP.
3. Patriotic appeals by government leaders to the public to adopt preventive innovations are seldom effective. Examples of this point include energy conservation in the United States and family planning in the Third World. Exhortations from on high do not persuade individuals to change their behavior.
4. The perceived credibility of the communication source partly determines the success of a prevention campaign. For instance, electrical power companies and oil companies were not perceived to be credible sources of energy conservation information by the American public.
5. Decentralized diffusion systems (with wide sharing of decision-making power) can be effective in diffusing preventive innovations when the changes recommended are not highly technological (as in the case of solar and other energy conservation measures).
6. The mass media can create awareness or knowledge of preventive innovations and convey useful information about the skills needed for behavior change, but they should not be expected to change strongly held attitudes and behavior. The SHDPP utilizes the mass media to do what they do best – disperse information – and depends on interpersonal channels to complement the media, using small-group classes to bring about smoking cessation, dietary change, and stress management. Another illustration of the role of mass communication is provided by physician-broadcasters, who regularly convey health information (much of which is preventive in nature) via radio and television. These physician-broadcasters are able to inform the public, but they can seldom change overt behavior.[6]

In sum, we conclude that the diffusion perspective has contributed significantly to the effectiveness of a variety of prevention programs, but preventive behavior is particularly difficult to bring about, and a considerable potential remains for improving prevention campaigns.

Notes

1 The material in this section is adapted from Rogers (1983: 5–32).
2 A review of the many studies supporting this five-stage model of the innovation decision process is provided by Rogers (1983: 163–209).
3 In addition, as stated previously, the consequences of innovations can be classified as immediate versus delayed and as relatively certain versus uncertain.
4 A thorough summary of the main conclusions from Phase I of the SHDPP study is contained in Farquahar (1977).
5 Formative evaluation is a type of research conducted while an activity, process, or system is being developed or is ongoing in order to improve its effectiveness. Two main types of formative evaluation are (a) pretesting and (b) designing program activities on the basis of existing knowledge about the intended audience.
6 With Linda Adler of Stanford University, the present author is involved in an investigation of the effects of physician-broadcasters in health education, sponsored by the National Association of Broadcasters and by the Kaiser Family Foundation.

References

Bandura, A. 1977. *Social Learning Theory.* Englewood Cliffs, N.J.: Prentice-Hall.
Bickel, R. C., and N. D. Reppuci. 1983. "Social networks, information-seeking, and the utilization of services." *American Journal of Community Psychology, 11:* 185–205.
Farquahar, J. W. 1977. "Community education for cardiovascular health." *Lancet, 1:* 1192–5.
Gourash, N. 1978. "Help-seeking: a review of the literature." *American Journal of Community Psychology, 6:* 413–23.
Maccoby, N., and D. S. Solomon. 1981. "Heart disease prevention: Community studies." In *Public Communication Campaigns,* eds. R. E. Rice and W. J. Paisley, pp. 104–17. Beverly Hills, Calif.: Sage.
McGuire, W. J. 1984. "Public communication as a strategy for inducing health-promoting behavior change." *Preventive Medicine, 13:* 299–319.
Morgan, D. L. 1983. "Beyond the crisis mentality: Preventive aspects of social support." University of California at Riverside, Department of Sociology, unpublished paper.
Rogers, E. M. 1973. *Communication Strategies for Family Planning.* New York: Free Press.
Rogers, E. M. 1983. *Diffusion of Innovations.* New York: Free Press.
Rogers, E. M., and D. Lawrence Kincaid. 1981. *Communication Networks: Toward a New Paradigm for Research.* New York: Free Press.
Rogers, E. M., and J. K. Larsen. 1984. *Silicon Valley Fever: Growth of High-Technology Culture.* New York: Basic Books.

5 Cultural influences on prevention and the emergence of a new health consciousness

Robert Crawford

Introduction

Americans have increasingly come to see themselves at risk. Despite all the attention given to the difficulty of modifying hazardous behaviors – and in part because of the attention these behaviors have received – the past decade has been characterized by a dramatic turn toward self-protection. Millions of people are making new efforts to reduce their exposure or susceptibility to physical health hazards and millions more are declaring their desire to do more for their health.

We are witnessing the most massive reversal of smoking behavior in our history. More than 30 million people have stopped smoking since 1964, when 42% of adults smoked. By the end of 1983, the percentage had dropped to 29 (USDHHS, 1983: 260, *Chicago Sun Times,* 1984). A number of studies indicate that the consumption of salt, total fat, saturated fat, and cholesterol is down (USDHHS, 1983: 263). The streets, gymnasiums, parks, and a rapidly expanding number of health clubs are overflowing with joggers and exercisers. For 1979, estimates were that between 15 and 25 million were jogging. A Harris poll the same year found that 37% of those interviewed were regularly exercising (Gillick, 1984: 379). A 1979 Yankelovich survey found that "46% of American adults reported recently changing the lifestyles of themselves and their families in the interest of good health" (USDHHS, 1980: 293–4). Some recent data suggest that even alcohol consumption, which along with seat belt use has been the behavior to be least affected by the new health consciousness, may be declining (*Time,* 1985: 68–73). Among much of the professional middle class, those who reject the prevention ethic, especially as applied to smoking, are practically regarded as deviants.

This chapter offers an interpretation of these changes in two separate but interrelated arguments. The first relies on the assumption that physical health is a practical matter that individuals manage in various ways

95

and with various degrees of awareness and concern. The definitions of health employed in these efforts are essentially medical. My interpretation will emphasize not only a series of "events" important to the development of a new health consciousness, but also the multiple health hazard and health promotion discourses to which Americans have been recently exposed. These discourses, defined here as publicly communicated configurations of knowledge, are essential for understanding the social construction of both problem and solution regarding health concerns. What we think and do about health, in other words, is the product of a social process that defines the nature of the problem (to what extent a problem is perceived at all, what kind of a problem) and promotes selective strategies for its solution (e.g., medical, political, personal).

My second argument proceeds from the premise that beliefs and actions are not only practical; they are also metaphorical. That is, beliefs and actions concerned with health express meanings that cannot be grasped simply in terms of the instrumental or practical logic of physical health promotion and protection. I am not suggesting that instrumental purposes are irrelevant, only that the significance of practical activity can best be understood if the cultural meanings attached to such activity are considered (Sahlins, 1976). The challenge of a cultural interpretation is to explore the multiple meanings that practical activity may signify at a particular time and place.

A practical interpretation

Throughout the 1960s and 1970s, diverse medical, political, commercial, and social-movement discourses (shaping and shaped by concrete events) conveyed to a vast number of Americans a sense of somatic vulnerability. Americans acquired the perception that their environment was hazardous, their lifestyle had become health denying, and customary preventive and therapeutic practices no longer provided adequate protection. The turn toward self-protection must be understood in part as a response to this acquired vulnerability and to the practical solutions perceived to be available, efficacious, and normatively reinforced.

Any explanation of the new health consciousness must begin with the historical shift from infectious to chronic disease. Although, in 1900, eleven major infectious diseases accounted for 40% of all deaths, by 1973, they were the cause of only 6% (McKinlay & McKinlay, 1977: 19). By 1979, 75% of all deaths were due to chronic diseases, mostly cardiovascular diseases and cancer. Even though the shift from infectious to chronic diseases has been occurring for some time, attention continued to be focused on the former through the 1950s. This, I believe, was due to the medical practice of continuing to solidify and extend the gains made through vaccines and antibiotics in the 1930s and 1940s. Moreover, the therapeutic promise of medicine was never greater. The conquest of polio in 1955 only strengthened the belief that medicine was well on its way to delivering the utopian dream of a life free of disease (Dubos, 1959).

Americans could not long ignore, however, the mounting toll from heart disease and cancer. Personal experience and growing public attention forced a redefinition of the problem of health and strategies for protection. By the 1960s, the "new" dread diseases were thrust before the public by national associations, such as the American Heart Association and the American Cancer Society, in their efforts to gain public and governmental support for research. These maladies were presented as the next target for a triumphant (if only adequately funded) medical science. Not only did these organizations bring to public awareness the extent and human costs of these diseases; they also effectively conveyed the message that, for the moment at least, no medical cures existed. They intended to direct hope toward a therapeutic solution, but as the years wore on without the appearance of the promised magic bullet, the public's sense of vulnerability and fear, particularly of cancer, intensified. Even President Nixon's War on Cancer, declared in 1972 and also directed toward medical research, carried this double message. Medically guaranteed health no longer seemed so believable.

Concurrently, public education campaigns based on a growing body of epidemiological research were initiated. As early as the late 1950s, the links between smoking and cancer and heart disease received publicity, culminating in 1964 in the influential Surgeon General's report on smoking and health (USDHEW, 1964). Other reports followed, as did several years of public service announcements on television, warning the public of the dangers of smoking. The Framingham Study also began reporting results by the late 1950s, and by the 1960s the concept of "risk factor" became common parlance among middle-class men in their forties and fifties (Kannel & Gordon, 1968).

By the 1970s, the scale and intensity of health hazard communication escalated and continued to grow exponentially throughout the decade. The relatively limited set of medical prescriptions and proscriptions believed necessary for protection against infectious disease (primarily vaccination, personal hygiene, and avoidance of contagious persons) was replaced by a vastly expanded list of dos and don'ts. Modest therapeutic advances could not offset the psychological effects of a continuous flow of media reports describing newly discovered hazards. Unlike infectious diseases, chronic diseases erased the clear distinction between health and illness, between predisposing conditions and the actual disease. One no longer "caught" a disease; it was acquired. The critical time frame for prevention was lengthened. Present behaviors would bear results twenty or thirty years later.

Health hazards also became politicized and thus all the more visible. In the late 1960s and 1970s, the nation discovered environmental and occupational health hazards. We moved through a succession of disasters and alarms that seemed to grow increasingly more ominous. Harmful chemicals were identified in our rivers and lakes, food, drinking water, air, factories, offices, schools, and homes. Never before had the public been subjected to such a barrage of environmental warnings. New federal agencies – the Environmental Protection Agency, Occupational Safety and Health Administration, Consumer Product Safety Commission, Nuclear Regulatory Commission, National Highway Traffic Safety Commission – and their state counterparts initiated research and investigations that contributed to public awareness of the scale of the problem. Health hazard regulation generated its own politics and mobilized both public interest groups and industry. Throughout the 1970s, the public was subjected to claims and counterclaims about risk, the necessity for regulation, regulatory inadequacies, and the effects of regulation on the economy. Despite considerable confusion about competing scientific claims as to the extent of risk and the development by mid-decade of a defensive "everything causes cancer" cynicism, public support for legislation and regulation of environmental health hazards grew dramatically. Such support has remained high. In one public opinion survey, for example, 58% of respondents agreed with the statement that "protecting the environment is so important that requirements and standards cannot be too high, and continuing environmental improvements must be made regardless of cost" (CBS–New York Times, 1983).

As the political controversies generated by environmental and occupational health regulation intensified, still another politicized discourse was added to the flood of attention being given to the problem of health. Stimulated by support from foundation, insurance, academic, and governmental sources, the problem of disease prevention became explicitly formulated as one of individual behaviors or lifestyles. Building on the already substantial attention devoted to at-risk behaviors over the previous decade, a new cadre of prevention advocates argued that the most promising strategy for improving the nation's health required the assumption of "individual responsibility" (see, e.g., Knowles, 1977). Beginning in the mid-1970s, this theme, often highly moralized, competed with the regulatory approach and became for many the cornerstone of prevention policy.

The National Consumer Health Information and Health Promotion Act of 1976, for example, provided support for health education efforts aimed at changing individual behavior. Political leaders took up the theme of individual irresponsibility, as when Secretary of Health, Education, and Welfare Joseph Califano wrote of "indulgence in 'private' excesses" and the necessity for "individual discipline and will" (USDHEW, 1979; viii–ix). The public interest, it was claimed, required that public policy and voluntary efforts be mobilized to change individual "bad habits."

The emphasis on individual responsibility must, in part, be understood as political. In the mid-1970s, escalating medical care costs came to be defined as *the* critical problem in medical care policy–this in a period of broad public support for the extension of rights and entitlements to medical care, including the adoption of national health insurance. The discovery of the "limits of medicine" (i.e., more sober judgments about the therapeutic determinants of health) and turn toward prevention–no matter what else might be said in their behalf–also contributed a justification for shifting the burden of medical care costs back to labor and consumers. At the same time, the emphasis on personal efforts to control health hazards provided an attractive alternative for those hoping to curtail expensive and politically contentious environmental and occupational health policies (Crawford, 1977).

The moralization of health behavior under the rubric of individual responsibility derives from other sources as well. The theme of individual responsibility resonates with a deeply rooted American cultural tradition of individualism and self-reliance. Self-improvement has been a central motif of the myriad health and fitness movements of the past century and a half (Whorton, 1982). Prevention campaigns in the past have employed the theme of individual responsibility in their rhetoric (Brandt, 1985). By the late 1970s, the idea that self-protection against health hazards was a moral responsibility reverberated through the media and the mass of health promotion material filling bookstore shelves. It also acquired a commonsense logic. In the increasingly conservative climate of the 1980s, with both political and economic authorities repeatedly warning that our jobs and the country's economic health are dependent on giving business a free hand and on reducing the scale of governmental activity, personal health promotion, along with the moral claims that help sustain such actions, may appear to be a practical necessity. As with crime, the absence of adequate social protection inclines individuals to take matters into their own hands.

The popular health movements that emerged in the 1970s drew still more attention to health hazards and to the role of the individual in protecting against them. These movements developed in conjunction with the growing health consciousness among the middle class, both feeding from and contributing to health awareness. The holistic health movement, for example, combines the new interest in health promotion with a remarkably diverse challenge to orthodox medicine. It offers an array of alternative therapeutic and preventive practices and has marketed these services to a growing number of clients (Kopelman and Moskop, 1981). Sometimes called the wellness movement, it also shares themes with the natural foods, human potential, and environmental movements. The emphasis is on the attainment of positive health of both mind and body. Although recognition is given to the importance of a health-enhancing environment, the practical emphasis is on host resistance and adaptation, that is, on restructuring attitudes, emotions, and behaviors, with or without the help of holistic healers. Illustrative is an introduction to a holistic health handbook in which the author counsels against the "negativity" of blaming the environment and proclaims that "health and happiness *can* be ours if we desire; we can create our personal reality, down to the finest detail" (Bauman, 1978: 19). Or as another writer puts it, "We choose our sickness when, through neglect or ignorance, we allow it to spread within us" (Muramoto, 1973: 116). I believe (Crawford, 1980) that the holistic health movement has contributed to a strident moralism about "self-destructive" behaviors and about the attitudinal and behavioral requisites for "high level wellness." As one advocate admonishes, "To abuse [the gift of health] or to fail to seek it out with all our power is a denial of the value of self. Anyone who disregards the magnificence of life deserves only pity" (Grant, 1978: 10). Holistic health elevates the value of health and makes a health-promoting lifestyle synonymous with good living, a pan value or standard by which an expanding number of behaviors, attitudes, and social phenomena are judged.

Self-help and self-care are two additional movements that have contributed to an emphasis on individual health promotion. Both movements share a rejection of dependence on physicians and drugs and, as their names imply, hope to create the conditions for autonomous health seeking or health protection. Self-care is the more individualistic, having as its goal the transfer of medical competence to the individual or, generally, providing individuals with essential health information and skills. The movement has contributed to the dissemination of health hazard information and to the elevation of health as a goal requiring attention and conscious effort. Instead of depending on medical treatment, individuals are urged to be more self-reliant. Self-help groups have evolved, in part, from an American tradition of mutual aid and have often been formed by people with disabilities and chronic diseases. Groups provide mutual support, and some are politically active, seeking benefits and improvements in services. Women's self-help groups, for example, were an important part of the women's movement in the 1970s. This collective and political dimension of self-help, however, does not entirely negate the effects of a rhetoric of individual responsibility adopted by many of its professional and popular advocates. (For an exchange on the political implications of self-help, see Crawford, 1980; Katz & Levin, 1980; Sidel & Sidel, 1981.)

It should also be noted that movements seeking social equality have promoted health consciousness as well. The black movement in this country has often emphasized personal transformation as an essential step in altering the social conditions of oppression. Framed in these terms, health promotion is a rejection of the self-destructive practices and self-hatred often associated with subjugation. Health of body and mind is an expression of black pride. Health consciousness among women has also been stimulated by a feminist-inspired enhancement of self-worth.

By the 1980s, cause and effect become all the more difficult to distinguish. The cultural diffusion of health consciousness animates still more institutional, professional, and commercial activity, which in turn augments and shapes the expanding health culture. Hospitals are now rushing to establish wellness programs and community health education projects. Health hazard appraisals, questionnaires that produce scores of statistically defined vulnerability, have now been administered to millions of Americans. Corporate health promotion programs reward healthy behavior, provide health promotion counseling, and sponsor athletic contests. Corporations are increasingly prohibiting smoking in the work place. New state laws are also mandating health and safety behavior – for example, seat belt use and smoking restrictions – drawing still more attention to these hazard areas and adding to the social pressures on recalcitrants. Health education is a burgeoning profession, and fitness cheerleaders like Jane Fonda, Diana Nyad, and Richard Simmons have become national celebrities. Jamnastics, Jazzercise, Kinetics, Nautilus, and a profusion of health clubs are seeking clientele in a highly competitive market. Themes become entangled: body shape, fitness, strength, disease prevention, longevity, youth, beauty, and, of course, sex appeal.

The commercialization of health promotion and fitness is truly astounding. "Health foods" are now marketed by major food chains. In 1981, health foods, vitamins, bottled water, and diet products alone were claiming more than $13 billion in sales, and health and fitness had turned into an estimated $30 billion per year market (*Time*, 1981). A deluge of specialty magazines and books now offer information and products for every conceivable health and fitness desire. Health fashion projects the conventionally desirable image. Marathons and triathalons have become national media events, with a full list of corporate sponsors. Body conscious and self-care-oriented Americans have turned to an array of home, do-it-yourself medical testing devices, such as blood pressure monitors or kits that test for diabetes (*New York Times*, 1984). Health spas have never done better. How much these expanding markets are a response to pre-existing demand and how much demand is being created by marketing is a matter of conjecture.

The discourses reviewed here (and others, such as doctor–patient communications) must be examined in much more detail before we can fully understand the precise ways that our conceptions of hazard, risk, self-protection, and health itself are socially structured. Medical knowledge underlies all of these discourses (with the partial exception of holistic health), shaping our conception of self as biological individuals and governing our activities in maintaining ourselves as biophysical entities. My argument has been that in the past two decades, and especially since the 1970s, numerous discourses have had the effect of increasing Americans' sense of vulnerability to physical health hazards, enhancing the goal of health, and provoking far-reaching changes in self-protective behavior.

Health as metaphor

In contrast to the discussion of the preceding section, the argument here is that meaning cannot be fully grasped by isolating social and experiential subsystems (like health, illness, or risk) from their larger social and cultural contexts (Comaroff, 1983). Concerns in one domain of experience, such as physical health, are often conflated or converge with anxieties in another, for example, personal relationships. Frequently, displacements occur in which emotions and thoughts are shifted through a common point of association from an initial experience to a substitute. Powerful symbolic media, such as the body and bodily concerns, condense meanings from diverse spheres of thought, emotion, and action (Freud, 1965). In every culture, the body and its signs are among its richest symbolic vehicles – both source and object of metaphorical thinking. The body, in sickness and health, in youth and age, in its femininity and masculinity, in its shades of color, is a key marker by which social definitions of the self are acquired and communicated. From this, the metaphorical perspective, it is important to ask how thoughts and actions apparently having to do with physical hazards and self-protection take on meanings in relation to larger sociocultural processes and historical events. It is important to know how health discourse references aspects of our cultural order. Just as Susan Sontag (1977) has attempted in relation to serious illness, I shall argue that health is a metaphor, a moral discourse, an opportunity to express and reaffirm shared values, and an extremely important cultural site where the social self is constructed (Haley, 1978).

My thoughts on this subject are provoked by a series of 60 interviews carried out in 1981. Those interviewed were selected through several chains of association, each interviewee being asked to recommend two others. Initial interviewees were chosen through recommendations made by people known to the author. By the end, although they were all drawn from the Chicago metropolitan area, the people I interviewed had widely divergent demographic characteristics, varying in class, race, gender, and age. Almost all of those interviewed would be considered healthy by medical definitions. These in-depth, open-ended interviews sought to discover how people think about and define health, what threats they perceive to their health, and what resources, strategies, and explanations they considered important for maintaining health. This kind of research cannot produce conclusions about the distribution and prevalence of beliefs. Instead, the goal is to explore how people talk about health, to search for the symbolic structures through which health is conceived.

Health is about many things. Amid the diversity, however, two dominant themes will be the focus of my discussion here. It is my contention that these two themes structure our concepts of health, and, in turn, our thoughts and experience of health contribute to the expression of these themes in American culture. Following Phillip Rieff (1966), although using the terms somewhat differently, I refer to these themes as *control* and *release*.

Health as control

The words "self-control," "self-discipline," "self-denial," and "willpower," or words like them, were spoken throughout the interviews. They were spoken most frequently, although by no means exclusively, by professional middle-class people. These values and qualities of character were often considered essential for the achievement of health, defined mostly in physical, and occasionally in emotional or psychosomatic terms. Sometimes, these concepts provided the substance of what health was believed to be. That is, when people talked about threats to health, explanations for health, or prescriptions for maintaining or improving health, one or more of these related values framed the discussion and set the moral tone. Health, in other words, appears to be a moral quality as well as a physical and emotional one.

For those emphasizing control, health was often held to be a major goal, requiring choice, effort, and determination. As one professional woman put it, "I think I have to have more perseverence with the problem, make it a goal. Just like I have this goal for work, I should have this goal for health." Health, in other words, must be achieved. It does not flow naturally from a way of life. Actions must be taken and time must be found. Other valued activities have to be sacrificed. As one might expect, the pursuit of health does not always win out. Many voiced a desire to be doing more and guilt about not doing enough. The failure to keep up with contemporary health behavior norms seemed to require an explanation. It was an explanation that stressed deficits of character, particularly the lack of those personal qualities of control believed essential for successful goal accomplishment. "Maybe I don't press myself enough," complained a professional woman, after listing the copious activities that consumed her time. "Maybe I should have less down time." Here there is a sense that leisure, or "down time," must be converted to the "up time" of health promotion. The work of self-improvement, so characteristic of the middle class, requires a continuous striving. The Protestant world view is extended to the body. Leisure must be transformed into instrumental activity. The goal of health is likened to the goal of work, along with all the latter's moral imperatives that putatively guarantee success.

The more the achievement of health is defined as a moral project, the more people are likely to confuse means with ends:

Q: How do you know you are healthy?
A: I guess I judge it by the standards that I would read about if people are healthy. I get exercise. I don't smoke. I don't eat a lot of red meat. I don't have a lot of cholesterol. I take vitamins. I get a physical every year. I think I'm healthy. . . . I try to do all of those things, so I think I'm healthy.

But what is the end and what the means is precisely the issue I am raising here. "Health" may be a means by which the end of developing and/or displaying the values of control can be expressed. Practically all of the middle-class people with whom I spoke either voiced disappointment and guilt about insufficient willpower or discipline or conveyed a sense of moral achievement about their healthy lifestyle. They also expressed admiration and sometimes harsh judgments about other people's health behaviors: "You have to be man enough, woman enough, you have to be adult enough to control your life." "Unhealthiness for me has connotations of neglect." "Anybody who wanted could be healthy." "People bring it on themselves." "If only I were more disciplined." "I'm disappointed that I don't have more control." "There is just not enough willpower in me." "It's a matter of realizing that I can get back the strength of will that I had a few years ago." "Everybody knows that I have no self-control." "I let myself go."

The language of control as applied to health and the body can be found throughout contemporary culture. Admonitions about self-control saturate the personal health columns of newspapers and magazines. *American Health* magazine advertises that a subscription will allow you to "take control of your life." A brand of vitamins is promoted by an appeal to "body control – the formula for the '80s." A widely advertised exercise machine is boosted by the slogan No Pain, No Gain. Both thinness and muscle are the perfect metaphors for virtuous self-denial and disciplined determination (*Time*, 1982). In our weight-conscious society, fat is a confirmation of loss of control, a moral failure, a sign of impulsiveness, self-indulgence, and sloth. As one person in an interview told me, "Within a second you make a judgment saying this person is healthy or not."

The values of self-control, self-discipline, self-denial, and willpower are, of course, fundamental to our culture. In their contemporary form, they are largely the products of the Protestant and industrial revolutions. They have provided the foundation for a personality structure congruent with the requirements of capitalist industrialization (Weber, 1930; Thompson, 1966, 1967). In the nineteenth century, these values, increasingly secularized, became a mark of achievement, the bedrock of an ideology of self-determination that continues to function both pragmatically as a guide to action and morally as a legitimation of privilege. Despite the significant modification of these values in the twentieth century (to be discussed in the following pages), the work ethic and its associated values persist at the very center of American culture. The work ethic survives in middle-class codes of achievement and professionalism and in working-class values of hard work, manhood, craftsmanship, and sacrifice. It is through the discipline of work that the American dream of deserved status and material reward is to be realized. Hard work, self-reliance, and the drive to succeed are the professed keys to social mobility, the means by which one moves up in a putatively open class structure.

It is my contention that since the 1970s, the values of control have become more prominent in American society and that health promotion is one domain of belief and action in which these values are articulated. Underlying the strengthening of these values have been significant changes in the demands of the labor market, the experience of work, and the level of consumption. For the majority of Americans, the post–World War II era of sustained economic growth – the longest in our history – meant stable employment and rising real incomes. Real incomes rose 38% in the 1950s, followed by another 33% in the 1960s (*New York Times,* 1985). Americans moved into their own homes, became two-car families, bought more medical care, education, and entertainment, and began to worry sociologists and theologians. Americans appeared to many to have become oriented more toward release than control (Rieff, 1966). Even in the 1960s, despite the disquieting distractions of civil rights, urban riots, assassinations, Vietnam, and rebellious youth, the American middle class remained secure in its abundance.

All this changed in the 1970s. Under inflationary and recessionary pressures, real income began to fall – more than 9% from 1973 to 1982 (*New York Times,* 1985). The pinnacle of the American dream – buying a home – became difficult or impossible to achieve as the costs of housing and financing soared. Those still able to purchase a home began to pay a larger portion of their incomes for the privilege. Two incomes per family, overtime, and additional part-time jobs became typical means of maintaining an expected standard of living. Many more were not able to do so. People moved into smaller houses, lowered room temperatures in order to save on heating costs, and held on to their deteriorating automobiles.

Moreover, as the economy contracted, unemployment rose, imposing its own discipline as competition to obtain and keep jobs intensified. "Getting down to business," "productivity," and the Japanese became the mobilizing symbols for the disciplining of labor. The mandate was not only imposed; it was also internalized as Americans began to experience a new economic vulnerability. In assessing what would be required to succeed in the new era, middle-class Americans embarked on a project of personal reconstruction. They drew on the storehouse of an old American axiom: Failure is an individual matter, the consequence of personal flaws, and success can be regained only by renewed individual effort. The best-selling nonfiction book in the spring of 1984 was entitled *Tough Times Never Last but Tough People Do* (Schuller, 1984).

Health and fitness provided a readily available discourse and practice through which Americans could construct and express the new, disciplined self. Body provides the metaphor; it is the nature within that can be harnessed and transformed in conformity with our consciously chosen designs. We tighten our belts, cut out the fat, build resistance, and extend endurance. "If you're in shape, you've got the edge," proclaims an adver- tisement for a deodorant. "Everyone's a winner!" we are assured by the official song of the New York City marathon. The healthy or fit every- woman and everyman (not just successful athletes) have become symbols of America's renewed spirit of determination. Whatever the practical reasons and concerns that have led Americans to discipline their bodies in the name of health or fitness, the ritualized response to economic vul- nerability (i.e., personal reconstruction) finds in health and fitness a com- patible symbolic practice. The middle class, pressed and anxious, is in training. Faced with physical vulnerabilities, Americans are hardening their bodies. Experiencing economic vulnerability, they are fortifying their character and mobilizing their personal resources for the competi- tive struggle. Both are moral projects. In the ritual of personal regenera- tion, middle-class identity is secured. Personal effort will distinguish those who "deserve" to succeed or "deserve" to live longer, free of debilitating disease. In the lexicon of American individualism, it is called "taking responsibility."

I am suggesting that in the 1970s a homology developed between physical concerns and these other dimensions of our social and cultural experience. The fact that our lifestyle had been labeled hazardous and that our living and working environments could no longer be considered benign appeared at precisely the same historical moment that economic misfortune became a part of our reality. Life became unsafe. America discovered "limits." Both kinds of vulnerabilities are undoubtedly rein- forced by the angst of living in a nuclear world amidst increasing inter- national tensions. In this context, vulnerabilities to physical health haz- ards take on an added significance. They become a physical location for this wider range of concerns. Both our physical and our social worlds seem to demand a reordering of life. In both spheres, Americans are being asked to give something up. As medical authorities reveal a grow- ing list of physical dangers along with their requisite, self-protective behaviors, political authorities proclaim the nation at risk from declining productivity, declining standards in the schools, uncontrollable govern- ment expenditures, and military vulnerability.

Health as release

Of course, this is all too neat. The transition to a culture of control has not been so smooth. The internalization of mandates for discipline have been neither automatic nor pervasive. Working-class and poor people, for example, are more likely to view the new mandates as additional burdens. Adaptations to hard times may be seen as necessary, but hardly an opportunity for self-improvement. It is not that values of control are unimportant for working-class people. They, too, have a Protestant heritage. Nor are they free from the self-blame inflicted by individualist ideology (Sennett & Cobb, 1972). The virtue of self-control is not an exclusive property of the middle class, but for most nonprofessional and nonmanagerial wage workers, self-direction and continuous striving are not the usual job requirements, nor are rewards for such efforts plentiful. Supervision and imposed disciplines of time, activity, behavior, speech, and body are the more prevalent type of work experience (Foucault, 1977). Thus, mandates for more control are likely to be experienced by these workers as another imposition by external authorities, be they political, economic, or medical. Demands for bodily controls during *time off* are likely to be regarded as an invasion of time reserved for enjoyment. There is no need to recreate the self for "the competitive edge," no need to run marathons in order to demonstrate a capacity for endurance. As a steel worker put it to me in rejecting health-promoting activities:

I'm saying that I'm not going to worry about when my time is up. I just worry about when my time is here. . . . It's that enjoyment thing again. You want to get something out of it. . . . You got every right in the world to satisfy yourself. So I say do it. . . . I'm going to work and I'm going to enjoy the fruits of my work.

The structuring of time for an uncertain payoff in the distant future is thought to be an infringement of a right – the right to be free of restraint, the right of enjoyment. There is no value in delaying gratification. "Enjoy it. Shoot, you only go around once."

In the release conception, health is not rejected as a value, but it is often repudiated as a goal to be achieved through instrumental actions. It is perceived more as an outcome of the enjoyment of life and the positive state of mind derived from such enjoyment. In the interviews, I did not predefine health, and in the course of these conversations it became clear that, for many, emotional and physical health could not be separated in an arbitrary way – this in spite of the medical, political, and commercial discourses that continually make that separation. Many considered emotional health to be more important – both in itself and in its effects on physical health. Conceptions of control were not absent from these discussions of emotional health. I frequently detected, for example, a kind of mind-over-matter, positive-thinking psychosomatics. But when people talked about stress, which was often, they were more likely to think of health in terms of "not worrying," "letting things go," "getting things out of your system," and, again, enjoying life. In such thinking, health is a matter of coping with the pressures and tensions of overwork, family obligations, or life crises such as the death of a loved one, divorce, or career disappointment.

Thus, these people consider themselves to be threatened by different kinds of hazards. Since they generally view these hazards as unavoidable, they feel it is the way they respond to them that is important for their health. For some, even physical hazards can be dealt with in this way. In the absence of a capacity to control one's life situation and life events (only be degree more characteristic of working-class and poor people's experience), the prescription for health is to adopt a positive and easygoing attitude and, most of all, *not to worry.*

The two conceptions of health – control and release – are not necessarily seen as incompatible. A person may be concerned with both aspects of health and be committed to both sets of values, seeking a healthful and ethical balance between them. It is interesting, for example, that several people spoke of exercise both in terms of a desire for more discipline and as a release from stress. Release conceptions, however, were often seen as conflicting with the control demanded by self-protection from physical hazards. Several people, for example, complained of being inundated by the multitude of warnings about physical health hazards. For them, the problem of health was a public discourse that instills fears and demands actions as if one were constantly in danger. "With that kind of thinking I'm going to be scared to death," a construction worker told me. "And if I'm afraid and full of fear, I'm not going to be healthy."

For others, health-mandated controls conflict not only with a specific pleasurable activity, but with a style of living that has come to mean the very definition of the good life – a life free of constraints. For this professional man, it was a matter of identity:

When you hear about something causing a problem – a doctor comes up with a study and says you shouldn't have coffee any more, and people keep responding to all these things – "you shouldn't eat, you shouldn't have butter, you shouldn't have starches, you shouldn't have – " Your whole lifestyle becomes prone to – You become a reactionary. Instead of a person living your own life, you are living a life where people are saying you are being threatened by this or that. . . . You live in a shell. You don't enjoy life. The fact is that I want to live a certain lifestyle.

A perfectly healthy body will do no good if its achievement demands a self-denying load of constraints. Worrying about physical health will undermine one's well-being and will interfere with the pleasures that make life worthwhile. As a salesman expressed it, "Ideal health is being able to do what you want to do when you want to do it." In this view, health is pursuing a free lifestyle, individually chosen and externally obstructed by no one. Physical health merges with a more inclusive well-being and the values believed essential for securing that well-being. Listen, for example, to another salesman responding to the question of whether men or women are healthier:

I think men are on the whole healthier than women due to the fact that I think they feel better. I think they feel healthier. They may have the same aches and pains, but if a man doesn't notice it, or doesn't want to notice it, I would tend to think that's healthier. The woman may live longer because she does notice it and maybe takes care of it, but if he feels better, who is healthier? It gets back to what my interpretation of being healthy is: if you feel healthy, you are healthy. Now a doctor may have a different interpretation than that. You may have a foreign body invading your system; he would say you are not healthy. And from his reality he is right. But not from my reality. Because I don't go to a doctor everyday and ask him, do I have a foreign body invading my system? From day to day it is how do I feel? And if I feel healthy, I'm healthy. If I feel sick, I'm sick.

There are interesting issues of gender raised here that need more systematic exploration (see, e.g., Nathanson, 1977). My point is that in this comment one can see that the cosmology of instrumental, future-oriented control (the reality of the doctor) is rejected in favor of an immediate, experiential ethic (social–emotional or day-to-day reality). Physical health hazards and behavioral controls are subordinated to an opposing definition of well-being. "Who's healthier?" he asks.

If space permitted, it would be useful to trace the medical, political, social movement, and commercial discourses that have promoted a release orientation aimed specifically at maintaining physical and emotional health. For example, considerable attention has been given to "stress" in the past decade. Such concepts as type A and cancer-prone personalities have become widely diffused. Medical authorities have increasingly emphasized the role of stress in a number of diseases. Pharmaceutical companies have developed their own approach to healthful release via the world of chemicals. The alcohol industry, with only a modicum of subtlety, identifies its products with robust healthiness. Stress management has become a component of employee relations and "burnout" a growing concern in the professions. Holistic health practitioners offer a range of "relaxation therapies." Much can be heard about "runner's high." These discourses warrant careful examination. Is there, for example, an ideological and political context shaping the emergence of stress as a concept and model of prevention similar to the model of prevention emphasizing the physical hazards of individual lifestyle? In the stress paradigm, how is the problem defined (where is stress located?) and what solutions are proposed?

In the few pages remaining, however, I would like to suggest the outlines of an interpretation similar to that of health as control. That is, it may well be that, along with a practical logic of release as a means to physical or emotional health, health discussed in terms of release may be a means of expressing notions of well-being and self deeply rooted in our cultural life. As with control, what we think and do about health may be in part an acting out of a larger cultural drama.

Every culture organizes releases from its normal renunciations (Rieff, 1966). American culture provides abundant opportunities, channels, and endorsements for release. Release, however, has acquired a more fundamental significance: It has become indispensable to our economic system. The culture of consumption or what has also been called the culture of abundance (Susman, 1984) began to take root in the late nineteenth century. Urbanization and industrialization were radically transforming American life. Liberal Protestantism eased the ascetic renunciations of its Puritan predecessor as a growing middle class discovered the possibility and importance of leisure. Traditional and communal forms of self-realization and definition began to erode. Into the ferment of a culture of newly detached individuals seeking to discover viable ways of reconstituting the self, advertising began to contribute its own model. As historian Jackson Lears has argued, the conception was therapeutic. The new consumer ethic promised personal transformation. Consuming "would contribute to the buyer's physical, psychic, or social well-being." It would provide a "richer, fuller life" (Lears, 1983: 18–19). It is this fastening of a "therapeutic ethos" to consumption that provided the moral foundations for the consumer ethic in the twentieth century. The connection also supplied a powerful cultural logic for a concept of health defined in terms of release.

As a system imperative, advanced capitalism requires that well-being be conceived in ways that promote release. Rather than delay gratification, the imperative is to indulge. Rather than deny the self, the premise is instant contentment through commodified pleasures. A personality must be produced that is compatible with consumption. For whatever reasons (and there are many) that people seek release from control or freedom from restraint, the consumer ethic has provided a vehicle and sociocultural reinforcement. Abundance has created the material conditions, "a gorgeous variety of satisfactions" (Rieff, 1966) through which well-being can be realized. Since World War II the need and desire for release have become a consuming passion.

Contemporary Americans are the objects and subjects of two opposing mandates, two opposing approaches to the achievement of well-being.

The opposition is structural. The culture of consumption demands a modal personality contrary to the personality required for production. The mandate for discipline clashes with the mandate for pleasure. To the extent that well-being and self-realization have come to be defined in terms of release, the emerging mandates for controls will be resented and perhaps resisted. This will be particularly true for people who already experience the weight of externally imposed controls or believe they have little to gain by becoming more disciplined. In the current period, when both economic and physical vulnerabilities and culturally prescribed solutions have raised the value of control exponentially, many will endeavor to retain a concept of well-being that continues to be generated by a culture of release. Others, feeling the opposition internally, will attempt both.

It should not be surprising that health is a site where this conflict is experienced and expressed. First, a practical logic exists for both control and release. Numerous discourses structure that logic. In contemporary American life, physical and emotional health require both controls and releases. Second, health is a metaphor for generalized well-being. As such, health is a moral discourse, a discourse through which the culture's values about individual and social well-being are communicated. In everyday experience, one must question the extent to which the two dimensions of health – the practical and the metaphorical – can be separated. Both physical and emotional well-being are inextricably bound to society and culture. The choices we make about health are choices derived from the complex fabric of our social and moral lives.

References

Bauman, E. 1978. Introduction to holistic health. In *The Holistic Health Handbook,* ed. Berkeley Holistic Health Center, pp. 17–19. Berkeley, Calif.: And/Or Press.

Brandt, Allen. 1985. *No Magic Bullet: A Social History of Venereal Disease in the United States since 1880.* New York: Oxford University Press.

CBS–*New York Times.* 1983. Poll. April 7–11, 1983.

Chicago Sun Times. 1984. Cigarette smoking declines. April 2: 4.

Comaroff, J. 1983. The defectiveness of symbols or the symbols of defectiveness? On the cultural analysis of medical systems. *Culture, Medicine and Psychiatry* 7: 3–20.

Crawford, R. 1977. You are dangerous to your health: The ideology and politics of victim blaming. *International Journal of Health Services* 7: 663–80.

Crawford, R. 1980. Healthism and the medicalization of everyday life. *International Journal of Health Services 10:* 365–88.

Dubos, Rene. 1959. *The Mirage of Health.* New York: Anchor Books.

Foucault, Michel. 1977. *Discipline and Punish: The Birth of the Prison.* New York: Vintage.

Freud, Sigmund. 1965. *The Interpretation of Dreams.* New York: Avon Books.

Gillick, M. 1984. Health promotion, jogging, and the pursuit of the moral life. *Journal of Health Politics, Policy and Law 9:* 369–87.

Grant, L. 1978. *The Holistic Revolution.* Pasadena, Calif.: Ward Ritchie Press.

Haley, Bruce. 1978. *The Healthy Body in Victorian Culture.* Cambridge, Mass.: Harvard University Press.

Kannel, W., and Gordon, T., eds. 1968. *The Framingham Study.* Washington D.C.: U.S. Government Printing Office.

Katz, A., and Levin, L. 1980. Self care is *not* a solipsistic trap: A reply to critics. *International Journal of Health Services 10:* 329–36.

Knowles, J. 1977. The responsibility of the individual. In *Doing Better and Feeling Worse: Health in the United States,* ed. J. Knowles, pp. 57–80. New York: Norton.

Kopelman, L., and Moskop, J. 1981. The holistic health movement: A survey and a critique. *Journal of Medicine and Philosophy 6:* 209–35.

Lears, J. 1983. From salvation to self-realization: Advertising and the therapeutic roots of the consumer culture, 1880–1930. In *The Culture of Consumption,* ed. R. Fox and J. Lears, pp. 1–38. New York: Pantheon.

McKinlay, J., and McKinlay, S. 1977. The questionable contribution of medical measures to the decline of mortality in the United States in the twentieth century. *Health and Society 55:* 405–28.

Muramoto, N. 1973. *Healing Ourselves.* New York: Avon Books.

Nathanson, C. 1977. Sex roles as variables in preventive health behavior. *Journal of Community Health 3:* 142–55.

New York Times. 1984. Flood of health kits widens home tests for early symptoms. October 1: A1.

New York Times. 1985. Owning a home: the dream persists. February 28: 17.

Rieff, Phillip. 1966. *The Triumph of the Therapeutic.* New York: Harper & Row.

Sahlins, Marshall. 1976. *Culture and Practical Reason.* University of Chicago Press.

Schuller, Robert. 1984. *Tough Times Never Last but Tough People Do.* New York: Bantam.

Sennett, Richard, and Cobb, Jonathon. 1972. *The Hidden Injuries of Class.* New York: Knopf.

Sidel, V., and Sidel, R. 1981. All self-care is not solipsistic, but selective citation surely is: A reply to Katz and Levin. *International Journal of Health Services 11:* 653–7.

Sontag, Susan. 1977. *Illness as Metaphor.* New York: Farrar, Straus & Giroux.

Susman, Warren. 1984. *Culture as History.* New York: Pantheon.

Thompson, E. P. 1966. *The Making of the English Working Class.* New York: Vintage Books.

Thompson, E. P. 1967. Time, work discipline, and industrial capitalism. *Past and Present 38:* 56–97.

Time. 1981. The fitness craze: America shapes up. November 2: 94–106.

Time. 1982. The new ideal in beauty: Coming on strong. August 30: 70–2.

Time. 1985. Water, water everywhere. May 20: 68–83.

USDHEW. 1964. *Smoking and Health: Report of the Advisory Committee to the Surgeon General of the Public Health Service.* Washington, D.C.: U.S. Government Printing Office.

USDHEW. 1979. The Secretary's Forward. In *Healthy People: The Surgeon General's Report on Health Promotion and Disease Prevention.* Washington, D.C.: U.S. Government Printing Office.

USDHHS. 1980. *Health: United States 1980.* Washington, D.C.: U.S. Government Printing Office.

USDHHS. 1983. *Health: United States 1983.* Washington, D.C.: U.S. Government Printing Office.

Weber, Max. 1930. *The Protestant Ethic and the Spirit of Capitalism.* London: Allen & Unwin.

Whorton, James. 1982. *Crusaders for Fitness: The History of American Health Reformers.* Princeton, N.J.: Princeton University Press.

Part II

Research and prevention programs for specific hazards

The preceding section of this volume offered theoretical perspectives that apply to any situation in which people face the threat of harm. The chapters in this section, in contrast, describe the findings of research and actual prevention programs in several specific fields: health promotion and disease prevention, natural hazards, crime prevention, consumer safety, and occupational safety and health. This group of topics does not exhaust the possibilities for self-protective behavior in our lives. Financial planning, contraceptive use, antiwar protests, and environmental action are other steps that people may take to reduce their risk of being harmed. Nevertheless, the topics included here cover many different hazards and a wide variety of protective actions. The relevant literature is vast.

Each of the general topics of health, natural hazards, and crime is represented in this section by several chapters. The first chapter in each of these subsections attempts to answer the question, Why do people take precautions against this hazard? The second chapter (two additional chapters in the case of health) describes the kinds of programs that have attempted to encourage protective behavior and summarizes our knowledge of what works best. Consumer safety and occupational safety and health are discussed in separate chapters that emphasize actual program experience. The task accepted by these authors was difficult. Within a few pages they attempt to give a comprehensive overview of their topic that is current, accurate, and yet understandable to readers who are not familiar with that particular hazard. The chapters provide a rich source of ideas for understanding and encouraging self-protective behavior.

Although the chapters have similar goals – to summarize research or program experience – each introduces some unique ideas into the discussion of preventive behavior. Paul Cleary reminds us that many behaviors that prevent illness or increase the risk of becoming ill are not performed because of their health consequences. Weight control is an obvious example of a health-relevant action in which health protection is usually a

115

minor motive. Cleary's observation, undoubtedly correct, raises the daunting prospect that explaining health behavior will require us to develop a model of human behavior in general. Examining two specific health issues, autoimmune deficiency syndrome (AIDS) and adolescent smoking, Cleary offers a way out. He suggests that we should forget about a comprehensive model of health behavior and instead develop mini models for individual health problems. Such mini models can incorporate the health and nonhealth factors that are relevant to the particular problem.

The attention that health promotion programs have received probably exceeds that given to natural hazards preparedness, citizen crime prevention, and safety combined. The health promotion field is not only larger in volume; it has taken a much greater variety of approaches and has more often seen these approaches tested through properly designed evaluations. A comprehensive review of this work would take many chapters (for an overview, see Green, 1984).

Reviewers of preventive health programs typically tackle only a small portion of the field. They focus on a particular setting for health promotion (schools, hospitals, work sites, the community), on members of a particular age group (infants, children, teenagers, adults, elderly) or on a particular problem (cardiovascular disease, weight loss, smoking, alcohol abuse). Readers can consult the *Annual Review of Public Health, Health Education Quarterly,* and *Behavioral Health* (Matarazzo, Weiss, Herd, Miller, & Weiss, 1984) for recent reviews.

The two chapters on health promotion programs in this volume do not attempt to provide a complete summary of these programs. Both focus only on smoking, and each emphasizes a single type of setting, one the community and the other schools. Yet because the problem of smoking has received so much attention, these two chapters describe and evaluate a very wide range of interventions. The chapters are particularly strong in discussing the methodological and strategic problems that must be faced in field research on prevention. McCaul and Glasgow's careful review of school-based smoking prevention efforts points out enormous gaps in our knowledge of how these programs work. It should make us pause before we rush into large-scale, community programs with multicomponent treatments whose effects we do not fully understand.

Natural hazards researchers, unlike those studying health behavior, can seldom employ experimental methods. Cause-and-effect relations are extraordinarily difficult to establish, especially from post hoc investigations of natural disasters, the most common type of study. Dennis Mileti and John Sorensen have collaborated in preparing the two chapters that summarize our knowledge about this field. Their chapters are particularly valuable because the literature in this field is so scattered. Many discussions of natural hazards behavior are incidental segments of reports, often unpublished, that assess the accuracy of the disaster warning system, the magnitude of the disaster damage, and the performance of emergency personnel. Programs to encourage preparedness are rarely described in written publications, and evaluations are even more uncommon.

Mileti and Sorensen's discussion of why people take precautions is based on a decision-making model of protective action. Their review of the research identifies factors that influence the taking of precautions against future hazards and also steps taken in response to warnings of imminent disaster. Attempts to encourage people to take steps that will reduce their vulnerability to natural hazards have a wide variety of forms, including legal regulations, economic incentives, information, and persuasion. Examples described in the chapter show that the success of these approaches has been mixed. The author's pay particular attention to programs that provide information and that seem to expect rational self-protective behavior on the part of the public. The chapter describes the types of information that are provided and critically examines the data concerning the effectiveness of this general strategy.

Stephanie Greenberg brings together the scattered literature on why people take precautions against crime. In addition to individual actions, such as acquiring a weapon or learning self-defense,[1] avoiding certain high-crime areas, and purchasing special door locks, other frequently practiced crime prevention strategies, such as block watch programs, require the cooperative efforts of many individuals. These different actions often have different determinants. Fear has been regarded as a very important aspect of reactions to crime, much more so than for the other hazards discussed in this book, and Greenberg delineates the complex relations between fear and protective behaviors.

Fred Heinzelmann looks specifically at programs that attempt to increase crime prevention activities. These, too, have a variety of goals, ranging from changes in specific, individual behaviors to the establishment of permanent, communitywide organizations. Although the scientific literature on crime prevention is relatively small, there have been several state-of-the-art reviews, and Heinzelmann discusses the characteristics that seem to distinguish successful from unsuccessful programs.

Leon Robertson's provacative chapter tells a cautionary tale of unsuccessful safety programs, particularly projects dealing with seat belt use and driver education. He suggests that behavioral scientists are often unrealistically optimistic about their ability to change behavior, partly because people exposed to prevention campaigns exaggerate the extent to which they have adopted recommended measures. His chapter forces one to think about the limits of voluntary programs and the situations in which they can succeed. Robertson reminds us that an overemphasis on behavioral issues may divert our attention from technological solutions – safer cars, childproof medicine containers, food products with less salt and cholesterol – that might be much more effective in promoting safety and health.

Alexander Cohen's concluding chapter examines health and safety efforts in work place settings. He describes an attempt by the National Institute for Occupational Safety and Health to develop guidelines, derived from research on risk communication, for improving the health and safety messages that most programs rely on. The work place offers unusual opportunities for prevention programs because relevant behaviors are often easily observed and because management has greater control over its employees than public health officials, for example, have over the general population. Sanctions and incentives are certainly much easier to apply in a work setting than in the community. Cohen describes some careful applications of behavior modification strategies to increase the self-protective behavior of workers.

Note

1 In the crime prevention literature, only carrying a weapon and learning self-defense are termed "self-protection" measures.

References

Green, L. W. (1984). Modifying and developing health behavior. *Annual Review of Public Health, 5,* 215–36.
Matarazzo, J. D., Weiss, S. M., Herd, J. A., Miller, N. E., & Weiss, S. M. (1984). *Behavioral health.* New York: Wiley.

6 Why people take precautions against health risks

Paul D. Cleary

Introduction

The question Why do people take precautions against health risks? implicitly defines a domain of behaviors – behaviors that people deliberately engage in to protect themselves from what they perceive to be health risks. Several well-known models of illness behavior have been applied to preventive behavior. These models are based on the premise that people estimate the seriousness of risk or symptoms, evaluate the costs and benefits of action, and then choose a course of action that will maximize their expected outcome. If people have accurate information and carefully consider the advisability of alternative behaviors, these models may describe well the factors that influence behavior. However, most illness behaviors are more complex than the models imply. People sometimes act on the basis of behaviors learned in childhood or adolescence; evaluating the seriousness of a condition is usually difficult; people are not always aware of the factors that influence their behavior; and behaviors often serve multiple, non-health-related functions. Preventive health behavior is even more difficult to model because, in addition to the complexities listed above, the consequences of preventive behaviors are often delayed and probabilistic, and estimating the extent to which particular actions will reduce risk is difficult.

In this chapter I shall review several of the most widely cited theoretical models relevant to volitional preventive behaviors. These models have stimulated a tremendous amount of research, and the resultant data have provided important insights into health behavior. However, these models focus primarily on cognitive factors and are inherently limited in their capacity to explain many health-relevant behaviors. To emphasize how

An earlier version of this chapter was presented at a conference on self-protective behavior, Rutgers University, June 1984. Work on this chapter was supported by grants from the Commonwealth Fund and the Robert Wood Johnson Foundation. I thank Sue Levkoff and Neil Weinstein for helpful comments on an earlier draft.

complex preventive behaviors can be and the variety of factors that must be taken into account in explaining them, I shall briefly refer to two examples of health risks: smoking and acquired immune deficiency syndrome (AIDS). If one considers the range of factors that can influence whether and how people quite smoking or "protect" themselves from AIDS, it is clear how inadequate these widely used models of behavior are. These examples emphasize that it is necessary to be aware of the broad matrix of factors influencing health behavior if we are to understand variations in preventive actions. Next, I shall describe a number of studies that represent a variety of theoretical perspectives.

Preventive behaviors in the different areas described in this book tend to share a number of characteristics, but this does not make it easy to develop a general model for these behaviors. Clearly, certain processes such as risk perception will be affected by the same variables in many situations. However, it is not feasible to develop a general model to predict the conditions under which different people will initiate and maintain all preventive behaviors. Rather, I suggest that it is more useful to develop an in-depth understanding of the psychological, social, and cultural factors motivating and sustaining specific behaviors. For example, rather than simply measure risk and assume that perceived risk will be related to behavior in a similar way for all behaviors, it would be more reasonable to develop an understanding of the factors affecting risk assessment and apply those findings to the behavior in question.

Cognitive models of health behavior

Numerous models of behavior have been developed on the assumption that people act to maximize the perceived benefits of their behavior. These include the work of Kasl and Cobb (1966), the health belief model (Janz & Becker, 1984), the theory of reasoned action (Ajzen & Feishbein, 1980), subjective expected utility theory (Edwards, 1954), the protection motivation theory (Rogers, 1983), and models of evacuation behavior (Fritz, 1961; Houts et al. 1984; Perry, Lindell, & Green, 1981). Probably the two most frequently cited paradigms in research on health behavior are the health belief model and the theory of reasoned action.

The health belief model

The health belief model was developed by Becker, Hochbaum, Rosenstock, Kirscht, Leventhal, and others (Becker, 1974; Becker, Kaback, Rosenstock, & Ruth, 1975; Becker & Maiman, 1975; Hochbaum, 1958;

Leventhal, Hochbaum, Rosenstock, 1960; Rosenstock 1960, 1966, 1974; Rosenstock & Kirscht, 1979). This approach to explaining health behaviors is a synthesis of social psychological theories of value expectancy and decision making (Maiman & Becker, 1974). As such, it focuses on behaviors that are under an individual's control and is concerned primarily with conscious decisions about the utility of specific actions. Variables used to predict an individual's behavior are (a) perceived susceptibility to a health threat, (b) perceived severity of the consequences of a disease or health threat, (c) the individual's evaluation of the efficaciousness of possible protective actions, (d) the perceived costs of or barriers to possible protective actions, (e) cues to action such as symptoms or mass media communications, and (f) demographic, structural, and social psychological factors that act as "enabling" factors.

Janz and Becker (1984) reviewed studies of the health belief model published between 1974 and 1984. They discussed four investigations of vaccination behavior, three studies of screening behaviors, and eight studies of risk factor behaviors. In addition, they tabulated the results of 13 studies of preventive health behaviors conducted before 1974. In general, the results of these studies show that the factors described by the health belief model are related to prevention behaviors. In one of the earlier studies on protective behavior Hochbaum (1958) found that people who believed they could unknowingly contact tuberculosis or have asymptomatic tuberculosis were more likely to get a screening x ray than people who did not hold this belief. Leventhal, Hochman, and Rosenstock (1960) found that beliefs about vulnerability to Asian flu were related to the probability of getting a flu shot. Cummings, Jette, Brock, and Haefner (1979) prospectively studied factors that predisposed individuals to receive swine flue vaccination in 1976. In that study, more than 40% of the variation in inoculation behavior was explained by the predictors used. The authors found that beliefs concerning the efficacy of the behavior and barriers to the behavior, along with reported family problems, were consistent predictors. Other beliefs and characteristics did not contribute significantly to the explanatory model.

Harris and Guten (1979) examined the relation between a range of health-protective behaviors and selected variables from the health belief model among a sample of 842 randomly selected adults. They found that practically everyone in the sample performed at least some regular, protective behavior. Furthermore, they found that health belief model variables moderately influence the number of different kinds of health practices, safety practices, and preventive care activities performed. However, no variable was predictive of behavior in all three clusters, and safety practices were least explained. It is important to note that all of the relations reported by Harris and Guten are weak. Their main measure of association is the proportion of the total sum of squares explained by the predictors, and the highest figure for any of the health belief model variables is .015. Both family income and education had stronger associations with the health behaviors described (the strongest association was .044 for the effect of family income on preventive care). Langlie (1977) was more successful in her attempts to predict risk behavior. In her analyses, the health belief model variables accounted for 34% of the variance in direct-risk behaviors and 22% of the variance in indirect-risk behaviors among the subset of her sample that she defined as consistent responders. The most important variables in her models were low cost, favorable attitudes, and belief in control.

Calnan and Moss (1984) conducted a prospective study examining how well the health belief model would predict attendance at a class on breast self-examination and compliance with the recommendations given in the class. They found that both previous positive health activities and beliefs about personal vulnerability to breast cancer were important in explaining class attendance. However, counter to the health belief model predictions, perceived control over health was negatively correlated with attendance. The best predictors of changes in the practice of breast self-examination were beliefs about the costs and benefits of self-examination, but the authors emphasized that a large amount of the variance remained unexplained, indicating the limited utility of the health belief model in this particular case.

The health belief model has also been applied to studies of polio vaccination (Rosenstock, Derryberry, & Carriger, 1959), preventive dental care (Kegeles, 1963; see also Antonovsky & Kats, 1970), hypertension control (Taylor, 1979), smoking behavior (Swinehart & Kirscht, 1966), checkups (Haefner & Kirscht, 1970), compliance (Becker et al., 1979), and dieting (Becker, Maiman, Kirscht, Haefner, and Drachman, 1977).

In their review of these studies, Janz and Becker (1984) conclude that the research to date provides substantial empirical evidence that the dimensions identified by the health belief model are important predictors of health-related behaviors. In general, they conclude that susceptibility appears to be somewhat more important for preventive health behaviors than sick role behaviors, and the reverse seems to be the case for benefits. Most studies have found a positive association between susceptibility and preventive behavior (Becker et al., 1975; Fink, Shapiro, & Roeser, 1972; Kelly, 1979; Rundall & Wheeler, 1979), but several negative results also have been reported (Ben-Sira & Padeh, 1978; Howe, 1981; Weisenberg, Kegeles, & Lund, 1980). Interestingly, perceived severity of consequences was relatively unimportant in predicting preventive behaviors. With respect to preventive health behavior, susceptibility, benefits, and barriers are consistently associated with outcomes. Variables representing barriers to behaviors were significantly associated with behavior in all of the 13 studies reviewed. In an earlier review, Becker and Maiman (1983: 544) point out that several studies utilizing health belief model variables have not yet yielded the anticipated results. Also, only about half of the relevant studies have been prospective. Calnan and Moss (1984) have emphasized that in retrospective studies it is often difficult to determine whether beliefs determine behavior or whether people rationalize their beliefs to be consistent with their behavior (McKinlay, 1972). Of the 13 studies reviewed by Janz and Becker (1984), only three were prospective. However, those prospective studies uniformly supported the importance of health belief model variables.

The theory of reasoned action

The theory of reasoned action (Ajzen & Fishbein, 1980; Fishbein, 1967; Fishbein & Ajzen, 1975) is a general model of behavior that has been applied to a number of health behaviors and tested in a wide variety of laboratory and applied settings (Ajzen & Fishbein, 1970, 1977; Fishbein, 1967, 1973; Fishbein & Jaccard, 1973; Hecker & Ajzen, 1983; Jaccard, 1975; Seibold & Roper, 1979). This theory is relevant only to behaviors that are under volitional control; it deals with "rational" thought processes based on available information. In this sense, it is similar to the health belief model in the domain of behaviors to which it refers. The attitudes included in the theory of reasoned action are the same as the beliefs in the health belief model, and like the health belief model, the theory of reasoned action is premised on a value-expectancy theory of behavior. Indeed, as Kirscht (1983) and others have pointed out, the elements of the health belief model can be mapped onto the theory of reasoned action.

The main differences between the health belief model and the theory of reasoned action are that the latter incorporates subjective norms and specifies several additional explanatory constructs and the relations among those constructs. According to the theory of reasoned action, a person's intention to perform a behavior is the immediate determinant of the action. This intention is hypothesized to be a function of two basic factors: the individual's attitude toward the behavior and subjective norms. Attitudes are determined by beliefs about the outcomes. Subjective norms, on the other hand, reflect one's beliefs that specific individuals or groups think that one should or should not behave in a particular way. Attitudes toward the behavior and subjective norms are posited as acting to influence intentions, which are the most important predictors of behavior.

Perhaps the most distinguishing feature of the theory of reasoned action is that it makes no reference to determinants of behavior other than subjective norms and attitudes. Variables explicitly excluded from consideration include personality characteristics, demographic variables, social role, status, socialization, intelligence, and kinship patterns. Ajzen and Fishbein (1980) state that "one of the major disadvantages of relying on external variables to explain behavior is that different kinds of external variables have to be invoked for different behavior domains . . . such a multitude of theories is not only unnecessary, but it actually impedes scientific progress" (p. 9). They also state, "We have examined the potential effects of variables external to our theory, such as demographic characteristics, personality traits, and traditional measures of attitudes toward persons, institutions, and policies. We argued that such variables have no necessary relation to any particular behavior, since they have no consistent effects on the beliefs underlying these behaviors" (p. 91). Ajzen and Fishbein (1980) have reviewed an extensive literature supporting the theory of reasoned action and a more recent variation, the theory of planned behavior (Ajzen, 1984).

Kirscht (1983) has outlined several weaknesses in this literature. For example, he points out that, although impressive findings have emerged from the Fishbein–Ajzen model, much of the research has been conducted on college students. He suggests that verification with noncollege samples would be desirable. Kirscht also notes that both the health belief model and the Ajzen–Fishbein model have been less successful in explaining the modification and maintenance of personal health habits, and he observes that quite different factors may be involved in different stages of health behavior (see also Dishman, 1982; Kasl, 1974, 1978). For example, factors related to the initiation of a behavior may not play as large a role in the maintenance of that behavior.

Two examples of complex behaviors

AIDS: behavior or contagion?

To demonstrate the limitations of the health behavior models reviewed so far, I would like to consider preventive behavior among persons with HTLV-III antibodies in their blood. HTLV-III is a virus that currently is thought to be the main etiologic agent for acquired immune deficiency syndrome (AIDS). Recently, screening tests for HTLV-III have been developed and refined so that after a series of tests we can now be relatively certain whether a person's blood contains HTLV-III antibodies. People are currently being screened for HTLV-III and being informed of those test results.

Public health and medical personnel would like to structure the way information is provided and influence patient behavior to achieve several goals. First, it is important that information be given in an informative and intelligible way, a difficult task. Persons with HTLV-III antibodies are at high risk of developing a fatal disease, but the nature of the risk and whether it can be altered is confusing. Second, we want to maximize people's ability and motivation to behave in ways that are functional for both themselves and the public at large. The information about HTLV-III in one's blood and the knowledge that one may develop AIDS can be devastating. Furthermore, the behavioral recommendations for persons with positive results include not having unprotected sex, not kissing, not having children, and notifying physicians and dentists. Adhering to these recommendations would have a tremendous impact on most people's lives, and the factors related to whether people comply are extremely complex. Perhaps most important, we would like to help these people. We would like to provide the appropriate support or enable people to mobilize support from other sources and potentiate their ability to cope effectively with their new knowledge.

This is one of the most important yet elusive and complicated public health problems in history. Do traditional illness behavior models provide a theoretical or practical guide for addressing these issues? To a certain extent, they do. Clearly, perceived susceptibility, perceived severity of the AIDS, the individual's evaluation of the efficacy of behaviors, the costs of behaviors, cues to action, and enabling factors are important. However, these models fall far short of telling us all we need to know in this situation. For example, consider the variable perceived susceptibility. This variable likely will be related to subsequent behavior. However, what we really need to know is what accounts for the variations in the ways people process information and develop models of susceptibility. Furthermore, in order to understand how perceived risk will be related to preventive behaviors in different groups, it is necessary to take into account people's ideas of AIDS and how it is transmitted.

For people with HTLV-III antibodies, the probability of developing AIDS within five years is between 5 and 10% but we do not understand the factors that discriminate between those who will and those who will not develop the disease. Epidemiologists with the most current information find it difficult to estimate aggregate risk and differentiate persons at high and low risk. A recent *Time* article compared the situation to playing Russian roulette with one bullet and 10 chambers. Imagine how confusing this situation is for someone who has little statistical or medical knowledge, is highly anxious, and perceives a fatal threat associated with the information.

One of the groups of people identified as being at high risk of contracting AIDS comprises homosexual men. Let us assume that we are interested in the general questions of how homosexual men respond to the threat of AIDS, whether they take protective action, and what type of protective action they take. One approach would be to measure the variables specified by the health belief model and develop a predictive equation based on the individuals' scores on the various variables. Another approach would be to develop an inventory of attitudes, beliefs, and intentions with respect to AIDS, measure those variables, and use the theory of reasoned action to develop an equation to predict how people will behave. I think that, in the context of the AIDS situation, the limitations of these approaches are clear. Individuals may have various degrees of knowledge about the syndrome, they may be reacting to different types of information, fear may play a prominent role in their behavior, social groups and network influences may play critical roles in their reaction, and so on. If we expanded the study to include intravenous drug users, Haitians, and people who frequently receive transfusions, the complexity of the problem is overwhelming.

Let me suggest a different approach to the problem. I would argue that the first question to be addressed should be people's conceptualizations of AIDS "risk factors." Recent data suggest that AIDS is caused by an infectious agent that is transmitted by intimate contact or by blood products (see, e.g., Popovic, Sarngadharan, Read, & Gallo, 1984). However, it has also been reported that there are a number of "risk factors" for AIDS, such as frequent intimate sexual contact, use of amyl nitrate, and anal intercourse. If one read only the popular press, one might develop one of two distinct disease models. The first is that certain types of behavior, such as taking drugs intravenously, sniffing amyl nitrate, and engaging in frequent homosexual sex with multiple partners increase one's risk of developing AIDS because those behaviors make one "vulnerable" to AIDS. That is, those behaviors weaken a person's resistance in some way and increase the risk of contracting AIDS. A second, very different perspective is what I refer to as a contagion model of AIDS. In this model, the risk factors mentioned increase one's risk of contracting AIDS by bringing one into contact with carriers of the vector that transmits AIDS. This model is supported not only by recent work on AIDS-related retroviruses but also by the striking geographic concentrations of AIDS incidence (Popovic et al., 1984).

Predictions about protective behavior would be very different depending on which model of risk a person held (Kleinman, 1980; Lau & Hartman, 1983; Leventhal, Meyer, & Nerenz, 1980). If a person held the notion that frequent sex increases the risk of AIDS irrespective of whether one's partner has previously come into contact with the infectious agent, then reducing sexual activity would seem like an efficacious action. One would have a clear-cut idea about the risk factor, would be motivated by both knowledge and fear to reduce risk, would assess one's protective action as efficacious, and would be likely to take action (in this case inaction).

If, on the other hand, one held the notion that AIDS clusters among individuals with similar characteristics or behaviors primarily because those individuals live in close proximity and have a high probability of having contact with one another, then one would make different predictions. The history of a number of infectious diseases indicates that people have difficulty distinguishing when casual contact transmits a disease and when intimate contact is necessary. In such a situation, since contact with infected individuals may seem inevitable, one might be much less likely to take certain protective actions, such as reducing sexual contacts.

These considerations are especially important now that a relatively inexpensive screening test for HTLV-III is available. The risk model that one holds may be critical to how efficacious one views screening. A large anxiety component is associated with the AIDS risk in the minds of many homosexual men, and this fear may inhibit screening if the individual does not see a way of reducing risk. Other variables, such as perceived self-efficacy, social support, and cultural influences, could all be brought to bear in a systematic study of preventive health behavior. Although the behavior is complicated, it is possible to derive a number of hypotheses about protective behavior and test them. Just because the simple multivariate models are not applicable to a large number of situations does not mean that it would be difficult to derive a more appropriate model, given the special characteristics of the risk under consideration.

Adolescent smoking: health or social behavior?

In analyzing the development of health behavior, it is very important to take into account the meaning of the behaviors for the actor. Traditional models of health behavior take into account only health-related attitudes and beliefs, but some behaviors serve many purposes for people. Consider, for example, smoking. Smoking is especially interesting because most smokers start at a relatively young age, and adolescents are particularly likely to attach social significance to certain behaviors. It is possible to outline a typology of the functions of smoking that is substantially different from the one assumed by most health behavior models. In addition to being thought of as a health-related behavior, smoking can facilitate cultural identification, and it can be used for social, psychological, and physical regulation.

In deciding to smoke, adolescents may consider the health consequences of their behavior. Proponents of the theory of reasoned action would contend that smoking behavior can be understood by looking at the way parents and peers help an adolescent form subjective norms and the ways those norms are related to behavioral intentions. However, one of the most compelling models for smoking behavior and interventions is based on theories of social modeling, in which cognitive mediation is not a necessary component. Anyone who has smoked or knows a smoker can describe a situation in which a cigarette was smoked without deliberation. Furthermore, almost everyone has witnessed a situation in which all the behavioral intentions in the world could not stop a smoker from smoking another cigarette (Schelling, 1984). Although the theory of reasoned action may help describe smoking behavior under certain circumstances, smoking behavior is probably determined primarily by variables and processes not considered in that model.

Smoking can also be described as a mechanism of group or subculture identification. Adolescents may smoke, shave their hair, wear a leather jacket, dye their hair purple, or take certain drugs as a means of identifying with a particular group. One theory as to why a person would be motivated to identify with such a group is that such responses are prompted by a low opinion of self and function to assuage distressing self-rejecting attitudes. Central to this theory is the postulate that people characteristically behave so as to minimize the experience of negative self-attitudes and to maximize the experience of positive self-attitudes. Partially overlapping social psychological perspectives are Jessor and Jessor's (1977) field theory of problem behavior, Akers's (1977) social learning theory, and Kandell's adolescent socialization theory (Kandel & Adler, 1983). Other, related theoretical perspectives include the strain, cultural deviance, and social disorganization theories developed by Merton (1938), Sutherland (1942), and Shaw and McKay (1931), respectively.

Finally, smoking can be described as a social, psychological, or physiological regulator (Leventhal & Cleary, 1980). Adolescents (or adults for that matter) may smoke to improve their image in social settings, to give themselves confidence, or to reduce tension.

Critique

A superb summary of the health belief model, the theory of reasoned action, and other models of health-related behavior has been presented by Becker and Maiman (1983), and the interested reader is referred to that review for additional details. A number of models that include a broader range of variables have been developed and tested (e.g., Fabrega, 1973; Kosa & Robertson, 1975; Suchman, 1964, 1965, 1966, 1967), but the health belief model and the theory of reasoned action have received by far the most attention in the literature on health behavior. Models of conscious decision making about health and illness behavior describe well certain of the variables influencing behavior and have stimulated a great deal of research. However, the examples in the previous section emphasize the need to move beyond these traditional models if we are to develop a true understanding of the behaviors we are trying to predict. Perhaps the major limitation is that they deal primarily with psychosocial influences (Janz & Becker, 1984) and assume that people usually attempt to maximize a value-expectancy function. It is necessary to recognize that people constantly act without conscious consideration of the consequences of their actions and sometimes act irrationally. For example, many health behaviors are learned in childhood or adolescence and are not always based on explicit decision-making processes. When people do make conscious decisions, their behaviors do not always correspond to those decisions (Schelling, 1984). Slovic, Fischhoff, and Lichtenstein, in Chapter 1, review data showing that people prefer to insure themselves against relatively high probability, low-loss hazards and tend to reject insurance in situations in which the probability of loss is low and expected loses are high – tendencies counter to economic theory.

Even when people do attempt to behave rationally, the estimation of risk and efficacy of behavior is extremely difficult. There is frequently uncertainty as to whether a particular act will have an impact on health status, and if it does what that impact will be. For example, it is very difficult to specify whether regular exercise will change any given individual's health. Even in situations in which there is sound scientific evidence that a variable is linked to morbidity or mortality, the type of behavior necessary to reduce risk may be extremely complicated. There is good reason to believe that serum cholesterol levels are related to the probability of developing arterial disease. However, it is not clear whether the most efficacious way of achieving a reduction in risk is to lead a more relaxed lifestyle, to reduce one's intake of low-density lipoproteins, to take certain medications, or to get more exercise.

A further complexity is that the outcome of self-protective behaviors is usually delayed for a substantial time. For example, the effect of diet and exercise among teenagers may not become evident for 30 years or more. Also, the outcome of self-protective behaviors is probabilistic. Morbidity and mortality are influenced by a broad range of factors, and the impact of self-protective behaviors can be modified by many factors, so it is unlikely that there will be more than a weak link between any specific protective behavior and any particular outcome. Exceptions are easy to think of (e.g., inoculation in an area with a high prevalence of disease), but in general the predictive value of any given behavior is likely to be low.

It is important to realize that "health behaviors" serve many functions and are related to numerous factors other than health, many of which an individual may not be aware of. Almost everything we do in the course of a day increases or decreases our health risks. As Veatch (1980) has pointed out, "Behaviors as highly diverse as smoking, skiing, playing professional football, compulsive eating, omitting exercise, exposing one-self excessively to the sun, skipping needed immunizations, automobile racing, and mountain climbing all can be viewed as having a substantial voluntary component" (p. 50), and these behaviors can have an important impact on morbidity and mortality. When trying to explain health-relevant behavior, one confronts the awesome task of explaining human behavior in general.

It is instructive to note how similar these characteristics are to four characteristics that Weinstein (1977) has suggested are shared by a wide range of natural and nonnatural threats: (a) It is difficult or impossible for us to determine the actual magnitude of the risks; (b) it is unclear what precautionary actions we should take; (c) most people's knowledge of risks is based on indirect and undependable sources of information; and (d) effective preparation requires more than a one-time mobilization of resources. Health behaviors are more likely to be developed over the course of the life span and to serve multiple functions, but cognitive models also have serious limitations when applied to other types of pre-ventive behaviors. If we are to develop a true understanding of protective behaviors, it is important to focus more on developing a better under-standing of how people process cognitive and emotional information, how social context conditions these processes and influences responses, and how culture and ethnicity influence these relationships. In the following sections, I shall review findings from a number of empirical studies that incorporate these variables.

Other influences on preventive behavior

Genetic influences

Variation in some health behaviors may be due to genetic factors, environmental factors, social and cultural factors, and early socialization processes. Furthermore, each of these types of influence may interact to affect the eventual adoption of a behavior. Smoking is an interesting example. Until recently, smoking cigarettes was a normative behavior among a substantial proportion of the U.S. population. The models reviewed earlier suggest that information, social context, fear, expense, expected outcome, and other factors influence decisions about smoking. However, that there is also a genetic component of smoking behavior has been suggested on the basis of the finding that identical twins are more likely than fraternal twins to demonstrate concordance of their smoking habits. Furthermore, these results hold for twins reared together as well as apart, and there is a correlation between smoking status and the smoking status of natural but not of adoptive parents (Eysenck & Eaves, 1980). A number of researchers have noted that smoking and drinking are more concordant in monozygotic than in dizygotic twins (Cederlof, 1966; Cederlof, Friberg, & Lundman, 1977; Eysenck & Eaves, 1980; Friberg, Kaij, Dencker, & Jonsson, 1959; Johnsson & Nilsson, 1968; Partanen, Bruun, & Markkanen, 1966; Shields, 1962). Also, Goodwin, Schulsinger, Hermansen, Guze, and Winokur (1973) found that among adoptees with natural parents who were alcoholic there were higher rates of alcoholism than among a matched control group of adoptees (see also Goodwin, 1976, 1979).

Although the reader should be warned that the interpretation of twin studies is complex and controversial (Kamin, 1974; see also Cavalli-Sforza & Bodmer, 1971; Cederlof, Friberg, & Lundman, 1977; Oestlyngen, 1949; Smith, 1974; Vandenberg, 1976), they are extremely provocative. We do not have to resolve the nature versus nurture argument to benefit from these data. The most important point for our consideration is the fact that information about family characteristics and genotype can help predict whether an individual will smoke, drink to excess, or take drugs. The results of these studies, especially the differences between monozygotic and dizygotic pairs, suggest that the role of "background factors" may be more subtle and important than many social scientists acknowledge.

Influences during childhood and adolescence

Having discussed the "social heredity" aspects of health behavior, we shall examine several studies that focused on the development of health behaviors and the role of social background factors. Health behavior may reflect, in part, broad social processes. For example, there are well-known sex differences in health behavior (Cleary, Mechanic, & Greenley, 1982). Although there are numerous explanations for such differences, research indicates that gender role socialization and obligations may have a considerable influence on health attitudes, beliefs, and behaviors (see, e.g., Hibbard, 1984). The importance of socialization processes is also suggested by research on the relation of both socioeconomic status and education to health behavior.

In 1961, David Mechanic selected a sample of 350 mother–child pairs for a study of health and health behavior. Independent data were collected from mothers, children, teachers, and official records. In addition, 198 mothers completed daily illness diaries for 15 days after the interview. In 1977, a follow-up was initiated, and 91% of the original children completed detailed questionnaires concerning their health and illness attitudes and values as well as their experience and behavior in relation to health concerns (Mechanic & Cleary, 1980). Like other researchers, Mechanic and Cleary found that the behaviors of interest (i.e., taking risks, being prepared for health emergencies, drinking, smoking, wearing seat belts, engaging in preventive medical care, being physically active, and exercising) were either independent of one another or only modestly correlated.

Rather than focus on individual behaviors, they followed Belloc and Breslow's (1972) strategy and created an index of health behavior and examined the correlates and predictors of the index. A wide range of variables from both the 1961 and 1977 interviews were examined, but the variables most substantially related to the index of positive health behavior were being female and having more education. Other analyses suggested that a sense of responsibility for health maintenance is integrated into an overall style of living reflecting social values, psychological well-being, and cultural integration.

A number of other researchers have also found that education is associated with health status and health practices. However, the relation is still poorly understood. Using the data just described, Mechanic (1980) attempted to test several theories explaining the link between education and health and health behavior. First, he tested Pratt's (1976) concept that certain types of families encourage freedom, responsiveness, and active coping among members and promotes flexible role relation. A second hypothesis was that children of parents who show concern for their own health and the health of their children, who are good models, and who encourage such behavior in their children will develop better health. The third hypothesis was that health practices and perceived good health are related to self-esteem and coping capacities. Interestingly, Mechanic found that only one adult behavior was related to the mother's education (seat belt use). However, five of the six adult behaviors were related to the respondent's education. Various models testing the previously mentioned hypotheses were estimated. In every case, education remained the key variable, although in the case of smoking and assessment of health, parental interest was an independent predictor. In short, the essential variables mediating the relation between educational attainment and health behavior continue to elude us. Attitudes, influence of classmates, availability of cigarettes in the home, and so on cannot account for such a persuasive and elusive relation. The fact that various health behaviors are related to such a general dimension as education and the fact that physical and mental health perception as well as specific behaviors are involved and interrelated reinforce the view that there is an underlying factor that accounts for a substantial part of the variance in health behavior.

There is increasing recognition that mental health and perhaps general social competence are related to class and are indicative of a generalized competence. Kessler and Cleary (1980) analyzed the relation between social class and distress using data from a longitudinal study of mental disorder in New Haven, Connecticut. When they examined the impact of physical health problems on the respondents, they found that the data were consistent with the childhood socialization perspective, which views social origins as important in shaping patterns of interpretation and coping. They interpreted the data as supporting the view that social origins determine beliefs, values, and behavior styles that exert lifelong influences on one's response to health-related challenges. Further support for this view was provided by analyses of health care behavior. The authors speculated that upper-status people who were born in the lower classes might retain some of their lower-class health care behaviors. To examine this possibility they determined the percentage of respondents who reported having a personal physician. Among the members of the sample in the upper social strata, 80% reported having a personal physician, but only 48 and 38% of those born in the lower two strata, respectively, reported having a personal physician. Clearly, the upwardly mobile members of the upper strata had retained at least one important component of the health care practices characteristic of their lower-class origins.

A number of studies have looked at smoking behavior among young people in an attempt to identify related developmental factors. Hirschman, Leventhal, and Glynn (1983) interviewed 386 youngsters and found that those who had tried a cigarette were more likely to have friends and parents who smoked. They found that the first cigarette is typically smoked with friends and that it is frequently borrowed from a parent or older sibling. Krohn and co-workers (Krohn, Massey, Skinner, & Lauer, 1984; Lauer, Akers, Massey, & Clarke, 1982) conducted a two-wave panel study of 1,405 seventh- through twelfth-grade students. Of respondents who reported both parents as nonsmokers and whose best friends were nonsmokers, 80% had never smoked and 3% were regular smokers. Of those with both parents and best friends who smoked, only 11% had never smoked and 74% were frequent smokers. The results of the second wave of the study also generally supported the hypothesis that adolescents' ties to aspects of conventional society are important in constraining deviant behavior. Specifically, commitment to education and beliefs were found to have the strongest constraining effect. Having friends and/or parents who smoke is the best predictor of smoking. However, it is not clear whether this association develops through social learning or is spurious.

Chassin et al. (1984) interviewed 3,015 sixth- through eleventh-grade students twice over a one-year period. They found that smoking initiation was predicted by greater intentions to smoke, a larger number of friends who smoked, fewer negative health beliefs about smoking, greater tolerance for deviance, lower expectations for attaining academic success, and more positive attitudes about smoking. Although the variables predicting transition from trying cigarettes to regular smoking were similar, family variables and personality variables were not important for this group.

Adult social and cultural influences

Ethnicity. There is accumulating evidence that ethnicity is an important determinant of individuals' perception of and response to symptoms (see, e.g., Angel & Cleary, 1984). Furthermore, ethnicity may partially determine the relative importance of different health behavior predictors. For example, Bullough (1972) questioned low-income mothers from three Los Angeles poverty areas that were predominantly inhabited by three ethnic groups (black, white, and Mexican-American) about preventive health care. She found that common barriers to the use of preventive services were reinforced by alienation, including feelings of powerlessness, hopelessness, and social isolation. Therefore, certain barriers might have a greater impact on low-income patients than on higher income patients. Fabrega (1977) studied illness episodes in a panel of families living in Mexico. The two socioethnic groups studied differed significantly in terms of perceived illness and reported symptoms, and their illness behaviors were different.

Social support. The literature on social support is extensive (Broadhead et al., 1983). There are several ways that social support could influence health care use. It may be that patients use medical services as an indirect means of seeking help for mental health problems. If this is the case, and social support fulfills some of those needs, social support should be negatively associated with medical care use. Certain role obligations may act as a barrier to seeking help for mental health problems. Social support may allow people to meet their obligations and free them to seek help. In such a situation, social support would be expected to be positively related to the use of services.

It is likely that people communicate with members of their social support network about whether to seek care (e.g., Booth & Babchuk, 1972; Suchman, 1965). Depending on the advice of others, social support may be positively or negatively associated with service use. There may also be an interaction between a person's beliefs and the beliefs of network members. For example, Berkanovic, Telesky, & Reeder (1981) examined the impact of congruent and incongruent patterns of symptom beliefs and social network advice on the decision to seek medical care. They concluded that social network influences may be most influential when beliefs and advice are incongruent. The nature of the influence may also depend on who is consulted. Thus, McKinlay (1973) found that mothers who consulted family members were less likely to use prenatal care than those who consulted friends and spouse. Salloway and Dillon (1973) and Horwitz (1977, 1978) have shown that help-seeking patterns depend on whether a person is a member of a compact family-based network or a less compact friendship network. Positive associations between social support and health behavior have been found by Geertsen, Klauber, Rindfleish, Kane, and Gray (1975) and Langlie (1977), although Suchman (1965) found no relationship between family ties and service use. Salloway and Dillon (1973) found a positive association with promptness of help seeking. These studies have focused on utilization behavior, but it is reasonable to expect that social support and social networks would have similar effects on preventive behavior.

Suchman (1964, 1965, 1966, 1967) also has written extensively on health and illness behavior. Suchman's work is important because of its emphasis on the role of social context in influencing preventive health behavior. Specifically, he hypothesized that individuals who belong to a "parochial" social group are more likely to adhere to "popular" health beliefs. He defines parochialism as high ethnic exclusivity, high friendship group solidarity, and high family orientation to tradition and authority. Unfortunately, several studies (e.g., Berkanovic et al., 1981; Farge, 1978; Geersten et al., 1975) have failed to replicate Suchman's results.

Langlie (1977) attempted to develop a model of preventive behavior that incorporated both the social psychological factors specified in the health belief model and the social group characteristics of Suchman's work. She notes that previous work (e.g., Bullough, 1972; Moody & Gray, 1972; Tash, O'Shea, & Cohen, 1969) demonstrated that social group properties have a significant impact on preventive health behavior even when other social psychological factors are controlled. She analyzed 11 preventive health behaviors and concluded that they can be described as either direct-risk preventive health behaviors or indirect-risk preventive health behaviors. Direct-risk behaviors include such activities as driving or walking recklessly or putting oneself in contact with smoke or germs. Indirect-risk behaviors include, for example, failure to follow medical recommendations. Langlie's analyses showed that appropriate indirect-risk preventive health behaviors are more common among people belonging to a high socioeconomic status social network that is characterized by frequent interaction between nonkin.

Langlie (1977) notes that, although few studies have systematically specified the relations between social group properties and preventive health behavior, several studies demonstrated that social group properties have a significant impact on preventive health behavior even when other social psychological factors are controlled. For example, the work by Pratt (1976) cited earlier indicated that high levels of family interaction, support, encouragement among family members, and low levels of family conflict were related to positive health behavior. Both Slesinger (1976) and Bullough (1972) argue that social integration is positively related to the use of preventive care. Although the link between preventive behavior and social support has not been studied often, there is suggestive evidence that such a link might be important.

Assessment of risk

In most models dealing with conscious decisions about health protection, perceptions of risk or danger are assumed to be a major determinant of whether a person takes protective action. Surprisingly, although we know a fair amount about the factors related to the perception of risk, almost none of this work has been applied to studies of health or illness behavior. Most researchers assume that people are aware of the risks they face or that perception of risk is directly related to the information available. An implicit assumption in much research on protective behavior is that educating people about their risks will result in more protective behavior. There are several problems with this approach. Although we still need to know a great deal more about risk perception, it is clear from the research that there may be substantial systematic biases in the way people evaluate danger. The estimation of risk is a complex process that depends on the context in which information is presented, the personality of the individual, and cultural factors. For example, a fascinating program of research conducted by Tversky and Kahneman (1981) has demonstrated that seemingly inconsequential changes in the formulation of choice problems causes predictable and significant shifts in preference. The main determinants in such shifts are variations in the framing of acts, contingencies, and outcomes and the characteristic nonlinearities of values and decision weights.

Slovic, Fischhoff, and Lichtenstein, in Chapter 1, review the data showing that, in general, people tend to overestimate the frequency of rare causes of death and underestimate the frequency of more common causes of death. Furthermore, they note that the causes of death that are overestimated tend to be dramatic and sensational. These data support the importance of an availability heuristic for the estimation of risk. That is, people tend to judge events as likely or frequent if the events are easy to imagine or recall. One consequence of this tendency is that people may view themselves as personally immune to certain hazards.

A number of studies have shown that there is a general tendency for people to underestimate risk (Harris & Guten, 1979; Kirscht, Haefner, Kegeles, & Rosenstock, 1966; Larwood, 1978; Robertson, 1977; Weinstein, 1982; Weinstein & Lachendro, 1982). For example, Weinstein (1982) consistently finds that college students are generally unbiased about hereditary risk factors and are even somewhat pessimistic about environmental risk factors, but they remain optimistic about their chances of avoiding health and life-threatening problems. Few acknowledge actions or psychological attributes that increase their risk, or emphasize those behavioral and psychological risk factors in estimating their overall vulnerability.

The complexities of risk assessment suggest that a linear, additive model such as the health belief model is probably inadequate to predict protective behavior. It is reasonable to expect that individuals who believe in their self-efficacy and in the efficacy of a particular behavior are more likely to engage in that behavior to reduce risk. However, Weinstein's findings suggest that the risks most commonly thought to be preventable by private action are the most likely to evoke unrealistic optimism about vulnerability, so interest in preventive action may be weakened by optimism.

Social psychological factors

Introspection. Mechanic has written extensively on help-seeking behavior and has outlined a number of the factors that may influence how people perceive, evaluate, and act on symptoms (Mechanic, 1979). He has advanced the hypothesis that attention to inner feelings and bodily changes increases awareness of and intensity of distress and the prevalence of reported symptoms (Mechanic, 1983). His work is concerned primarily with the perception of and response to symptoms and has not been applied to self-protective behavior. However, it may well be that people who frequently attend to internal sensations and symptoms are more likely than those who do not to be concerned about their health and thus more likely to engage in protective actions.

Distress and fear. Mechanic has also studied the role of stress in stimulating health behavior. Understanding how the desire to reduce distress motivates health behavior is important because threatening materials are used so frequently in messages aimed at increasing protective behavior (Higbee, 1969; Leventhal, 1970). In a review chapter on fear communications, Leventhal (1970) pointed out that most studies of fear communication use messages with two components: (a) information describing a danger and (b) recommendations for avoiding the danger. Implicit in much fear communication research is the assumption that fear is a motivator of change. Subjects are assumed to follow recommendations in order to reduce the tension resulting from the fear message. As an alternative to this assumption, Leventhal proposed that emotional and instrumental behaviors are simultaneous, parallel responses and do not give rise to another. Leventhal argued that fear control is often independent of danger control, although the two processes interact. The preponderance of the data on fear shows a positive association between fear and acceptance of health recommendations. However, Leventhal argues that both facilitating and inhibiting effects of fear (e.g., Janis & Feshbach, 1953) are compatible with his parallel response model and that it is important to specify in more detail the conditions under which the processes of fear reduction and danger control will interact to produce different outcomes. In their empirical work, Leventhal and colleagues (Leventhal and Singer, 1966; Leventhal, Singer, & Jones, 1965; Leventhal & Trembly, 1958; Leventhal, Watts, & Pagano, 1967) typically manipulated fear in combination with (a) action plans for taking protective action, (b) information on the effectiveness of action, and (c) manipulations of perceived vulnerability. They also examined personality variables such as self-esteem (Leventhal et al., 1980).

On the basis of his theoretical and empirical work, Leventhal argues that the effects of fear tend to be short-lived and that behaviors motivated by fear tend to be automatic as opposed to voluntary. The effect of fear, moreover, is conditioned by how efficacious or noxious a person perceives the preventive or protective recommendations to be. For example, if taking a protective action such as screening for a disease may result in awareness of danger about which a person thinks he or she can do little, the fear-arousing message may reduce the probability of action. If, however, there is a response to the danger that is perceived to be efficacious and have few costs, the person motivated by fear is more likely to follow a recommendation. However, the issues are even more complicated. The probability that a person takes action is determined partially by perceived self-efficacy. If fear reduces self-esteem or induces a sense of vulnerability, the message may disrupt coping behavior. "In summary, long-term compliance with protective recommendations (stopping smoking or taking a tetanus shot) seems to require exposure to information about the danger and about a specific plan for action. The level of fear stimulated by the information at the time of exposure seems to be irrelevant, but exposure to information about threat can lead to action if accompanied by behavioral planning" (Leventhal et al., 1980: 8).

Self-efficacy. Bandura and his associates (Bandura, 1977, 1982; Bandura, Adams, & Beyer, 1977; Bandura, Adams, Hardy, & Howells, 1980) makes a persuasive case that perceived self-efficacy helps to account for such diverse phenomena as changes in coping behaviors, intensity of stress reactions, reactions to failures in health promotion activities, and achievement striving. There are important distinctions among perceived self-efficacy, self-esteem, and beliefs about action-outcome contingencies (Lefcourt, 1976; Simmons, Rosenberg, & Rosenberg, 1973; Wallston & Wallston, 1978). Whereas perceived locus of control is concerned primarily with beliefs about the causes of certain outcomes, perceived self-efficacy is a function of a person's perceived skills to effect a change that is under the control of human action.

Strickland (1978) has reviewed a substantial body of theoretical and empirical work suggesting that beliefs about locus of control of reinforcement are influential in relation to health. However, she notes several limitations of the research, such as the lack of clear-cut or substantial results and the fact that the variance accounted for by perceived locus of control is probably quite small in most situations. She also notes, as does Folkman (1984), that a tendency to believe events are under one's control may not always be facilitative. That is, attempts at mastery of events are most appropriate when events are controllable. Seeman and Seeman (1983) documented the significance of perceived locus of control for health-related behaviors. They reviewed three types of health behavior: preventive care, health knowledge and perspectives, and acute and chronic illness. In a longitudinal study of 931 adults, they found that a sense of a low level of control was associated with less self-initiated preventive care, less optimism concerning the efficacy of early treatment, poorer self-rated health, as well as more illness episodes, more bed confinement, and greater dependence on the physician. Interestingly, they differentiated luck denial and personal mastery and found that the luck denial score tended to be a somewhat better predictor in the preventive health areas, whereas personal mastery was a somewhat better predictor in the illness area. In the work cited earlier, Langlie (1977) concluded that indirect-risk preventive behaviors are related to the perception that one has control over one's health status, not just the cost–benefit ratio of the preventive action.

Ajzen (1984) has investigated the possibility that perceived control affects behavioral intention independently of attitude and subjective norm. In fact, Ajzen and Timko (in press) have revised the theory of reasoned action and taken issues of control into account in a theory of planned behavior. They compared this revised theory, which assumes a direct effect of perceived control on intention, with the theory of reasoned action, in which the effect of perceived control is completely mediated by attitude and subjective norm. Using sample of 113 undergraduates, they found that perceived control had a significant effect on intention, over and above the effects of attitude and subjective norm, and it influenced behavior independent of intention.

Conclusions

The social, cultural, and psychological factors reviewed in this chapter clearly are important determinants of health behavior. The study of AIDS and smoking, for example, would benefit from a careful consideration of the factors cited here. But how are these variables to be incorporated into a better model of health behavior? Leventhal and colleagues have developed what they refer to as a general-systems model of health behavior (Leventhal, 1983; Leventhal and Nerenz, 1983; Leventhal, Prohaska, & Hirschman, 1985). In their formulation, attitudes and beliefs are included under the category of conceptual control. However, conceptual control is only one of four components of their general-systems model. Other important determinants include social control, affective/stress control, and symptom-based control.

In a chapter reviewing models of health-related behavior, Becker and Maiman (1983) also attempt to develop a unified conceptual framework. Partly motivated by the fact that the number of truly distinct concepts in these various models is substantially smaller than the number of variables mentioned by each group of authors, Becker and Maiman attempted to reduce the multitude of concepts using data from the theorists themselves. Cummings, Becker, and Maile (1980) contacted 8 of the 11 authors they considered to be responsible for the main models of health-related behavior. Acting as judges, the authors placed each of 109 variables from the models into categories on the basis of their similarity. They found that the variables clustered into six relatively distinct categories: perception of illness, threat of disease, knowledge of disease, social network variables, access to care, and attitude toward health care.

Becker and Maiman, Leventhal and colleagues, and others (e.g. Wallston & Wallston, 1981) have made an important contribution by ordering and trying to synthesize the variables in the literature. However, rather than try to reduce these variables to a manageable number of dimensions, I think it more reasonable to admit that such a task is impossible and that it is more useful to adopt an eclectic theoretical approach to understanding self-protective behaviors.

The variables reviewed in this chapter are staggering in their breadth. They may influence behavior in complex ways that cannot be described by simple, linear models. It would be possible to catalogue, once again, the variables in the literature and the variance explained by each, but I think such an exercise would be as pointless as it would be difficult. What is the solution? It is my opinion that there is no solution; we are asking the wrong questions. Instead of developing more elaborate predictive "models," we should be trying to understand the meaning of the behaviors to individuals and the processes involved in encoding the acting on information. A more process-oriented approach to the study of health behavior would be much more useful than a giant, predictive model that predicts a little, some of the time. The diverse nature of health behaviors makes it unreasonable to attempt to develop a single theory applicable to all health or self-protective behaviors or to attempt a synthesis of the research findings in this area. Instead, what I have attempted to do is to indicate the broad range of processes that must be taken into account by anyone trying to understand protective behavior.

I think that only by analyzing the processes leading to particular acts can we begin to unravel the complex factors that explain them. It is important to define clearly the class of behaviors one is interested in, to determine their characteristics and the factors that are likely to influence them, and then to assess which theories of behavior are applicable. It is especially important to keep in mind that behaviors vary tremendously in the extent to which they are conscious, considered behaviors. Avoiding salt may be a newly acquired behavior that involves a fair amount of conscious thought each time one eats a meal. In contrast, exercise may be such an integrated part of one's lifestyle that it involves little or no thought.

Inevitably, however, we shall return to asking whether a model that is useful for understanding one health behavior is applicable to others; whether the processes are the same or different; what classes of behaviors are most similar to health behaviors; and so on. Probably, whether or not the behavior is health related has little to do with the applicability of the models, processes, and variables renewed here. What is more important are the characteristics of a risk. Is it common or rare; what is the meaning of the risk to individuals and communities; is knowledge about the risk complex or simple, relevant or not; what is the meaning of a behavior required to increase protection; are there social models who do or do not perform the behavior; is the protective behavior a new behavior or a learned behavior that must be activated; in what social context must the behavior be adopted; are there facilitators or barriers to the behavior; is the behavior one that people typically perform with consideration, or is the relevant behavior a habit? The important questions concern the meaning of risks, protective behaviors, and the context in which both occur. Once questions concerning those variables have been answered, we can turn to the psychological, economic, sociological, and anthropological literatures, which are rich with answers to the question of how people can be expected to behave.

References

Ajzen, I. 1984. From intentions to actions: A theory of planned behavior. In *Action-Control: From Cognition to Behavior*, ed. J. Kuhl and J. Beckman. New York: Springer-Verlag.

Ajzen, I., and Fishbein, M. 1970. The prediction of behavior from attitudinal and normative variables. *Journal of Experimental Social Psychology 6:*466–87.

Ajzen, I., and Fishbein, M. 1977. Attitude–behavior relations: A theoretical analysis and review of empirical research. *Psychological Bulletin 84:*888–918.

Ajzen, I., and Fishbein, M. 1980. *Understanding Attitudes and Predicting Social Behavior.* Englewood Cliffs, NJ: Prentice-Hall.

Akers, R. L. 1977. *Deviant Behavior: A Social Learning Approach,* 2d ed. Belmont, CA: Wadsworth.

Angel, R., and Cleary, P. D. 1984. The effects of social structure and culture on self-reports of health among Mexican Americans. *Social Science Quarterly 65:*814–28.

Antonovsky, A., and Kats, R. 1970. The model dental patient: An empirical study of preventive health behavior. *Social Science and Medicine 4:*467–79.

Bandura, A. 1977. Toward a unifying theory of behavioral change. *Psychological Review 84:*191–215.

Bandura, A. 1982. Self-efficacy mechanism in human agency. *American Psychologist 37:*122–47.

Bandura, A., Adams, N. E., and Beyer, J. 1977. Cognitive processes mediating behavioral change. *Journal of Personality and Social Psychology 35:*125–39.

Bandura, A., Adams, N. E., Hardy, A. B., and Howells, G. N. 1980. Tests of the generality of self-efficacy theory. *Cognitive Therapy and Research 4:*39–66.

Becker, M. H. (ed). 1974. *The Health Belief Model and Personal Health Behavior.* Thorofare, NJ: Slack.

Becker, M. H., Kaback, M., Rosenstock, I., and Ruth M. 1975. Some influences of public participation in genetic screening programs. *Journal of Community Health 1:*3–14.

Becker, M. H., and Maiman, L. A. 1975. Sociobehavioral determinants of compliance with health and medical care recommendations. *Medical Care 13:*10–23.

Becker, M. H., and Maiman, L. A. 1983. Models of health-related behavior. In *Handbook of Health, Health Care, and the Health Professions,* ed. D. Mechanic. New York: Free Press, pp. 539–68.

Becker, M. H., Maiman, L. A., Kirsch, J. P., Haefner, K. P., and Drachman, R. H. 1977. The health belief model and prediction of dietary compliance: A field experiment. *Journal of Health and Social Behavior 18:*348–66.

Becker, M. H., Maiman, L. A., Kirsch, J. P., Haefner, K. P., Drachman, R. H., and Taylor, D. W. 1979. Patient perceptions and compliance: Recent studies of the health belief model. In *Compliance in Health Care,* ed. R. B. Haynes, D. W. Taylor, and D. L. Sackett. Baltimore, MD: Johns Hopkins University Press, pp. 78–109.

Belloc, N. B., and Breslow, L. 1972. Relationship of physical health status and health practices. *Preventive Medicine 1:*409–21.

Ben-Sira, A., and Padeh, B. 1978. Instrumental coping and affective defense: An additional perspective in health promoting behavior. *Social Science Medicine 12:*163–8.

Berkanovic, E., Telesky, C., and Reeder, S. 1981. Structural and social psychological factors in the decision to seek medical care for symptoms. *Medical Care 19:*693–709.

Booth, A., and Babchuk, N. 1972. Seeking health care from new resources. *Journal of Health and Social Behavior 13:*90–9.

Broadhead, W. E., Kaplan, B. H., James, S. A., Wagner, E. H., Schoenbach, V. J., Grimson, R., Heyden, S., Tibblin, G. & Gehlbach, S. H. 1983. The epidemiologic evidence for a relationship between social support and health. *American Journal of Epidemiology 117:*521–37.

Bullough, B. 1972. Poverty, ethnic identity, and preventive health care. *Journal of Health and Social Behavior 13:*347–59.

Calnan, M. W., and Moss, S. 1984. The health belief model and compliance with education given at a class in breast self-examination. *Journal of Health and Social Behavior* 25:198–210.

Cavalli-Sforza, L. L., and Bodmer, W. F. 1971. *The Genetics of Human Populations.* San Francisco: Freeman.

Cederlof, R. 1966. *The twin method in epidemiologic studies on chronic disease.* Stockholm: Karolinska Institutet.

Cederlof, R., Friberg, L., and Lundman, T. 1977. The interaction of smoking, environment, and heredity. *Acta Medica Scandinavica* Suppl. 612.

Chassin, S. J., Presson, C. C., Sherman, S. J., Corty, E., Olshavsky, R., and Bensenberg, M. 1984. Predicting the onset of cigarette smoking in adolescents: A longitudinal study. *Addictive Behaviors* 9:383–90.

Cleary, P.D., Mechanic, D., and Greenley, J. R. 1982. Sex differences in medical care utilization: An empirical investigation. *Journal of Health and Social Behavior* 23:106–19.

Cummings, K. M., Becker, M. H., and Maile, M. C. 1980. Bringing the models together: An empirical approach to combining variables used to explain health actions. *Journal of Behavioral Medicine* 3:123–45.

Cummings, K. M., Jette, A. M., Brock, B. M., and Haefner, D. P. 1979. Psychosocial determinants of immunization behavior in a swine influenza campaign. *Medical Care* 17:639–49.

Dishman, R. 1982. Compliance/adherence in health-related exercise. *Health and Psychology* 1:237–67.

Edwards, W. 1954. The theory of decision making. *Psychological Bulletin 51:* 380–417.

Eysenck, H. J., and Eaves, L. J. 1980. *The Causes and Effects of Smoking.* London: Smith.

Fabrega, H. Jr. 1973. Toward a model of health behavior. *Medical Care 11:*470–84.

Fabrega, H. Jr. 1977. Perceived illness and its treatment: A naturalistic study in social medicine. *British Journal of Preventive and Social Medicine 31:*213–19.

Farge, E. J. 1978. Medical orientation among a Mexican-American population: An old and a new model reviewed. *Social Science Medicine 12:*277–82.

Fink, R., Shapiro, S., and Roeser, R. 1972. Impact of efforts to increase participation in repetitive screening for early breast cancer detection. *American Journal of Public Health, 62:*328–36.

Fishbein, M. 1967. Attitude and the prediction of behavior. In *Readings in Attitude Theory and Measurement,* ed. M. Fishbein. New York: Wiley, pp. 477–92.

Fishbein, M. 1973. The prediction of behavior from attitudinal variables. In *Advances in Communication Research,* ed. C. D. Mortensen and K. K. Sereno. New York: Harper & Row, pp. 3–31.

Fishbein, M., and Ajzen, I. 1975. *Belief, Attitude, Intention and Behavior: An Introduction to Theory and Research.* Reading, MA: Addison-Wesley.

Fishbein, M., and Jaccard, J. J. 1973. Theoretical and methodological considerations in the prediction of family planning intentions and behavior. *Representative Research in Social Psychology 4:*37–51.

Folkman, S. 1984. Personal control and stress and coping processes: A theoretical analysis. *Journal of Personality and Social Psychology 46:*839–52.

Friberg, L., Kaij, L., Dencker, S. J., and Jonsson, E. 1959. Smoking habits of monozygotic and dizygotic twins. *British Medical Journal 1:*1090–2.

Fritz, C. E. 1961. Disaster. In *Contemporary Social Problems,* ed. R. K. Merton, and R. A. Nisbet. New York: Harcourt, Brace, & World, pp. 682–94.

Geersten, R., Klauber, M. R., Rindfleish, M., Kane, R. L., and Gray, R. 1975. A reexamination of Suchman's views on social factors in health care utilization. *Journal of Health and Social Behavior 16:*226–37.

Goodwin, D. W. 1976. *Is Alcoholism Hereditary?* New York: Oxford University Press.

Goodwin, D. W. 1979. Alcoholism and heredity: A review and hypothesis. *Archives of General Psychology 36:*57–61.

Goodwin, D. W., Schulsinger, F., Hermansen, L., Guze, S. B., and Winokur, G. 1973. Alcohol problems in adoptees raised apart from alcoholic biological parents. *Archives of General Psychology 28:*238–43.

Haefner, D., and Kirscht, J. 1970. Motivational and behavioral effects of modifying health beliefs. *Public Health Reports 85:*478–84.

Harris, D. M., and Guten, S. 1979. Health-protective behavior: An exploratory study. *Journal of Health and Social Behavior 20:*17–29.

Hecker, B. L., and Ajzen, I. 1983. Improving the prediction of health behavior: An approach based on the theory of reasoned action. *Academie Psychology Bulletin 5:*11–19.

Hibbard, J. H. 1984. Sex differences in health and illness orientation. *International Quarterly of Community Health Education 4:*95–104.

Higbee, K. 1969. Fifteen years of fear arousal: Research on threat appeals, 1953–1968. *Psychological Bulletin 92:*426–44.

Hirschmann, R., Leventhal, L., and Glynn, L. 1983. The development of smoking behavior: Conceptualization and supportive cross-sectional data. Unpublished manuscript.

Hochbaum, G.M. 1958. *Public Participation in Medical Screening Programs: A Sociopsychological Study.* Washington, DC: U.S. Government Printing Office.

Horwitz, A. 1977. Social networks and pathways to psychiatric treatment. *Social Forces 56:* 86–105.

Horwitz, A. 1978. Family, kin and friend networks in psychiatric help-seeking. *Social Science Medicine 12:* 297–304.

Houts, P. S., Lindell, M., Hu, T. W., Cleary, P. D., Tokuhata, G., and Flynn, C. B. 1984. The protective action decision model applied to evacuation during the Three Mile Island Crisis. *International Journal of Mass Emergencies and Disasters 2:*1–13.

Howe, H. 1981. Social factors associated with breast self-examination among high risk women. *American Journal of Public Health 71:*251–5.

Jaccard, J. 1975. A theoretical analysis of selected factors important to health education strategies. *Health Education Monographs 3:*152–67.

Janis, I. L., and Feshbach, S. 1953. Effects of fear-rousing communications. *Journal of Abnormal and Social Psychology 48:*78–92.

Janz, N. K., and Becker, M. H. 1984. The health belief model: A decade later. *Health Education Quarterly 11:*1–47.

Jessor, R., and Jessor, S. C. 1977. *Problem Behavior and Psychosocial Development: A Longitudinal Study of Youth.* New York: Academic Press.

Jonsson, E., and Nilsson, T. 1968. Alcohol consumption in monozygotic and dizygotic twin pairs. *Nordisk Hygienish Tidskrift 49:*21–5.

Kamin, L. J. 1974. *The Science and Politics of IQ.* Hillsdale, NJ: Erlbaum.

Kandel, D. B., and Adler, I. 1983. Socialization into marijuana use among French adolescents: A cross-cultural comparison with the United States. *Journal of Health and Social Behavior 23:*295–309.

Kasl, S. V. 1974. The health belief model and behavior related to chronic illness. *Health Education Monographs 2:*433–54.

Kasl, S. V. 1978. A social psychological perspective on successful community control of high blood pressure. *Journal of Behavioral Medicine 1:*347–81.

Kasl, S. V., and Cobb, S. 1966. Health behavior, illness behavior and sick role behavior: I. Health and illness behavior. *Archives of Environmental Health 12:*246–66.

Kegeles, S. 1963. Why people seek dental care: A test of a conceptual formulation. *Journal of Health and Human Behavior 4:*166–73.

Kelly, P. 1979. Breast self-examinations: Who does them and why. *Journal of Behavioral Medicine* 2:31–8.

Kessler, R. C., and Cleary, P. D. 1980. Social class and psychological distress. *American Social Review* 45:463–78.

Kirscht, J. P. 1983. Preventive health behavior: A review of research and issues. *Health Psychology* 2:277–301.

Kirscht, J. P., Haefner, D. P., Kegeles, S. S., and Rosenstock, I. M. 1966. A national study of health beliefs. *Journal of Health and Social Behavior* 7:248–54.

Kleinman, A. 1980. *Patients and Healers in the Context of Culture: An Exploration of the Borderland between Anthropology, Medicine, and Psychiatry.* Berkeley: University of California Press.

Kosa, J., and Robertson. 1975. The social aspects of health and illness. In *Poverty and Health: A Sociological Analysis,* ed. J. Kosa and I. K. Zola. Cambridge, MA: Harvard University Press, pp. 40–79.

Krohn, M. D., Massey, J. L., Skinner, W. F., and Lauer, R. M. 1983. Social bonding theory and adolescent cigarette smoking: A longitudinal analysis. *Journal of Health and Social Behavior* 24:337–49.

Langlie, J. K. 1977. Social networks, health beliefs, and preventive health behavior. *Journal of Health and Social Behavior* 18:244–60.

Langlie, J. K. 1979. Interrelationships among preventive health behaviors: A test of competing hypotheses. *Public Health Reports* 94:216–25.

Larwood, L. 1978. Swine flu: A field study of self-serving biases. *Journal of Applied Social Psychology* 8:283–9.

Lau, R. R., and Hartman, K. A. 1983. Common sense representations of common illnesses. *Health Psychology* 2:167–85.

Lauer, R. M., Akers, R. L., Massey, J., and Clarke, W. R. 1982. Evaluation of cigarette smoking among adolescents: The Muscatine study. *Preventive Medicine* 11:417–28.

Lefcourt, H. M. 1976. *Locus of Control: Current Trends in Theory and Research.* New York: Halstead.

Leventhal, H. 1970. Findings and theory in the study of fear communications. In *Advances in Experimental Social Psychology,* Vol. 5, ed. L. Berkowitz. New York: Academic Press, pp. 119–86.

Leventhal, H. 1983. Behavioral medicine: Psychology in health care. In *Handbook of Health, Health Care, and the Health Professions,* ed. D. Mechanic. New York: Free Press, pp. 709–43.

Leventhal, H., and Cleary, P. D. 1980. The smoking problem: A review of the research and theory in behavioral risk modification. *Psychological Bulletin* 88:370–405.

Leventhal, H., Hochbaum, G. M., and Rosenstock, I. M. 1960. Epidemic impact of the general population. In *The Impact of Asian Influenza on Community Life: A Study of Five Cities.* Washington, DC: U.S. Department of Health, Education, and Welfare, Public Health Service, Publ. No. 706.

Leventhal, H., Meyer, D., and Nerenz, D. 1980. The common sense representation of illness behavior. In *Medical Psychology,* ed. S. Rachman. New York: Pergamon, Vol. 2, pp. 7–30.

Leventhal, H., and Nerenz, D. 1983. A model for stress research and some implications for the control of stress disorders. In *Stress Prevention and Management: A cognitive behavioral approach,* ed. D. Meichenbaum and M. Jaremko. New York: Plenum.

Leventhal, H., Prohaska, T. R., and Hirschman, R. S. 1985. Preventive health behavior across the life-span. In *Preventing Health Risk Behaviors and Promoting Coping with Illness,* Vol. 8, ed. J. C. Rosen and L. J. Soloman. Vermont Conference on the Primary Prevention of Psychopathology. Hanover, NH: University Press of New England, pp. 191–235.

Leventhal, H., and Singer, R. 1966. Affect arousal and positioning of recommendations in persuasive communications. *Journal of Personality and Social Psychology 4:*137–46.

Leventhal, H., Singer, R., and Jones, S. 1965. Effects of fear and specificity of recommendations upon attitudes and behavior. *Journal of Personality and Social Psychology 2:*20–9.

Leventhal, H., and Trembly, G. 1968. Negative emotions and persuasion. *Journal of Personality and Social Psychology 36:*154–68.

Leventhal, H., Watts, J., and Pagano, F. 1967. Effects of fear and instructions on how to cope with danger. *Journal of Personality and Social Psychology 6:*313–21.

Maiman, L. A., and Becker, M. H. 1974. The health belief model: Origins and correlates in psychological theory. *Health Education Monographs 2:*236–53.

McKinlay, J. B. 1972. Some approaches and problems in the study of the use of services: An overview. *Journal of Health and Social Behavior 13:*115–52.

Mechanic, D. 1979. Correlates of physician utilization: Why do major multivariate studies of physician utilization find trivial psychosocial effects? *Journal of Health and Behavior 20:*387–96.

Mechanic, D. 1980. Education, parental interest, and health perceptions and behavior. *Inquiry 17:*331–8.

Mechanic, D. 1983. Adolescent health and illness behavior: Review of the literature and hypotheses for the study of distress in youth. *Journal of Human Stress 9:* 4–13.

Mechanic, D., and Cleary, P. D. 1980. Factors associated with the maintenance of positive health behavior. *Preventive Medicine 9:*805–14.

Merton, R. K. 1938. Social structure and anomie. *American Social Review 3:*672–82.

Moody, P., and Gray, R. 1972. Social class, social integration, and use of preventive health services. In *Patients, Physicians and Illness,* ed. E. G. Jaco. New York: Free Press, pp. 250–61.

Oestlyngen, E. 1949. Possibilities and limitations of twin research as a means of solving problems of heredity and environment. *Acta Psychologica 6:*59–90.

Partanen, J., Bruun, K., and Markkanen, T. 1966. *Inheritance of Drinking Behavior: A Study on Intelligence, Personality and Use of Alcoholic Adult Twins.* Stockholm: Almquist & Wiksell.

Perry, R. W., Lindell, M. K., and Green, M. R. 1981. *Evacuation Planning in Emergency Management.* Lexington, MA: Heath.

Popovic, M., Sarngadharan, M. G., Read, E., and Gallo, R. C. 1984. Detection, isolation, and continuous production of cytopathic retroviruses (HTLV-III) from patients with AIDS and pre-AIDS. *Science 224:*497–500.

Pratt, L. 1976. *Family Structure and Effective Health Behavior: The Energized Family.* Boston: Houghton Mifflin.

Robertson, L. S. 1977. Car crashes: Perceived vulnerability and willingness to pay for crash protection. *Journal of Community Health 3:*136–41.

Rogers, R.W. 1983. Cognitive and physiological processes in fear appeals and attitude change: A revised theory of protection motivation. In *Social Psychophysiology,* ed. J. T. Cacioppo and R.E. Petty. New York: Guilford, pp. 153–76.

Rosenstock, I. M. 1960. What research in motivation suggests for public health. *American Journal of Public Health 50:*295–302.

Rosenstock, I. M. 1966. Why people use health services. *Milbank Memorial Fund Quarterly 44:*94–127.

Rosenstock, I. M. 1974. Historical origins of the health belief model. *Health Education Monographs 2:*409–19.

Rosenstock, I. M., Derryberry, M., and Carriger, B. 1959. Why people fail to seek poliomyelitis vaccination. *Public Health Reports 74:*98–103.

Rosenstock, I. M., and Kirscht, J. 1979. Why people use health services. In *Health Psychology*, ed. G. Stone, F. Cohen, and N. Adler. San Francisco: Jossey-Bass, pp. 161–88.

Rundall, T., and Wheeler, J. 1979. The effect of income on use of preventive care: An evaluation of alternative explanations. *Journal of Health and Social Behavior 20:*397–406.

Salloway, J. C., and Dillon, P. B. 1973. A comparison of family networks and friends networks in health care utilization. *Journal of Comparative Family Studies 4:* 131–42.

Schelling, T. C. 1984. Self-command in practice, in policy, and in a theory of rational choice. *American Economic Review 74:*1–11.

Seeman, M., and Seeman, T. E. 1983. Health behavior and personal autonomy: A longitudinal study of the sense of control in illness. *Journal of Health and Social Behavior 24:*144–60.

Seibold, D., and Roper R. 1979. Psychosocial determinants of health care intentions: Test of the Triandis and Fishbein models. In *Communication Yearbook,* Vol. 3, ed. D. Nimmo. New Brunswick, NJ: Transaction Books.

Shaw, C., and McKay, H. 1931. *Juvenile Deliquency and Urban Area.* University of Chicago Press.

Shields, J. 1962. *Monozygotic Twins Brought up Apart and Brought up Together.* New York: Oxford University Press.

Simmons, R. G., Rosenberg, F., and Rosenberg, M. 1973. Disturbance in the self-image at adolescence. *American Social Review 38:*553–68.

Slesinger, D. 1976. The utilization of preventive medical services by urban black mothers. In *The Growth of Bureaucratic Medicine,* ed. D. Mechanic. New York: Wiley, pp. 197–219.

Smith, C. 1974. Concordance in twins: Method and interpretation. *American Journal of Human Genetics 26:*454–66.

Strickland, B. R. 1978. Internal–external expectancies and health related behaviors. *Journal of Consulting and Clinical Psychology 46:*1192–1211.

Suchman, E. A. 1964. Sociomedical variations among ethnic groups. *American Journal of Sociology 70:*319–31.

Suchman, E. A. 1965. Social patterns of illness and medical care. *Journal of Health and Social Behavior 6:*2–16.

Suchman, E. A. 1966. Health orientation and medical care. *American Journal of Public Health 56:*97–105.

Suchman, E. A. 1967. Preventive health behavior: A model for research on community health campaigns. *Journal of Health and Social Behavior 8:*197–209.

Sutherland, E. H. 1942. *Principles of Criminology.* Chicago: Lippincott.

Swinehart, J., and Kirscht, J. 1966. Smoking: A panel study of beliefs and behavior following the PHS report. *Psychological Reports 18:*519–28.

Tash, R.H., O'Shea, R. M., and Cohen, L. K. 1969. Testing a preventive-symptomatic theory of dental health behavior. *American Journal of Public Health 59:*514–21.

Taylor, D. W. 1979. A test of the health belief model in hypertension. In *Compliance in Health Care,* ed. R. B. Haynes, D. W. Taylor, and D. L. Sackett. Baltimore, MD: Johns Hopkins University Press, pp. 103–9.

Tversky, A., and Kahneman, D. 1981. The framing of decisions and the psychology of choice. *Science 211:*453–8.

Vandenberg, S. G. 1976. Twin studies. In *Human Behavior Genetics.* ed. A. H. Kaplan. Springfield, IL: Thomas.

Veatch, R. M. 1980. Voluntary risks to health: The ethical issues. *Journal of the American Medical Association 243:*50–5.

Wallston, B. S., and Wallston, K. A. 1978. Locus of control and health: A review of the literature. *Health Education Monographs 6:*107–17.

Wallston, B. S., and Wallston, K. A. 1981. Toward a unified social psychological model of health behavior. In *The Social Psychology of Health and Illness*. ed. G. Sanders and J. Seels. Hillsdale, NJ: Earlbaum.

Weinstein, N. D. 1977. Coping with environmental hazards: Reactions to the threat of crime. Paper presented at the American Psychological Association Meetings, San Francisco, August.

Weinstein, N. D. 1982. Unrealistic optimism about susceptibility to health problems. *Journal of Behavioral Medicine 5:*441–60.

Weinstein, N. D., and Lachendro, E. 1982. Egocentrism as a source of unrealistic optimism. *Personal and Social Psychological Bulletin 8:*195–200.

Weisenberg, M., Kegeles, S., and Lund, A. 1980. Children's health beliefs and acceptance of a dental preventive activity. *Journal of Health and Social Behavior 21:*59–74.

7   Community studies of smoking cessation

Surgeon General's Report

Community studies of smoking cessation refer to research in which geographically defined populations or age cohorts are selected for experimental intervention or as control or comparison groups. In this chapter, two major studies of cessation are described, and related research findings are briefly considered. The theoretical background for these studies is outlined, methodological issues are discussed, and directions for future research are suggested. It is concluded that community studies represent a significant emerging paradigm for public health research.

Characteristics of a controlled community study

For this discussion, a controlled community study is defined according to the scope of intervention and quality of research design, with the essential feature being the identification of natural, location-based aggregations of individuals as well as formal and informal social systems. In a community study, the entire population of a geographic area is considered, so that a church or worksite is not a community itself, but one of many systems constituting the total network of interactions.

Because the population size to be addressed is a limiting factor in any social program, the large numbers of people involved in a community study dictate selection of intervention methods. Clinical or other people-oriented approaches that typify behavioral research on smoking cessation and prevention (Bernstein, 1969; Bernstein & McAlister, 1976; Pechacek & McAlister, 1980; Lando & McGovern, 1982; Lichtenstein, 1982) are not feasible for programs directed toward many thousands of people. Community studies instead emphasize large-scale delivery systems such as

This chapter is an abbreviated version of the article "Community Studies of Smoking Cessation and Prevention," which appeared in the Report of the Surgeon General, *The Health Consequences of Smoking: Chronic Obstructive Lung Disease.* Washington, D.C.: U.S. Government Printing Office, 1984.

the mass communication media. Because community participation is now considered essential for success, such studies also include community organization programs seeking to stimulate interpersonal communication in ways that are feasible on a large-scale basis. Community studies also may involve environmental change, such as programs to modify the purchase price or availability of consumer products or to sanction public behaviors.

Because the emphasis herein is on controlled community research, attention is limited to studies in which valid inferences can be made concerning the effects of intervention on smoking rates in an entire population. The essential elements are use of adequate measures of smoking behavior applied over time in order to estimate long-term trends, and equally important, the inclusion of control or reference areas for the purpose of comparison. There are, of course, many questions and controversies regarding the usefulness and validity of large-scale experimental or quasi-experimental research (Campbell & Cook, 1979). Social policies such as those needed to sharply reduce smoking are not likely to be introduced without experimental trials, however, and the studies reported herein probably represent the best currently attainable compromise between external and internal validity. Given the very small number of studies meeting even the minimal methodological criteria, it would be unwise to restrict the review to the standards required by laboratory or clinical studies.

Theoretical background

Effective mass communication, community organization, and environmental change require a theoretical basis for planning. Most community studies of health promotion and disease prevention are based on fundamental theories and concepts from the behavioral sciences. The most important of these are briefly outlined below.

Mass communication

Theories on mass media effect have changed during the recent history of communication research, and several clear stages have been identified (Klapper, 1960; Griffiths & Knutson, 1960; Atkin, 1979; Flay, Ditecco, & Schlegal, 1980; Wallack, 1981). Media were initially considered nearly omnipotent in directly altering behavior, but it was later discovered that they are incapable of producing effects independent of other, more powerful social forces. The most recent view is that mass media may have effects, but that they are small and largely dependent on facilitation from interpersonal influences and favorable environmental circumstances. Notwithstanding these limitations, shifts of a few percentage points in consumer preferences may be very significant in product marketing, while similar reductions in chronic disease-promoting behaviors may have enormous absolute significance in a population of several millions. One mass media effect that is agreed upon by most communication scientists is termed the "agenda-setting function" (McCombs & Shaw, 1972), in which the media powerfully influence topics generated in formal and informal social gatherings. Media communication can also inform and teach simple skills (Bandura, 1977). But the manner in which people actually behave with regard to a particular topic of discussion, and whether or not information or skills are actually used, depends more upon interpersonal forces than upon the media messages themselves.

Community organization

The theories and concepts that underlie community organization are less well developed than those applied to media planning. Although there is broad agreement that the effects of the media are enhanced by interpersonal factors, there is no clear consensus on the exact identity of those factors or how they can be feasibly modified in entire communities. A useful principle is derived from Bandura's (1977) distinction between factors influencing acquisition of new behaviors and those influencing performance of new behaviors. Media communications can model new behaviors so that they are learned (acquired) on a cognitive level (the person knows how to perform the behavior). However, cueing and feedback (direct social reinforcement) are usually needed for behavioral learning, or actual performance of the new behavior. Numerous studies of learning via media communication show that when a complex behavior is being learned, effectiveness is sharply enhanced by providing supplementary interpersonal communication for encouragement, feedback, and reinforcement (Bandura, 1977). To create feedback and reinforcement in a community setting, organizations must be involved to provide roles and structure for interpersonal communication. Where formal social networks are not involved, communication and influence will be diffused through families and other informal systems (Meyer, Maccoby, & Farquhar 1977). The effectiveness of interpersonal communication can be greatly enhanced, however, by organizing formal or semiformal structures, such as learning groups using leaders trained to lead discussions, answer questions, and provide encouragement and followup. Various campaigns in agricultural development illustrate these principles (Green, 1970; Rogers & Shoemaker, 1971).

A related factor is the notion of generalized social support (Caplan, Cobb, & French, 1975), which refers not to the differential social reinforcement of specific behaviors, but to the general extent and quality of interpersonal relationships. Social relations appear to be generally helpful, probably because of their "stress-buffering" effects. Social ties within the family probably enhance cessation and prevention of tobacco use. For example, spousal support leads to higher successful quit rates (West, Graham, Swanson, & Wilkinson, 1977; Mermelstein, Lichtenstein, & McIntyre, 1983), and lower rates of teenage smoking occur in families in which neither parent smokes (National Institute on Education, 1979). The general enhancement of interpersonal support networks is, of course, a primary objective of religious groups and social work and most other helping professions.

Environmental change

There are also theories and concepts from which environmental changes can be planned (Bandura, 1977; Craik, 1973), the basic principle of which is to modify the availability and cost of products or behaviors (such as by limiting supply or prohibiting behaviors in public settings). Not all such measures can be applied by communities as defined herein. For example, regulations on mass media advertising can probably be controlled in most cases only at the Federal level, although billboard advertising may be amenable to more local control. Other promising interventions such as taxation (Lewit, Coate, & Grossman, 1981; Fugi, 1980) can be applied within fairly small localities, but the risk of "black market" competition is lessened when economic controls are fairly uniform across larger geographic units. Product availability and regulation of behavior can be achieved by towns or countries, but restrictive regulations almost invariably arouse opposition unless the public is willing to self-enforce the restrictions. Therefore, it is legitimate to favor voluntary restraints over those that require formal policing. Syme and Alcalay (1982) call for intervention and prevention efforts at the community level using a public education agenda. Such programs will seek to increase public awareness of the health consequences of smoking, create an atmosphere in which smoking is recognized as a minority behavior, influence public policy, and increase antismoking advertisements.

Breslow (1982) has recently reviewed the environmental and public policy approaches to smoking control and calls for a "comprehensive strategy that will mobilize all available resources most effectively" (p. 149). He advocates federal, state, and local legislation as the most important forms of social action directed toward action alternatives as well as research. He states that "protection and advancement of economic interests will generally follow prevailing ideology. Finding ways of cutting through the economic barriers, as always, will pose a challenge to public health. While compromises will be necessary, the objective of steady movement toward the goal now seems attainable" (p. 149).

Cessation studies

Controlled community studies on smoking cessation are still relatively scarce. However, community trials for cardiovascular disease prevention, in which cigarette smoking is the major risk factor, are providing some of the best examples of research in this area. These studies have tended to focus on cessation among adults because primary outcomes of the trials include possible short-term (5- to 10-year) effects on cardiovascular mortality and morbidity rates that could hypothetically result from widespread adult cessation. These studies were reviewed in depth in the 1983 Report of the Surgeon General, *The Health Consequences of Smoking* (U.S. Department of Health and Human Services, 1983).

Stanford three-community study

The most well known U.S. cardiovascular community study was conducted in California by Farquhar, Maccoby, and colleagues at Stanford University (Farquhar et al. 1977; Maccoby & Alexander, 1980; Meyer, Nash, McAlister, Maccoby, & Farquhar, 1980). Beginning in 1972 and ending in 1976, the study was supported through the National Institutes of Health research grant program and involved three small communities (population of each was approximately 20,000) nonrandomly assigned to control, media-only, or media and face-to-face programs. The three towns are all within 100 miles of Stanford University. The control town, Tracy, is located in an inner valley and not exposed to media sources common to the other two towns, Gilroy and Watsonville. Gilroy, assigned to the media-only condition, is situated in a coastal valley, and Watsonville, receiving a small additional interpersonal communication program, is on the coast. In Watsonville, a cardiovascular high risk group including many smokers (n = 169) was identified, and 113 cases were randomly assigned at a 2:1 ratio for face-to-face intervention. The three towns are demographically similar, although the proximity of Watsonville and Gilroy to the larger cities of Santa Cruz and San Jose gives them more cosmopolitan features than Tracy. Nevertheless, the research design was probably the best balance of feasibility and external and internal validity that could have been achieved in that setting given the limited available resources.

In each town, multistage probability samples of households were contacted and invited to a survey station where questionnaires and physiological measures were administered. These surveys were applied in the autumn months, beginning in Watsonville in September and ending in Tracy in November. Approximately 600 persons aged 35 to 59 were sampled at each location. The measurements included questions about smoking, and serum samples from high risk participants were analyzed to estimate thiocyanate concentrations as a check on inaccurate reporting of smoking status (Meyer et al., 1980). These measurements were taken annually for 4 years, yielding a picture of 3-year smoking trends among the survey participants in the three communities.

The program of media communication was conducted over 3 years (1973 to 1975), with greatest intensity in the first and second years of work. Television, newspapers, radio, billboards, and direct mail advertising were designed to provide information and to model attitudes and skills that would promote behavioral changes associated with lowered cardiovascular risk, such as weight reduction, lowered fat consumption, and increased exercise. To encourage cessation of smoking, information about its harmful effects was given, along with advice on how to stop smoking. In booklets mailed to the sampled households in Gilroy and Watsonville, instructions were provided for simple self-control skills (Meyer et al., 1980). In brief television and radio communications, actors were shown recommending or modeling cessation of smoking in a variety of authoritative and entertaining ways.

The face-to-face, intensive instruction program was provided for 113 randomly assigned high risk participants in Watsonville, of whom 107 started treatment, and 77 continued for the second annual examination. Activities were based on principles of behavioral psychology and group dynamics and were designed to reinforce and train skills for behavior change (Meyer et al., 1980). The first-year program consisted of classes and home visits, mostly during the summer of 1973. During the summer of the following year, aggressive followup activities were conducted to reinforce smokers who reported cessation and to encourage and train those who were not yet able to quit. This maintenance program included training in stress management and other intensive, individual counseling for those who consented to continuing contact. In the third year, the activities were gradually reduced to telephone contacts and a small "reunion" in the summer of 1975.

The results of the program among high risk participants differed considerably across the three communities. Over the 3 years of study, the prevalence of smoking decreased markedly among the group receiving media and face-to-face communication. The group receiving media intervention showed an initital decline as compared with the control group, but the change did not differ from the modest reduction observed in Tracy over the entire 3-year period. Because the high risk samples included most of the older smokers in the survey samples from each community, the data on cessation in the complete samples corresponded closely to that of the high risk group. The serum thiocyanate tests indicated very slight overreporting of cessation (Farquhar et al., 1977), but self-reported cessation rates were not adjusted for thiocyanate findings (Kasl, 1980). There was some attrition in this longitudinal study, but not enough to account for the clear differences in cessation rates between the intensively instructed and the other participants. Adjusting for attrition, 32 percent reported sustained cessation in the intensive intervention group (Meyer et al., 1980). This research supports the hypothesis that face-to-face communication is a necessary part of a successful community program to reduce smoking. Farquhar and his colleagues (Farquhar, Magnus, & Maccoby, 1981) conclude that the question of how such communication can be feasibly and cost-effectively provided on a widespread basis remains to be answered by further studies, and this conclusion will be noted in a later section. A number of critical comments can be made in regard to the Stanford three-community study, and these have been thoroughly discussed in numerous publications (Leventhal & Cleary, 1980; Meyer et al., 1980). The primary shortcomings concern the quasi-experimental research design and the inability to generalize from the longitudinally followed study group to the entire community.

The North Karelia project

The best documented long-term community study is being conducted in Finland by Puska and colleagues (Puska et al., 1979; Puska, McAlister, Pekkda, & Koskela, 1981; Puska, Nissinen, Salonen, & Tuomilehto, 1983a; Puska & Koskela 1983; McAlister, Puska, Salonen, Tuomilehto, & Koskela, 1982). Also beginning in 1972 and continuing to the present, the research is comparing changes in cardiovascular disease risk factors in two neighboring counties of eastern Finland, Kuopio and North Karelia.

Both are large rural areas with numerous small farming, lumber, or mining communities and a single major town. North Karelia is representative of eastern Finland as a whole in having one of the world's highest rates of cardiovascular disease (Pyörälä, 1974; World Health Organization, 1975). Financial support for the intervention came from the Finnish Ministry of Health, following a formal request from leaders in North Karelia for help in reducing the high mortality and morbidity levels. Research funds were awarded by the Academy of Finland. The neighboring county of Kuopio was selected as a reference or control location. In North Karelia, a broad program was implemented to provide new services, education, and training through community health centers, the mass media, and a variety of community organizations. During the second 5 years of the project, media programs were carried out on a national level, with special organizing and support for activities in North Karelia.

In both counties, independent samples of households were drawn in 1972, 1977, and 1982, with approximately 5,000 persons aged 25 to 59 in 1972 sampled in each area in the first two surveys and about 4,000 aged 25 to 64 sampled in the 1982 measurement. Response rates were generally excellent, and nearly 90 percent of the sample participated by attending local survey centers in the spring of each of the survey years (1972, 1977, 1982). Self-reported cigarette-smoking behavior was measured in all three surveys. In the 1977 survey, serum thiocyanate values were estimated for a subsample, and in the 1982 survey, for all participants. For the 1977 sample, there was 99 percent agreement in smoking status (smoker/nonsmoker), and when classified by intervals of 5 or 10 cigarettes, the agreement between results was 93 and 97 percent, respectively (Puska et al., 1979). The age-adjusted partial correlation between daily reported number of cigarettes and serum thiocyanate in 1982 was approximately 0.7 among men and women in both areas. In the years when the larger surveys were not conducted, smaller samples (1,200 to 3,500) were selected yearly for a postal survey of North Karelia. Together, these measurements provide a comparative view of trends over 10 years in the populations of both counties and a year-to-year picture of the changes in North Karelia.

The program of service, education, and training was very broad in scope. Initially, an intensive educational campaign was conducted for reduction of cigarette smoking with cooperation from the news media. Physicians and public health nurses staffing community health centers were provided special training and were encouraged to recommend cessation to all patients visiting the centers. Tens of thousands of leaflets and posters were distributed to encourage nonsmoking. With assistance from

Heart Association volunteers in each small community, informal restrictions on smoking and point-of-purchase advertising were adopted. During 1976 and 1977, these measures became part of a package of national legislation that increased cigarette tax revenue, directed health services to provide information services, limited public smoking, and banned tobacco advertising.

During the second 5-year period, an effort was made to provide nationwide applications, while maintaining intensive community work in North Karelia. A series of programs was broadcast nationally on television to demonstrate how "average" people stop smoking (Puska et al., 1981). In association with these broadcasts, special organizing campaigns were conducted in North Karelia to increase social support for people attempting to quit. These activities occurred in the winters of 1978, 1979, 1980, and 1982 and were seen nationally by a majority of the population, with higher viewership in North Karelia. During the first broadcast series, an effort was made to encourage the formation of informal volunteer-led self-help groups to view the broadcasts together. Very few volunteers succeeded in establishing groups, however, and focus in subsequent years has been on training volunteers to provide even less formal cueing, reinforcement, and support in their incidental, day-to-day contacts with cigarette smokers (Puska et al., 1981).

The results to date are presented in Puska and Koskela (1983). Over the 10-year period, self-reported numbers of cigarettes smoked per day fell by more than one-third among men in North Karelia. In the control or reference area, a less than 10 percent reduction was observed. Changes in prevalence of smoking account for most of this difference. No evidence of an effect occurred among women, with rates of smoking going up in both areas. The year-to-year data for 25- to 29-year-old men and women in North Karelia show an interesting pattern, with the sharpest declines among men associated with the first year of work and with the television broadcasts and associated activities in 1978 to 1980 and in 1982. Since 1978, when new antismoking laws were passed, the proportion of male smokers aged 15 to 64 has changed from 44 to 31 percent in North Karelia, and from 39 to 35 percent in the rest of the country, a difference of 9 percent in absolute rates of change over that 4-year period. Although the effect of changes in smoking cannot be separated from the effects of new hypertension services and other measures to prevent cardiovascular disease, there is some early indication that mortality rates may have been influenced by the program: a 24 percent decline in cardiovascular deaths has been observed in North Karelia, compared with a 12 percent decline nationally in Finland (Puska et al., 1983a, b).

The North Karelia Project has received much attention, and various points of controversy have been widely discussed. The methodology of the study does not compare with that achieved in controlled clinical trials, but it may have been the optimal design that was feasible in the circumstances. Puska and his colleagues point out that "it is easy to say that the North Karelia Project was successful because of the unique historical background and because the conditions in North Karelia were favorable for the program. However, at the planning stage, great concern was expressed because the area was rural, of low socioeconomic status with high unemployment, and so forth." Because a large number of independent units were not randomly assigned to experimental and control conditions, the Finnish study cannot be taken as a conclusive test of the effects of community programs, but it does provide a promising illustration and evaluation of what can be achieved through broad and vigorous intervention to reduce smoking behavior. Its major strengths are the relatively large number of different communities that were studied and the 10-year followup interval.

Other large-scale studies

Two other community studies are the Australian North Coast Project (Egger et al., 1983) and the Swiss National Research Program (Autorengruppe Nationales Forschungprogramm, 1984; Gutzwiller & Schwiezer, 1983). There have also been a number of other large-scale controlled studies, single and multifactor clinical trials, and worksite trials that provide a context for the consideration of the community-level intervention studies described above. These include the London Civil Servants Smoking Trials (Rose & Hamilton, 1978; Rose, Heller, Pedoe, & Christie, 1980; Rose, Hamilton, Colwell, & Shipley, 1982), the Göteborg (Sweden) study (Werko, 1979; Wilhelmsen, 1981; Wilhelmsen, Tibblin, & Werlo, 1972), the Oslo (Norway) study (Hjermann, Velve Byre, Holme, & Leren, 1981; Holme, Helgeland, Hjermann, & Leren, 1981), the World Health Organization European Collaborative Trials (World Health Organization European Collaborative Group, 1974; Kornitzer, De-Backer, Dramaix, & Thilly, 1980; Kornitzer, Dramaix, Littel, & De-Backer, 1980), and the Multiple Risk Factor Intervention Trial (MRFIT) (Hughes, Hymowitz, Ockene, Simon, & Vogt, 1981; Multiple Risk Factor Intervention Group, 1982). Comparison of the results from the four community studies with those from the other large-scale studies, as shown in Table 7.1, indicates distinct similarities. The individual studies each have somewhat different weaknesses, but all indicate that absolute reduc-

Table 7.1 *Results of community studies compared with other large-scale studies*

Study	Years of study	Net percent reduction in smoking[a]	Strengths	Weaknesses
Stanford Three-Community Study	3	15–20	Matched communities	Panel study only
Australian North Coast Study	3	15	Independent samples	Problems with comparability of groups
Swiss National Research Program	3	8	Randomization, independent samples	Small size and number of study sites
North Karelia Project	10	25[b]	Numerous communities, independent samples	Nonrandom assignment
Other large-scale studies[c]	2–10	5–25	Internal validity	External validity

[a]Difference between percent reduction in proportion of smokers in the maximum intervention versus control conditions.
[b]Difference between percent reduction in the mean number of cigarettes smoked per day among men.
[c]Clinical and worksite trials, the London Civil Servants Smoking Trial, the Göteborg study, the Oslo study, the WHO Collaborative Trial, and the Multiple Risk Factor Intervention Trial.

tions in smoking prevalence in intervention sites are about 12 percent greater than reductions in comparison communities.

Several ambitious community studies of cardiovascular disease prevention are currently in progress. Because it has become clear that community studies are the most natural and cost-effective method for testing new public health services to reduce chronic disease (Farquhar, 1978; Puska et al., 1983a), more of these efforts may be useful, particularly if costs can be reduced and, where possible, absorbed into existing services.

Related studies of cessation

A number of recent efforts have increased understanding of and confidence in the methods employed in large-scale community studies. Research on methods of stimulating interpersonal support for mass media programming is particularly relevant (Colletti & Brownell, 1982). In quasi-experimental studies, McAlister, Puska, Koskela, Pallsren, and Maccoby (1980) and Puska et al. (1981) have reported methods for facilitating the effectiveness of televised smoking cessation classes in Finland. Formal self-help groups appear difficult to organize, but reorganization of less formal social reinforcement in natural interaction settings appears feasible and effective. Related studies of television and other media-based methods are described by Danaher, Berkanovic, and Gerber (1983), Best (1980), Leathar (1981), and others. Dubren (1977a,b), Brengelmann (1976), and the American Cancer Society (1981) found that effects of media programs may be enhanced if a telephone hotline is offered. Flay, Hansen, Johnson, and Sobel (1983) used a school-based, family-oriented prevention program that included a five-segment television component to be aired the following week to encourage participation of cigarette-smoking parents. Overall, parents of students in experimental groups were over three times more likely to view the cessation segment than parents of control students, with similar differences observed for the proportions of successful parental attempts to quit. Within the experimental groups, teacher training had a significant effect (p<.01) on raising participation rates by parents of program students. Considering only homes with smokers, 51 percent of the students with trained teachers reported that at least one cigarette smoking adult viewed one or more cessation segments, compared with 37 percent of students with untrained teachers. Furthermore, 38 percent of parents with trained teachers attempted to quit smoking, compared with 24 percent of parents of students with untrained teachers (p<.001). At 1-year followup, the cessation rates in the two groups were 19 and 13 percent, respectively, according to children's reports of parental behavior. The validity of the indicators of adult smoking behavior is at issue; student reports could contain bias, which will be estimated in further analyses. Nevertheless, these results suggest that children can enhance the effectiveness of a media program in encouraging parents to stop smoking, and that organized social reinforcement is important in mass media smoking cessation programming (Flay et al., 1983). More research is needed on these and other methods of large-scale social reinforcement and support for cessation of smoking.

Some attention has been given to environmental changes that might contribute to the cessation of cigarette smoking. Evidence indicates that smoking can be regulated by counteradvertising, restrictions on advertising, warning labels, and symbolic or governmental actions such as the Surgeon General's Report of 1964 (Warner, 1977). Complete prohibition of smoking is not an acceptable alternative, but restrictions on smoking locations may be helpful for people attempting to quit voluntarily (Horwitz, Hindi-Alexander, & Wagner, 1982). Taxation of cigarettes has provided an effective deterrent in some population groups, particularly among younger men (Lewit, et al., 1981). In Finland, cigarette taxes have been increased and a portion (0.5 percent) of the funds are dedicated to support services to reduce the prevalence of smoking (Puska & Koskela, 1983). Similarly, integrated environmental and educational interventions may be useful in further large-scale efforts.

Methodological issues

In view of the high costs of clinical trials, such as those incurred by the Multiple Risk Factor Intervention Trial, a strong argument can be made for the cost effectiveness and generalizability of community studies of chronic disease prevention (e.g., Farquhar, 1978). However, there are methodological problems with the community studies that deserve careful consideration. In order to ensure strict adherence to assumptions of the statistical theories supporting experimental inference, independent units of observation must be sampled. Because the behavior and disease rates of people within a community are obviously not independent, the data from geographic units must be aggregated at various levels, such as family, neighborhood, community, and region. Thus, for example, smoking rates in three communities assigned to three different experimental conditions must be treated as three discrete observations, but having only one observation per condition does not permit use of traditional statistical procedures for hypothesis testing. By assigning more than one community to each condition, between-community variance can be estimated to provide more valid tests of program effect. Future research may be expected to involve more sites, with fewer cases sampled in each site.

Another problem concerns the comparability of groups. Unless a large number of communities are randomly assigned to conditions, the strict methodologist can identify obvious threats to experimental validity. For example, it might be natural to expect a bias toward the application of experimental programs in settings favorable to the adoption of innovation, while using "less interested" communities for the control group. This inevitably raises questions about the comparability of communities with regard to socioeconomic status, cosmopolitan features, or other hard-to-measure social characteristics.

Problems are also introduced by the possibility of experimental contamination or confounding effects of competing experimental programs. This issue must be thoroughly analyzed with respect to the North Karelia Project, where it appears that program results for dietary change and control of hypertension have been diluted by program spillover and the establishment of new health services in the reference (control) area.

Related to the issue of comparability of groups within a study is the problem of generalization to broader populations. For example, some groups that fall into the lower socioeconomic strata have not followed the general population trend toward smoking cessation and may also be at increased risk for smoking-related disease from concurrent industrial exposures.

Another difficulty is raised by studies that rely primarily on self-reports to assess behavior change, since such reports may be biased by intervention involvement (Evans, Hansen, & Mittlemark, 1977; Benfari, McIntyre, Benfari, Baldwin, & Ockene, 1977; Pechacek, Fox, Murray, & Luepker, 1984). Numerous other methodological points are pertinent to the review of community studies. For example, cohort studies that track individuals over time may be much less generalizable than those that involve repeated independent samples, but are critical for studying the development of certain behaviors, such as smoking onset.

Directions for future studies

There is a clear need for further research on community-level intervention to reduce smoking. The challenge is to develop relatively inexpensive methods that can be easily implemented on a large-scale basis. This will involve refinements in three broad activity categories: (1) education and instruction related to smoking, smoking cessation, and smoking prevention; (2) social reinforcement in support for nonsmoking behavior; and (3) environmental changes related to cigarettes and cigarette smoking.

Education and instruction methods are needed to convey information, attitudes, and skills more effectively as they relate to the cessation and prevention of smoking. For example, as the factors contributing to the process of smoking cessation and prevention are identified (DiClemente & Prochaska, 1982; McAlister, 1983; Leventhal, Cleary, Safer, & Gutmann, 1980), they can be modeled via television or other forms of mass communication. Although the schools have an obvious role in smoking prevention, the kinds of educational activities that appear to produce results are not easily adopted by traditional educators. Innovative education and training programs can be marketed to those willing to pay for therapeutic or consultative services related to smoking cessation and prevention, but less costly methods need to be developed for communitywide application. The establishment of smoking cessation programs within existing health services and the integration of chronic disease prevention with mental health promotion are also needed to effect broad-scale societal education and change.

Growing evidence indicates that the social reinforcement and support provided in formal therapies can be effectively evoked at far less expense by self-help groups and natural helping networks. In the North Karelia Project, community volunteers were taught to reinforce learning of smoking cessation skills from television (Puska et al., 1981). Children may also be powerful, natural sources of social reinforcement (Flay et al., 1983). Related methods are being applied in other ongoing community studies to harness the influence of natural social networks for antismoking campaigns (Pechacek et al., 1984). In addition to reinforcing specific behaviors and attitudes related to smoking prevention and cessation, social environments can give more general support and assistance to people trying to cope with stress, strain, and conflict. Given the relationship between chronic smoking, stress, and alienation, it is reasonable to expect a positive effect from interventions that reduce stress, improve coping, and increase social support (Colletti & Brownell, 1982).

Other community efforts are being made in noncontrolled contexts, as in the following examples. First, the American Cancer Society has introduced an "Adopt a Smoker" program to involve exsmokers in the annual Great American Smokeout Day. Second, community physicians are being urged to increase the frequency and intensity of cessation advice given to smokers. Finally, the television and newspaper media have become involved in the antismoking campaign, frequently including programming and articles that feature behavioral scientists discussing smoking behavior and the techniques of quitting.

Options for environmental change and public policy are varied and complex (Farquhar et al., 1981). The outright prohibition of smoking is not feasible, but limited prohibitions on smoking in public and some private places can have desirable effects in shifting negative attitudes. Restrictions on marketing are difficult on a local level, but constraints on advertising or availability may have a powerful effect. As indicated in a previous section, new taxes or other broad environmental changes are more likely to affect young smokers among whom dependence is not firmly established. Thus, they may be expected to have cumulative, long-term effects on future smoking rates. There is a role for research in clarifying optimal forms of restriction, but such research has not been implemented, not even in worksites where the effects of restrictions could be evaluated (Orleans & Shipley, 1982).

Future students must also develop an integrated model for combining cessation and prevention activities. Although the processes involved in the adoption of smoking are clearly different from those involved in its discontinuance, there are commonalities to be explored to find more efficient strategies for smoking reduction.

References

American Cancer Society. *A Study of the Impact of the 1980 Great American Smokeout. Summary Report.* National program sponsored by Gallup Organization, Inc., and analyzed by Lieberman Research, Inc., January 1981, 7 pp.

Atkin, C. Research evidence on mass mediated health communication campaigns. In: Nimmo, D. (Editor). *Communication Yearbook III.* New Brunswick, New Jersey, Transaction Books, 1979.

Autorengruppe Nationales Forschungsprogramm. *Wirksamkeit der Gemeindeorientierten Pravention Kardiovascularer Krankheiten.* [Effectiveness of Community-Oriented Prevention of Cardiovascular Disease.] Bern, Hans Huber, 1984.

Bandura, A. *Social Learning Theory.* Englewood Cliffs, New Jersey, Prentice-Hall, 1977.

Benfari, R. C., McIntyre, K. Benfari, M. J. F., Baldwin, A., Ockene, J. The use of thiocyanate determination for indication of cigarette smoking status. *Evaluation Quarterly 1*(4): 629–38, November 1977.

Bernstein, D. A. Modification of smoking behavior: An evaluative review. *Psychological Bulletin 71*(6): 418–40, June 1969.

Bernstein, D. A., McAlister, A. L. The modification of smoking behavior: Progress and problems. *Addictive Behaviors 1*(2): 89–102, 1976.

Best, J. A., Mass media, self-management, and smoking modification. In: Davidson, P.O., Davidson, S. M. (Editors). *Behavioral Medicine: Changing Health Lifestyles.* New York, Brunner/Mazel, 1980, pp. 371–90.

Brengelmann, J. L. *Experimente zur Behandlung des Rauchens.* [Experiments in the Treatment of Smoking.] Stuttgart, Verlag W. Kohlhammer, 1976.

Breslow, L. Control of cigarette smoking from a public policy perspective. In: Breslow, L., Fielding, J. E., Lave, L. B. (Editors). *Annual Review of Public Health.* Volume 3. Palo Alto, California, Annual Reviews Inc., 1982, pp. 129–51.

Campbell, D. T., Cook, T. D. *Quasi-Experimentation: Design and Analysis for Field Settings.* Chicago, Rand McNally College Publishing Company, 1979.

Caplan, R. D., Cobb, S., French, J. R. P., Jr. Relationships of cessation of smoking with job stress, personality, and social support. *Journal of Applied Psychology 60*(2): 211–19, April 1975.

Colletti, G., Brownell, K. D. The physical and emotional benefits of social support: Application to obesity, smoking, and alcoholism. In: Hersen, M., Eislee, R. M., Miller P.M. (Editors). *Progress in Behavior Modification,* Volume 13. New York, Academic Press, 1982, pp. 109–78.

Craik, K. H. Environmental psychology. *Annual Review of Psychology 24:* 403–22, 1973.

Danaher, B. G., Berkanovic, E., Gerber, B. Smoking and television: Review of extant literature. *Addictive Behaviors 8*(2): 173–82, 1983.

DiClemente, C. C., Prochaska, J. O. Self-change and therapy change of smoking behavior: A comparison of processes of change in cessation and maintenance. *Addictive Behaviors 7*(2): 133–42, 1982.

Dubren, R. Evaluation of a televised stop-smoking clinic. *Public Health Reports 92*(1): 81–84, January–February 1977a.

Dubren, R. Self-reinforcement by recorded telephone messages to maintain nonsmoking behavior. *Journal of Consulting and Clinical Psychology 45*(3): 358–60, June 1977b.

Egger, G., Fitzgerald, W., Frape, G., Monaem, A., Rubinstein, P., Tyler, C., McKay, B. Result of large scale media antismoking campaign in Australia: North Coast "Quit For Life" Programme. *British Medical Journal 286:*1125-8, 1983.

Evans, R. I., Hansen, W. E., Mittlemark, M. B. Increasing the validity of self-reports of smoking behavior in children. *Journal of Applied Psychology 62*(4): 521-3, April 1977.

Farquhar, J. W. The community-based model of life style intervention trials. *American Journal of Epidemiology 108*(2): 103-11, August 1978.

Farquhar, J. W., Magnus, P. F., Maccoby, N. The role of public information and education in cigarette smoking controls. *Canadian Journal of Public Health 72*(6): 412-20, November-December 1981.

Farquhar, J. W., Wood, P. D., Breitrose, H., Haskell, W. L., Meyer, A. J., Maccoby, N. Alexander, J. K., Brown, B. W., Jr., McAlister, A. L., Nash, J. D., Stern, M. P. Community education for cardiovascular health. *Lancet 1*(8023): 1192-5, June 4, 1977.

Flay, B. R., Ditecco, D., Schlegel, R. P. Mass media in health promotion. *Health Education Quarterly 7:*127-43, 1980.

Flay, B. R., Hansen, W. B., Johnson, C. A., Sobel, J. L. *Involvement of Children in Motivating Smoking Parents to Quit Smoking With a Television Program.* Paper presented at the Fifth World Conference on Smoking and Health, Winnipeg, Manitoba, July 1983.

Fuji, E. The demand for cigarettes. *Applied Economics 12:*479-89, 1980.

Green, L. W. Identifying and overcoming barriers to the diffusion of knowledge about family planning. *Advances in Fertility Control 5*(2); 21-9, 1970.

Griffiths, W., Knutson, A. L. The role of mass media in public health. *American Journal of Public Health 50*(4): 515-23, April 1960.

Gutzwiller, F., Schweizer, W. Intervention on smoking. An individual and collective challenge. In: Schettler, F. G., Gotto, A. M., Middlehoff, G., Habenicht, A. J. R., Jurutka, K. R. (Editors). *Atherosclerosis: Proceedings of the Sixth International Symposium.* New York, Springer-Verlag, 1983.

Hjermann, I., Velve Byre, K., Holme I., Leren, P. Effect of diet and smoking intervention on the incidence of coronary heart disease: Report from the Oslo study group of a randomized trial in healthy men. *Lancet 2*(8259): 1303-10, December 12, 1981.

Holme, I., Helgeland, A., Hjermann, I., Leren, P. The Oslo study: Social indicators, risk factors and mortality. In: Bostrom, H., Ljungstedt, N. (Editors). *Medical Aspects of Mortality Statistics.* Skandia International Symposia. Stockholm, Sweden, Almquist and Wiksell International, 1981, pp. 165-81.

Horwitz, M. B., Hindi-Alexander, M., Wagner, T. J. *Psychosocial Mediators of Long-Term Abstinence Following Smoking Cessation.* Paper presented at the 90th meeting of the American Psychological Association, Washington, D.C., August 24, 1982.

Hughes, G. H., Hymowitz, N., Ockene, J. K., Simon, N., Vogt, T. M. The Multiple Risk Factor Intervention Trial (MRFIT). V. Intervention on smoking. *Preventive Medicine 10*(4):476-500, July 1981.

Kasl, S. V. Cardiovascular risk reduction in a community setting. Some comments. *Journal of Consulting and Clinical Psychology 48*(2): 143-9, April 1980.

Klapper, J. T. *The Effects of Mass Communication.* New York, Free Press, 1960.

Kornitzer, M., DeBacker, G., Dramaix, M., Thilly, C. The Belgian Heart Disease Prevention Project: Modification of the coronary risk profile in an industrial population. *Circulation 61*(1): 18-25, January 1980.

Kornitzer, M., Dramaix, M., Kittel, F., DeBacker, G. The Belgian Heart Disease Prevention Project: Changes in smoking habits after two years of intervention. *Preventive Medicine 9*(4): 496-503, July 1980.

Lando, H. A., McGovern, P. G. Three-year data on a behavioral treatment for smoking: A follow-up note. *Addictive Behaviors 7*(2): 77–81, 1982.

LaSater, T. *The Pawtucket Heart Program.* Paper presented at ADAMHA Community Prevention Research Technical Review, June 1983.

Leathar, D. S. The use of mass media health education campaigns in Scotland. *Journal of International Health Education 19*(4): 122–9, 1981.

Leventhal, H., Cleary P. D. The smoking problem: A review of the research and theory in behavioral risk reduction. *Psychological Bulletin 88*(2): 370–405, 1980.

Leventhal, H., Cleary, P., Safer, M., Gutmann, M. Cardiovascular risk modification by community-based programs for life-style change: Comments on the Stanford Study. *Journal of Consulting and Clinical Psychology 48*(2): 150–8, April 1980.

Lewit, E., Coate, D., Grossman, M. The effects of government regulation on teenage smoking, *Journal of Law and Economics 24:* 545–73, December 1981.

Lichtenstein, E. The smoking problem: A behavioral perspective. *Journal of Consulting and Clinical Psychology 50*(6): 804–19, 1982.

Maccoby, N., Alexander, J. Use of media in lifestyle programs. In: Davidson, P. O., Davidson, S. M. (Editors). *Behavioral Medicine: Changing Health Lifestyles.* New York, Brunner/Mazel, 1980.

McAlister, A. Social-psychological approaches. In: National Institute on Drug Abuse. *Preventing Adolescent Drug Abuse: Intervention Strategies.* NIDA Research Series, Volume 47. U.S. Department of Health and Human Services, Public Health Service, Alcohol, Drug Abuse, and Mental Health Administration, DHHS Publication No. (ADM)83–1280, 1983, pp. 36–50.

McAlister, A., Puska, P., Koskela, K., Pallonen, U., Maccoby, N. Psychology in action: Mass communication and community organization for public health education. *American Psychologist 35*(4): 375–9, April 1980.

McAlister, A., Puska, P., Salonen, J. T., Tuomilehto, J., Koskela, K. Theory and action for health promotion: Illustrations from the North Karelia Project. *American Journal of Public Health 72*(1): 43–50, January 1982.

McCombs, M. E., Shaw, D. L. The agenda-setting function of mass media. *Public Opinion Quarterly 36*(2): 176–87, Summer 1972.

Mermelstein, R., Lichtenstein, E., McIntyre, K. Partner support and relapse in smoking-cessation programs. *Journal of Consulting and Clinical Psychology 51*(3): 465–6, June 1983.

Meyer, A., Maccoby, N., Farquhar, J. The role of opinion leadership in a cardiovascular health education campaign. In: Ruben, B. D. (Editor). *Communication Yearbook I.* New Brunswick, New Jersey, Transaction Books, 1977.

Meyer, A. J., Nash, J. D., McAlister, A. L., Maccoby, N., Farquhar, J. W. Skills training in a cardiovascular health education campaign. *Journal of Consulting and Clinical Psychology 48*(2): 129–42, April 1980.

Multiple Risk factor Intervention Research Group. Mutliple Risk Factor Intervention Trial: Risk factor changes and mortality results. *Journal of the American Medical Association 248*(12): 1465–77, September 24, 1982.

National Institute on Education. *Teenage Smoking: Immediate and Long-Term Patterns.* U.S. Department of Health, Education, and Welfare, National Institute on Education, November 1979.

Orleans, C. S., Shipley, R. H. Worksite smoking cessation initiatives: Review and recommendations *Addictive Behaviors 7*(1): 1–16, 1982.

Pechacek, T. F., Fox, B. H., Murray, D. M., Luepker, R. V. Review of techniques for measurement of smoking behavior. In: Matarazzo, J. D., Miller, N. E., Weiss, S. M.,

Herd, J. A. (Editors). *Behavioral Health: A Handbook of Health Enhancement and Disease Prevention*. New York, John Wiley and Sons, 1984, pp. 729–54.

Pechacek, T. F., McAlister, A. Strategies for the modification of smoking behavior: Treatment and prevention. In: Ferguson, J. M., Taylor, C. B. (Editors). *Extended Applications and Issues*. The Comprehensive Handbook of Behavioral Medicine, Volume 3. Jamaica, New York, Spectrum Publications, 1980, pp. 257–98.

Puska, P., Koskela, K. Community-based strategies to fight smoking: Experiences from the North Karelia Project in Finland. *New York State Journal of Medicine 83*(13): 1335–8, December 1983.

Puska, P., McAlister, A., Pekkola, J., Koskela, K. Television in health promotion: Evaluation of a national programme in Finland. *International Journal of Health Education 24*(4) 238–50, October–December 1981.

Puska, P., Nissinen, A., Salonen, J. T., Tuomilehto, J. Ten years of the North Karelia Project: Results with community-based prevention of coronary heart disease. *Scandinavian Journal of Social Medicine 11*(3): 65–8, 1983a.

Puska, P., Salonen, J. T., Nissinen, A., Tuomilehto, J., Vartiainen, E., Korhonen, H., Tanskanen, A., Ronnqvist, P., Koskela, K., Huttunen. J. Coronary risk factor changes during ten years of a preventive community programme, the North Karelia Project. *British Medical Journal 287:* 1840–4, 1983b.

Puska, P., Tuomilehto, T., Salonen, J., Neittaanmaki, L., Maki, J., Virtamo, J., Nissinen, A., Koskela, K., Takalo, T. Changes in coronary risk factors during comprehensive five-year community programme to control cardiovascular diseases (North Karelia Project). *British Medical Journal 2*(6198): 1173–8, November 10, 1979.

Pyörälä, K. The epidemiology of coronary heart disease in Finland: A review. *Duodecim 90:* 1605–22, 1974.

Rogers, E., Shoemaker, F. *Communication of Innovations: A Cross-Cultural Approach.* New York, Free Press, 1971.

Rose, G., Hamilton, P. J. S. A randomised controlled trial of the effect on middle-aged men of advice to stop smoking. *Journal of Epidemiology and Community Health 32*(4): 275–81, December 1978.

Rose, G., Hamilton, P. J. S., Colwell, L., Shipley, M. J. A randomised controlled trial of anti-smoking advice: 10-year results. *Journal of Epidemiology and Community Health 36*(2): 102–8, June 1982.

Rose, G., Heller, R. F., Pedoe, H. T., Christie, D. G. S. Heart disease prevention project: A randomized controlled trial in industry. *British Medical Journal 1*(6216): 747–51, March 15, 1980.

Syme, S. L., Alcalay, R. Control of cigarette smoking from a social perspective: In: Breslow, L., Fielding, J. E., Lave, L. B. (Editors). *Annual Review of Public Health,* Volume 3. Palo Alto, California, Annual Reviews Inc., 1982, pp. 179–99.

U.S. Department of Health and Human Services. *The Health Consequences of Smoking: Cardiovascular Disease. A Report of the Surgeon General.* U.S. Department of Health and Human Services, Public Health Service, Office of the Assistant Secretary for Health, Office on Smoking and Health. DHHS Publication No. (PHS)84–50204, 1983.

Wallack, L. M. Mass media campaigns. The odds against finding behavior change. *Health Education Quarterly 8*(3): 209–259, Fall 1981.

Warner, K. E. The effects of the antismoking campaign on cigarette consumption. *American Journal of Public Health 67*(7): 645–50, July 1977.

Werko, L. Prevention of heart attacks. A multifactoral preventive trial in Gothenberg, Sweden. *Annals of Clinical Research 11*(2): 71–9, April 1979.

West, D. W., Graham, S., Swanson, M., Wilkinson, G. Five year follow-up of a smoking withdrawal clinic population. *American Journal of Public Health* 67(6): 536–44, June 1977.

Wilhelmsen, L. Risk factors for disease according to population studies in Göteborg, Sweden. Paper presented at Skandia International Symposia, September 23–25, 1980. In: Bostrom, H., Ljungstedt, H. (Editors). *Medical Aspects of Mortality Statistics.* Stockholm, Sweden, Almquist and Wiksell International, 1981, pp. 73–88.

Wilhemsen, L., Tibblin, G., Werko, L. A primary preventive study in Gothenburg, Sweden. *Preventive Medicine* 1(1–2): 153–60, March 1972.

World Health Organization. *Vital Statistics and Causes of Death, 1972,* Volume 1. Geneva, 1975.

World Health Organization European Collaborative Group. An international controlled trial in the multifactorial prevention of coronary heart disease. *International Journal of Epidemiology* 3(3): 219–24, September 1974.

8   Preventing adolescent smoking[1]

Kevin D. McCaul and Russell E. Glasgow

Introduction

Because adults often find it difficult to stop smoking (Glasgow & Bernstein, 1981; Leventhal & Cleary, 1980; Pechacek, 1979), a great deal of attention has been given to programs designed to prevent children from becoming smokers. Most of these efforts have taken place in school settings. This emphasis on smoking prevention is not new, but researchers' tactics are different from those used before 1970.

Early smoking prevention progress typically included one-sided attempts to increase adolescents' knowledge about the dangers of smoking. Reviews have been consistent in concluding that such programs were successful in improving knowledge, less successful in changing attitudes, and ineffective in preventing actual smoking behavior (Evans, Henderson, Hill, & Raines, 1979; Thompson, 1978; Williams, 1971). More recent programs have introduced multicomponent interventions that address a variety of psychosocial factors associated with the development of adolescent smoking. For example, interventions have been designed to counteract peer and media pressure to experiment with cigarettes. Most reviews of the newer smoking prevention programs conclude that they have had sizable effects on smoking behavior (e.g., Botvin & McAlister, 1981; Botvin & Willis, 1985; Coates, Perry, Killen, & Slinkard, 1981; Evans, Smith, & Raines, 1984; Johnson, 1982a; McAlister, Perry, & Maccoby, 1979; Pechacek & McAlister, 1980). The great variety of programs that have been developed may suggest new directions for the prevention of other health and nonhealth hazards as well.

In this chapter we shall describe the various ingredients of these prevention programs. We shall consider carefully what has been learned about the impact of these ingredients and the reasons they may be successful. We shall also illustrate the difficulties of interpreting the

170

results of multicomponent programs. In effect, we shall attempt in this review to move adolescent smoking prevention beyond the stage of finding interventions that work to the next stage of understanding how they work.

We should note that the designs of these programs usually offer considerably more control and interpretive clarity than the large-scale community interventions reviewed in Chapter 7 of this volume. Nevertheless, they are not laboratory experiments, and successful smoking prevention programs are often characterized by potentially serious design problems (Biglan & Ary, 1985; Flay, d'Avernas, Best, Kersell, & Ryan, 1983; Flay et al., 1985). In many of the studies, random assignment procedures have not been employed; treatment implementation has been at the level of an entire school, thus confounding treatment and school; the time frame used makes it uncertain whether the programs actually prevent or simply delay the onset of smoking; and there are a significant number of dropouts. Still, at least some of the outcomes are replicable (see Botvin & Eng, 1982) and hold up under more stringent methodological conditions (Flay et al., 1985).

The treatments that we shall review represent many novel activities in comparison with earlier prevention research. New methods of delivering programs, including role playing and the use of peer leaders, were introduced. Novel materials and activities were also developed, including (a) information about peer, parental, and media pressures to smoke; (b) information about the short-term, negative interpersonal and health effects of smoking; (c) behavioral rehearsal on combating pressures to smoke; (d) skills training in decision making and coping with anxiety; and (e) public commitment to nonsmoking. These strategies seem so diverse as to defy categorization, but all the prevention activities are hypothesized to influence one or more of five mediating variables related to smoking behavior.

The program components and these five mediating variables are shown in Figure 8.1, and the review of the literature will be organized around the mediating variables seen in the figure.[2] In discussing each variable, we shall consider 13 studies (Table 8.1) that used multicomponent programs and produced statistically significant reductions in adolescent smoking. Prevention programs that did not reduce smoking or that did not report any information about treatment effects on mediating variables have been excluded from this review. Without collecting process measures (data on mediating variables) one can only speculate about the aspect of the multicomponent treatment that was responsible for the effects observed.

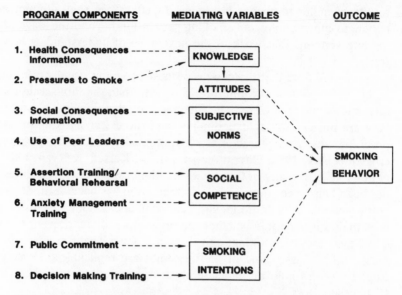

Figure 8.1. Program components of recent smoking prevention programs and associated mediating variables. Arrows reflect possible causal paths suggested by researchers using the program components as part of their treatment.

Knowledge and attitudes

As noted previously, reviewers have repeatedly concluded that earlier prevention programs influenced knowledge (or beliefs about cigarette smoking and smokers), had a minor impact on attitudes (affective responses to smoking and smokers), but failed to affect smoking behavior (Leventhal & Cleary, 1980; Thompson, 1978). It is intriguing, then, that the same pattern of results is obtained on knowledge and attitude measures in more recent studies. Table 8.1 reveals that every study except one (Evans et al., 1978) produced significant changes in knowledge. Furthermore, the failure to obtain belief differences in that study was attributed to ceiling effects (i.e., all subjects believed that smoking has negative effects on health).

In contrast to belief changes, reliable attitudinal changes were not typically produced by the prevention programs summarized in Table 8.1. This may be attributed in part to the relatively uniform negative attitudes toward smoking held by adolescents (Flay et al., 1983). Still, the data do not suggest that attitudinal changes are responsible for program effectiveness. Only one study (Botvin, Baker, Renick, Filazzola, & Botvin, 1984) reported both attitudinal and behavior change at the end of the program.

Table 8.1. *Improvement of process measures relative to control conditions from studies that reduced smoking behavior*

Study	Knowledge	Attitudes	Subjective norms	Social competence	Intentions
Botvin & Eng (1982)	Yes	NR	NR	NR	NR
Botvin et al. (1980)	Yes	NR	NR	NR	NR
Botvin et al. (1983)	Yes	No[a]	NR	Yes	NR
Botvin et al. (1984)	Yes	Yes	NR	No	NR
Coe et al. (1982)	NR	No	Yes	NR	NR
Evans et al. (1978)	No	NR	NR	NR	NR
Evans et al. (1981)	Yes	NR	NR	NR	Yes
Flay et al. (1982)	Yes[b]	NR	NR	NR	No
Flay et al. (1983)	Yes	No	No	NR	No
Iammarino, Heit, Kaplan (1980)	Yes	NR	NR	NR	NR
Perry, Killen, Slinkard, & McAlister (1980a)	Yes	No	NR	NR	Nr
Schinke & Blythe (1981)	Yes	No[a]	Yes	Yes	Yes
Schinke & Gilchrist (1983)	Yes	NR	NR	Yes	Yes

Note: NR indicates not reported; Yes indicates reliable treatment–control differences for that measure; No indicates no group differences.
[a]In these studies, no attitudinal differences were obtained at post-test, but differences were observed at follow-up.
[b]Flay et al. found reliable differences in knowledge related to "social perceptions" (e.g., whether the media honestly portray cigarette smoking) but not in knowledge related to health.

Five studies obtained smoking reductions without consistent increases in negative attitudes toward smoking. Two of these studies did report attitudinal differences (Botvin, Renick, & Baker, 1983; Schinke & Blythe, 1981), but only at follow-up assessment; smoking reductions were seen immediately after treatment. This discrepancy calls into question the directionality of the attitude–behavior relation depicted in Figure 8.1.

It is thus tempting to propose that changes in knowledge, but not attitude underlie the effectiveness of smoking prevention programs in reducing smoking. However, this suggestion is suspect. To support this conclusion, program effects on smoking should have been examined after controlling for knowledge. If changes in knowledge were important for program success, this analysis would show no effects, but none of the studies portrayed in Table 8.1 reported such analyses. Though we will not belabor the point in subsequent sections, this criticism could be applied to each of the process variables listed in Table 8.1.

The failure to demonstrate program effects on attitudes also complicates speculation that differences in knowledge underlie program effectiveness. As Figure 8.1 shows, attitudes are thought to be later in the causal chain than beliefs (knowledge changes), suggesting that beliefs do not affect behavior independently of attitudinal changes. The lack of consistent attitudinal changes simultaneously suggests that the knowledge changes may be unimportant or, at least, that they act in a manner different from that portrayed.

A final reason for caution here, noted earlier, comes from the numerous demonstrations of program effects on knowledge without accompanying behavioral changes. It may be that changes in knowledge are necessary but insufficient for reducing smoking. Alternatively, what may differentiate more recent programs in this respect is the type of beliefs that were changed. Whereas early programs focused on the long-term health effects of smoking, the programs shown in Table 8.1 were designed to change beliefs concerning the immediate, negative health effects of smoking and/ or knowledge about pressures to smoke. It is conceivable that changes in these beliefs are more important for adolescents than are long-term health beliefs.

Experiments that specifically compared the effects of these innovative messages and those of information on long-term health effects might shed light on this possibility. Unfortunately, we uncovered no experiments that examined the specific effects of providing information about social pressures on adolescents to smoke (e.g., peer, parental, and media influences), although this component is presumed to be an important aspect of recent prevention programs (Coates et al., 1981; Evans et al., 1981). Several experiments, however, have addressed the relative efficacy of information on immediate health consequences and information on remote effects (e.g., cancer, heart disease; see Evans, 1976; Fodor & Glass, 1971; Horn, 1960).

Health educators have been reminded that information about the "immediate" effects of smoking may be more persuasive to adolescents than the "scare" tactics associated with long-term health effects information (Ellis, Indyke, & Debevoise, 1980). There are several reasons for this. First, most adolescents are aware of long-term health consequences, but they are less cognizant of the immediate effects of smoking a cigarette (Glasgow, McCaul, Freeborn, & O'Neill, 1981). Thus, information emphasizing the immediate health effects of smoking is new and potentially more persuasive. Second, many adolescents who smoke fail to label themselves as smokers and do not believe that they will smoke in the future (Leventhal & Cleary, 1980), thus diminishing the impact of information about future health consequences. Finally, children are more present oriented than are adults (Mittelmark, 1978), again suggesting that information on immediate effects will be more salient than that on long-term effects.

Five experiments have evaluated the hypothesis that information on immediate health effects will add to prevention efforts, but unfortunately, the contribution of such information has proved to be minimal. Mittelmark (1978) assigned sixth-grade children to an experimental condition that emphasized the immediate effects of smoking on carbon monoxide levels in the body or to a second condition that emphasized the long-term effects of smoking (e.g., a film on lung cancer; depiction of a black lung). The results showed increases in knowledge in both experimental groups, compared with measurement-only, control conditions (attitudes were not assessed). There were no reliable differences between conditions on intentions to smoke or self-reports of smoking. The results of a similarly designed study conducted by Hill (1979) were also negative.

Two other experiments obtained somewhat more promising results, but with important qualifications. Glasgow et al. (1981) varied the presence of short- and long-term health information in a 2 × 2 factorial design. The information on immediate effects produced stronger belief changes and was more easily remembered, presumably because it was newer to subjects than the information on long-term effects. In addition, the information on immediate effects tended to reduce subjects' intentions to smoke in the next year relative to a control condition (actual smoking behavior was not measured). It should be noted, however, that there were no differences between the immediate- and long-term-effects conditions on the intention-to-smoke measure. The long-term-effects condition was also successful in altering intentions, and the combination of both types of information was the most successful.

Henderson (1979) obtained positive results with an informational film about the immediate physiological effects of smoking, but in comparison with a message emphasizing strategies used by adolescents to resist social pressures to smoke rather than in comparison with a long-term-effects condition. Measures taken at a nine-week post-test showed that both experimental messages led to increased knowledge relative to a control condition, although neither produced reliable attitudinal differences. The film on immediate effects also produced a lower intention to smoke in the future than did the other conditions, but only among students who had previously experimented with smoking. There were no post-test differences on reported smoking.

Finally, Arkin et al. (1981) implemented several interventions in different schools and relied on smoking behavior to test treatment effects. At a one-year post-test, a short-term-effects condition (that included information on both negative health and social consequences) proved less effective than both a long-term-health-effects condition and a standard curriculum condition in reducing the onset of experimental smoking.

We speculated earlier that the increase in knowledge about the effects of smoking produced by recent prevention programs might be more effective in reducing smoking than similar increases obtained in earlier research, because immediate-consequences information would prove to be more powerful than long-term-consequences information. The data directly assessing this hypothesis fail to support it: None of the studies showed that immediate-effects information was superior to long-term-effects information. (Indeed, the final study cited showed the opposite pattern of results.) Immediate-effects information sometimes produced better outcomes than no treatment, but that finding was inconsistent, and it suffers from alternative, placebo effect explanations.

We have spent a disproportionate amount of space reviewing studies concerned with the immediate effects of smoking on health. We have done so, in part, because the value of this prevention component has seemingly been uncritically accepted and incorporated into many recent prevention programs. And despite the negative results of experimental studies concerning the efficacy of information on immediate health effects, it may be premature to abandon the hypotheses on which this prevention component was initially constructed. The operationalization of immediate-effects information has usually focused on effects that are in some ways as remote as long-term effects. One cannot "feel" carbon monoxide, and it may be difficult for adolescents to tie such information to beliefs about sickness. Leventhal and his associates (Leventhal, Meyer, & Nerenz, 1980; Leventhal, Safer, & Panagis, 1983; Safer, Tharpe, Jackson, & Leventhal, 1979) have proposed that protective health behaviors are initially motivated by the perception of concrete symptoms that trigger an illness "schema." This notion suggests that researchers should focus on short-term symptoms that can be experienced by novice smokers (e.g., coughing, burning throat, being out of breath). Furthermore, these symptoms should be tied to adolescents' existing notions of the long-term effects of smoking on health.

Subjective norms

Measures of subjective norms were obtained infrequently in the studies listed in Table 8.1 and the measures were different across studies. Ajzen and Fishbein (1980) define subjective norms as the individual's "perception that important others desire the performance or nonperformance of a specific behavior" (p. 57). The measures that we used for completing Table 8.1., however, were not nearly as specific as this definition would require. For example, Coe, Crouse, Cohen, and Fisher (1982) found that program students lowered their opinions of smoking as "cool." Schinke and Blythe (1981) found that experimental subjects were more likely to predict that a refusal to smoke would not be met with highly negative responses from peers. Finally, Flay et al. (1983) failed to find differences on an unspecified measure of social normative beliefs.

Several researchers have suggested that normative changes in the school environment may be primarily responsible for program effectiveness (Leventhal & Cleary, 1980; McCaul, Glasgow, Schafer, & O'Neill, 1983). In describing their successful intervention, McAlister et al. (1979) noted that intensive interviews "indicate that the intervention may have influenced the entire social atmosphere regarding smoking. The students report that hardly anyone smokes now, and that it's not cool to smoke any more" (p. 655). Unfortunately, those authors did not report more systematic assessments of subjective norms. There is thus some evidence and additional speculation that prevention programs achieve their effectiveness by altering subjective (and perhaps actual) norms. Specific tests of prevention components thought to influence norms, however, provide a less optimistic picture.

Figure 8.1 shows two components of recent prevention programs that may be tied to changes in norms: information about the negative social consequences of smoking and the use of peer leaders to assist in presentations. Information about peer disapproval of smoking would be expected to influence normative beliefs directly, whereas peer leaders (especially when selected for their "Fonzie" appearance; see McAlister et al., 1979) might indirectly reduce beliefs in the social acceptability of smoking (Fisher, 1980). We will discuss each of these intervention components separately.

Social consequences

In a small-scale study with seventh-grade students, O'Neill, Glasgow and McCaul (1983) evaluated the effects on intentions to smoke of a videotaped social consequences message relative to a control message discussing general facts about smoking. Results from both an immediate posttest and a one-month follow-up revealed a consistent pattern of results: There were no differential effects for students who were nonsmokers, but Sex × Treatment interactions were obtained for students who had previously experimented with smoking. The interaction pattern showed that the social consequences message reduced the intention to smoke of female experimental smokers but actually increased the intention to smoke of male smokers. A similar interaction finding was obtained for a measure of whether subjects perceived persons who smoke cigarettes to be more "mature."

A much larger study by Arkin et al. (1981) compared the effects of information about social consequences with the effects of a long-term health consequences curriculum. Their social consequences curriculum included videotaped presentations of the negative social consequences of smoking, discussion of peer, family, and media pressures to smoke, and role playing of situations involving refusals to smoke. This program also focused on the immediate physiological effects of smoking, making it a less than pure manipulation of information on social consequences. When only students who were nonsmokers at pretest were considered, both the social pressure and long-term health consequences curriculum reduced the probability of experimental smoking compared with a no-treatment control condition. (As noted earlier, the long-term condition showed some advantages over the social consequences curriculum.) Unfortunately, no process measures were reported, and neither of the interventions was more effective than no treatment in reducing the probability of initial experimental smokers becoming regular smokers.

These two studies suggest that information about the negative social consequences of smoking might be a useful aspect for some participants in prevention programs. Arkin et al. (1981) showed that such information reduced first time smoking, although their "social consequences" condition could more accurately be described as a multicomponent treatment. Using a more straightforward manipulation, O'Neill et al. (1983) found effects on general subjective norms and intentions to smoke, although only for a selected group of adolescents (i.e., female "experimenters"). As we noted previously, investigators have underemphasized the possible role of such moderating variables. An accumulation of similar reports could, in the future, assist in the understanding of the processes by which programs achieve their effects and of the optimal types of programs for different subgroups of adolescents.

Peer versus adult leaders

Three experiments have been conducted to examine the importance of using peer leaders to present prevention programs. In the earliest of these, Irwin, Creswell, and Stauffer (1970) evaluated the effects of type of instructor (regular classroom teachers versus member of the smoking research team) and teaching method (individual self-study versus peer discussion versus teacher-directed discussion) on students' attitudes and knowledge about smoking. The pattern of results was intriguing. Overall, the peer-led approach was the least effective method. Despite these early negative results, several researchers have subsequently selected and trained peer discussion leaders to interact with their classmates; indeed, the component has become almost "institutionalized" among major prevention efforts (Flay et al., 1983; Johnson, 1982b; McAlister, Perry, Killen, Slinkard, & Maccoby, 1980).

Investigators at the University of Minnesota have evaluated the effects of adding peer leaders in the context of a multicomponent treatment program for seventh-grade students. The results of these studies have been inconsistent. Hurd et al. (1980) reported a nonsignificant trend (p = .10; one-tailed) toward an incremental effect of adding peer opinion leaders in addition to adult discussion leaders. In a three-year follow-up of that study, Luepker, Johnson, Murray, and Pechacek (1983) found that the addition of peer leaders reduced smoking behavior compared with the adult-led program. However, Arkin et al. (1981) failed to find an additive effect of peer opinion leaders.

None of the studies evaluating the use of peer leaders has presented data on subjective norms; thus, it is unclear whether using peer leaders influences such beliefs. Some authors have proposed that peer discussion leaders are preferable to adults, because adolescents are frequently rebellious and may react negatively to adult "preaching" (McAlister et al., 1979). In addition, it is suggested that, during adolescence, peers become more important sources of social influence than adults, a hypothesis that has received some support (Krosnick & Judd, 1982). But these rationales for using peer leaders must be balanced against the probably greater credibility of adults and implementation problems that may result from using adolescents. The inconsistent results of the above studies should lead investigators to question the assumption that peers will necessarily be more influential with their classmates than will adults (see Johnson, 1982b).

Social competence

Like subjective norms, social competence has been measured infrequently and inconsistently in the studies portrayed in Table 8.1. In two studies, Botvin and colleagues gathered identical measures of reported assertiveness (Botvin et al., 1983, 1984). As shown in Table 8.1., their

Life Skills Training Program produced assertiveness in one study but not the other. Botvin's research design has frequently made use of other measures that could be broadly labeled social competence (only assertiveness outcomes are presented in Table 8.1), including resistance to "influenceability," self-esteem, and social anxiety. No consistent effects have been observed across studies for any of these measures.

Three studies by Schinke and his colleagues, in which training of social skills was included (Schinke & Blythe, 1981; Schinke & Gilchrist, 1983, 1984), found strong and consistent effects. In these studies, the subjects were individually tested and videotaped in simulated social encounters in which they were pressured to smoke. Experimental subjects differed from controls by showing greater eye contact, and more use of "no" and "I" statements (Schinke & Blythe, 1981; Schinke & Gilchrist, 1983). Skills-building subjects complied less with, and showed greater resistance to, suggestions to smoke, and they suggested better alternatives (Schinke & Gilchrist, 1984). Finally, at follow-up assessments, the experimental subjects reported more refusals of offers to smoke (Schinke & Blythe, 1981; Schinke & Gilchrist, 1983).

There is an important difference between the earlier two experiments by the Schinke group and the others shown in Table 8.1. Specifically, the number of participants in these two experiments was quite low (total Ns = 28 and 56) compared with the "norm" (e.g., N = 281 in Botvin, Eng, & Williams, 1980, and N = 3296 in Evans et al., 1981). The smaller samples lend themselves to more intensive work (eight 60-minute sessions) on social skills and make possible the sorts of individual behavioral assessments that were conducted. Other investigators are encouraged to develop similar measures of hypothesized mediating variables. Although such assessment may be impractical in larger studies, self-report instruments related to social skills are available (e.g., Michelson & Wood, 1980); alternatively, a random sample of subjects could be drawn for more intensive study.

Specific manipulations of the two program components shown in Figure 8.1 that are expected to influence social competence are lacking. No studies have experimentally evaluated procedures for improving skills for coping with anxiety. In the only study that has experimentally tested the effects of behavioral versus attitude modification approaches to training adolescents to resist pressures to smoke (Schinke & Gilchrist, 1984), the behavioral skills training condition reduced reported cigarette use relative to both the attitude modification and a no-treatment comparison condition. Finally, two experiments (Jason, Mollica, & Ferrone, 1982; Spitzzerri & Jason, 1979) compared role playing with alternative techniques for encouraging nonsmoking among adolescents, but both were directed primarily toward encouraging cessation rather than preventing initiation. Furthermore, these studies failed to demonstrate a strong effect for behavioral rehearsal. Spitzzerri and Jason (1979) found that an intervention that included role playing and group discussion and that focused on resisting pressures to smoke helped current smokers to stop compared with a condition in which a single film on the health hazards of smoking was shown. In an extension of this study, Jason, Mollica, and Ferrone (1982) discovered that this behavioral rehearsal and discussion intervention was no more effective than a discussion-only program.

The data reported on general measures of social competence (e.g., assertiveness, self-esteem) certainly do not make a strong case for the importance of this component of prevention programs. However, the careful assessments of specific refusal skills on the part of Schinke and colleagues suggest promise for that component as an important aspect of prevention. Some skills training programs are effective in reducing smoking, improving refusal skills, and increasing the reported use of those skills (Schinke & Blythe, 1981; Schinke & Gilchrist, 1983). Further analyses, in line with the questions outlined previously, might address whether refusal skills influence outcomes (with treatment controlled) and whether the treatment shows no effects when refusal skills are controlled.

Intentions

The final mediating variable shown in Figure 8.1 is one's intention to smoke in the future. In Fishbein & Ajzen's (1975) model of attitude–behavior linkages, intentions are the most direct precursor of behavior. Thus, one would expect a strong relationship between intent to smoke and actual smoking behavior, and the data in Table 8.1 tend to support this prediction. Of the five studies measuring intentions, three produced reliable reductions in intent to smoke, one produced means in the predicted direction (Flay, Johnson, Hansen, & Grossman, 1982), and the final study (Flay et al., 1983) suffered from "floor" effects (i.e., both experimental and control subjects uniformly planned not to smoke).

Behavioral intentions are clearly predictive of later performance across a variety of behaviors (Ajzen & Fishbein, 1980), and the smoking behavior of adolescents is no exception (Allegrante, O'Rourke, & Tuncalp, 1977; McCaul, Glasgow, O'Neill, Freeborn, & Rump, 1982; NIE, 1979). Again, it is crucial that in the future researchers evaluate the impact of intentions on smoking behavior after controlling for prior mediating variables (and for treatment). Also, further investigations of program components expected to influence intentions are warranted.

Of the two components listed in Table 8.1 that may affect smoking intentions, no experiments have been conducted to test the separate or comparative effects of teaching decision-making skills to adolescents, although such skills are purported to be an important aspect of prevention programs (e.g., Flay et al., 1983). Several reports have described experimental manipulations of public commitment to nonsmoking. Hurd et al. (1980) included public commitment as one part of a multicomponent program. In one experimental school, half of the subjects received a peer-led social consequences intervention (described previously), and the other half received that intervention and, in addition, made public commitments not to smoke. Students expressed their commitment by making a statement about why they would not smoke; the statement was delivered in front of the class and was videotaped. Self-reported smoking was measured, and Hurd et al. (1980) concluded that "commitment appeared to have some effect, but the prevalence of smoking was low at baseline" (p. 24). There were, in fact, no statistically significant commitment effects, but due to the success of the basic social consequences curriculum (only one person began smoking after project onset), one could only speculate about the incremental effects of the commitment procedure. In a 10-month follow-up to this study, Murray et al. (1979) reported that both social consequences conditions "involving peer leaders differed from the other two conditions though not from each other" (p. 12). Thus, commitment did not add to the effectiveness of the basic social consequences intervention. Again, however, these negative results may have been due to floor effects, given the very low rate of recruitment to smoking in both conditions.

We included public commitment as a component that would influence intentions to smoke, because that rationale has been suggested by researchers who have used the strategy (e.g., Flay et al., 1983), but we are unaware of evidence that commitment changes intentions to perform a behavior. Instead, public commitment to an attitudinal position theoretically enhances resistance to persuasion, assuming that a commitment is freely made by the individual (Kiesler, 1971). McCaul et al. (1983) tested the resistance to persuasion hypothesis in a series of three experiments. In commitment conditions, small groups of seventh graders were asked to write speeches on "why you believe it is bad to smoke." The speeches were then audiotaped (or videotaped in one study), and adolescents stated their intention not to smoke in the future. Subjects were then presented with persuasive arguments about why smoking is OK. Unfortunately, commitment failed to produce differential effects in any of the three experiments on either resistance to persuasion or intent to smoke

compared with several control conditions. McCaul et al. (1983) speculated that the processes set into motion after a commitment is made by
adults may not be operative for adolescents.

Although there are potential problems with each of the commitment
studies reviewed, the existing evidence is negative. There are no data to
support the hypothesis that public commitment to nonsmoking reduces
intentions to smoke or actual smoking behavior. Hurd et al. (1980) hint
that the manipulation of commitment may heighten interest and participation, and commitment may also persuade students that the prevalence
of smoking among their peers is lower than they had expected (i.e., a
change in subjective norms). These possible effects of public commitment, however, are purely conjectural at this point.

Discussion

The preceding review leads to a straightforward conclusion: It is still
unclear what specific treatment components are responsible for reducing
adolescent smoking. Many ingenious programs have been developed, and
their results seem clearly superior to those of previous educational approaches, but we do not know why they work. So far, the evidence has
failed to support consistently any of the following plausible research hypotheses (many of which have been almost routinely adopted in prevention programs; see Ellis et al., 1980):

1. Information about the immediate physiological effects of smoking has
   greater impact than more traditional information about long-term health
   effects.
2. Peer leaders are more effective in altering social norms and reducing
   smoking among adolescents than adults or regular classroom teachers.
3. Behavioral rehearsal is more effective than classroom discussion (although there is some evidence to support this notion).

Investigators interested in future research on smoking prevention have
several design options. They may profitably utilize the multicomponent,
treatment/no-treatment designs reviewed here if careful measures of process variables and analyses addressing the relation between possible mediating variables and treatment outcome are included. The large-scale
studies that have taken this approach have the advantage of external
validity and sufficient sample sizes to conduct multivariate analyses and to
detect small changes in smoking behavior. However, this approach is
costly and often presents methodological difficulties – for example, the
problem of assigning schools rather than individuals to conditions.

Alternatively, investigators may perform small-scale experiments in which variables that purportedly mediate behavior change can be carefully assessed (Leventhal & Cleary, 1980; McCaul et al., 1983). Such designs might prove to be cost effective in that ineffective strategies could be discarded early and more promising components could be incorporated into broader-scale interventions. However, there is the possibility that prevention components work in concert and cannot be studied one at a time or that a program acts by changing the social climate of a whole school or community, an effect that could not be achieved in a small-scale experiment. Clearly, both types of research designs have limitations.

In this chapter we have attempted to progress beyond the question of whether some smoking prevention programs work, a question of internal validity, to the question of why beneficial effects are obtained, a question of construct validity. Construct validity is essential for theory testing and development, but it is equally important for generalization purposes. It is questionable whether program users (e.g., school districts or communities) can or will adopt a prevention program in its entirety – reproducing all of the intervention's components (Newman, 1981). But if it is clear how and why a program works, exact duplication is unnecessary, and different versions can be developed with the reasonable expectation that they will have similar effects. Finally, an understanding of construct validity may lead to more efficient programs. Ineffective components can be discarded and additional effort can be focused on intervention components that prove effective.

Efforts to prevent adolescent smoking have come a long way from earlier, didactic approaches, but the field is not yet on firm ground. Our present knowledge base is not adequate to recommend the adoption of any existing programs on a large scale. The sophistication of smoking prevention programs and evaluation procedures is growing, but there remains a clear need for further research.

Notes

1 This chapter is a revision of the article "Preventing Adolescent Smoking: What Have We Learned About Construct Validity?" which appeared originally in *Health Psychology*, 1985, *4*(4), 361–87.

2 Although most of the mediating variables shown in Figure 8.1 are included in the theory of reasoned action (Ajzen & Fishbein, 1980), the sequential nature of that theory is not represented here. For example, the theory hypothesizes that intentions mediate the link between attitudes and behavior, but we have merely included intention as one of several potential mediating variables.

References

Ajzen, I., & Fishbein, M. (1980). *Understanding attitudes and predicting social behavior.* Englewood Cliffs, NJ: Prentice-Hall.

Allegrante, J. P., O'Rourke, T. W., & Tuncalp, S. (1977). A multivariate analysis of selected psychosocial variables on the development of subsequent youth smoking behavior. *Journal of Drug Education, 7,* 237–48.

Arkin, R. M., Roemhild, H. F., Johnson, C. A., Luepker, R. V., & Murray, D. M. (1981). The Minnesota Smoking Prevention Program: A seventh-grade health curriculum supplement. *Journal of School Health, 51,* 611–16.

Biglan, A., & Ary, D. V. (1985). Current methodological issues in research on smoking prevention. In C. Bell & R. Battjes (Eds.), *Prevention research: Deterring drug abuse among children and adolescents* (NIDA Research Monograph, pp. 170–95). Washington, DC:U.S. Government Printing Office.

Botvin, G. J., Baker, E., Renick, N., Filazzola, A. D., & Botvin, E. M. (1984). A cognitive-behavioral approach to substance abuse prevention. *Addictive Behaviors, 9,* 137–48.

Botvin, G. J., & Eng, A. (1982). The efficacy of a multicomponent approach to the prevention of cigarette smoking. *Preventive Medicine, 11,* 199–211.

Botvin, G. J., Eng, A., & Williams, C. L. (1980). Preventing the onset of cigarette smoking through life skills training. *Preventive Medicine, 9,* 135–43.

Botvin, G. J., McAlister, A. (1981). Teenage cigarette smoking: Causes and prevention. In C. B. Arnold (Ed.), *Annual review of disease prevention.* New York: Springer-Verlag.

Botvin, G. J., Renick, N., & Baker, E. (1983). The effects of scheduling format and booster sessions on a broad-spectrum psychosocial approach to smoking prevention. *Journal of Behavioral Medicine, 6,* 359–79.

Botvin, G. J., & Wills, T. (1985). Smoking prevention: A social skills approach. In C. Bell & R. Battjes (Eds.), *Prevention research: Deterring drug abuse among children and adolescents* (NIDA Research Monograph, pp. 8–49). Washington, DC: U.S. Government Printing Office.

Coates, T. J., Perry, C., Killen, J., & Slinkard, L. A. (1981). Primary prevention of cardiovascular disease in children and adolescents. In C.K. Prokop & L. A. Bradley (Eds.), *Medical psychology: Contributions to behavioral medicine* (pp. 157–96). New York: Academic Press.

Coe, R. M., Crouse, E., Cohen, J. D., & Fisher, E. B., Jr. (1982). Patterns of change in adolescent smoking behavior and results of a one year follow-up of a smoking prevention program. *Journal of School Health, 52,* 348–53.

Ellis, B. H., Indyke, D., & Debevoise, N. M. (Eds.). (1980). *Smoking programs for youth* (National Cancer Institute). Washington, DC: U.S. Government Printing Office.

Evans, R. I. (1976). Smoking in children: Developing a social psychological strategy of deterrence. *Preventive Medicine, 5,* 122–7.

Evans, R. I., Hansen, W. B., & Mittlemark, M. B. (1977). Increasing the validity of self-reports of smoking behavior in children. *Journal of Applied Psychology, 62,* 521–3.

Evans, R.I., Henderson, A. H., Hill, P. C., & Raines, B. E. (1979). Current psychological, social, and educational programs in control and prevention of smoking: A critical methodological review. In A. M. Gotto & R. Paoletti (Eds.), *Atherosclerosis reviews* (pp. 203–245). New York: Raven.

Evans, R. I., Rozelle, R. M., Maxwell, S. E., Raines, B. E., Dill, C. A., Guthrie, T. J., Henderson, A. H., & Hill, P. C. (1981). Social modeling films to deter smoking in adolescents: Results of a three-year field investigation. *Journal of Applied Psychology, 66,* 399–414.

Evans, R. I., Rozelle, R. M., Mittelmark, M. B., Hansen, W. B., Bane, A. L., & Havis, J. (1978). Deterring the onset of smoking in children: Knowledge of immediate physiological effects and coping with peer pressure, media pressure, and parent modeling. *Journal of Applied Social Psychology, 8,* 126–35.

Evans, R. I., Smith, C. K., & Raines, B. E. (1984). Deterring cigarette smoking in adolescents: A psycho-social–behavioral analysis of an intervention strategy. In A. Baum, J. Singer, & S. Taylor (Eds.), *Social psychological aspects of health* (pp. 301–18). Hillsdale, NJ: Earlbaum.

Fishbein, M., & Ajzen, I. (1975). *Belief, attitude, intention and behavior: An introduction to theory and research.* Reading, MA: Addison-Wesley.

Fisher, E. B., Jr. (1980). Progress in reducing adolescent smoking. *American Journal of Public Health, 70,* 678–79.

Flay, B. R., d'Avernas, J. R., Best, J. A., Kersell, M. W., & Ryan, K. B. (1983). Cigarette smoking: Why young people do it and ways of preventing it. In P. J. McGrath & P. Firestone (Eds.), *Pediatric and adolescent behavioral medicine* (pp. 132–183). New York: Springer-Verlag.

Flay, B. R., Johnson, C. A., Hansen, W. B., & Grossman, L. M. (1982). *The USC/KABC-TV Smoking Prevention/Cessation Program: Preliminary short-term results* (HBRI Technical Publication Series). University of Southern California, Los Angeles.

Flay, B. R., Ryan, K. B., Best, J. A., Brown, K. S., Kersell, M. W., d'Avernas, J. R., & Zanna, M. P. (1985). Are social psychological smoking prevention programs effective? The Waterloo study. *Journal of Behavioral Medicine, 8,* 37–59.

Fodor, J. T., & Glass, L. H. (1971). Curriculum development and implementation of smoking research: A longitudinal study. *Journal of School Health, 41,* 199–202.

Glasgow, R. E., & Bernstein, D. A. (1981). Behavioral treatment of smoking behavior. In C. K. Prokop & L. A. Bradly (Eds.), *Medical psychology: Contributions to behavioral medicine.* New York: Academic Press.

Glasgow, R. E., McCaul, K. D., Freeborn, V. B., & O'Neill, H. K. (1981). Immediate and long term health consequences information in the prevention of adolescent smoking. *Behavior Therapist, 4,* 15–16.

Henderson, A. H. (1979). *Examination of a multivariate social-psychological model of adolescent smoking decisions and of the impact of antismoking messages.* Unpublished doctoral dissertation, University of Houston, Houston, TX.

Hill, P. C. (1979). *The impact of immediate physiological consequences versus long-term health consequences on the smoking beliefs, intentions, and behavior of adolescents.* Unpublished doctoral dissertation, University of Houston, Houston, TX.

Horn, D. (1960). Modifying smoking habits in high school students. *Children, 7,* 63–5.

Hurd, P. D., Johnson, C. A., Pechacek, T., Bast, L. P., Jacobs, D. R., & Luepker, R. V. (1980). Prevention of cigarette smoking in seventh grade students. *Journal of Behavioral Medicine, 3,* 15–28.

Iammarino, N., Heit, P., & Kaplan, R. (1980). School health curriculum projects: Long term effects on student cigarette smoking and behavior. *Health Education, 11,* 29–31.

Irwin, R. P., Creswell, W. Jr., & Stauffer, D. J. (1970). The effect of the teacher and three different classroom approaches on seventh grade students' knowledge, attitudes and beliefs about smoking. *Journal of School Health, 40,* 335–9.

Jason, L. A., Mollica, M., & Ferrone, L. (1982). Evaluating an early secondary smoking prevention intervention. *Preventive Medicine, 11,* 96–102.

Johnson, C. A. (1982a). Prevention in adolescence: Initiation and cessation. In *The Health consequences of smoking: Cancer 1982* (U.S. Dept. of Health and Human Services). Washington, DC: U.S. Government Printing Office.

Johnson, C. A. (1982b). Untested and erroneous assumptions underlying antismoking programs. In T. Coates, A. Peterson, & C. Perry (Eds.), *Promoting adolescent health: A dialog on research and practice* (pp. 149–165). New York: Academic Press.

Kiesler, C. A. (1971). *The psychology of commitment: Experiments linking behavior to beliefs.* New York: Academic Press.

Krosnick, J. A., & Judd, C. M. (1982). Transitions in social influence at adolescence: Who induces cigarette smoking? *Development Psychology, 18,* 359–68.

Leventhal, H., & Cleary, P. D. (1980). The smoking problem: A review of the research and theory in behavioral risk modification. *Psychological Bulletin, 88,* 370–405.

Leventhal, H., Meyer, D., & Nerenz, D. (1980). The common sense representation of illness danger. In S. Rachman (Ed.), *Contributions to medical psychology* (Vol. 2, pp. 7–30). Elmsford, NY: Pergamon.

Leventhal, H., Safer, M. A., & Panagis, D. M. (1983). The impact of communications on the self-regulation of health beliefs, decisions and behavior. *Health Education Quarterly, 10,* 3–29.

Luepker, R. V., Johnson, C. A., Murray, D. M., & Pechacek, T. F. (1983). Prevention of cigarette smoking: Three year follow-up of an education program for youth. *Journal of Behavioral Medicine, 6,* 53–62.

McAlister, A., Perry, C., Killen, J., Sinkard, L. A., & Maccoby, N. (1980). Pilot study of smoking, alcohol and drug abuse prevention. *American Journal of Public Health, 70,* 719–21.

McAlister, A. L., Perry, C., & Maccoby, N. (1979). Adolescent smoking: Onset and prevention. *Pediatrics, 63,* 650–8.

McCaul, K. D., Glasgow, R. E., O'Neill, H. K., Freeborn, V. B., & Rump, B. (1982). Predicting adolescent smoking. *Journal of School Health, 52,* 342–6.

McCaul, K. D., Glasgow, R. E., Schafer, L., & O'Neill, H. K. (1983). Commitment and the prevention of adolescent smoking. *Health Psychology, 2,* 353–65.

Michelson, L., & Wood, R. (1980). Behavioral assessment and training of children's social skills. In M. Hersen, R. M. Eisler, & P. M. Miller (Eds.), *Progress in behavior modification,* Vol. 9, pp. 241–92. New York: Academic Press.

Mittelmark, M. B. (1978). *Information on imminent versus long term health consequences: Impact on children's smoking behavior, intentions, and knowledge.* Unpublished doctoral dissertation, University of Houston, Houston TX.

Murray, D. M., Johnson, C. A., Luepker, R. V., Pechacek, T. F., Jacobs, D. R., & Hurd, P. D. (1979, September). *Social factors in the prevention of smoking in seventh grade students: A follow-up experience of 1 year.* Paper presented at the meeting of the American Psychological Association, New York.

National Institute of Education. (1979). *Teenage smoking: Immediate and longterm patterns (USDHEW, Contract No. 400-79-001). Washington, DC: U.S. Government Printing Office.*

Newman, I. M. (1981). School based education programs: Past progress, present problems, future potentials. In *National Conference on Smoking or Health: Developing a Blueprint for Action* (pp. 34–55). New York: American Cancer Society.

O'Neill, H. K., Glasgow, R. E., & McCaul, K. D. (1983). Component analysis in smoking prevention research: Effects of social consequences information. *Addictive Behaviors, 8,* 419–23.

Pechacek, T. F. (1979). Modification of smoking behavior. In *Smoking and health: A report of the Surgeon General* (U.S. Dept. of Health, Education and Welfare, Publication No. PHS 79-50066, pp. 19-1–19–63). Washington, DC: U.S. Government Printing Office.

Pechacek, T. F., & McAlister, A. L. (1980). Strategies for the modification of smoking behavior: Treatment and prevention. In J. M. Ferguson & C. B. Taylor (Eds.), *A comprehensive handbook of behavioral medicine. Extended applications and issues*, Vol. 3, pp. 257–98. New York: SP Medical and Scientific.

Perry, C. L., Killen, J., Slinkard, L. A., & McAlister, A. L. (1980). Peer teaching and smoking prevention among junior high students. *Adolescence, 15*, 277–81.

Perry, C. L., Maccoby, N., & McAlister, A. L. (1980). Adolescent smoking prevention: A third year follow-up. *World Smoking and Health, 5*, 40–5.

Safer, M. A., Tharpe, Q. J., Jackson, T. C., & Leventhal, H. (1979). Determinants of three stages of delay in seeking care at a medical clinic. *Medical Care, 17*, 11–27.

Schinke, S. P., & Blythe, B. J. (1981). Cognitive–behavioral prevention of children's smoking. *Child Behavior Therapy, 3*, 25–42.

Schinke, S. P., & Gilchrist, L. D. (1983). Primary prevention of tobacco smoking. *Journal of School Health, 53*, 416–19.

Schinke, S. P., & Gilchrist, L. D. (1984). Preventing cigarette smoking with youth. *Journal of Primary Prevention, 5*, 48–56.

Spitzzeri, A., & Jason, L. A. (1979). Prevention and treatment of smoking in school age children. *Journal of Drug Education 9*, 285–96.

Thompson, E. L. (1978). Smoking education programs 1960–1976. *American Journal of Public Health, 68*, 250–7.

Williams, T. M. (1971). *Summary and implications of review of literature related to adolescent smoking.* Report to USDHEW, Health Services and Mental Health Administration, Center for Disease Control, National Clearinghouse for Smoking and Health.

9   Natural hazards and precautionary behavior

Dennis S. Mileti and John H. Sorensen

Introduction

Efforts to determine how people deal with natural disaster began more than half a century ago. Researchers have examined a wide range of geological and climatological events, including hurricanes, earthquakes, tornadoes, tsunamis (tidal waves), and volcanoes. Early studies (e.g., Kutak, 1938; Prasad, 1935; Prince, 1920) focused on the responses of individuals and communities during and after a disaster, a type of natural hazards study that has become known as disaster research. Explanations of disaster responses have been based on theories of collective behavior and theories of social organization and disorganization (Dynes, 1970). Summaries of this research are available (Fritz, 1961, 1968; Mileti, Drabek, & Haas, 1975; Quarantelli & Dynces, 1977).

A second research tradition places emphasis on human precautions, actions taken to reduce the risk of future natural hazards rather than actions that are a response to an experienced disaster. Such "natural hazards research" began with work (White, 1945) that investigated why some precautions were taken more frequently than others and why losses seemed to be on the rise despite attempts to encourage protective actions (White, Burton, & Kates, 1958). A number of theorists have attempted to identify the mechanisms that lead people to take precautions (Burton, 1962; Kates, 1962; Simon, 1956; White, 1964).

The difference between disaster research and natural hazards research is mainly a matter of emphasis. In this chapter we seek to answer the question of what leads people to take precautions against natural hazards. Our focus, therefore, is on the mitigation of natural hazards risks, on preparedness for disaster, and on responses to warnings of impending disaster. The first and second topics draw the findings of natural hazards research, whereas information about the third topic comes from the disaster research field.

189

Consequences of Natural Disasters

If human precautions against natural hazards were totally successful, disaster would be avoided, but these measures are usually only partially effective. In fact, given the low probability of some types of natural disaster – a one-hundred-year flood or an earthquake powerful enough to devastate an entire city – complete protection is impractical. It is unjustifiable from a cost–benefit perspective. Society is not willing to relocate cities or bear the costs of building totally earthquake resistant structures. And no matter how prudent one's efforts to prepare for a natural disaster may be, there is no guarantee that they will be sufficient to protect one against the whims of the natural environment. Nevertheless, discovery of the basic mechanisms that shape precautionary behavior can help to make prevention strategies more cost effective and reduce the risk imposed by natural environmental extremes even though the risk can never be totally eliminated.

Both costs and benefits are produced when a disaster occurs. Costs can be assessed in many alternative ways, focusing on deaths, injuries, loss of property, monetary loss from the disruption of economic activities, social disruption, or psychic distress (White & Haas, 1975). These harmful effects generally appear to be short-lived. In fact, long-term effects of disaster have not been detected (Rossi, Wright, Wright, & Weber-Burdin, 1978). On a national level, average per capita losses from large-scale disasters are small because of the low probability of occurrence in any one year.

The costs of a natural disaster are borne unequally, even among those who experience the event. Some die, are injured, or are dislocated; many experience damage; and most are affected in other small ways (Bowden & Kates, 1974). Members of the lower class lose more in disasters than other segments of society because they frequently live in more hazardous structures (Cochran, 1975).

Understanding responses to natural hazards also requires an appreciation of the benefits people may receive. In fact, three kinds of benefits have been discerned (Sorensen & White, 1980): (a) benefits from the occupancy of hazardous zones, (b) direct benefits from a disaster, and (c) benefits from human response. The benefits from continuing to occupy a high risk zone may be substantial. The continued economic productivity of occupancy of the San Francisco peninsula, for example, far outweighs the costs of some future earthquake disaster in the minds of residents. Floods may provide direct benefits by irrigating parched agricultural lands and may be welcomed by farmers as a benefit rather than as a disaster. In addition, human responses during and after disasters typically increase social cohesion and ease preexisting conflicts between citizens (Fritz, 1961; Mileti et al., 1975). These responses facilitate the adoption of additional precautions to reduce future risk (Burton, Kates, & White, 1978; Haas, Kates, & Bowden, 1977) and yield other benefits.

Not only are the costs and benefits of disasters difficult to measure; each risk-mitigating policy that is adopted by a community and each action that is taken by a homeowner also has costs and benefits associated with it. The costs sometimes outweigh the benefits.

Examples of precautions taken to mitigate and prepare for natural disasters

People can take a variety of actions to prepare for a natural disaster (Mileti, Hutton, & Sorensen, 1981; White & Hass, 1975). Examples of measures that reduce the likelihood of experiencing harm include flood-proofing and earthquake reinforcement for houses, moving out of areas subject to landslides or mud flows, and evacuating in response to hurricane warnings. "Emergency preparedness," in contrast, refers to the ability to respond to an experienced disaster in ways that reduce the cost and the anguish of recovery. Actions that enhance emergency preparedness include purchasing insurance, stockpiling emergency supplies, and developing emergency response plans. The costs of taking such actions are incurred as soon as the precautions are adopted; the benefits will be experienced only if the low-probability event actually occurs.

Actions taken at a societal level have a greater potential for reducing losses and enhancing emergency preparedness than actions by individuals and families, since societal decisions affect so many people. For example, when the United States restricted development of flood plains through the National Flood Insurance Program, it kept many more families from being at risk than would have resulted from individual family decisions not to live in flood-prone areas. The most effective precautions, consequently, are not ones taken by individuals but those legislated or adopted by communities (e.g., emergency planning) and by nations (e.g., restricting the development of flood plains).

Determinants of precautionary action

Much research has sought to discover the factors that determine the adoption of precautions against natural disaster (see Cochran, 1975). Investigations have examined the full range of units of analysis, including individuals (Kates, 1978, 1971; Kunreuther, 1978; Saarinen, 1966; White, 1964; White et al., 1958), organizations (Anderson, 1969; Haas, 1970; Mileti et al., 1981), communities (Hutton & Mileti, 1979; Miller, Brinkmann, & Barry, 1974; Murton & Shimabukuro, 1974), and even whole societies (Anderson, 1968; Visvader & Burton, 1974; White, 1974).

This research has employed a variety of theoretical perspectives, including theories of organizations (Drabek, 1969; Hutton & Mileti, 1979; Lindbolm & Braybrooke, 1963; Mileti, 1975), decision-making theory and the bounded rationality model of humans (Kunreuther, 1978; Slovic, Kunreuther, & White, 1974; Simon, 1955, 1956), and symbolic interactionism, as well as combinations and integrations of different perspectives (Burton et al., 1978; Hutton & Mileti, 1979; White, 1974; White & Haas, 1975). Contributions have come from most of the social sciences, including geography (Burton et al., 1978; Kates, 1962; Sorensen & White, 1980), social psychology (Kunreuther, 1978; Sims & Bauman, 1972; Slovic et al., 1974), economics (Cochrane, 1975; Dacey & Kunreuther, 1969), and sociology (Anderson, 1969; Haas, 1970; Hutton & Mileti, 1979; Quarantelli & Dynes, 1977).

Despite differences in theoretical orientation, methods, type of precautionary behavior under study, unit of analysis, and type of natural disaster, research has produced relatively consistent conclusions. Strong evidence exists concerning (a) the basic process of adjusting to environmental extremes and (b) the key variables in the precaution adoption process.

The general precaution adoption process

The process that best describes how people adopt precautions against natural disasters has been described in a simple ideal type by Slovic et al. (1974). The process is composed of four steps in which people (a) assess the probabilities of a hazardous event, (b) review the behaviors available to mitigate risk, (c) evaluate the impacts of these behaviors in terms of their risk abatement potential and their consequences for other aspects of life, and (d) decide which precaution, if any, to adopt.

A number of factors may detract from the reasonableness of the outcomes of each stage: inaccurate estimates of risk, inadequate knowledge about the effectiveness of a precaution, errors in the processing of information, self-serving biases, and other factors. The variables of each step in the precaution adoption process are summarized in the next section. They comprise the existing state of knowledge and theory about the adoption of precautionary behaviors against natural disaster.

The emerging theory of precautionary behaviors

Research suggests that three categories of theoretical constructs play key roles in the adoption of protective actions: (a) risk perceptions, (b) characteristics of the people considering an action (e.g., their location in the social structure and the resources available to them), and (c) external incentives (e.g., those imposed by government). These three categories serve well to organize the research findings.

Perceptions of risk. The adoption of precautions against a natural hazard is dramatically influenced by what people believe about the risk associated with that hazard. Despite faults in human thinking about risk, the odds that people will take a precaution increase as a positive function of the amount of risk they perceive. The greater the potential damage expected, the more likely it is that people will act.

Risk perceptions are affected by a variety of factors. Tversky and Kahneman (1974), for example, demonstrated that most people have a difficult time thinking probabilistically. The probabilities of some natural disasters, however, are more easily estimated than others (Hewitt & Burton, 1971). People tend to overestimate small-frequency disasters and underestimate high-frequency events. Furthermore, people's perceptions of their personal risk have little relation to scientific evidence (Burton & Kates, 1964; White, 1964). For the most part, what scientists say about risk and what people think about risk are two different items.

Burton et al. (1978) provided evidence that beliefs about the cause of a natural disaster have a dramatic impact on the risk people perceive. Perceived causes included God, nature, technology, and government decisions (such as decisions about where people should and should not build homes). People who believe that an earthquake is God's will tend to discount risk. Experience with disaster usually enhances perceived risk (Burton et al., 1978; Mileti et al., 1975; White & Haas, 1975), but this effect diminishes as time passes. Thus, protective actions are usually adopted on a large scale shortly after a disaster, because risk perceptions are high (Danzig, Thayer, & Galanter, 1958; Mileti et al., 1975; White & Haas, 1975), but often they are discarded or ignored only a few years later.

Risk perceptions also differ according to whether or not society has done something about the risk. For example, people who live in a community that has a flood protection work, such as a dam, are likely to think that the risk from a flood that exceeds the protective capacity of the dam is low even if it is, in fact, substantial (White & Haas, 1975). Interestingly, the adoption of some precautions, by lowering perceived risk, can give people a false sense of security and constrain the adoption of other needed precautions. Mileti and colleagues (1981) illustrated this phenomenon with respect to earthquake hazard. They discovered that people with earthquake insurance refrain from adopting other earthquake precautions because insurance reduces their perceived potential loss.

Two other factors that affect risk perception, and consequently the adoption of protective actions, are the propensity of people to deny risk and people's access to information about risk. Residents of hazardous areas typically deny the risk of natural disasters by discounting the possibility that anything serious will ever happen to themselves or their possessions (Burton & Kates, 1964; Kunreuther, 1978; Mileti et al., 1975; White & Haas, 1975). In addition, perceptions of the magnitude of risk (and precautionary action) have been shown to become more realistic when people are given access to the best available scientific information (Burton & Kates, 1964; Kunreuther, 1978; National Academy of Sciences, 1978). The reason is straightforward. If people are told by scientists about risk over and over again, they will eventually stop ignoring or underestimating the risk.

In summary, behavior generally follows a rational cost–benefit decision-making model. However, it does so imperfectly, given people's reluctance to admit that they could be victims of a large-scale disaster.

Characteristics of people. Two characteristics have an important influence on the adoption of precautions. One is the capacity of an individual to assess the costs and benefits of taking a precaution in relation to social values and general personal goals (Clifford, 1956; Craik, 1970; Hutton & Mileti, 1979; Kunreuther, 1978; Luft, 1976; McCahill, 1974; Salisbury & Heinz, 1970; Smith, 1973; Sorensen & White, 1980; Stallings, 1971; Stea, 1970; van Meter & van Horn, 1975; White & Haas, 1975; Whyte, 1977). The second factor is the capacity to implement a precautionary measure. This is determined largely by an individual's place in the social structure (Dynes & Wenger; Fritz, 1961; Hutton & Mileti, 1979; Mileti, 1975; Moore, Bates, Layman, & Parenton, 1963; Quarantelli, 1965; Sjoberg, 1962; Speigel, 1957) and by the resources available (Burton et al., 1978; Dynes & Wenger, 1971; Fritz, 1961; Hutton & Mileti, 1979; Kates, 1977; Kennedy, 1970; Sjoberg, 1962; Sorensen & White, 1980).

Both societal values and the goals of individuals affect the adoption of precautions, because they influence the perception of the costs and benefits of precautions (Hutton & Mileti, 1979). Although the values of the individuals comtemplating action are the most germane (see Clifford, 1956; Kunreuther, 1978; Sorensen & White, 1980; Stallings, 1971; White & Haas, 1975), general social values may also be predictive. For example, the value most Americans place on self-reliance and individualism works against the adoption of community-level protective measures. Americans have a difficult time letting anyone tell them what they can and cannot do with their private property. Profit and monetary goals may work against a policy that might diminish property values in a high-risk zone.

Several types of resources facilitate the implementation of precautionary behaviors. First, communities that make intensive use of such resources as capital and labor like urban centers, are more likely to implement protection policies than areas without high resource utilization. Second, the amount of surplus capital available is positively related to action, so that financial constraints are less likely to be a problem for more affluent members of society (Burton, Kates, & White, 1978; Hutton & Mileti, 1979; Kates, 1977; Kennedy, 1970; Mileti et al., 1981; Sorensen & White, 1980).

To conclude, people take actions to mitigate risks if the actions do not contradict basic values and goals and if the costs are easy to bear.

Incentives. At larger levels of aggregation, such as state and national government, the perception of risk is greater than at the individual level. Few preventive measures would be enacted by individuals were it not for the policies and regulations established by these larger units. Among these governmental actions are the dissemination of information, the provision of incentives, the enforcement of regulations, and combinations of these. However, the effect of macro-level policies on the actions of individuals has been studied to only a limited extent. Illustrative studies of precautions related to the National Flood Insurance Program have been conducted by Hutton and Mileti (1979) and by Kunreuther (1978).

Protective actions in reponse to warnings of imminent danger

In the preceding discussion we looked at why people do or do not take protective actions against future natural disasters. In this section, we shall provide an interview of research findings on determinants of actions in response to warnings of likely and impending disaster. These findings stem from investigations of an action, like evacuation, that is performed as a result of warnings of an imminent hazard such as a flood, tornado, or tsunami.

The general warning response process

Reactions to warnings are not well represented by a simple stimulus–response model of human behavior. Rather, people make decisions in response to warnings, considering what actions, if any, should be taken. This warning–decision process can be described in terms of the following steps: (a) hear warning, (b) understand, (c) believe, (d) personalize, (e) decide, and (f) take action.

The first stage in the process is hearing that there is an emergency. This information may be received in the form of a public warning such as a siren or a publicly broadcast message. It cannot be assumed that all people will hear a broadcast public emergency warning. Even when the warning can be heard, people may fail to listen because of habituation (the siren has been used frequently in the past and they fail to notice it on this occasion) or selective perception (they hear only what they want to hear).

If it is heard, the emergency information must be understood. This means that the appropriate meaning must be attached to the message. For example, a flood warning may be understood as a wall of water by one person but as ankle-high runoff by another. Ashfall may be construed as a suffocating blanket or a light dusting. A 50% probability may be understood as almost certain by some and as unlikely by others. The meaning attached to a warning is related to people's knowledge and frame of reference. For example, it may be difficult for people to under-stand a tsunami warning if they do not know what tidal waves are like. Emergency information must attempt to provide the public with accurate understanding – in this broad sense of understanding – of the emergency situation.

Once the warning is understood, it is necessary for people to believe that the problem is real and that the contents of the message are accurate. Believability is influenced by the method of delivery, the content of the warning, the consistency of information, and the situation in which the warning is issued. If people believe the warning, they attempt to person-alize it, considering its implications for themselves and their social group, usually their family. If people do not think that the emergency informa-tion is applicable to them (the "it can't happen to me" syndrome) they are likely to ignore it. If they do believe that they are the intended targets of the warning (the "it must be me" syndrome), they are more likely to follow its recommendations. When emergency information does not in-clude a clear description of the location of the risk, for example, people frequently underrespond or overrespond.

When a person has heard the warning, come to an understanding of its meaning, believes the message, and believes that he or she will be personally affected, the individual must then decide what to do. Even if the warning message recommends a response, people will not necessarily follow the recommendation. People usually act on their decisions about which protective actions to take unless constraints prevent them from doing so (e.g., the lack of an automobile in which to evacuate a threatened area.)

This general warning response sequence is actually quite similar to the general precaution adoption sequence described in the preceding section. In both instances, people engage in a decision process and ultimately or do not take protective actions as a function of their perceptions about the risks and benefits of response alternatives.

Characteristics of effective warning messages

The key determinant of the actions taken by the public in response to an imminent disaster is the emergency warning message they receive. Ten message variables largely determine public response (Mileti, 1975; Mileti et al., 1975, 1981).

The first of these variables is the source of the emergency warning. Warnings must be credible to their audience (Mileti et al., 1981). Since people have different views about who is credible, warning messages should contain endorsements by scientists, organizations, and officials.

Second, a warning message should be consistent in both content and tone. Inconsistency creates uncertainty. In a study of the Rio Grande flood, Clifford (1956) found that inconsistent information caused confusion, making people less likely to understand or believe that a flood was going to occur. Fritz (1957) reached the same conclusion in a study of warning messages for a range of disasters. A message should be especially consistent in its discussion of the level of risk. For example, a message should not say that something bad is happening but there is no cause for concern. Rather, it should suggest *how* concerned people should be in light of the situation.

Third is the accuracy of what is said. A warning message must contain timely, accurate, and complete data. If people learn or suspect that they are not receiving the whole truth, they are likely to ignore instructions about how to respond and act in ways consistent with their own suspicions. Mileti et al. (1975) have suggested that errors in disaster warnings can cause people to disbelieve subsequent emergency messages.

Fourth is the clarity of the emergency information. A warning message must be worded clearly in simple language.

Fifth, a message should convey a high level of certainty about the events taking place and what people should do. Even in a low-probability or ambiguous situation, the message should be stated with certainty (even about the ambiguity). Certainty determines the level of belief in a warning and affects decision making. In a study of response to earthquake predictions, Mileti et al. (1981) found that warnings became more believable as the probabilities they contained became greater. If warnings are certain, people are more likely to take action.

Sixth, the message must contain sufficient information. Insufficient information creates confusion, uncertainty, and anxiety. Although the message must not overwhelm people with detail, it should not leave an information void that people will fill with misperceptions or fears. The amount of information provided affects the understanding, personalization, and decision-making phases of warning response. A study of family response to hurricane and flood warnings (Leik, Carter, & Clark, 1981) revealed that when warnings were general and vague, people did not take protective actions. In a study of response to the Mount St. Helens eruption (Perry & Greene, 1983) it was found that more detailed information led to higher levels of perceived risk and more protective actions taken by more people.

Seventh, a warning message should offer clear guidance as to what people should do and how much time they have in which to act. A study of the Big Thompson Canyon flood (Gruntfest, 1977) revealed that people who received warnings were not necessarily advised on what actions to take. As a consequence, many attempted to drive out of the canyon and were killed.

Eighth, the frequency of public messages should be stated so that people will know when they will hear the original message again or a new message (Mileti, 1975). Such information can reduce the anxiety of not knowing when one can confirm what is happening or learn more details. In addition, frequent messages can help to reduce misinformation and misperceptioins. Frequency affects many phases of the response process, including hearing, understanding, believing, and deciding. Numerous studies underscore the importance of repeated exposure to a warning.

Ninth is the specification of the location of the disaster. The warning should clearly state the areas that are affected or may be affected by the event. It must be clear to people whether or not the warning applies to them (personalization; Perry & Greene, 1983). Location information can also enhance believability. Diggory (1956) showed that the greater the proximity to a threatened area, the more likely it is that a message will be believed.

Finally, the use of more than one channel of information dissemination maximizes the number of people reached in a given period of time and facilitates the confirmation of warnings (Mileti, 1975).

Personal and situational factors that modify warning response

Good warning messages, ones with the attributes delineated in the preceding section, can help most people form accurate risk perceptions and take appropriate action. Often, however, warnings are not optimal, and personal characteristics can determine whether precautions are taken or ignored.

The factors that have been identified fall into eight categories. First, physical attributes of the emergency and the setting may be important. Visibility of the hazard is one such consideration. For example, it is difficult to get the public to believe a flood warning on a sunny day (Mileti, 1975). Such perceptual cues are significant aids to threat confirmation. When no cues exist, as in a radiation emergency at a nuclear power plant, it is important that an artificial stimulus disrupt the routine-appearing environment. Sirens can help accomplish this. Perceptual cues can affect believing, personalizing, and deciding. For example, people often wait to evacuate an area threatened by a hurricane until they see the weather change. Distance from the hazard is obviously important. At the Three Mile Island nuclear power plant, perceived physical distance from the hazard was a strong predictor of evacuation behavior.

Second, social-setting factors must be considered. These include whether a family is united when a warning is received (see Drabek & Stephenson, 1971; Drabek, 1969), what activities are being performed, and how others are responding. The social setting affects beliefs, decisions, and response. Mack and Baker (1961) reported that families united at the time of a warning are more likely to believe the warning message, and Drabek and Stephenson (1971) note that united families are more likely to take action. The importance of family unity has also been established in studies of the Three Mile Island accident. Almost 90% of the households behaved as family units, with all evacuating or all staying. Furthermore, Cutter and Barnes (1982) noted that some people at Three Mile Island evacuated because a neighbor had evacuated.

Third, social ties affect decisions to respond. Perry (1979) found that, as family cohesion increased, the likelihood of evacuating in response to a flood warning increased. Sorensen and Richardson (1983) found that knowing someone who worked for the utility that owned the power plant on Three Mile Island was associated with the decision not to evacuate during the reactor accident.

Fourth, social structural characteristics of the message receiver, including age, gender, resources, and socioeconomic class, can influence warning response. In a study of the Rapid City flood, Mileti (1975) found that older people were less likely than others to hear warnings regardless of their source. Sorensen and Richardson (1983) and other researchers found that older people were less likely than others to evacuate at Three Mile Island. Women are more likely to believe a warning than men, but the basis for this finding is not well understood.

Fifth, psychological characteristics of the listener, such as cognitive abilities, personality, and attitudes, can also influence perception. Limits on the ability to process information are a constraint for all people. Too much information makes it difficult to assimilate the information and reach a decision. The personality trait investigated most extensively in the context of warning response is locus of control. Simply stated, people with an "internal" locus of control believe that outcomes are determined by their own efforts; people with an "external" locus of control believe that their fate is determined by luck, the actions of others, or the will of God (Sims & Bauman, 1972). Several investigations have demonstrated that people with an internal locus of control are more likely to respond to a warning than are people with an external locus of control.

Sixth, prewarning attitudes affect hearing and decision making. People filter information to conform to their existing views (selective perception). If these views are biased and the warning message is not adequate to dispel these biases, people may disregard the message. For example, people who believed that a disastrous flood simply would not occur in their community would be less likely than others to respond to flood warnings.

Seventh, preemergency knowledge about a hazard or about relevant protective actions is a particularly interesting factor. Most scholars and officials are quick to assume that the dissemination of information through public education results in increased knowledge, which leads to actions that are more protective as well as more protective actions by more people when disaster warnings are issued (see Sorensen, 1983). Education, however, is not highly effective in enhancing public response to natural hazards (Baker, 1979; Burton et al., 1978; Mileti, 1975; Sorensen, 1983). Research on floods (Roder, 1961; Waterstone, 1978) shows that knowledge gained through public education increases awareness but does not influence protective action. In addition, people who have experienced a disaster respond to subsequent disaster warnings in ways that they wish they would have responded to previously experienced disaster warnings.

Eighth, and last, physiological characteristics of the persons receiving warnings can affect whether precautions are taken or ignored. For example, the deaf cannot hear sirens, and the physically impaired are less mobile than the healthy. To date, there has been little systematic research on this topic.

Cross-cutting issues: a consideration of selected factors

In the preceding pages we have attempted to provide an overview of what is known about why people take precautions against natural hazards, both during nondisaster periods and when warned of an impending disaster. In this concluding section we shall attempt to use this knowledge to formulate some answers to questions regarding the adoption and maintenance of protective actions against natural hazards.

Perceived risk, unit of analysis, and action

Most individuals regard natural hazards as low-probability events, and largely ignore them until disaster strikes. Although few people deny the possibility that a natural disaster, will eventually occur, few believe that they themselves will be affected or that disaster is sufficiently imminent to require the adoption of risk-reducing actions. Research in the United States and other nations, however, has revealed exceptions to this general rule. Individuals who experience natural disasters frequently (e.g., the Japanese and those who live along some American rivers) do adjust to the hazard. Thus, action is taken only when the risk is perceived to be high, a perception honed by repeated disaster experience. Even then, however, people are reluctant to adopt more costly measures, such as moving out of a flood plain.

As the unit of human aggregation becomes larger, the probability of harm increases from small values to total certainty. For example, at the national level, it is quite certain that losses to natural disasters will occur every year. Action by larger units, like the nation, is therefore more likely, but it is subject to political constraints. States and nations typically overcome these constraints primarily on the heels of major catastrophes.

Adoption of precautions: the effectiveness of public information and education

Individuals do take protective action against natural disasters in response to information, but generally they do so only when disaster is not far off and the probability is near certainty. Even in these circumstances, those responsible for issuing the warnings must labor hard to convince people that they are actually at risk and that they must act. The characteristics of an effective warning message have been reviewed in previous pages. To bring about large-scale public action in the absence of an impending disaster would require a huge public information campaign. An effort of this magnitude has never been attempted when a natural disaster has not been imminent. Public information campaigns to encourage the adoption of protective actions during nondisaster times have generally been ineffective. Research has shown that the general threat from a possible future hazard is easily discounted; a specific impending disaster cannot be ignored if the public information effort is sound.

Fear arousal is ineffective if not tied to a specific impending disaster. The limited evidence available suggests that fear arousal is a productive strategy when disaster is imminent. Positive incentives, such as those provided by the National Flood Insurance Program, enhance precautionary action, but experience suggests that the effects are more pronounced when the incentive is available to larger social units (e.g., communities) than when they are available to individuals.

Adoption of precautions: social pressure, social influence, and modeling

The extent of voluntary adoption of precautions depends largely on the degree of risk that is perceived. There is considerable evidence, however, that individual decisions are influenced by the behavior of other people such as neighbors. Kunreuther (1978), for example, found that a strong predictor of having earthquake insurance was having a neighbor with earthquake insurance. Though modeling influences behavior, most often its effect on preparedness is negative because precautions are not the norm and most of the people one would observe have not taken any action. However, research on reactions to warnings has repeatedly disclosed that people's decisions are shaped by their observations of what others are doing (see Mileti, 1975; Mileti et al., 1975, 1981). People are more likely to evacuate an area if their neighbors evacuate. However, the information that people receive in warning messages has a far greater influence than neighbors' actions on the adoption of protective action.

Modeling may operate at the state level if legislators believe that the risk in their own state is as high as that in a state that has adopted some hazard reduction policy. For example, Utah has followed the lead of California in seismic hazard reduction. Other states with earthquake risk, such as Missouri, have resisted efforts to model earthquake hazard policies on those of California.

Social pressure can operate in another way, when major disasters create political pressure to legislate risk-reducing policies. Intersystem incentives to adopt risk-mitigating measures (as when the national government offers incentives to local communities) can influence precautionary action. However, success is not likely if the incentive requires compliance.

Adoption of precautions: appeals to motives other than self-protection

Attempts to encourage the voluntary adoption of natural hazard precautions by reference to motives like well-being, by cost–benefit analysis, and by a focus on other possible future gains have accomplished little. The reason is straightforward. Few individuals, families, or small groups stand to benefit from risk-reducing actions. In a very real sense, most cost–benefit analyses would favor nonaction. The same is true from the perspective of major private-sector corporations. Only when the risk of future disaster cannot be discounted – largely because of the past frequency of losses – are appeals to well-being and financial savings successful, but only then because they address the obvious for their audience. Such appeals are also successful in the immediate aftermath of disaster.

Nevertheless, the National Flood Insurance Program has done much to increase the adoption of flood insurance by individuals. From a cost–benefit perspective the advantages of insurance are relatively clear: the federal government will not provide postdisaster aid to flood victims unless they have purchased insurance.

The maintenance of precautions

Once actions have been taken, maintaining them over time is often a major problem. Unless they are institutionalized – as in building codes – or unless additional disasters occur, interest in continuing precautionary behavior is low. Evidence suggests that it is helpful to make behaviors that result in risk mitigation part of the routine jobs of local community workers.

Key determinants of the adoption process for natural hazards

People protect themselves from natural hazards either when they perceive a need or when they are required to act by some element of the social system, as when actions are legislated. Few cases of government-mandated behavior exist, though the Alquist–Priolo Special Studies Act in California and the National Flood Insurance Program are two examples. Unless disasters occur frequently, people seldom act voluntarily, so efforts at the national, state, and community levels are essential to reduce losses from natural disasters.

References

Anderson, Jon. 1968. "Cultural Adaptation to Threatened Disaster." *Human Organization* 27:298–307.
Anderson, William A. 1969. "Disaster Warning and Communication Processes in Two Communities." *Journal of Communication* 19(2):92–104.
Baker, E. J. 1979. "Predicting Response to Hurricane Warnings." *Mass Emergencies 4*:9–24.
Bowden, M., and R. Kates. 1974. "The Coming San Francisco Earthquake: After the Disaster." In H. Cochrane, J. Eugene Haas, and R. Kates (eds.), *Social Science Perspectives on the Coming San Francisco Earthquake.* Boulder: University of Colorado, Institute of Behavioral Science, Natural Hazards Paper 25, pp. 62–81.
Burton, Ian. 1962. *Types of Agricultural Occupance of Flood Plains in the United States.* University of Chicago, Department of Geography, Research Paper 75.
Burton, Ian, and Robert Kates. 1964. "The Perception of Natural Hazards in Resource Management." *Natural Resources Journal 3*:412–41.
Burton, Ian, Robert Kates, and Gilbert White. 1978. *The Environment as Hazard.* New York: Oxford University Press.
Clifford, Roy. 1956. *The Rio Grande Flood: A Comparative Study of Border Communities.* Washington, D.C.: National Academy of Sciences, National Research Council.
Cochran, Anita. 1975. *A Selected Annotated Bibliography on Natural Hazards.* Boulder: University of Colorado, Institute of Behavioral Science, Natural Hazards Paper 22.
Cochrane, Harold. 1975. *Natural Hazards: Their Distributional Impacts.* Boulder: University of Colorado, Institute of Behavioral Science, Monograph 14.
Craik, K. 1970. "The Environmental Disposition of Environmental Decision Makers." *Annals of the American Academy of Political and Sociological Science* (May): 87–94.
Cutter, A., and Kent Barnes. 1982. "Evacuation Behavior and Three Mile Island." *Disasters 6*(1):116–24.
Dacey, D., and H. Kunreuther. 1969. *The Economics of Natural Disaster.* New York: Free Press.
Danzig, Eliott, Paul Thayer, and Lila Galanter. 1958. *The Effects of a Threatening Rumor on a Disaster-Stricken Community.* Washington, D.C.: National Academy of Sciences, National Research Council.

Diggory, James. 1956. "Some Consequences of Proximity to a Disaster Threat." *Sociometry* 19(March):47–53.

Drabek, Thomas. 1969. "Social Processes in Disaster: Family Evacuation." *Social Problems* 16(3):336–49.

Drabek, Thomas E., and John Stephenson. 1971. "When Disaster Strikes." *Journal of Applied Social Psychology* 1(2):187–203.

Dynes, Russell. 1970. *Organized Behavior in Disaster.* Lexington, Mass.: Heath.

Dynes, Russell, and Dennis Wenger. 1971. "Factors in the Community Perception of Water Resources." *Water Resources Bulletin* 7(August):644–51.

Fritz, Charles E. 1968. "Disasters." In *International Encyclopedia of the Social Sciences.* New York: Macmillan, pp. 202–7.

Fritz, Charles E. 1961. "Disaster." In Robert Merton and Robert Nisbet (eds.), *Contemporary Social Problems.* New York: Harcourt, Brace, Jovanovich, pp. 651–94.

Fritz, Charles E. 1957. "Disaster Compared in Six American Communities." *Human Organization* 16(Summer):6–9.

Gruntfest, Eve. 1977. *What People Did During the Big Thompson Flood.* Boulder: University of Colorado: Institute of Behavioral Science, Working Paper 32.

Haas, J. Eugene. 1970. "Lessons for Coping with Disaster." In Committee on the Alaska Earthquake of the National Research Council (ed.), *The Great Alaska Earthquake of 1964.* Washington, D.C.: National Academy of Sciences, pp. 39–51.

Haas, J., R. Kates, and M. Bowden (eds.). 1977. *Reconstruction Following Disaster.* Cambridge, Mass.: MIT Press.

Hewitt, K., and Ian Burton. 1971. *The Hazardousness of a Place.* Toronto: University of Toronto Press.

Hutton, Janice, and Dennis Mileti. 1979. *Analysis of Adoption and Implementation of Community Land Use Regulations for Floodplains.* San Francisco: Woodward-Clyde.

Kates, Robert. 1978. *Risk Assessment of Environmental Hazard.* New York: Wiley.

Kates, Robert. 1977. "Experiencing the Environment as Hazard." In S. Wapner, S. Cohen, and B. Kaplan (eds.), *Experiencing the Environment.* New York: Plenum, pp. 133–56.

Kates, Robert. 1971. "Natural Hazards in Human Ecological Perspective." *Economic Geography* 47:438–51.

Kates, Robert. 1962. *Hazard and Choice Perception in Flood Plain Management.* University of Chicago, Department of Geography, Research Paper 78.

Kennedy, Will C. 1970. "Police Departments: Organization and Tasks in Disaster." *American Behavioral Scientist* 13(3):354–61.

Kunreuther, Howard. 1978. *Disaster Insurance Protection: Public Policy Lessons.* New York: Wiley.

Kutak, Robert I. 1938. "The Sociology of Crises." *Social Forces* 17(2):66–72.

Leik, Robert, J. Michael Carter, and John P. Clark. 1981. *Community Response to Natural Hazard Warnings.* Minneapolis: University of Minnesota, Unpublished Report.

Lindbolm, Charles E., and David Braybrooke. 1963. *A Strategy of Decision.* New York: Free Press.

Luft, Harold. 1976. "Benefit Cost Analysis and Public Policy Implementation." *Public Policy (24)*:437–62.

Mack, Raymond, and George Baker. 1961. *The Occasion Instant.* Washington, D.C.: National Academy of Sciences, National Research Council.

McCahill, Edward. 1974. "Florida's Not So Quiet Revolution." *Planning* 40:10–14.

Mileti, Dennis S. 1975. *Natural Hazard Warning Systems in the United States.* Boulder: Institute of Behavioral Science, Monograph 13.

Mileti, Dennis, Janice Hutton, and John Sorensen. 1981. *Earthquake Prediction Response* and *Options for Public Policy*. Boulder: University of Colorado, Institute of Behavioral Science, Monograph No. 31.

Mileti, D., T. Drabek, and J. Haas. 1975. *Human Systems in Extreme Environments: A Sociological Perspective*. Boulder: University of Colorado, Institute of Behavioral Science, Monograph 2.

Miller, D. J., W. Brinkmann, and R. Barry. 1974. "Windstorms: A Case Study of Wind Hazard for Boulder, Colorado." In Gilbert White (ed.), *Natural Hazards: Local, National, Global*. New York: Oxford University Press, pp. 80–6.

Moore, Harry E., Frederick L. Bates, Marvin V. Layman, and Vernon J. Parenton. 1963. *Before the Wind: A Study of Response to Hurricane Carla*. Washington, D.C.: National Academy of Sciences, National Research Council.

Murton, Brian, and Shinzo Shimabukuro. 1974. "Human Adjustment to Volcanic Hazard in Puna District, Hawaii." In Gilbert White (ed.), *Natural Hazards: Local, National, Global*. New York: Oxford University Press, pp. 151–9.

National Academy of Sciences. 1978. *A Program of Studies on the Socioeconomic Effects of Earthquake Predictions*. Washington, D.C.: National Academy of Sciences, National Research Council.

Perry, Ronald. 1979. "Incentives for Evacuation in Natural Disaster." *Journal of the American Planning Association* 45(4):440–7.

Perry, Ronald, and Marjorie Green. 1983. *Citizens' Response to Volcanic Eruptions*. New York: Irvington.

Prasad, J. 1935. "The Psychology of Rumor." *British Journal of Psychology* 26(3):126–39.

Prince, Samuel H. 1920. *Catastrophe and Social Change*. New York: Columbia University, Unpublished Ph.D. dissertation.

Quarantelli, E. L. 1965. "Mass Behavior and Government Breakdown in Major Disaster." *Police Yearbook* 21:105–12.

Quarantelli, E. L., and Russell R. Dynes. 1977. "Response to Social Crisis and Disaster." *Annual Review of Sociology* 3:23–49.

Roder, Wolf. 1961. "Attitudes and Knowledge on the Topeka Flood Plain." In Gilbert White (ed.), *Papers on Flood Problems*. Chicago: Unviersity of Chicago, Department of Geography, Research Paper 70.

Rossi, Peter, James D. Wright, Sonia R. Wright, and Eleanor Weber-Burdin. 1978. "Are There Long Term Effects of American Natural Disasters?" *Mass Emergencies* 3:117–32.

Saarinen, Thomas F. 1966. *Perception of Drought Hazard on the Great Plains*. University of Chicago, Department of Geography, Research Paper 106.

Salisbury, R., and J. Heinz. 1970. "A Theory of Political Analysis and Some Preliminary Applications." In I. Sharkansky (ed.), *Policy Analysis in Political Science*. Chicago: Markham, pp. 39–60.

Simon, H. A. 1956. "Rational Choice and the Structure of the Environment." *Psychological Review* 63:129–38.

Simon, H. A. 1955. "A Behavioral Model of Rational Choice." *Quarterly Journal of Economics* 69(2):99–118.

Sims, J., and D. Bauman. 1972. "The Tornado Threat: Coping Styles of the North and South." *Science* 176:1386–92.

Sjoberg, Gideon. 1962. "Disasters and Social Change." In George Baker and Dwight Chapman (eds.), *Man and Society in Disaster*. New York: Basic Books, pp. 356–84.

Slovic, Paul, Howard Kunreuther, and Gilbert White. 1974. "Decision Processes, Rationality, and Adjustment to Natural Hazards." In G. White (ed.), *Natural Hazards: Local, National, Global*. New York: Oxford University Press, pp. 187–204.

Smith, Thomas B. 1973. "The Policy Implementation Process." *Policy Sciences* 4:197–209.

Sorensen, John H. 1983. "Knowing How to Behave Under the Threat of Disaster: Can it Be Explained?" *Environment and Behavior 15*(4):438–57.

Sorensen, John, and Brad Richardson. 1983. *Evacuation Behavior at TMI: Review and Reexamination.* Oak Ridge, Tenn. Oak Ridge National Laboratories.

Sorensen, John, and Gilbert F. White. 1980. "Natural Hazards: A Cross-Cultural Perspective." In I. Altman, A. Papaport, and J. Wohwill (eds.), *Human Behavior and the Environment.* New York: Plenum, pp. 279–318.

Spiegel, John. 1957. "The English Flood of 1953." *Human Organization 16*(Summer):3–5.

Stallings, Robert A. 1971. *A Comparative Study of Community as Crisis Management Systems.* Columbus: Ohio State University, Unpublished Ph.D. dissertation.

Stea, D. 1970. "From the Outside Looking In at the Inside Looking Out." *Environment and Behavior 2:*3–12.

Tversky, A., and D. Kahneman. 1974. "Judgement under Uncertainty: Heuristics and Biases." *Science 185:*1124–31.

van Meter, Donald, and Carl Horn. 1975. "The Policy Implementation Process." *Administration and Society 6:*445–88.

Visvader, Hazel, and Ian Burton. 1974. "Natural Hazards and Hazard Policy in Canada and the United States." In Gilbert White (ed.), *Natural Hazards: Local, National, Global.* New York: Oxford University Press, pp. 219–30.

Waterstone, M. 1978. *Hazard Mitigation Behavior of Urban Flood Plain Residents.* Boulder: University of Colorado, Institute of Behavioral Science, Monograph No. 30.

White, Gilbert F. (ed.) 1974. *Natural Hazards: Local, National, Global.* New York: Oxford University Press.

White, Gilbert F. 1964. *Choice of Adjustments to Floods.* University of Chicago, Department of Geography, Research Paper 93.

White, Gilbert F. 1945. *Human Adjustment to Floods.* University of Chicago, Department of Geography, Research Paper 29.

White, Gilbert F., Ian Burton, and Robert Kates. 1958. *Changes in Urban Occupancy of Flood Plains in the United States.* University of Chicago, Department of Geography, Research Paper 57.

White, Gilbert F., and J. Eugene Haas. 1975. *Assessment of Research on Natural Hazards.* Cambridge, Mass.: MIT Press.

Whyte, A. 1977. *Guidelines for Field Study in Environmental Perception.* Paris: UNESCO, MAB Technical Note 5.

10 Programs that encourage the adoption of precautions against natural hazards: review and evaluation

John H. Sorensen and Dennis S. Mileti

Introduction

Each year natural disasters take a significant toll of life and impart enormous costs to people in the United States. Virtually everyone is at some degree of risk from climatological or geophysical events, and certainly all help to pay for some of the damage these events inflict. Thus, it is in the interest of all to attempt to prevent losses and to support programs designed to reduce losses. Despite the inherent rationality of this statement people are, in general, reluctant to act until a nearby disaster stimulates their concern or they become victimized by disaster. Losses from natural disasters fluctuate but generally continue to rise. The potential for catastrophic events and losses has increased dramatically. As a result, numerous private and public programs have been developed to stimulate preparedness for disaster and to encourage the adoption of risk-reducing and protective actions.

One of the purposes of this chapter is to review attempts to encourage the adoption of actions that increase protection against natural hazards and disasters. In addition, examples of specific programs designed to influence human behavior and response to natural hazards are described.[1] Special attention is given to methods of providing the public with information and to some of the educational programs developed to do so. The chapter also reviews the rather limited attempts that have been made to evaluate the programs discussed here. It concludes with a discussion of the success and failure of these programs. To initiate this review, a brief discussion of concepts central to natural hazard research is needed.

Hazard preparedness: Some basic concepts

Definition of hazard

A critical distinction between social and physical science approaches to disaster protection is apparent in their definitions of a natural hazard. To

208

the physical scientist it is a geophysical process. To the social scientist it is a complex interaction between human and environmental systems. That is, such natural events as floods, earthquakes, and volcanoes are not hazards unless they interact with and affect human systems.

These different definitions have significant implications for loss reduction approaches. Viewing a hazard as a physical phenomenon has typically promoted attempts to engineer the problem away (e.g., build dams or levees to control floods, dig more wells to cope with drought, build sea walls to prevent wave damage) or to eliminate the event (seed hurricanes to dissipate energy, lubricate earthquake faults to generate releases of energy [White, 1945; White et al., 1958; Burton & Kates, 1964]).

As a reaction against the definition of hazard as a physical event, several researchers have offered a new way to view the problem. White (1945, 1961), for example, canvassed the range of actions people took to prevent or reduce flood losses. This was followed by conceptual and field work by Burton and Kates (1964), who sought to define a general model of human response to hazard. Kates (1962, 1971) developed an explicit ecological approach to understanding human response to hazard. Taken together, the thrust of this research was to identify the ways in which people could take protective actions to reduce losses from disaster. These actions were labeled "adjustments."

Hazard adjustment

Adjustments are defined as those actions that people both consciously and unwittingly take to cope with natural hazard. Burton, Kates, and White (1978) identify three general categories of adjustment. *Adaptations* are long-term changes that affect human ability to cope with hazard. *Incidental adjustments* affect the way one deals with and experiences loss from hazard, but are done without that intent. *Purposeful adjustments* are actions consciously performed to cope with hazard events. Table 10.1 illustrates a range of purposeful adjustments for the earthquake hazard. It is distinguishes between actions individuals can take and those society can take. In this chapter, adjustments are synonymous with self-protective behavior and preparedness.

Thus, Table 10.1 illustrates the wide range of behaviors that can protect people against earthquakes. Individuals can move away from hazardous areas, stockpile emergency supplies such as food and water, develop an emergency plan, invest in a hazardproofed house, build small engineering works to reduce hazard, buy insurance to compensate for loss, or self-insure. Such actions are taken before a disaster warning. Protective

Table 10.1. *Typology of adjustment for earthquakes*

	Adjustment category		
Change human systems	Reduce loss		Accept loss
1. Change location of activity *Individual adjustment* Relocate *Societal adjustment* Land-use planning or zoning Eminent domain 2. Change use of land *Individual adjustment* Adopt new functions *Societal adjustment* Land-use planning or zoning	1. Affect cause *Individual adjustment* No known way *Societal adjustment* Earthquake fault lubrication (experimental) 2. Modify event *Individual adjustment* No major way feasible *Societal adjustment* Prevent various earthquake effects (e.g., landslides), 3. Prevent loss *Individual Adjustment* Emergency plans Emergency supplies Earthquake-resistant design and construction Evacuation *Societal adjustment* Building codes Warnings and protection Major engineering works Emergency planning		1. Share loss *Individual adjustment* Insurance Seek relief *Societal adjustment* Disaster relief funds Loans Emergency services

Table 10.2. *Examples of adaptive and nonadaptive behavior*

Hazard	Increase survival and minimize loss	Decrease survival and maximize loss
Earthquake	Stand in door frame	Run out of building
Hurricane	Evacuate low-lying areas before storm	Have hurricane party
Flash flood	Climb up and out of canyon	Stay in house or climb onto roof
Tornado	Seek shelter in basement or protected structure	Attempt to drive to safer place
Avalanche	Evacuate perpendicular to flow	Attempt to outrun avalanche
Tsunami	Move to high ground	Go to the beach after first wave
Lightning storm	Seek low-lying area	Stand under tree

behavior, however, also includes knowing what to do when a hazard is about to occur.

Adaptive behavior

Adaptive behaviors (not to be confused with long-range adaptation) are defined as actions that will increase the probability of surviving or saving property from damage in the face of disaster. The definition itself implies uncertainty. There is no certainty that any of these behaviors will achieve what they are intended to achieve. Evacuation after the receipt of a warning may expose people to the risk of an auto accident or may lead them to areas of greater risks. For example, some people who evacuated the Big Thompson Canyon in Colorado after the issuance of a flood warning became fatalities when caught in their cars by the rapidly rising waters. Likewise, following tornado warnings in Wichita Falls, Kansas, people attempting to leave a shopping mall for safer locations were caught unprotected. Table 10.2 provides examples of potential behaviors in various disasters. Some actions are adaptive, and others increase the likelihood of harm. A chief goal of protective action programs is to increase the incidence of adaptive behaviors following a warning of impending disaster.

Approaches to encouraging protective behavior

Given the inherent limitations of human decision making and the gaps between knowledge, adoption, and implementation, how does one convince the public to prepare for and react adaptively to disaster? To address this question, it is necessary to examine the approaches that can be used to affect human behavior.

Mechanisms for affecting behavior

Extensive literatures exist on how human behavior can be guided, manipulated, changed, or somehow affected. Several attempts have been made to classify such strategies. For example, Dahl and Lindblom (1953) discuss a tripartite set of strategies governments can adopt to influence the behavior of their constituents. Moral power is providing information to influence behavior. Economic power is providing incentives or penalties to influence choice through market intervention. Regulatory power is compelling people to behave in conformity with some set of guides. Burton et al. (1978) present four types of interventions designed to effect the adoption of hazard adjustment. These are preemption, mandates, influences, and facilitation. Precise definitions are not offered, but examples are provided. Preemption includes forceful transfer of property rights. Mandates include building codes or regulations. Influences include subsidies or political pressure. Facilitation includes the dissemination of information or advice.

Within each category identified by these two models, further differentiation is possible. There are a variety of regulatory approaches (Baram, 1982), economic or noneconomic incentives (Carnes et al., 1983; Sorensen, Soderstrom, & Carnes, 1984), and types of information (Whyte, 1977; Rodgers, 1983).

To expand on these efforts, a typology of influences is presented here. This typology defines the following guides to behavior:

1. Regulatory mandate and enforcement. Public laws, orders, and regulations mandate certain behaviors.
2. Enforcement. Behavior is changed through legal actions.
3. Economic sanctions. Penalties are imposed for incorrect behavior.
4. Economic incentives. Behavior is rewarded and reinforced through various incentives.
5. Information and persuasion. Behavior is influenced through education or information.

It should be recognized that these strategies are not mutually exclusive. Information is necessary to describe incentives; regulations establish information programs; legal actions enforce regulations; sanctions come about due to the enforcement of regulations. Nevertheless, the typology provides a useful framework for understanding attempts to influence protective behavior.

Sample programs

Table 10.3 classifies some existing programs as to the approach used to influence behavior and the types of protective action involved. The categorization of protective action is based on the examples in Table 10.1 and is believed to encompass all major programs.

If Table 10.3 is comprehensive, it should reveal some patterns in the methods of influencing the public to adopt hazard adjustments. The major mechanism by which action is encouraged is the dissemination of information. Virtually every hazard adjustment has been promoted by some informational or educational program. This, in part, reflects the assumption that behavior can be influenced by indirect social intervention. More direct means, such as economic sanctions or incentives, have been applied less frequently, reflecting general inexperience with the use of such factors to influence behavior. Regulatory experience is somewhat greater. Though few in number, certain regulations such as building codes have had widespread impacts on hazard protection. Though not widespread, enforcement mechanisms are beginning to be exploited as means of achieving hazard protection.

The patterns of Table 10.3 reflect other forces that shape social program development and implementation in general. First, there is a general reluctance to allocate large sums of money to protective action programs and policies; rather, quick, low-cost methods are favored. Second, programs that are complex to administer and implement are generally avoided. Third, public agencies are often reluctant to intervene in the affairs of people or impose inconveniences on the public. As a result, complex programs such as the National Flood Insurance Program (NFIP) are rare.

Program descriptions

Using the classification developed in the previous section, we can now discuss programs designed to promote the adoption of protective actions. The purpose is not to inventory all existing efforts but to show how some concepts of affecting behavioral change have been implemented. Table 10.4 lists programs designed to influence individual-level action. Some

Table 10.3. *Existing and potential measures to encourage family-level protective actions for natural hazards*

Measure	Engineering or structural adjustments	Preparedness plans and emergency supplies	Insurance	Locational choice
Regulatory mandates	Building codes (standard), floodproofing requirements	Legislation requiring home plan and emergency supplies (hypothetical)	Lending requirements	Land-use regulation (floods), seismic safety elements, coastal setbacks
Enforcement	FEMA suit against Louisiana parishes that failed to adopt various flood plain adjustments	Probably not feasible	Condemnation of damaged building (floods)	Monitoring of new building activity (hypothetical)
Economic sanctions	Fines for subcode buildings in hazard areas (hypothetical)	Probably not feasible	Withholding of federal aid for nonparticipation in flood insurance, denial of mortgages	Penalties for building in hazardous areas (hypothetical)
Economic incentives	Local cost sharing for drainage projects	Insurance rebates for having a plan (hypothetical)	Subsidized insurance	Relocation after property purchase
Information programs	Various information programs for earthquakes; exist for many hazards	Preparedness programs	Flood hazard information brochures	Alquist–Priolo Act, disclosure in California

Table 10.4. *Examples of protective action programs*

Regulatory mandates
    San Francisco ordinance prohibits construction of parapets and requires that existing ones
      be removed
    Building codes require floodproofing of new construction in flood plains (NFIP)
    California law requires communities to develop seismic safety elements for planning and
      regulating development in hazardous areas

Enforcement actions
    Reconstruction is prohibited after floods if structure is more than 50% damaged
    Eminent domain is used to acquire flood plain land for use as a park
    Unsafe unreinforced masonry buildings are condemned because of lack of earthquake
      safety

Sanctions
    Flood relief is withheld from communities not participating in the NFIP

Incentives
    Federal flood insurance subsidized premiums
    Private insurance rate reductions for safety equipment
    NFIP purchases homes for relocation out of the flood plain

Influences
    NOAA Public Information Program to increase hurricane, tornado, and flood awareness
    NOAA Schools Program to develop hazard curriculum
    Texas Marine Council Awareness Program to increase hurricane awareness
    California Earthquake Education Act mandates development of an awareness and educa-
      tion program
    FEMA Earthquake Awareness Programs in Memphis, Charleston, to alert public to risk
    Southern California Earthquake Preparedness Project to develop comprehensive program
    Alquist–Priolo Act: earthquake information disclosure to purchasers of homes

---

directly influence the individual, whereas others seek to work through existing social and political institutions.

National Flood Insurance Program. The NFIP uses three approaches to stimulate protective action against flood damage. First, it employs sanctions to stimulate community participation. Under the NFIP, no federally guaranteed loans can be provided for properties in a flood hazard area unless that area is in the program. In addition, federal disaster assistance for restoration in a flood-damaged community is denied if the community has not participated in the program. Assistance can be withheld if a community fails to implement the land-use regulations necessary for participation.

Second, the NFIP produces incentives to participate. Initially, highly subsidized insurance is provided to flood plain residents. As more precise information becomes available, premiums are raised to reflect more closely the actuarial rate. In addition, the NFIP provides funds to communities for the acquisition of flood plain property and land.

Third, the NFIP provides information to encourage protective adjustments. Federal Emergency Management Agency (FEMA) regional offices work with communities to adopt and implement the program. Each state develops information brochures to promote the purchase of insurance. Under the NFIP, detailed maps are prepared to outline the extent of various risks of flooding. Attempts to inform the public about insurance vary among communities and states.

FEMA legal action. In 1981, FEMA filed lawsuits against two parishes in Louisiana that were participants in the NFIP. The suits alleged negligence by the government of St. Bernard and Jefferson parishes and by builders, developers, and consultants in allowing improper flood plain development. As a result, the government paid $93 million in flood insurance claims in 1978 and 1979. Specifically, FEMA maintained that the defendants (a) failed to enforce elevation requirements, (b) failed to enforce floodproofing requirements, (c) failed to develop adequate drainage systems, and (d) allowed development without provisions for flood water control or retention. The suit also requested court-ordered actions to improve flood mitigation by improving canals, ditches, and culverts and adopting measures to reduce flooding and stop flood plain development.

Flood plain land acquisition. Several federal programs provide funding to local governments for the relocation of vulnerable structures or the acquisition of flood plain land and property. For example, after extensive flooding on the Red River, the community of East Grand Forks, Minnesota, used money from a Department of Housing and Urban Development (HUD) discretionary grant to acquire flood-damaged property and assist occupants in relocating.

Section 1362 of the NFIP authorizes funds for the purchase of properties damaged by floods when they incur damages on three occasions in a five-year period. For example, residents of the River Oaks subdivision in Clay County, North Dakota, received flood insurance claim payments of $75,000, $304,000, and $375,000 from three successive floods. After denial of the HUD funds, the county used Section 1362 to purchase housing for River Oaks residents.

Southern California Earthquake Preparedness Project (SCEPP). SCEPP is one of the few comprehensive regional programs designed to encourage multiple-method protective planning and response. It pursues the following functions:

1. The development of prototype preparedness plans
2. The coordination of existing preparedness activities
3. Assistance in developing an earthquake prediction and warning system
4. The development of earthquake awareness and educational programs

SCEPP was funded by the California State Legislature and FEMA for an initial $11.5 million. Its goal is to accelerate preparedness planning in both the private and public sectors before a damaging earthquake occurs in southern California.

This effort has recently been expanded to the northern California–San Francisco Bay area. In addition, as part of the National Earthquake Hazards Reduction Act, the approach will be implemented in many more seismically hazardous areas throughout the United States, including the Puget Sound area, Missouri, and Massachusetts.

Alquist–Priolo act. Under a 1975 revision of the 1972 Geologic and Hazard Acts, California law requires disclosure of earthquake hazards to prospective buyers. If property is located in a "special study zone," sellers or their agents must inform persons of a potential earthquake hazard before final closing. The disclosure, however, is implemented just before final closing and has little effect on purchase decisions. Several evaluations of the requirement have been made (Palm, 1981).

California earthquake education. In 1981 California passed the California Earthquake Education Act (SB843). This legislation provides funds for developing public and school education programs about earthquake preparedness and response. After the development of curriculums and programs, they will be tested in selected schools and communities.

These educational programs are currently being developed at the University of California, Berkeley, Lawrence Hall of Science. A model junior-high-level curriculum involves three major activities: (a) an earthquake-preparedness scavenger hunt at home, (b) a coloring book of home hazards, and (c) lesson plans for teachers on the science of earthquakes, damage, individual protection, and preparedness.

FEMA earthquake awareness. In 1983 FEMA initiated a comprehensive earthquake hazard education program. The purpose is to enhance the public's understanding of earthquakes and teach people how to reduce their vulnerability. The program will develop such educational materials as brochures, maps, homeowner handbooks, and press releases. It will also develop curriculum packages and aids to teachers. The curriculum is being pilot-tested in Seattle, Washington.

In addition, earthquake awareness centers are being developed in Memphis, Tennessee, and in Charleston, South Carolina. These centers are to develop libraries, recruit speakers, train outreach volunteers, and stimulate local interest in preparedness.

National Oceanographic and Atmospheric Administration (NOAA) programs. The NOAA has several programs geared toward encouraging protective action. Its central approach is through programs that provide general information for the public, educational materials for classroom use, and factual accounts of previous disasters. These cover a variety of media; brochures are the most popular, but films, maps, workbooks, radio and television spots, and slides are also provided. Regulska (1982) prepared an extensive documentation of these efforts, some of which have been developed in conjunction with other agencies. The NOAA (1983) also publishes a list of its information resources.

Texas Coastal and Marine Council. At the state level, the Texas Coastal and Marine Council has mounted a major effort to educate the public about hurricanes and other coastal hazards (Davenport, 1978; Davenport & Waterstone, 1979). The council has combined the use of brochures, maps, atlases, information kits, radio and television spots, public displays, and media reports to elevate hazard awareness. Their work is closely coordinated with that of NOAA. It is a model for multimedia and multiple-approach educational efforts that systematically apply behavioral science principles to program design. The program emphasizes two-way communication, participation of users, and continued evaluation and feedback mechanisms.

Seismic safety elements. Since 1971 the state of California has required each city and county to include a seismic safety element in general land-use plans. The intent of the requirement is to obtain sound decisions regarding the development of hazardous areas. The element requires an identification and appraisal of seismic hazards including surface rupture from faulting, ground shaking, ground failures, tsunami, mudslide, landslide, and slope stability.

Local governments vary in the way they implement this requirement. Although it is not specified by legislation, many governments have used the seismic safety element as a basis for developing and implementing zoning or setback codes. Some communities have used overlay or grid-type information systems to develop indexes of development suitability. Others have made few attempts to use the hazard information for decision making.

Program directions

The 10 programs described in the preceding section illustrate the variety of approaches to encouraging self-protective behavior before natural disasters strike. The programs range from attempts to force compliance with standards designed to protect property and lives, to the use of either the carrots or the stick to modify behavior, to the provision of information that is hoped to influence behavior.

Many programs are based on the optimistic assumption that, if provided with information, people will make good judgments and decisions about protective actions. But this optimism has been met by growing doubts as the toll inflicted by disasters continues to rise. In some more recent programs, information is augmented by inducement or threat. The success of these approaches, however, is largely unevaluated. Attempts to influence behavior are reinforced by mandates to live outside high-risk areas, to build in a risk-resistance manner, or to insure against loss. Finally, when all else fails, the courts are called on to achieve compliance with normative views of safety. Efforts to provide better education and information are also proceeding in the hope that more rigid solutions to ensuring safety will not be needed.

Providing information to encourage protective action

Many emergency preparedness programs assume that the public is unaware of hazards, their consequences, and actions that can be taken to reduce losses. As a result, many hazard reduction programs include a public education or information provision component. The underlying assumption of this practice is that, with a higher level of awareness, people will seek more information and will engage in more appropriate behaviors before and during a disaster. Over time, it is concluded, losses from hazards and their impact on society will be reduced. As a result of these beliefs, hazard awareness programs, education, and information dissemination have become well-accepted elements of any comprehensive natural hazard management scheme.

Regulska (1982) reviews many of the programs developed to increase hazard awareness. It appears that little thought beyond some general principals of education and information dissemination has been devoted to such programs. This section of the chapter attempts to sort out some of the underlying philosophies of or conceptual approaches to the dissemination of information about natural hazards. The discussion builds on the descriptions of information programs in the preceding section, but rather than describe programs, it seeks to analyze, in a qualitative fashion, some of the characteristics of programs. In doing so, it builds on the review of educational efforts by Sims and Baumann (1983), the research of Sorensen (1983), and Saarinen's (1982) review of relevant literature.

Nine basic strategies can be identified. Many programs or publications involve several of these, although often one dominates the others. The approaches include the following:

1. *Practical instructions.* This represents one of the most popular means of encouraging protective action. It is based on the assumption that people are unaware of what they can do to prepare for a disaster and that preparation involves minimal effort. For example, one brochure evaluated contains straightforward instructions concerning emergency preparedness and precautionary reactions for storm and flood waters, about water purification, and related matters. Although the materials appear to be common-sensical, they provide the information necessary to prepare for the interruption of normal services.

2. *Scientific information.* Information is provided to the public on the assumption that people who are ignorant of a potential hazard should know something about the physical mechanism that may cause the disaster and, upon learning, will be stimulated to take appropriate actions. It differs from the previous category by focusing on the risks rather than the response. This philosophy pervades most of the earth-science-dominated programs. For example, many brochures promoting the NFIP rely on maps depicting the extent of the floodway, 100-year flood plain, and/or standard project flood plain to convey risk information to the public. Similarly, underlying earthquake hazard information programs is the belief that it is desirable to inform people of the theory of plate tectonics as a cause of earthquakes in their area.

3. *Educational model.* Quite different from the previous approach, educational models seek to reduce information to an extremely simplistic format without much scientific detail or explanation. Techniques for teaching basic science concepts to elementary school children are used to inform the public of the risks of nature hazards. Clever or cute techniques may be used to generate attention. For example, NOAA uses a cartoon-like character named Owlie Skywarn to tell children about various hazards and how to prepare for them. It is unclear, however, whether the information is really targeted for children or for adults.

4. *Persuasive (norm-oriented) communications.* Information is disseminated in order to modify behavior so that it conforms to a predetermined notion of socially acceptable or necessary behavior. Though this approach is not common, it emphasizes the need for altruism and support for the community after a disaster, even at personal sacrifice.

5. *Modeling.* People with whom the public identifies or who are widely admired serve as models of appropriate protective behavior. It is assumed that people will imitate or be persuaded by these models. Although this strategy is not widely employed, it is not difficult to imagine a well-known actor demonstrating earthquake-resistant building practices or purchasing earthquake insurance. The potential of this strategy remains largely unexploited.

6. *Attribute portrayal.* Selected attributes or key characteristics of a practice are highlighted. Frequently used in Madison Avenue–type advertisement, the approach seeks to sell an audience about a feature of the desired product or practice. For example, to encourage the purchase of flood insurance, information brochures highlight its low cost and subsidized premium and the ease with which it is obtained.

7. *Fear arousal.* This strategy is not commonly used by itself, but it may enter into a general information program. It is natural to capitalize on the desire to avoid the danger and losses caused by natural disasters. For example,, a menacing storm is labeled "a killer from the skies" on a weather poster. This attracts the observer's attention to the more informational aspects of the poster. Presentations by NOAA on hurricanes involve before and after shots of buildings destroyed by storm surge and wind. Pictures of losses from disasters are common in many informational publications. Such strategies prevail despite checkered record of fear arousal in prompting protective behavior.

8. *Prompts.* Repetitive exposure to recommendations may elicit desirable behavior. A prime example is the sign program for flash floods in Colorado canyons. These signs, positioned along roads going through canyons, instruct people to climb the canyon walls instead of drive out when flooding occurs. The program is based on a study of evacuation behavior in the 1977 Big Thompson Canyon flood, in which it was shown that climbing was an extremely prudent action (Gruntfest, 1978). To date, the use of prompts in promoting hazard adjustment has been minimal, but research suggests it is a strategy worthy of pursuit.

9. *Learning through participation.* This strategy adheres to the logic of the statement "Doing is learning." Although they do not have broad exposure, several programs exist to educate the public through participation in a hazard mitigation effort. For example, a Girl Scout program in Santa Clara, California, implemented a Quake-Safe Program, in which scouts earned badges by adopting various hazard adjustments such as developing family emergency plans, stockpiling emergency supplies, and learning first aid. Development of the program was assisted by the U.S. Geological Survey, the Red Cross, and local emergency planning personnel.

Evaluating protective action programs

Methodological issues

Despite reasonable theories concerning information, incentives, penalties, decision making, and human behavior, we cannot always predict how the public will respond to mitigation programs. Consequently, empirical evaluations are particularly important. Yet the methodological problems are severe. It is difficult to evaluate information programs and clearly identify the specific causes of observed behavior changes. It is difficult to isolate the effects of a program from other possible influences not related to the program, and it is difficult to attribute effects to one part of a program rather than another.

To illustrate, consider a brochure encouraging flood plain residents to purchase flood insurance and develop a household contingency plan. To estimate its effectiveness, a sample of 100 households that receive the brochure are compared with 100 households not given the brochure. Six months later, members of those households are interviewed to determine their response to the brochure. Let us assume that 25% of the group that received the brochure purchased flood insurance and developed a plan but that only 2% of the noninformed control group did likewise. Still, we cannot conclude that the brochure is responsible for the behavioral changes. For example, the brochure may have been only one of several pieces of information on floods received during the intervening period. It is possible that those who acted did so only because of the combination of information they received. The brochure may have only initiated discussions about the protective actions, so that adoption was actually part of a more complex process in which interactions with previous adopters, such as friends or relatives, were crucial. Finally, public announcements about the brochures by trusted authorities may have been more persuasive than the brochures themselves.

Previous research and evaluations

Due partly to such methodological difficulties as well as to budgetary constraints, few formal program evaluations have been conducted to measure program implementation and effectiveness. As a result we have a very small empirical foundation on which to base the conceptualization, design, and implementation of new programs and the revision of existing ones. In this section most major efforts to evaluate programs that have been conducted to date are discussed. A distinction is made between information programs and other types of protective action programs.

Information programs. Palm (1981) evaluated the effects of the 1977 Alquist–Priolo Act disclosure requirement to determine whether the presence of special zones delineating areas of high earthquake risk and the mandatory disclosure of this information to home buyers affected people's adoption of earthquake mitigation measures or had an effect on house prices. Three groups of recent home buyers were surveyed, real estate agents were interviewed, and hedonic price indexes were analyzed. The homeowners included a group within the special zones, a group near the zones, and a subgroup of the first group who were particularly knowledgeable about the zones.

The results indicated that the disclosure had little impact on buyers or on housing prices. Few purchasers indicated that earthquake risk disclosure played a role in their decision to purchase. Many were not aware of the high-risk zones even if they resided within them. There was no difference in the adoption of protective actions among groups. Furthermore, prices had not been negatively affected by the disclosure.

The study has several shortcomings, however. First, any people who were affected by the disclosure and chose to locate away from earthquake risk were not identified and included in the study. This makes it impossible to infer that the program has had no impact. Second, the study is vulnerable to possible response bias. People may have downplayed the role of the hazard disclosure process in order to avoid admitting a poor decision. Furthermore, since the disclosure is made at the time of closing, the motivation to ignore new information when a decision has been made may be particularly strong, but the same information might have a much greater impact if provided earlier. Despite such issues, the research suggests that some changes in the program are probably needed.

Ruch and Christensen (1980) attempted to assess the effectiveness of a hurricane awareness program. Their findings were based on interviews with a randomly selected group of 381 households in Galveston, Texas. Three methods of information dissemination were involved: a checklist and map brochure, five-minute radio spots, and television ads and feature programs. The subjects were divided into four groups: one with no recall and three others, each composed of individuals remembering only one of the program elements.

The results suggest that the brochure increased knowledge but decreased perceptions of risk. Television had no significant effects. Radio slightly decreased risk perceptions. The results suggest that written information is more effective than electronic media in education but that all may have counterproductive impacts. Nevertheless, the questionable equating of program recall with program exposure seriously undermines our confidence in these conclusions.

Waterstone (1978) conducted a study of the hazard mitigation behavior of flood plain residents in Denver, Colorado. A major goal was to assess the effectiveness of an informational brochure among three groups of subjects from two areas similar in risk. Group 1 had received the brochure twice before the interview. Group 2 had not yet received the brochure. Group 3, from the same area as Group 2, had recently received the brochure.

Telephone surveys of 249 residents were conducted to ascertain the effectiveness of the brochure as well as to measure other variables postulated to affect protective behavior. The results indicated that people who remembered receiving the brochure were more knowledgeable about floods and were more concerned about flooding than those who had not. Furthermore, the brochure seemed to have increased their awareness of and interest in flood problems and encouraged the adoption of family contingency plans. Since people who remembered the brochure were more likely to have been concerned initially, conclusions about brochure effects based on brochure recall are questionable.

Haas and Trainer (1974) attempted to evaluate the effectiveness of a tsunami hazard public education effort in four Alaskan communities. Three education programs were implemented and one community was utilized as a control. The programs involved mass media, a mail-out brochure, or personal contact. Pre- and postquestionnaires were employed to measure various perceptions and knowledge about tsunamis and emergency response. The post-test, conducted four and a half months after the completion of the educational efforts, showed minimal effects. No significant changes were observed in what people knew about tsunamis, how reliable they felt the warning system was, or how they intended to act in response to a warning. The mass media and personal contact approaches did elevate perception of the severity of the local tsunami threat.

Baumann (1983) described a project designed to identify cost-effective programs. Three programs were offered to the public, each differing in the amount of information conveyed. Among those evaluated were four groups of people selected from flood-prone areas in the three program communities, as well as a control group. The communities were matched according to demographic characteristics and flood risks and subjects were randomly chosen.

The results indicated that the information programs elevated awareness of flood problems. Furthermore, program groups reported performing more activities to reduce flood losses than did the control group. Of major significance, however, was the finding that each program had about the same impact. The amount of information had no detectable effects. No attempt was made to examine the duration of effects, which might have been sensitive to the differences among the information programs.

Overall these investigations yield no conclusive evidence that people are more prepared and protected as a result of information programs. Furthermore, they are inconclusive about how programs could be improved to produce higher levels of protection. Finally, the experience gained with one program at a single location, even if evaluated, may not be useful in designing protective action schemes for different locations or for the entire country.

Noninformational adjustment programs. Efforts to evaluate other, noninformational programs are even more scarce. This is probably attributable to the difficulty of conducting evaluation research and the lack of established programs for which evaluation is appropriate. Several efforts warrant attention.

Mileti, Hutton, Lord, Sorensen, and Waterstone (1979) began an evaluation of the NFIP. They developed an evaluation design with theoretical justification and a methodology. They concluded, however, on the basis of case studies of selected communities, that any large-scale evaluation would be premature until communities had more experience with program implementation and until land-use controls had been in effect a sufficiently long time to alter development patterns.

Two studies have investigated the land-use provisions of NFIP in Columbus, Mississippi. Cheatham (1977) looked at changes in development rates in the flood plain before and after the adoption of land-use controls. A dramatic decrease in construction was documented. A study by Lee and Day (Waterstone, 1980) took the analysis one step farther by investigating whether the residual flood plain construction was being flood-proofed or elevated. The findings indicated that all buildings in flood areas had been elevated in compliance with the regulations.

Burby and French (1981) examined the performance of land-use management programs under the NFIP in protecting flood plains from urban encroachment. Their evaluation was based on a mail survey of 1,223 communities in the NFIP. Communities of fewer than 5,000 people and those that had not processed an application for flood plain construction were excluded from the sampling frame.

The study used a number of subjective and objective measures of program characteristics, implementation, and effectiveness. The results demonstrated that in some communities land-use regulations were not effective in preventing encroachment but in many communities they were. The data showed that, in communities where there was already significant building on the flood plain and pressure for further development because of a lack of less hazardous sites, encroachment was occurring at a rapid

Table 10.5. *Judged sources of learning about appropriate responses*
(n = *171*)

Source	Hazard (% of total)			
	Earthquake	Tsunami	Hurricane	Flash flood
School				
School (in general)	18	20	15	10
College	5	6	2	1
High school	9	4	3	1
K–8	12	11	5	5
Media				
TV	13	16	19	14
Radio	3	18	9	9
Newspaper	5	5	10	11
New media	5	6	10	9
Informal				
Family	7	16	6	9
Friends	2	1	1	2
Hearsay or common sense	12	11	6	7
Experience	2	2	2	5
Movies (disaster)	9	1	2	0
Formal or official				
Phone book	2	11	1	1
Civil defense alerts to public	3	8	3	3
Reading pamphlets or books	6	5	3	3
Never learned	22	11	33	37

Note: multiple responses possible.
Source: Sorensen (1983).

rate. To be effective, therefore, it seems that land-use programs must be implemented before significant development occurs.

Demand for and perceptions of protective action programs

Another way of evaluating protective action programs is to examine how people judge their utility. One attempt to do so was reported by Sorensen (1983). Though the information generated by this study is not generalizable to the public at large, it provides some insight into the way in which programs are perceived by the public.

Table 10.5 presents Hawaiian college students' perceptions of how they

Table 10.6. *Perceived usefulness of hazard information sources* (n = *171*)

Source	Usefulness		
	Very much/some (%)	Not very much/none (%)	Modal Response
Media	84.8	15.2	Some
Civil defense	69.0	31.0	Some
K–8 schooling	53.3	46.7	Some
Family	49.7	30.3	Some
Telephone book	42.1	57.9	None
Other government agencies	36.3	63.7	Not very much
Brochures	35.7	64.3	None
High school	33.3	66.7	Not very much
College	28.6	71.4	None
Friends	18.2	81.8	None

Source: Sorensen (1983).

have learned about protective actions appropriate to four hazards. The table indicates that official sources such as pamphlets, phone book instructions, or civil defense programs are not viewed as significant sources of learning. What has been learned is attributed primarily to school and the media, although knowledge provided by these sources may not be sustained over time. This suggests that efforts to disseminate information through special programs and efforts may not reach the intended audience unless efforts are made to target information.

Learning, however, is not necessarily a predeterminant of action, nor is advice always heeded. To understand whether information makes a difference, people's judgments about the usefulness of information were also tapped (Table 10.6). The results show that the media are perceived to be the most useful source of information on a range of hazards, yet from an expert's view, they may be an unreliable source. Despite the fact that the subjects felt they had not learned much from civil defense, this organization was perceived to offer useful information. This study also showed that neither the judged source of information nor the judged usefulness of the source was related to actual knowledge about adaptive responses to a hazard warning.

To date very little data on the process of acquiring good and bad information have been collected. In order to understand the role of education in protective action decision making, it is important to improve our understanding of how people acquire and use information about hazards. Similarly, the role the mass media play in shaping response and preparation is not well understood (Committee on Disasters and the Mass Media, 1980), although understanding is growing (Hartsough & Mileti, 1985). The extent to which information provided through normal communication channels can persuade the public to take protective action requires more detailed examination.

Conclusions

The extent to which predisaster protective action programs have been effective in reducing losses of life and property from natural hazards is still largely a matter of speculation. On one hand, proponents argue on intuitive grounds that programs are useful and have slowed the rising toll from disaster. On the other hand, critics argue that there is no evidence that programs have achieved their intent. Furthermore, critics claim that earmarking large expenditures for individual- and family-level protective actions is an inappropriate solution to what are essentially engineering problems.

For example, consider the NFIP. Supporters of the program cite growing insurance protection, expanding community participation, and more widespread adoption of land-use controls as signs that the program is successful. Critics cite growing loss payments, nonenforcement of codes, and increasing encroachment on flood plains as evidence of failure (Miller, 1980).

Information and education programs have similar supportive and critical constituencies. The limited evaluations to date suggest that few programs have stimulated extensive protective action behavior (Sorensen, 1983). As a result, critics suggest that such programs are a waste of time and effort. Supporters say that it is not possible to evaluate program effects that, they claim, are intuitively sound. It is more likely, however, that some evaluations have revealed ineffective program design and implementation and that other evaluations are themselves poorly carried out.

Overall, the need for better and more frequent evaluations of protective action programs is clearly demonstrated. Evaluation should be an integral part of the program, not an afterthought. Furthermore, evaluations should do more than measure program impacts. Better knowledge of what constitutes an effective program and implementation is greatly needed to design better protective action strategies.

Note

1 Interested readers may find such materials at their local civil defense or emergency services office and local Red Cross office. In addition, materials can be obtained by writing state civil defense or emergency services agencies. Specific information can also be obtained from public affairs offices in appropriate federal agencies such as the Federal Emergency Management Agency, National Weather Service, or U.S. Geological Survey.

References

Baram, M. 1982. *Alternatives to Regulation*. Lexington, Mass.: Heath.

Baumann, D. 1983. "Determination of the Cost Effectiveness of Flood Hazard Information Programs," *Papers and Proceedings of Applied Geography Conferences 6:* 292.

Burby, R., and French, S. 1981. "Coping with Floods: The Land Use Management Paradox," *Journal of the American Planning Association* (July): 289–300.

Burton, I., and Kates, R. 1964. "The Perception of Natural Hazards in Resource Management," *Natural Resources Journal 3:* 412–41.

Burton, I., Kates, R., and White, G. 1978. *The Environment as Hazard*. New York: Oxford University Press.

Carnes, S., Copenhaver, E., Soderstrom, J., Sorensen, J., Bjornstad, D., and Peele, E. 1983. "Incentives and Nuclear Waste Siting: Prospectives and Constraints," *Energy Systems and Policy 7:* 323–51.

Cheatham, L. 1977. *An Analysis of the Effectiveness of Land Use Regulations Required for Flood Insurance Availability*. State College: Mississippi State Water Resource Research Institute.

Committee on Disasters and the Mass Media. 1980. *Disasters and the Mass Media*. Washington, D.C.: National Academy of Sciences.

Dahl, R., and Lindblom, C. 1953. *Politics, Economics, Welfare*. New York: Harper & Row.

Davenport, Sally S. 1978. *Human Response to Hurricanes in Texas – Two Studies* (Natural Hazards Working Paper No. 34). Boulder: University of Colorado, Institute of Behavioral Science.

Davenport, S., and Waterstone, P. 1979. *Hazard Awareness Guidebook*. Austin: Texas Coastal and Marine Council.

Gruntfest, Eve C. 1978. *What People Did during the Big Thompson Flood* (Natural Hazards Working Paper No. 32). Boulder: University of Colorado, Institute of Behavioral Science.

Haas, J. Eugene, and Trainer, Patricia B. 1974. "Effectiveness of the Tsunami Warning System in Selected Coastal Towns in Alaska," in *Proceedings of the 5th World Conference on Earthquake Engineering*, Rome, Italy. International Association for Earthquake Engineering.

Hartsough, Don J., and Mileti, Dennis S. 1985. "The Media in Disaster," in *Perspectives on Disaster Recovery*, Jerri Laube and Shirley A. Murphy (eds.)., pp. 282–94. Norwalk, Connecticut: Appleton-Century-Crofts.

Kates, R. 1962. *Hazard and Choice Perception in Flood Plain Management*. University of Chicago, Department of Geography.

Kates, R. 1971. "Natural Hazards in Human Ecological Perspective: Hypotheses and models," *Economic Geography 47:* 438–51.

Mileti, D., Hutton, J., Lord, W., Sorensen, J., and Waterstone, M. 1979. *Analysis of Adoption and Implementation of Community Land Use Regulations for Floodplains.*

Final report to the National Science Foundation. San Francisco: Woodward-Clyde Consultants.

Miller, H. C. 1980. "Context and Impacts of Floodplain Regulations in the United States," in E. J. Baker (ed.), *Hurricane and Coastal Storms*. Tallahassee: Florida Sea Grant College, pp. 73–7.

National Oceanic and Atmospheric Administration. 1983. *Catalog of Weather and Flood Hazard Awareness Material*, NOAA/PA 82003. Washington, D.C.: National Oceanic and Atmospheric Administration.

Palm, Risa. 1981. *Real Estate Agents and Special Studies Zones Disclosure: The Response of California Home Buyers to Earthquake Hazards Information*. Boulder: University of Colorado, Institute of Behavioral Science.

Regulska, J. 1982. "Public Awareness Programs for Natural Hazards," in T. Saarinen (ed.), *Perspectives on Hazard Awareness*. Boulder: University of Colorado, Institute of Behavioral Science, pp. 35–65.

Rodgers, E. 1983. *Diffusion of Innovation*. New York: Free Press.

Ruch, C., and Christensen, L. 1980. "Hurricane Message Enhancement." College Station: Texas A&M University, Sea Grant College Program.

Saarinen, T. 1982. "The Relation of Hazard Awareness to Adoption of Mitigation Measures," in T. Saarinen (ed.), *Perspectives on Hazard Awareness*. Boulder: University of Colorado, Institute of Behavioral Science, pp. 1–38.

Sims, J., and Baumann, P. 1983. "Educational Programs and Human Response to Hazards," *Environment and Behavior 15:* 165–189.

Sorensen, J. 1983. "Knowing How to Behave Under the Threat of Disaster: Can It Be Explained?" *Environment and Behavior 15:* 438–57.

Sorensen, J., Soderstrom, E., and Carnes, S. 1984. "Sweet for the Sour: Incentives in Environmental Mediation," *Environmental Management 8:* 287–94.

Waterstone, M. 1978. *Hazard Mitigation Behavior of Urban Flood Plain Residents* (Natural Hazards Working Paper No. 35). Boulder: University of Colorado, Institute of Behavioral Science.

Waterstone, M. 1980. "Implementation of the National Flood Insurance Program," in E. J. Baker (ed.), *Hurricanes and Coastal Storms*. Tallahassee: Florida Sea Grant College, pp. 78–82.

White, G. F. 1945. *Human Adjustment to Floods: A Geographical Approach to the Flood Problem in the United States* (Research Paper No. 29). University of Chicago, Department of Geography.

White, G. F., ed. 1961. *Papers on Flood Problems* (Research Paper No. 70). University of Chicago, Department of Geography.

White, Gilbert F., Calef, W., Hudson, J., Mayer H., Schaeffer, J., and Volk, D. 1958. *Changes in Urban Occupance of Flood Plains in the United States* (Research Paper No. 57). Chicago: University of Chicago Press, Department of Geography.

Whyte, A. 1977. "The Role of Information Flow in Controlling Industrial Lead Emissions: The Case of the Avonmouth Smelter," in *Proceedings of the International Conference on Heavy Metals*. Toronto: Institute for Environmental Studies.

11 Why people take precautions against crime: a review of the literature on individual and collective responses to crime

Stephanie W. Greenberg

Introduction

As crime rates rose steadily in the decades following World War II, a trend toward citizen action to prevent crime developed. Law enforcement officials at all levels of government began to take the position that the police cannot – and should not – be everywhere and that private citizens must play an active role in protecting themselves, their homes, and their communities against crime. One result of this focus on citizen responsibility in crime prevention has been an effort among scholars to delineate the major categories of citizen responses and to investigate the determinants of these responses. The purpose of this chapter is to synthesize and assess what is currently known about responses to crime and the factors influencing these responses.

Three major dimensions of crime response have been identified: cognitive, affective, and behavioral. The cognitive dimension refers to beliefs about crime: about the extent of or change in the crime rate in a specific area (e.g., block, neighborhood, city, or nation), about the crime rate in the neighborhood in comparison with the rest of the city, or about the probability of victimization. Affective responses to crime refer primarily to fear, that is, feelings of threat when one is outside the home during the day or evening and worry or concern about oneself, one's home, or one's family being the target of crime. Behavioral responses include (a) avoidance (limiting one's activities in order to reduce the risk of victimization), (b) self-protection when outside the home (e.g., carrying weapons or learning martial arts), (c) household protection (e.g., installing special locks or burglar alarms, having neighbors watch the house when one is

This chapter is based on a larger study that was supported under the auspices of a grant from the Community Crime Prevention Division of the National Institute of Justice (Grant 81-IJ-CX-0080). The study was completed while the author was at the Research Triangle Institute and the Denver Research Institute. This chapter benefitted from the contributions of William M. Rohe, University of North Carolina-Chapel Hill.

231

away, or having a watchdog), and (d) collective action (e.g., participating in a crime prevention group or neighborhood patrol) (DuBow, McCabe, & Kaplan, 1979; Fowler & Mangione, 1974; Furstenberg, 1971; Garofalo & Laub, 1978; Lavrakas et al., 1980; Liang, Hwalek, Sengstock, 1983; Skogan & Maxfield, 1980). All of these behavioral responses to crime are attempts to prevent victimization of one's person or one's home. In addition, there is a behavioral response to crime, contacting the police, that may be either preventive or a reaction to being the victim of or witness to a crime.

This chapter focuses primarily on behavioral responses to crime. Cognitive and affective responses are discussed primarily in terms of their capacity to predict behavioral responses. The following topics are addressed: (a) definitions of behavioral responses to crime, (b) fear and other risk-related factors as motivating forces in responding to crime, (c) the relation between responses to crime and beliefs about the efficacy of different sources of help, (d) community differences in crime responses, and (e) initiation versus maintenance of crime responses.

Defining behavioral responses to crime

DuBow et al. (1979) define a behavioral response to crime as "an action or set of actions for which the presence of crime risks is believed to be a relevant consideration" (p. 30). Furstenberg (1972) distinguished two major types of responses: avoidance and mobilization. Avoidance involves isolating or removing oneself from situations that are believed to have a high risk of victimization. Mobilization, in contrast, is more aggressive and involves reducing one's openness to victimization. Mobilization implies an element of planning and the expenditure of financial resources; it includes both household protection and personal protection. Furstenberg's conceptual scheme does not, however, seem to apply to collective actions. Two typologies that do are Conklin's (1975) distinction between individual and collective behavior, and Schneider and Schneider's (1978) differentiation between private-minded and public-minded responses. Individual, or private-minded, responses are geared to reducing the risk of victimization for the individual or the household. Collective, or public-minded, responses are designed to reduce the risk of victimization for the neighborhood and include such activities as neighborhood patrolling, informal surveillance, and protective neighboring.

There are both conceptual and methodological problems with many of the typologies developed to describe behavioral responses to crimes. First, there is no common terminology for major categories of behavioral responses (DuBow et al., 1979). For example, the terms "collective action," "public-minded action," "territoriality," and "informal social control" have all been used to describe behaviors that enhance the safety of an area. However, it is not clear whether these terms refer to the same, or even similar, activities.

One reason for this lack of definitional clarity may be that few studies have demonstrated the validity of combining specific activities into a common category. Lavrakas and Lewis (1980) reviewed several typologies of crime prevention behaviors and found that in no case was there statistical evidence to indicate that the specific behaviors combined into a given type were actually intercorrelated. In a reanalysis of several large surveys with multiple measures of crime prevention responses, they found relatively strong correlations among a variety of indicators of avoidance (e.g., not going out at night or alone, driving instead of walking, avoiding certain locations). There was also evidence, albeit weaker, that household protection activities (installing special locks or bars, stopping deliveries when away from home, having neighbors watch the house when away) also tended to co-occur. Other behaviors, such as buying a gun or watchdog, seemed to occur independently of all others. These findings suggest a need to improve both the conceptual and the empirical coherence of the terms used to describe behavioral responses to crime.

The present author and associates reanalyzed the survey data collected in the Reactions to Crime Project conducted by Skogan and others. The survey examined a broad range of behaviors, including multiple measures of avoidance, self-protection, household protection, participation in a community organization involved in crime prevention, and contact with the police to report a specific crime or lodge a general complaint about neighborhood crime problems. The data were collected in a telephone survey in 1977 in three major cities: Chicago, Philadelphia, and San Francisco. (See Maxfield & Hunter, 1980, for the details of the data collection methods and Skogan & Maxfield, 1980, for an extensive discussion of the findings.) The reanalysis indicated that multiple measures within major response types were intercorrelated, giving statistical support to the typology used. The reanalysis also revealed only weak relations among the major response types (Greenberg, Rohe, & Williams, 1984b). This suggests that each of the major response categories is a function of a distinct set of individual or environmental determinants.

Another problem in categorizing responses to crime is that the motivations for specific behaviors are often unclear (DuBow et al., 1979). An individual may purchase a gun or a dog for recreational reasons, for crime prevention reasons, or both. Simply knowing that an individual has acquired a gun or a dog without probing for the motivation can result in a misleading classification.

Finally, some responses occur so infrequently or have such little salience to individuals that they may not even recall making them. Open-ended survey questions may therefore yield less information about behavioral responses than questions referring to specific behaviors. DuBow et al. (1979) demonstrated, in fact, that surveys with open-ended questions show lower incidence rates for a variety of crime prevention activities than do surveys with explicit questions.

Determinants of individual responses to crime

Fear as a motivating factor

Two opposing perspectives have developed concerning the role of fear in responding to crime. According to the perspective that developed out of the work of Emile Durkheim, a late-nineteenth-century sociologist, fear of crime can be an important impetus for the adoption of protective or preventive behaviors, especially at the community level. When members of a community perceive that norms for acceptable behavior are being violated, the community is motivated to make a strong response in order to restore order. Fear motivates behaviors that will not only reduce crime but will also reestablish and reinforce community norms for acceptable behavior. This perspective was implicit in many government-sponsored community crime prevention programs a decade ago. Skogan and Maxfield (1980) note a statement from the Law Enforcement Assistance Administration on organizing neighborhoods around crime: "Fear of crime can motivate citizens to interact with each other and engage in anti-crime efforts" (1977:5).

An opposing perspective has developed more recently. According to this perspective, fear may destroy the capacity of communities to address the crime problem. Fear, in this view, causes people to avoid public places, to stay off the streets, and to seek refuge in their homes behind locks and bars. As a result, a vicious cycle is created, in which a crime problem develops in a neighborhood (or, at least, residents perceive this to be the case), fear increases, the streets become deserted as people retreat to their homes, and the crime problem worsens as a result (Conklin, 1975; Lewis & Salem, 1980, 1981; Wilson & Kelling, 1982).

The first perspective suggests that fear should be related in similar ways to all of the major types of crime response, that is, as a general motivating factor. In contrast, the second perspective suggests that fear encourages individuals to protect themselves and their homes but inhibits community-based activities aimed at preventing or reducing crime. The research, as will be seen, is more supportive of the second perspective than of the first.

Of the five major behavioral responses to crime, the one that has the closest empirical association with fear is avoidance – not going to certain public places, traveling by car rather than walking or using public transportation, or staying at home (DuBow et al., 1979; Greenberg et al., 1984b; Lavrakas et al., 1980; Skogan & Maxfield, 1980). Studies indicate that more than half of the citizenry, particularly urban dwellers, engage in some form of avoidance in order to reduce their exposure to risk (Lavrakas et al., 1980). Women and the elderly, the two groups that express the most fear, are most likely to engage in avoidance and in more extreme forms of avoidance. (Biderman et al., 1967; Garofalo, 1977, Lavrakas et al., 1980; Lawton, Powell, Yaffe, & Feldman, 1976; Skogan & Maxfield, 1980). Blacks and people with low income also are more likely to engage in avoidance (DuBow et al., 1979).

In fact, avoidance is the stereotypical response to crime; the image of the urban dweller seeking safety behind locked doors, a prisoner in his or her own home, comes immediately to mind. The reality, however, seems to be considerably less dramatic. It appears that these actions usually represent relatively subtle changes in behavior, such as altering the time of day when people are willing to go out alone, driving instead of walking, and the like (Hindelang, 1978). In general, avoidance is a widespread and relatively easy means of responding to crime.

Although avoidance seems to be related to fear in a relatively straightforward manner, several aspects of this behavioral response are not well understood. First, the degree to which individuals engage in avoidance is likely to be heavily influenced by their need or desire to travel to certain locations. DuBow et al. (1979) note that avoidance is more convenient for women and the elderly because, on average, these individuals do not have as great a need as others to be at certain locations at specific times. It has also been found that working women and working elderly report lower levels of avoidance than those who are not working (Furstenberg, 1972). Thus, the question arises as to the degree to which lack of necessity to travel to public areas explains the high rates of avoidance among these two groups. If lack of necessity is an important factor, avoidance would appear to infringe less seriously on the freedom of movement of women and the elderly than is often believed.

Second, residential context is likely to affect the relation among demographic characteristics, fear, and avoidance. Elderly, black, and low-income people may report higher levels of fear and avoidance than do other groups because they are more likely to live in high-crime neighborhoods. Elderly and low-income people are also more likely to live alone. Liebowitz (1975) found that age was associated with high fear levels among people living in cities, among those living alone, and among those with low income. Age was not associated with fear among people living in small towns or rural areas, living with others, or with high income (see also Johnson, 1971; Sundeen & Mathieu, 1976).

Finally, it has been suggested that the high rates of avoidance among women and the elderly may be effective in reducing their victimization by reducing exposure to risk (DuBow et al., 1979). The high level of fear in these two groups, in view of their low overall rates of victimization, has been interpreted by some as an irrational response to crime. However, fear and the resulting avoidance behavior may not be irrational if, in fact, they are responsible for decreased victimization. It may also be the case that when exposure levels are equated, women and the elderly do not have lower rates of victimization than other groups, particularly for crimes to which they are especially vulnerable (e.g., rape or pursesnatch) (McPherson, 1978). But whereas avoidance may be effective at risk reduction, it may have negative consequences for individuals' sense of power and control over their environment (Cohn, Kidder, & Harvey, 1978).

At the opposite end of the spectrum from avoidance is self-protection – taking along a weapon or a dog when going out or learning self-defense. (Note that "self-protection" in the crime literature has a narrower definition than it does when applied to other hazards, like disease, injury, or natural disaster.) This is one of the least common responses to crime (Skogan & Maxfield, 1980). Men and young people are more likely to engage in self-protection than are women and older people (DuBow et al., 1979). Self-protection is likely to be unattractive to people who are unwilling to engage in violence with an attacker if need be. Simply avoiding those situations that are perceived to have a high risk of victimization is more likely to be acceptable. The problem in assessing the extent to which self-protection is practiced is that individuals purchase guns or dogs or learn self-defense for entertainment as well as for crime-related reasons.

Self-protection does not appear to be a consequence of fear in the way that avoidance is, but it does correlate with the assessment of the risk of victimization and with actual victimization (DuBow et al., 1979; Greenberg et al., 1984b). Whereas avoidance is oriented to reducing risk exposure, self-protection is an attempt to reduce the likelihood of being victimized when exposed to risk or reducing injury or property loss if actually victimized.

Studies have found that individuals who own a gun or take lessons in self-defense report lower levels of fear than those who engage in avoidance (Cohn et al., 1978; DuBow et al., 1979). These findings with respect to gun ownership may be spurious, however, because gun owners disproportionately are male and live in rural areas, two characteristics that tend to be associated with a lower level of fear (DuBow et al., 1979). However, Cohn et al. (1978) found that women enrolled in a self-defense course were less fearful and had a greater sense of environmental control at the end of the course than at the beginning. They also had a greater sense of control than did women of similar age who were not enrolled in the course. This study suggests that an important component of fear is perceived lack of environmental mastery. Strategies that increase the sense of control are likely to reduce fear.

It has been estimated that roughly 40% of households have purchased security devices, such as bars, special locks, burglar alarms, light timers, or outside lights, to protect their homes from crime (DuBow et al., 1979). This percentage is even higher when one considers other types of household protection, such as having the neighbors watch the house and having mail and newspaper delivery stopped when away from home for more than a day.

Research suggests that household protection is not related to fear or perceived risk of victimization. Rather, homeownership and social integration into the neighborhood are the most important determinants of household protection (Greenberg et al., 1984b; Lavrakas et al., 1980; Skogan & Maxfield, 1980). Homeownership affords the flexibility needed to take such precautions as installing special locks, alarms, or outside lights. In addition, homeownership is an indicator of economic investment. Household protection is an attempt to prevent or reduce damage to that investment. Social integration (i.e., feeling part of the neighborhood, knowing people in the neighborhood) is also associated with household protection, because some of these measures depend on the cooperation of neighbors (e.g., having neighbors check the house while one is away). In addition, information about how best to protect the home is often disseminated through neighborhood networks.

Studies have found that participation in community crime prevention organizations, though not as rare as self-protection, is less common than avoidance or household protection. On average, between 10 and 20% of all community residents are involved in such programs (Lavrakas et al., 1980; Podolefsky & DuBow, 1980; Skogan & Maxfield, 1980). This response to crime is very different from those discussed so far in that it represents an effort to prevent victimization in an area that extends beyond the individual or the household to an entire building, block, or neighborhood. This suggests that involvement in crime prevention organizations is more reflective of overall involvement in community activities than an expression of fear. Collective crime prevention programs tend to be sponsored by organizations that address a variety of local problems, not just crime, and are usually formed for some purpose other than crime prevention (Lavrakas et al., 1980; Podolefsky & DuBow, 1980). As a result, people typically become involved in collective crime prevention because they are already participating in organized community activities. Such people are generally joiners (Skogan & Maxfield, 1980).

Research has indicated that participation in community crime prevention is negatively related to fear and positively related to perceptions of crime as a local problem (Greenberg et al., 1984b). This suggests that awareness of local crime problems is an impetus to participation, but fear may be incapacitating. This supports Conklin's (1975) argument that fear of crime has a debilitating effect on the capacity of communities to deal with local problems. Cohn et al. (1978) found that individuals who participated in a community organization that addressed crime as well as other neighborhood problems experienced less fear and a greater sense of control than did individuals who did not participate and who engaged in avoidance activities.

An unintended consequence of participation in crime prevention programs appears to be increased concern about crime. As Skogan and Maxfield (1980) note:

One of the most common features of an anti-crime meeting is that people spend a great deal of time relating tales about victimization experiences. People report crime stories to others in attendance in order to illustrate the threat of crimes in their midst, and the necessity for taking some action. (p. 347)

As a result of knowing or hearing about neighbors who have been victimized, fear or at least concern about crime may be increased.

In addition to community involvement, several other individual characteristics are associated with membership in a community crime prevention organization. Blacks and older people are more likely to participate than are other groups of people (Greenberg et al., 1984b; Lavrakas et al., 1980; Skogan & Maxfield, 1980). Lavrakas et al. (1980) found that, whereas crime prevention organizations are more likely to be found in lower income and nonwhite areas than in other areas, individuals with relatively higher incomes in these communities are more likely to participate than are other community members. They also found that participation rates are highest in those programs that require relatively low levels of involvement. Programs that simply involve attending meetings or increasing informal surveillance in the neighborhood tend to have higher rates of participation than do programs with more active programs, such as citizen patrols or escort programs.

Finally, contacting the police either to report a specific crime or to complain about general crime conditions does not seem to be an expression of fear. Rather, it is related to perceptions about the seriousness of local crime, the experience of victimization, and the perception that neighbors are not a reliable helping resource (Boggs, 1971; Greenberg et al., 1984b; Hackler, Ho, & Urquhart-Ross, 1974). The stronger the perception that crime is a serious neighborhood problem and that neighbors would be indifferent if they witnessed a crime, the greater the likelihood of calling the police about a specific crime or to complain about neighborhood crime in general.

In summary, the research indicates that fear is not a generalized motivation for all types of crime responses. It is most closely associated with avoidance behavior. Women and the elderly, the two groups with the highest levels of fear, are most likely to engage in avoidance. Avoidance may be effective as a means of reducing exposure to the risk of victimization. However, its negative side effect is that it seems to reduce the sense of environmental mastery. Whereas the purpose of avoidance is to reduce the risk of victimization, self-protection is an attempt to reduce the likelihood of victimization when exposed to risk. It is most likely to be engaged in by men and young people, two groups with the lowest levels of fear. Individuals who engage in self-protection tend to feel less fearful and more in control. Another behavioral response that seems to enhance a sense of control is participation in community-based crime prevention activities. Awareness of local crime problems provides an impetus to participate, but fear seems to be incapacitating. In general, participation in community crime prevention is a result of involvement in organized community activities. Household protection, similarly, does not appear to be motivated by fear. Rather, it is an attempt to protect a major economic investment – one's home – from damage or property loss. Household protection is associated with both economic and social integration into the community. Finally, contacting the police is a function of the perception that the local area has a serious crime problem and that neighbors cannot be counted on to offer help. Therefore, a formal means of social control (i.e., the police) is called in for assistance.

There are several possible explanations for the finding that avoidance is the only behavioral response to crime that seems to be motivated primarily by fear. One explanation is that, in many studies, fear is measured by the extent to which people state that they are afraid to be outside on their block, in their neighborhood, or in the city at large during the day or at night. This measure is closely connected to avoidance. However, it would seem that self-protection and participation in community crime prevention would also be motivated by fear of being out alone. A second and, in the author's view, more convincing explanation is that an underlying assumption of avoidance, more than any other response to crime, is that individuals are powerless to protect themselves. The other responses are oriented toward "doing something about" crime at the individual, household, or community level. Stinchcombe et al. (1978) state that the distinctive characteristics of crime as a fear-provoking stimulus are its concentration in space, its association with signs of danger, and the inability to do much about it (also see Skogan & Maxfield, 1980). It is this sense of powerlessness that seems to set avoidance apart from the other responses.

Perceived risk and responses to crime

Behavior oriented toward disease prevention represents another model of individual responses to crime. Rosenstock (1966) presents a model of why and under what conditions people take action to prevent and detect disease (also see DuBow et al., 1979). The two major variables that determine health-related behavior, according to Rosenstock, are the psychological state of readiness to take a specific action and the perceived efficacy of a particular course of action in reducing a health threat. This model of responses to health risks has strong analogies to responses to crime risks. The psychological state of readiness to act is influenced by both perceived risk of contracting a disease or falling victim to a crime and the perceived seriousness of the disease or crime (Rosenstock, 1966).

In the crime context, perceived risk is conceptually distinct from fear in that the former represents an assessment of the likelihood of victimization, whereas the latter is an emotional response to this assessment. Perceived risk of crime victimization has been measured both directly and indirectly. Direct measures typically involve asking an individual to rate the likelihood or probability of being the victim of crime in general or of a specific crime. Indirect measures include knowing the victim of a crime or believing that people in one's social category (e.g., age, race, sex, income level) are likely to be crime victims (Skogan & Maxfield, 1980). Both knowing victims and believing oneself to be a member of a vulnerable group encourage a sense of susceptibility to crime victimization.

Perceived risk has been found to influence certain individual actions against crime but not others. Avoidance and self-protection are correlated with perceived risk; household protection, participation in community crime prevention, and contacting the police are not (Greenberg et al., 1984b). As noted in the previous section, the purpose of avoidance is to reduce exposure to risk, whereas self-protection is an attempt to reduce the likelihood or the seriousness of victimization when one is exposed to risk.

Although there are a number of important analogies between susceptibility to disease and to crime victimization, one of the major differences is the amount and credibility of information about the efficacy of risk-reducing behaviors. Information about the health risks of smoking and eating high-fat foods seems to have changed behavior in these areas. However, the effects of information on actions taken to reduce the risk of victimization are not as apparent.

Beliefs about the efficacy of different sources of help and responses to crime

Beliefs about the efficacy of various sources of help in combatting crime have been found to influence actual behavioral responses to crime. More specifically, perceptions of one's own responsibility for and effectiveness in dealing with crimes that are witnessed, neighbors as a helping resource, collective actions, and the court system influence behavioral responses.

The sense of personal responsibility for intervening in a crime predicts the likelihood of actual intervention, at least in experimental situations. The study of bystander intervention in crimes or other emergencies was instigated by the Kitty Genovese case in 1964, in which a woman was stabbed to death near her home while 38 people looked on and took no action. Studies have found that lone bystanders who are witnesses to a crime or other emergency are more likely to intervene, followed by pairs of people who know one another. A bystander who is among a group of strangers is least likely to respond. This was the situation in the Kitty Genovese incident. This pattern has been interpreted in terms of the diffusion of responsibility. When others are present, the total responsibility and guilt for nonintervention do not fall on one person. It is therefore easier to take no action than it is when an individual is alone. In this way, sense of personal responsibility appears to influence intervention, at least in simulated criminal events. (The classic work in bystander intervention has been done by Latane & Darley, 1970; see also Bickman, 1975; Bickman & Helwig, 1979; Bickman & Rosenbaum, 1977; Gelfand, Hartman,

Walder, & Page, 1973; Moriarty, 1975; Ross, 1971; Schwartz & Gottlieb, 1976).

Attitudes toward neighbors as a helping resource also appear to affect responses to crime. Studies have found a negative relationship between reliance on the police and reliance on informal means of dealing with crime and other neighborhood problems (Boggs, 1971; Hackler et al., 1974; Greenberg et al., 1984b). The lack of confidence in neighbors as a source of prevention or protection against crime encourages reliance on the police. Individuals may not trust the police or be satisfied with the service they receive, but they may believe that their neighbors would be indifferent if they witnessed a crime. As a result, they feel that they have no choice but to call the police. Thus, the less individuals believe in the efficacy of informal action, the greater is their reliance on formal means of social control.

Individuals involved in collective crime prevention activities are more likely than are nonparticipants to report that they have some control over crime and that citizens groups can make a difference (Cohn et al., 1978; Skogan & Maxfield, 1980). However, the direction of causation is unclear. Individuals who believe they can be effective in crime prevention may be more likely than others to participate in groups, or it may be that participation promotes a sense of efficacy.

Attitudes toward the criminal justice system, the courts in particular, have been found to be related to behavioral responses. One study found that people with unfavorable attitudes toward the court system were less likely to participate in community watch programs than were individuals with favorable attitudes (Rohe & Greenberg, 1984).[1] This finding suggests that individuals believe that community activities to reduce crime are in vain if the courts release criminals back to the streets. Individuals with such attitudes may choose a self-reliant strategy, such as avoidance or self-protection, rather than collective activities.

Community differences in crime responses

Patterns of response to crime are affected by community characteristics. Residents of low-income neighborhoods, particularly those that are culturally heterogeneous, are more likely to call the police and less likely to rely on informal means of control to deal with neighborhood problems than are residents of more affluent areas (Hackler et al., 1974). Boggs (1971) found that rural residents, suburban and central-city whites, and central-city blacks exhibited three different orientations toward response to crime. Rural residents were most likely to state that informal controls (i.e., neighbors) were responsible for neighborhood safety. Central-city blacks were most likely to state that the police were responsible for neighborhood safety and least likely to rely on informal control. Suburbanites and central-city whites had the most diversified set of responses, relying on informal controls, the police, and individual precautions.

These studies suggest that residents of low-income, particularly minority neighborhoods may have to rely on the police for a wide variety of problems, from troublesome teenagers to serious crimes. They may not trust the police or be satisfied with the service they receive, but residents of these areas may believe that there is no alternative. In contrast, residents of white, middle-class neighborhoods may utilize informal control – either their own intervention or the assistance of neighbors – for relatively minor problems and turn to the police if their own efforts do not alleviate nuisances or for serious crimes.

A corollary of these differences in response to crime is that community-based crime prevention programs are more difficult to organize and maintain in low-income, heterogeneous neighborhoods than in affluent, homogeneous areas (Abt Associates, 1980; McPherson & Silloway, 1980; Roehl & Cook, 1983). There are several possible explanations. First, participation in civic and other voluntary organizations tends to be lower in low-income, transient areas than in stable, middle-class areas. Economic pressures make volunteers less available in low-income areas, and often there is less economic stake in the community, whereas a greater economic stake in the community tends to encourage participation in more affluent areas (Greenberg, Rohe, & Williams, 1984a). As O'Brien (1975) states, "The nature of the environment they [poor people] have to cope with forces them to spend most of their resources on nonpolitical activities" (p. 20). Second, a low sense of efficacy has been offered as an explanation for low participation rates. Lower-income individuals as a group have a lower sense of personal efficacy in dealing with problems. This, it is suggested, leads to a belief that participation in an instrumental community organization will not lead to any real changes or benefits (Greenberg et al., 1984a). Third, suspicion of bureaucracies and lack of experience in participating in formal organizations may discourage participation. Gans (1962), in a classic study of the West End of Boston, noted that the person-oriented attitudes of residents led to a distrust of formal "impersonal" organizations. Finally, Piven and Cloward (1971) and Roberts (1973) suggest that low-income people have typically had little experience in participating in formal organizations and therefore have not developed the appropriate skills for forming and maintaining an organization.

Evidence of the difficulties involved in organizing crime prevention programs in low-income neighborhoods is offered by Podolefsky (1983). A police-sponsored program that was initiated in a low-income, culturally heterogeneous neighborhood was rejected by the residents, largely because the program organizers failed to involve community leaders in the initial planning of the program, and the program's approach to the causes of and solutions to the crime problem was at serious odds with that of the residents. The program emphasized victimization prevention (i.e., locks and property marking) as the primary solution to the crime problem, whereas the community stressed the need to address the broader social problems that were believed to cause crime (i.e., unemployment, idle youths, and poverty). Podolefsky and DuBow (1980) suggest that this dichotomy in the approach to crime prevention is associated with a community's economic status. Low-income neighborhoods tend to stress the social problems approach, whereas more affluent areas emphasize the prevention of victimization.

The difficulties that have been observed in organizing crime prevention programs in low-income communities point to a more general issue in collective responses to crime or to neighborhood problems in general. A basic assumption of crime prevention programs with a neighborhood orientation is that their success depends on collective citizen involvement. It is assumed that neighbors already know one another or would like to know one another, are willing to cooperate in such activities as watching each others' houses and intervening in crimes, and, most important, have shared norms for appropriate public behavior. Many of the activities of community crime prevention programs depend on mutual trust and a willingness to take responsibility for each others' safety. However, there are some neighborhoods where these assumptions do not apply, where mutual distrust and hostility prevail.

A number of studies have found that shared norms for public behavior are less likely to develop in low-income, culturally heterogeneous neighborhoods than they are in low-income, homogeneous neighborhoods or in middle-class neighborhoods. Residents of low-income, heterogeneous neighborhoods tend to be more suspicious of one another, to perceive less commonality among themselves, and to feel less control over their neighborhood than do residents of more homogeneous neighborhoods (Greenberg, Rohe, & Williams, 1982; Merry, 1981a,b; Rainwater, 1966; Suttles, 1968; Taub, Taylor, & Dunham, 1982; Taylor, Gottfredson, & Brower, 1981).

One explanation for this finding is that low-income, particularly minority neighborhoods are less stable than other neighborhoods. Some writers suggest that abandonment of these neighborhoods by mortgage-lending institutions and private industry has made it difficult for many of the residents to develop long-term ties to the neighborhood. Another explanation is that poor people tend to accept the views of the larger society that they are not trustworthy and will prey on one another at any opportunity (Suttles, 1968).

Low-income neighborhoods that do develop strong informal control tend to be characterized by the dominance of one ethnic group – Italian, Polish, Irish, or the like – but this does not necessarily mean that a majority of the population is of a single ethnic group. In several old Italian neighborhoods that have been studied, for example, Italians made up only 30 to 40% of the neighborhood. However, these neighborhoods had the reputation of being controlled culturally and politically by Italians. In addition, there was a perception that rules for behavior were firmly established and enforced by one group (Gans, 1962; Merry, 1981a; Spergel, 1964; Suttles, 1968).

The research also suggests that the cultural dominance of one group is more important than residential stability. One study examined a residentially stable housing project in which more than half of the residents were Chinese (Merry, 1981a). The Chinese, however, were isolated and alienated from other residents, and their social ties were with one another or with Chinese living outside the project. The Chinese, even though they were in the majority and had lived in the project for a number of years, were fearful of other residents, particularly teenagers. Black, white, and Hispanic residents of the project also viewed each other with suspicion. No single group in the project exercised authority or had the reputation of being able to establish and maintain control. The author of this study states that "the social order in a neighborhood depends on the presence of a dominant group that perceives itself as responsible for public order" (Merry, 1981a: 230–1). Because of the absence of such a group, the project was characterized by fear and hostility, and it was the police and courts who typically dealt with disputes and maintained order.

Some inner-city black neighborhoods suffer from similar problems. Though these neighborhoods are homogeneously black, the residents represent a mixture of classes and lifestyles (Erbe, 1975; Hannerz, 1976; Warren, 1969). It is difficult to establish agreed-on norms for public behavior in these areas because people of different classes, lifestyles, and family backgrounds have different conceptions of the appropriate use of public space. One consequence of this situation is that people living in the same neighborhood may have different definitions of undesirable public behavior.

The situation is typically very different in predominantly white, middle-class neighborhoods. Because whites have a greater choice of residential location than do blacks, predominantly white neighborhoods tend to be homogeneous in class and family type. As a result, the residents share many assumptions about appropriate public behavior, upkeep of property, control of children, and the like. These assumptions can be made even in the absence of frequent interaction and personal knowledge of others' backgrounds (Gans, 1967; Whyte, 1957). One study of a white, suburban neighborhood documented the rapidity and ease with which neighborhood norms developed (Gans, 1967). Gossip was an effective means of chastising people who violated norms because of the importance of maintaining the family's reputation in the community. In contrast, gossip is a relatively weak means of social control in heterogeneous, low-income neighborhoods where people do not necessarily care as much about what their neighbors think (Hannerz, 1967; Merry, 1979).

The research results suggest that it may be difficult to establish and maintain collective problem-solving activities in low-income, culturally heterogeneous areas. A reanalysis of survey data from 60 neighborhoods in three cities revealed that community crime prevention programs that require frequent contact and cooperation among neighbors, such as neighborhood watch, were less likely to be found in racially or economically heterogeneous areas (Greenberg et al., 1984b). Instead, these neighborhoods were more likely to have information dissemination programs, designed to teach people how to protect themselves and their homes, and police–community relations programs.

The research strongly indicates a need to tailor collective crime prevention strategies to community characteristics. Programs requiring frequent cooperative activity may be resisted in socially heterogeneous areas, where people may feel little in common with one another and therefore might not be interested in interaction. In addition, the more formal, bureaucratized approach that may be well accepted in middle-class areas is likely to be inappropriate in other contexts. A uniform, standard package is therefore likely to be ineffective in many neighborhoods.

Initiation versus maintenance of crime responses

Most research on the conditions favoring the maintenance of crime responses focuses on crime prevention groups rather than individual behavior. As a result, little is known about what motivates individuals to take a particular type of action and to maintain this behavior over a period of time. The following discussion, therefore, deals primarily with collective responses to crime.

As noted earlier, collective responses to crime typically develop in the context of general-purpose community organizations that add crime to their existing agenda of activities (Lavrakas et al., 1980; Podolefsky & DuBow, 1980). Evaluations of crime prevention programs have revealed that the victimization or reported crime rates of participating individuals or areas are substantially lower than are those of nonparticipating individuals or areas or that participating areas experience greater decreases in crime over time than do comparison areas (Greenberg et al, 1984a; Titus, in press; Washnis, 1976). For the most part, the programs evaluated in these studies adopted a comprehensive approach involving a variety of strategies to address crime and, sometimes, more general neighborhood problems. The programs that focus on single crime prevention strategies, such as property marking or crime reporting, appear to have less impact on crime than multiple-strategy programs, although this assertion has not been explicitly examined (Greenberg et al., 1984a).

Multi-issue groups may also be easier to maintain than single-issue groups. The effects of crime prevention programs on crime have been found to wane after 18 to 24 months (Cirel, Evans, McGillis, & Whitcomb, 1977; Fowler & Mangione, 1982). One reason may be that it is difficult to maintain the initial sense of purpose and enthusiasm among participants. Multi-issue groups have the advantage of being able to address new problems on a continuing basis as old problems are either successfully dealt with or deemed intractable.

In addition to program scope, other organizational characteristics are believed to affect program longevity and effectiveness. These include program sponsorship, staffing patterns, funding levels and sources, linkages with external agencies, and geographic area of program coverage. Although past research has suggested that these characteristics have an effect on levels of citizen participation, program longevity, the adoption of prescribed crime prevention behaviors, and ultimately on the reduction of crime and fear, these relationships have not been empirically examined.

Programs are usually sponsored and initiated by one of three types of organization: existing community organizations, citywide crime prevention agencies, or the police or sheriff's department. The major advantages of program initiation by community organizations are that the program is more likely to be tailored to the needs of the community, and they are more likely to draw on leadership resources in the community (Kidder, 1978; McPherson & Silloway, 1980; Podolefsky, 1983). A disadvantage of community-sponsored programs is that the leaders may lack knowledge as to how to obtain funding, technical assistance, and other resources. Communities may also lack a strong organizational base with which to initiate, organize, and maintain activities. These disadvantages are important advantages of externally sponsored programs. The advantages of external and internal sponsorship may be optimized by the coordination of community-sponsored programs through an umbrella coalition of neighborhood organizations, as was attempted in the Urban Crime Prevention Program (Roehl & Cook, 1983).

Staffing patterns refer to the balance between professional paid staff and volunteers. The advantages and disadvantages of a paid versus all-volunteer staff are analogous to those of external versus community sponsorship. It has been suggested that paid staff is more important for neighborhood-level than for block-level programs and for multi-issue than for single-issue groups (Green, 1979; Titus, in press); because of the extensive administrative and coordinating activities in programs covering large geographic areas or attempting to address a number of issues. Feins (1983), however, argues that participants in programs with a paid staff become passive consumers rather than active contributors to program activities and that functions performed by paid staff should be carefully defined and delimited for maximum effectiveness.

Sources and levels of funding are also believed to influence program effectiveness in ways that are analogous to staffing patterns and sponsorship. External funding is often required to purchase equipment or technical expertise. However, the danger of becoming totally dependent on a large amount of external funding should be avoided, given the uncertainties of funding continuation.

The capacity of a program to build and maintain strong links with external agencies has been viewed as an important component of program effectiveness (Roehl & Cook, 1983). A positive relationship between crime prevention groups and the police is regarded as a critical element in crime prevention (Feins, 1983; Greenberg, Rohe, & Williams, 1984c). However, there are a wide range of other external institutions and agencies that also affect neighborhoods in ways that could have a deleterious effect on local crime. These include courts, district attorneys, housing authorities, sanitation departments, and financial institutions. Thus, groups may also seek to make contacts with and exercise influence over these institutions in an effort to have a comprehensive approach to crime prevention.

The geographic area of program coverage may also have an effect on crime and fear reduction. It has been suggested that building- or block-level groups may be more effective than groups covering larger areas, because small, concentrated populations are easier to mobilize and coordinate. There is also likely to be more agreement on the crime problems and more active citizen participation in choosing and planning strategies than is the case in larger spatial areas (McPherson & Silloway, 1980; Yin, Vogel, Chaiken, & Both, 1977).

A variety of program maintenance activities have been suggested, such as training programs for volunteers, public recognition of volunteer efforts, block parties, and other highly visible activities (Greenberg et al., 1984c). These activities are all aimed at increasing a sense of cohesion and solidarity among participants, as well as creating an impression among the wider public (including potential offenders) that residents are actively concerned about the well-being of the community.

Summary and conclusions

Two major conclusions can be derived from the research on behavioral responses to crime. First, types of behavioral response tend to occur independently of one another. Since each type of response is a function of a different set of factors, strategies designed to encourage one type of response may be ineffective in encouraging, or may even work against the adoption of, others. Disseminating information about neighborhood crime in order to increase awareness of the problem may be one means of encouraging participation in crime prevention programs. If it is done in such a way as to produce fear, however, avoidance behavior may be increased but people may be less likely to become involved in collective activities.

Second, approaches to crime prevention must be tailored to the community. In general, collective approaches may be more difficult to establish in lower-income, heterogeneous neighborhoods, where residents sometimes fear and distrust one another and where there is generally a lower rate of participation in formal organizations. Unfortunately, these are the very areas that tend to have the most serious crime problems. Hence, special care is required in organizing activities in these areas. Programs introduced by an external agency that do not involve residents in the initial planning stages, defining the problem, or developing strategies are likely to meet with hostility and rejection in low-income areas. Strategies that emphasize protective measures and risk reduction, while at the same time ignoring the social problems that create crime, may also be ineffective in such communities. Thus, it is critical that crime prevention practitioners not approach all neighborhoods with a set, standard package. Rather, organized approaches to crime prevention must reflect the social structure of the neighborhoods they are designed to assist.

At present, there is little information on the relationship between the propensity to protect against crime and other hazards in the environment, at either the individual or the community level. Lavrakas et al. (1980) found that there is a generalized risk-avoidance disposition that causes people to feel threatened by a range of environmental hazards, including crime, disease, auto accidents, and household fires, and to expect dire consequences if they fall prey to one of these hazards. These individuals tend to be women, members of a minority, renters, and central-city residents and to have a low income; in other words, they are people who are surrounded by many environmental hazards and for whom the economic consequences of victimization would be the most serious. If generalized responses to a variety of hazards do exist, this would suggest a need for more information on the precautionary measures that are most likely to be adopted and the public education approaches that are most likely to be effective with different types of people.

Note

1 Community watch programs attempt to increase informal citizen surveillance of an apartment building, block, or neighborhood. Common activities include watching outside areas from inside the home, maintaining a telephone chain to keep an eye on strangers, and reporting suspicious or illegal events to the police. Information on improving home security is also typically a part of these programs.

References

Abt Associates. *Exemplary project validation report: Midwood-Kings Highway Development Corporation, Brooklyn, N. Y.* Report submitted to the National Institute of Justice. Cambridge, MA: Abt Associates, 1980.

Bickman, L. Bystander intervention in a crime: The effect of a mass-media campaign. *Journal of Applied Social Psychology,* 1975, *5*(4), 296–302.

Bickman, L., & Helwig, H. Bystander reporting of a crime. *Criminology,* 1979, *17*(3), 283–300.

Bickman, L., & Rosenbaum, D. P. Crime reporting as a function of bystander encouragement, surveillance, and credibility. *Journal of Personality and Social Psychology,* 1977, 35(8), 577–86.

Biderman, A. D., et al. *Report on a pilot study in the District of Columbia on victimization and the attitudes toward law enforcement.* Washington, DC: U. S. Government Printing Office, 1967.

Boggs, S. Formal and informal crime control: An exploratory study of urban, suburban and rural orientations. *Sociological Quarterly,* 1971, *12,* 319–27.

Cirel, P., Evans, P., McGillis, D., & Whitcomb, D. *Community crime prevention program in Seattle: An exemplary project.* Washington, DC: U. S. Government Printing Office, 1977.

Cohn, E. S., Kidder, L. H., & Harvey, J. Crime prevention vs. victimization prevention: The psychology of two different reactions. *Victimology,* 1978, *3,* 285–96.

Conklin, J. E. *The impact of crime.* New York: Macmillan, 1975.

DuBow, F., McCabe, E., & Kaplan, G. *Reactions to crime: A critical review of the literature.* Washington, DC: U. S. Department of Justice, National Institute of Justice, 1979.

Erbe, B. M. Race and socioeconomic segregation. *American Sociological Review,* 1975, *40*(6), 801–12.

Feins, J. D. *Partnerships for neighborhood crime prevention.* Washington, DC: U. S. Department of Justice, National Institute of Justice, 1983.

Fowler, F. J., Jr., & Mangione, T. W. *The nature of fear.* Boston, MA: University of Massachusetts, Survey Research Program, 1974.

Fowler, F. J., Jr., & Mangione, T. W. *Neighborhood crime, fear and social control: A second look at the Hartford Program.* Washington, DC: U. S. Department of Justice, National Institute of Justice, 1982.

Furstenberg, F. J., Jr. Fear of crime and its effects on citizen behavior. In A. Biderman (ed.), *Crime and justice: A symposium.* New York: Nailburg, 1972.

Furstenberg, F. J., Jr. Public reactions to crime in the streets. *American Scholar,* 1971, *40*(4), 601–10.

Gans, H. J. *The urban villagers.* New York: Free Press, 1962.

Gans, H. J. *The Levittowners.* New York: Pantheon Books, 1967.

Garofalo, J. *Public opinion about crime.* Washington, DC: Law Enforcement Assistance Administration, 1977.

Garofalo, J., & Laub, J. The fear of crime: Broadening our perspectives. *Victimology,* 1978, *3*(3–4), 242–53.

Gelfand, D. M., Hartman, D. P., Walder, P., & Page, B. Who reports shoplifters? A field experimental study. *Journal of Personality and Social Psychology,* 1973, *25*(2), 276–85.

Green, G. *Who's organizing the neighborhood?* Washington, DC: U. S. Department of Justice, Office of Community Anticrime Programs, 1979.

Greenberg, S. W., Rohe, W. M., & Williams, J. R. *Informal citizen action and crime prevention at the neighborhood level: Volume 1. Synthesis and assessment of the research.* Report submitted to the National Institute of Justice. Research Triangle Park, NC: Research Triangle Institute, 1984a.

Greenberg, S. W., Rohe, W. M., & Williams, J. R. *Informal citizen action and crime prevention at the neighborhood level: Volume 2. Secondary analysis of the relationship between responses to crime and informal social control.* Report submitted to the National Institute of Justice. Research Triangle Park, NC: Research Triangle Institute, 1984b.

Greenberg, S. W., Rohe, W. M., & Williams, J. R. *Informal citizen action and crime prevention at the neighborhood level: Volume 4. Workshop proceedings.* Report submitted to the National Institute of Justice. Research Triangle Park, NC: Research Triangle Institute, 1984c.

Greenberg, S. W., Rohe, W. M., & Williams, J. R. Safety in urban neighborhoods: A comparison of physical characteristics and informal territorial control in high and low crime neighborhoods. *Population and Environment,* 1982, *5*(3), 141–65.

Hackler, J. C., Ho, K. Y., & Urquhart-Ross, C. The willingness to intervene: Differing community characteristics. *Social Problems,* 1974, *21*(3), 328–44.

Hannerz, U. Gossip networks and culture in a black American ghetto. *Ethnos,* 1967, *32,* 35–60.

Hannerz, U. *Soulside.* New York: Free Press, 1976.

Hindelang, M. J. Race and involvement in crimes. *American Sociological Review,* 1978, *43,* 93–109.

Johnson, S. K. *Idle haven: Community building among the working-class retired.* Berkeley: University of California Press, 1971.

Kidder, R. L. *Community crime prevention: The two faces of de-legalization.* Philadelphia, PA: Temple University, Department of Sociology, 1978.

Latane, B., & Darley, J. *The nonresponsive bystander: Why doesn't he help?* New York: Appleton-Century-Crofts, 1970.

Lavrakas, P. J., & Lewis, D. A. The conceptualization and measurement of citizens' crime prevention behaviors. *Journal of Research in Crime and Delinquency,* 1980, *17,* 254–72.

Lavrakas, P. J., Normoyle, J., Skogan, W. G., Herz, E. J., Salem, G., & Lewis, D. A. *Factors related to citizen involvement in personal, household, and neighborhood anti-crime measures.* Executive Summary. Washington, DC: U. S. Department of Justice, 1980.

Law Enforcement Assistance Administration. *Guidelines manual: Guide to discretionary grant programs.* Washington, DC: Law Enforcement Assistance Administration, 1977.

Lawton, M., Powell, L. N., Yaffe, S., & Feldman, S. Psychological aspects of crime and fear of crime. In J. Goldsmith & S. Goldsmith (eds.), *Crime and the elderly.* Lexington, MA: Lexington Books, 1976.

Lewis, D. A., & Salem, G. Community crime prevention: An analysis of a developing strategy. *Crime and Delinquency,* 1981, *27*(3), 405–21.

Lewis, D. A., & Salem, G. *Crime and urban community: Towards a theory of neighborhood security.* Evanston, IL: Northwestern University, Center for Urban Affairs, 1980.

Liang, J., Hwalek, M., & Sengstock, M. *Measuring the fear of personal crime.* Paper presented at the annual meeting of the American Society of Criminology, Denver, CO, November, 1983.

Liebowitz, B. D. Age and fearfulness: Personal and situational factors. *Journal of Gerontology,* 1975, *30*(6), 696–700.

Maxfield, M. G., & Hunter, A. (eds.) *The reactions to crime papers: Volume 4. Methodological overview.* Evanston, IL: Northwestern University, Center for Urban Affairs, 1980.

McPherson, M. Realities and perceptions of crime at the neighborhood level. *Victimology,* 1978, *3,* 319–28.

McPherson, M., & Silloway, G. *Planning community crime prevention programs.* Minneapolis: Minnesota Crime Prevention Center, 1980.

Merry, S. E. Going to court: Strategies of dispute management in an American urban neighborhood. *Law and Society Review,* 1979, *13,* 891–925.

Merry, S. E. *Urban danger: Life in a neighborhood of strangers.* Philadelphia, PA: Temple University Press, 1981a.

Merry, S. E. Defensible space undefended. *Urban Affairs Quarterly,* 1981b, *16*(4), 397–422.

Moriarty, T. Crime, commitment, and the responsive bystander: Two field experiments. *Journal of Personality and Social Psychology,* 1975, *31*(2), 370–6.

O'Brien, D. J. *Neighborhood organization and the interest group process.* Princeton, NJ: Princeton University Press, 1975.

Piven, F. F., & Cloward, R. A. *Regulating the poor: The functions of public welfare.* New York: Vintage Books, 1971.

Podolefsky, A. Community response to crime prevention: The Mission District. *Journal of Community Action,* 1983, *1*(5), 43–8.

Podolefsky, A., & DuBow, F. *The reactions to crime papers: Volume 2. Strategies for community crime prevention.* Evanston, IL: Northwestern University, Center for Urban Affairs, 1980.

Rainwater, L. Fear and the house-has-haven in the lower class. *Journal of the American Institute of Planners,* 1966, *32,* 23–31.

Roberts, B. R. *Organizing strangers: Poor families in a Guatemala city.* Austin: University of Texas Press, 1973.

Roehl, J., & Cook, R. *National evaluation of the Urban Crime Prevention Program.* Reston, VA: Institute for Social Analysis, 1983.

Rohe, W. M., & Greenberg, S. W. Participation in community watch programs. *Journal of Urban Affairs,* 1984, *6*(3), 53–65.

Rosenstock, I. Why people use health services. *Milbank Memorial Fund Quarterly,* 1966, *44,* 94–127.

Ross, A. S. Effect of increased responsibility on bystander intervention: The presence of children. *Journal of Personality and Social Psychology,* 1971, *19*(3), 306–10.

Schneider, A. L., & Schneider, P. B. *Private and public-minded citizens responses to a neighborhood-based crime prevention strategy.* Eugene, OR: Institute of Policy Analysis, 1978.

Schwartz, S. H., & Gottlieb, A. Bystander reactions to a violent theft: Crime in Jerusalem. *Journal of Personality and Social Psychology,* 1976, *34*(6), 1188–99.

Skogan, W. G., & Maxfield, M. G. *The reactions to crime papers: Volume 1. Coping with crime: Victimization, fear and reactions to crime in three American cities.* Evanston, IL: Northwestern University, Center for Urban Affairs, 1980.

Spergel, I. *Racketville, Slumtown, Haulberg.* University of Chicago Press, 1964.

Stinchcombe, A., Heimer, C., Iliff, R. A., Scheppele, K., Smith, T. W., & Taylor, D. G. *Crime and punishment in public opinion: 1948–1974.* Chicago: National Opinion Research Center, 1978.

Sundeen, R. A., & Mathieu, J. T. The fear of crime and its consequences among elderly in three urban areas. *Gerontologist,* 1976, *16,* 211–19.

Suttles, G. D. *The social order of the slum.* University of Chicago Press, 1968.

Taub, R. P., Taylor, D. G., & Dunham, J. D. *Safe and secure neighborhoods: Territoriality, solidarity, and the reduction of crime.* Chicago: National Opinion Research Center, 1982.

Taylor, R. B., Gottfredson, S., & Brower, S. *Informal control in the urban residential environment.* Report submitted to the National Institute of Justice. Baltimore, MD: Johns Hopkins University, 1981.

Titus, R. M. Residential burglary and the community response. In R. V. G. Clarke (ed.), *Coping with burglary: Research perspectives on policy.* Boston: Kluwer-Nijhoff, in press.

Warren, D. I. Neighborhood structure and riot behavior in Detroit: some exploratory findings. *Social Problems,* 1969, *16,* 464–84.

Washnis, G. T. *Citizen involvement in crime prevention.* Lexington, MA: Heath, 1976.

Whyte, W. H., Jr. *The organization man.* Garden City, NJ: Doubleday Anchor, 1957.

Wilson, J. Q., & Kelling, G. L. The police and neighborhood safety: Broken windows. *Atlantic Monthly,* 1982, *127,* 29–38.

Yin, R. K., Vogel, M. E., Chaiken, J. M., & Both, D. R. *Citizen patrol projects* (Phase I Summary Report). National Evaluation Program. Washington, DC: U. S. Department of Justice, 1977.

12 Promoting citizen involvement in crime prevention and control

Fred Heinzelmann

Introduction

Crime and the fear of crime are high on the list of public concerns. The reality of the problem is reflected in Department of Justice figures indicating that more than one household in four will experience a serious crime during the year (Bureau of Justice Statistics, 1986). Violent crimes are, in fact, more frequent than many other serious life events. For example, the risk of being a victim of a violent crime is greater than the risk of injury in an auto accident, injury or death from a fire, or death from heart disease or cancer (Bureau of Justice Statistics, 1983).

Fear of crime is often linked to fear of victimization by a stranger, as in robbery and burglary, crimes that have shown dramatic increases in the past 20 years. The reported robbery rate, for example, increased 400% between 1960 and 1978, with 65% of these crimes involving armed offenders (National Institute of Justice, 1983). The rate of burglary has also increased significantly, recent national crime surveys indicating an annual rate of 1 of every 11 U.S. households.

Although the problem of crime has usually been seen as the responsibility of the criminal justice system, increased attention is being given to the contribution that citizens can make to their own security. During the past two decades, for example, several national commissions have emphasized the need for an active and involved citizenry, both in reducing crime and in improving the performance of the criminal justice system (President's Commission on Law Enforcement, 1967; National Advisory Commission on Criminal Justice Standards and Goals, 1973).

There is currently a greater willingness on the part of law enforcement agencies to involve citizens and community groups in the prevention and control of crime than there has been in the past. Several factors have influenced this development. Perhaps foremost among these is the fact that public funds are being curtailed in many communities. Thus, fewer police resources are available. In addition, accumulating evidence suggests that increases in the level of police patrol and changes in patrolling methods (such as using foot patrols rather then vehicle patrols) can have only a limited impact on crime rates (Kelling, Pate, Dieckman, & Brown, 1974; Kelling & Pate, 1981). Citizens and police alike are aware of these reductions in police resources and the limited impact of police operations on crime. A national survey, for example, found that 60% of the public believe that they and the police have equal responsibility for community security, and 80% indicated that crime prevention can work (Mendelsohn & O'Keefe, 1981). Police have also become more aware of the benefits of mobilizing citizen actions and response. Thus, both citizens and police appear to be receptive to collaborative efforts in dealing with crime.

Citizen concern about security has led to a sharpened focus on preventing victimization in specific situations (Clarke, 1983). The failure to control crime by changing the behavior of offenders has also prompted greater efforts to influence the behavior of citizens as potential victims of crime. A variety of citizen actions and environmental security strategies have therefore been designed to reduce criminal opportunities and to increase the likelihood of offender apprehension.

Citizens' involvement in and support for the criminal justice system (society's formal means of controlling crime) is also critical. Less than half of all the crimes that occur are ever reported to the police (Bureau of Justice Statistics, 1983). Whether a crime is reported depends on the victim's views about the seriousness of the crime, whether the victim was injured, the victim's attitudes about getting involved in the criminal justice process, the victim's perceptions of both police interest and their ability to do something about the incident (Bickman et al., 1977). The importance of encouraging citizen crime reporting has been clearly demonstrated. Delays in citizen reporting tend to nullify the potential impact of rapid police response to crime. In addition, citizens often provide crucial information and testimony leading to successful investigations, arrests, and convictions (Greenwood & Petersilia, 1975; Forst, Lucianovic and Cox, 1978; Spelman & Brown, 1981). Public cooperation with law enforcement personnel is often the most important factor influencing the outcomes of criminal justice efforts.

Community crime prevention activities

Community crime prevention efforts are directed at reducing both the incidence and the fear of crime and involve a variety of personal, household, and neighborhood anticrime activities (Lavrakas et al., 1981; Mendelsohn & O'Keefe, 1981; Podolefsky & DuBow, 1982; Greenberg, Rohe, & Williams, 1985). Through these crime-control measures, citizens along with police and other criminal justice personnel have been shown to influence community safety and security (Pennell, 1978; Percy, 1979; Yin, 1979; Rosentraub & Harlow, 1980).

Self-protective behavior

Self-imposed behavioral restriction appears to be the most common response citizens make to the risk of personal victimization. The goal is avoiding risk rather than resisting or deterring crime. Because such actions are directed at protecting the individual, they can be viewed as a "private-minded" form of crime prevention behavior. Women and the elderly, in particular, indicate that they avoid certain areas or individuals, that they do not travel at night, or that they travel only with others (Mendelsohn & O'Keefe, 1981). Other actions taken for personal protection include acquiring a weapon, developing self-defense skills, and taking actions (such as carrying credit cards rather than cash) to limit the amount of loss should victimization occur.

Household-protective behavior

A number of actions can be taken by citizens to provide household protection for both family and property. Most typical is "access control" to prevent unlawful entry or to deter offenders from targeting one's residence or goods. Security surveys of homes (usually conducted by police) can help to determine the most useful means of providing protection. More than 40% of burglaries involve entry through unlocked doors and windows (National Criminal Justice Information and Statistics Service, 1979). Therefore, recommended actions include the consistent use of bolt-locking doors and secured windows, marking portable goods with some form of personal identification, and using lighting and other methods to ensure that the household appears occupied. Studies suggest that when citizens carry out these kinds of actions, they are less likely to be victimized (Seattle Law and Justice Planning Office, 1975; Cirel, Evans, McGillis, & Whitcomb, 1977; Rubenstein, Murray, Motoyama, & Rouse, 1980). Household-protective measures are also examples of private-minded crime prevention behaviors, because the individual and immediate household are seen as the primary beneficiaries. Such measures are more common among homeowners than renters; the former have a greater economic and psychological investment in their homes and can exercise greater control over their property. It does not appear that one type of home-protective measure substitutes for others. Rather, the use of such household-based anticrime measures appear to be complementary so that people who take one precaution are more, not less, likely to adopt others (Lavrakas et al., 1981).

Neighborhood-protective behavior

Citizens can take actions in concert to promote neighborhood security. These activities usually involve groups of citizens working together in informal surveillance and reporting of suspicious events, in various kinds of citizen patrols, and in neighborhood escort activities. Fear of crime may lead to participation in collective anticrime efforts, but such participation more often follows from involvement in community organizations dealing with general neighborhood improvement that have added crime prevention to their agenda (Lavrakas et al., 1981; Podelefsky & DuBow, 1982). These neighborhood activities can be viewed as "public-minded" crime prevention behaviors, because the intended beneficiaries include all of the residents in the area. Although involvement in collective forms of citizen anticrime behavior is growing, the majority of citizens who are aware of such efforts do not get involved. There is some evidence that involvement in such activities may be "proactive" in suburban areas (where residents want to keep crime from becoming a problem), whereas inner-city residents who engage in such collective activities may be responding "reactively" to crime as an existing neighborhood problem.

It should be mentioned that neighborhood groups that address crime and fear of crime may help deal with other threats in the community. For example, neighborhood block watch groups often provide an organizational structure and a communication network for alerting citizens and mobilizing response regardless of whether the threat is crime, a natural hazard such as an earthquake or flood, a problem relating to neighborhood traffic safety, or a local health problem.

Citizen crime prevention programs

A number of crime prevention programs have been developed to encourage citizens to adopt behaviors intended to provide personal, household, or neighborhood protection. Assessments of these programs offer a measure of public response to them and also give some indication of their effects in reducing crime and fear.

Property-marking programs

Property-marking projects encourage citizens to mark their goods with some form of personal identification (often one's social security number) in order to deter theft or to enhance the likelihood that stolen goods will be identified and returned by the police. In short, the objective is both loss prevention and loss reduction. Property-marking (Operation Identification) projects were examined by Heller, Stenzel, Gill, Kolde, and Schimerman (1975). Nationwide data were collected by telephone from 99 projects, and more detailed site visits were made to 18 projects. It was found that participation rates of even 10% of the targeted households were difficult to achieve. This may be due in part to citizens' skepticism about the efficacy of property-marking procedures (O'Keefe & Mendelsohn, 1984). The more effective, personalized attempts to promote participation in these programs (through door-to-door contacts or personal presentations to citizen groups) were also the most costly. Although people who participated in the programs were burglarized significantly less often than nonparticipants, the results suggest that participants may also have implemented other protective measures. Perhaps due to the limited level of citizen participation, participating neighborhoods did not experience overall reductions in burglary rates. Increases were not achieved in burglary apprehensions or in the recovery or return of stolen property, although the latter finding may simply reflect the fact that police departments are not always sufficiently well organized to process recovered stolen property.

Security survey programs

Security surveys seek to identify the physical sources of vulnerability to burglary in residential and commercial buildings. On the basis of survey results, occupants take specific actions to reduce the opportunity for crime by "hardening the target" (e.g., installing better door locks, providing more adequate lighting, securing windows). In a national evaluation of programs providing building-security surveys (International Training, Research and Evaluation Council, ITREC, 1977), 206 programs were contacted by mail or telephone and 20 were assessed during site visits. Few of the programs had carried out physical security surveys in more than 10% of the households in their jurisdiction and less than 20% of the programs maintained any data on citizen compliance with the security recommendations that were made. Nonetheless, the authors suggest that "when survey recommendations are implemented, a recipient is less likely to be victimized." Here again it should be noted that other crime prevention measures may also have been implemented by the households participating in the program. The evaluation revealed that security surveys may improve police–community relations and may have some educational value in conveying other crime prevention information during the survey visit.

Citizen surveillance and reporting programs

Citizen surveillance and reporting programs teach citizens how to recognize suspicious events or crimes and how to report such events effectively. Although most of these programs are directed at residential settings, others encourage people to carry out surveillance and reporting while working. The latter programs often include delivery and trades personnel, letter carriers, realtors, and taxi drivers. They are encouraged to report anything suspicious that they observe as they make their routine rounds. Many of these people have ready access to two-way radios or telephones and can summon appropriate authorities quite rapidly.

Citizen crime-reporting projects were evaluated by Bickman et al. (1977), who obtained information from 78 projects nationwide, with site visits carried out in 20 locations. Although data limitations prevented the authors from making a precise evaluation, the findings suggest that information campaigns publicizing these programs can make large segments of the public aware of their existence. Effects on surveillance and crime-reporting behavior are more likely to be long lasting when presentations are made in home gatherings so that residents become acquainted and begin to establish continuing relationships. The authors also recommend that citizens give special attention to drivers of radio-equipped vehicles in "radio watch" programs.

Citizen patrol programs

Citizen patrols usually involve surveillance of particular areas on regular schedules. Such patrols aim to deter crime by reporting suspicious events to police rather than intervening in them. A national evaluation of citizen patrol projects was undertaken (Yin, Vogel, Chaiken, & Both, 1977). On the basis of limited evidence, the evaluators concluded that building patrols are likely to be more effective in reducing crime and fear than neighborhood patrols. The former serve a smaller and more clearly bounded area, which permits greater control to be exercised. Evidence on other types of patrol was too inconclusive for any assessment. Factors leading to patrol effectiveness included selection and training of members, established administrative procedures (schedules, rosters, etc.), affiliation with larger community organizations, and positive contacts with the police. In general, citizen patrols may reduce the fear of crime, and there is little evidence that they engage in vigilante-like behavior. The Guardian Angels consist of volunteers who patrol streets and subways in more than 50 cities. A recent evaluation of their activities indicates that such efforts can reduce fear and may also reduce property crimes to some extent (National Institute of Justice, 1986).

More comprehensive crime prevention programs

Several major themes emerge from a review of the preceding programs. First, it is evident that such efforts are far more likely to be effective if they are part of a comprehensive approach to community crime prevention, one that includes the use of security surveys, property marking, and some form of protective neighboring involving surveillance and crime reporting. Programs that are part of a more comprehensive crime reduction strategy must also address signs of disorder, such as broken windows, graffiti, vacant buildings, vandalism, abandoned cars, and littering, which may contribute to fear of crime as well as actual victimization. Second, a comprehensive approach can increase citizen participation levels beyond those commonly found in projects dealing with a single form of action, because there is a broader base for generating interest. Third, all program efforts are more likely to be successful if they (a) recruit citizens on a personal basis, (b) encourage interaction among citizens and between citizens and the police, and (c) provide consistent feedback to citizens on the operations and impact of the program.

A comprehensive approach to crime prevention is important because evaluations of such programs indicate that they can help to reduce crime and fear and improve the quality of life and viability of urban neighborhoods. (Rosenbaum, 1986). Fortunately, this approach to community crime prevention has become a more common strategy of both community groups and the police. Titus (1984a) provided a very useful review and synthesis of citizen crime prevention efforts that include home security, area surveillance, and reporting to police, features typical of neighborhood watch or block watch programs. The evidence suggests that these programs may be effective in reducing burglary and fear of crime while possibly offering other benefits as well. Such indirect benefits may include improved police–community relations and neighborhood revitalization. Although many opportunities exist for citizen involvement in such programs, actual participation in organized neighborhood crime prevention activities ranges from 7 to 20% (Greenberg et al., 1984). Thus, the proportion of citizens participating in these programs is modest, though an estimated 6 million Americans overall are currently involved in such efforts.

Key elements of citizen crime prevention programs

In the 1970s the federal government began to provide funds for the development of crime prevention activities, and from 1977 to 1981 more than $50 million were made available. Support for crime prevention programs was provided to local criminal justice agencies or directly to local community groups. In addition to neighborhood watch and similar activities, which focus on reducing opportunities for criminal activity, programs included antiarson projects, victim-assistance projects, dispute-resolution projects, and efforts to divert potential offenders from involvement in the criminal justice system. Research and program experiences have identified some of the aspects of these programs that make them effective (Feins, Peterson, & Rovetch, 1983; Krug, 1984; Roehl & Cook, 1984; Titus, 1984a).

Neighborhood programs can be organized through the cooperative efforts of police departments and interested citizens or through existing neighborhood organizations. The latter strategy has been found to be particularly useful. Citizen participation in planning and subsequent decision making was more evident in programs that were organized directly through local community groups than in programs that sought the involvement of citizens through the activities of law enforcement agencies or some other citywide agency. Such neighborhood groups are often attuned to the needs of residents, and they provide a structure within which collective actions can be organized and carried out. In addition, they often have their own resources. They may offer a communication system that provides residents with information about crime prevention activities and feedback about their success. The durability of such organizations also helps to sustain citizen anticrime activity. Two generalizations seem to be supported here. First, a strategy that involves direct dealings with local community groups is effective in promoting meaningful participation among neighborhood residents. Second, with a top-down approach, heavy citizen involvement can be expected only if a strong participatory neighborhood structure is already in place.

Getting to know the community and its concerns is an important initial step in the organizing process. It is necessary to understand what citizens consider to be feasible solutions. Awareness of the social composition of the community, the different attitudes and expectations of various sub-groups, and the neighborhood's leadership structure and social networks are all important.

Special attention should be given to problem identification, goal setting, and activity selections. It is important to identify both specific target-area crime problems and resources available for addressing them. A neighborhood's crime problems can be determined from police statistics, victimization surveys, and observations and discussions with residents. Because factors contributing to crime and fear vary, even over a small area, targeting is essential in order to select the most appropriate crime prevention activities for a given location. The strategies that are chosen should take into account the influence of the neighborhood's physical environment on the prevention and control of crime (Wallis & Ford, 1980; Heinzelmann, 1981). Research suggests that programs should begin by encouraging citizens to exercise control over their own immediate surroundings and property rather than attempt at the outset to create a feeling of responsibility for the entire block or neighborhood (Taylor, Gottfredson, & Brower, 1983).

Maintaining citizen interest and involvement in neighborhood anti-crime efforts is often a significant problem. Expanding a program's agenda to deal with other neighborhood problems can help; so can feed-back and periodic rewards to participants. It is useful to keep in mind that people's reasons for joining such programs may be primarily instrumental (problem solving), but their reasons for remaining active may be more expressive (social affiliation and enjoyment of activities). Crime prevention program efforts are more likely to be sustained if citizen groups establish effective working relationships with the criminal justice system and with other municipal agencies (e.g., fire departments and housing authorities) whose activities can also affect the community's sense of security.

Program monitoring and evaluation are important components of neighborhood crime prevention activities. Through monitoring, participants are apprised of one another's opinions concerning the program's strengths and weaknesses. They also learn what activities are actually taking place and discover ways of improving the program's operations. Evaluations should be undertaken to determine if a program is meeting its objectives. It is important to consider an array of consequences, since crime reduction may be difficult to document. Evaluation should include the assessment of fear reduction, resident satisfaction and use of the neighborhood, and effects on neighborhood revitalization. Because the development and implementation of a program evaluation plan may be complex, personnel at local colleges and universities should be considered as possible sources of assistance.

Success in promoting citizen involvement seems to depend on the nature of the crime prevention activity. Activities that include simple and direct forms of citizen action and that address problems of potential concern to everyone (e.g., personal risk reduction and mutual protection) are more likely to be effective in mobilizing citizens than are efforts that involve more complex and less tangible activities, such as efforts to document insurance coverage of arson-prone buildings. The evidence suggests that programs that develop collective forms of citizen response are more likely to become institutionalized and to have lasting effects, than programs that emphasize individual response.

Likewise, neighborhood characteristics influence the level of citizen involvement, participation being greater in relatively stable and culturally homogeneous neighborhoods than in socially fragmented and deteriorating areas. In low-income and culturally heterogeneous areas, immediate financial needs, a lower sense of efficacy, and greater suspicion of formal organizations may contribute to lower participation (Greenberg et al., 1985). Participation also seems to be higher in neighborhoods with loosely knit social networks than in neighborhoods with tightly knit social networks (Rohe & Greenberg, 1984). Tightly knit social networks – an individual's friends are also likely to be friends of one another – appear to provide considerable informal social control but discourage participation in formal community organizations. Such networks are often found in ethnic neighborhoods.

Some model crime prevention programs

A number of programs have been exemplary in involving citizens in the prevention and control of crime (Cirel et al., 1977; Feins et al., 1983; Greenberg et al., 1985). Many of these programs were developed and implemented with federal funding and they provide useful models for marshaling and sustaining citizen action.

The Seattle program focused on residential burglary with an effort made to target specific neighborhoods for crime prevention involvement (Cirel et al., 1977). Personal contacts with residents made by program personnel in a systematic, block-by-block sweep of the neighborhood produced a 40% participation rate. The program involved property marking, household security inspections, and block watch activities. Efforts were made to maintain citizen involvement through periodic meetings, publication of a newsletter, and other efforts to provide regular feedback to participants. The Seattle program was developed and implemented by citizens under the aegis of the city government and with the support of the local police. The evidence suggests that the civilian nature of the program increased the likelihood of citizen participation and compliance. The findings also suggest that project effects in reducing crime lasted 12 to 18 months before waning, indicating a need to maintain and periodically review program efforts.

The specific operations carried out in the Seattle program merit a more detailed review because they can provide a useful example for other communities. The key to the Seattle program is saturation. Focusing on the single crime of residential burglary, the program staff select a neighborhood and then methodically cover that area street by street until it has been saturated. The result is a continuum of organized and secure households rather than haphazard pockets of serviced homes.

After a neighborhood has been targeted by program personnel, the first step involves contacting the police and local citizen organizations. This makes it possible to learn about the neighborhood's crime problems and the areas that are considered unsafe or vulnerable. Existing groups can help in contacting citizens and generating support for the program. Resident contact is initially made by mail or telephone. Citizens are informed of the incidence of burglary in their neighborhood and the fact that free burglary prevention services will be made available. These include home security checks, property marking, and neighborhood block watch activities. Citizens are told that program staff will contact them in the near future to discuss the program, answer their questions, and enlist their participation.

The next contact phase involves "doorbelling," usually done in the evening when most residents are at home. During these contacts, program staff review the elements of the program and encourage participation in all program services, especially in the block watch component. Subsequently, a block watch meeting is held, usually in the home of an individual who has agreed to act as host for the initial meeting. That person is asked to invite all of his or her neighbors. At the block watch meeting, the program organizer provides information on burglaries in the neighborhood. He or she may indicate the number of burglaries that occurred during the past month (and during the same month a year ago), the types of residences burglarized, the days and times of the incidents, the places and methods of entry, an inventory of items stolen, and a map indentifying burglary locations. The program organizer then discusses facts about burglary that are particularly relevant to citizen action, pointing out that most incidents occur during the day, that it is possible for citizens to witness them, and that traditional police patrols can have only a minimal impact on the situation. Emphasis is placed on the idea that properly organized and informed citizens can effectively combat crime.

Residents are then counseled in some of the methods that burglars employ, how to look out for suspicious activity, what to observe and how best to report it, and the importance of calling the police promptly. The procedures involved in carrying out block watch activities are described. Residents are also advised to learn neighbors' routines and vacation schedules. Security measures, including the home security checklist and the use of an engraving tool to mark personal property, are demonstrated. In the small-group setting it is possible to provide a meaningful review of residential burglary and the problems it presents along with a discussion of realistic measures for dealing with the problem. Concern and responsibility to act are raised by getting individuals committed to the block watch concept and by providing instruction in specific actions judged to be effective.

A block watch captain is then elected, and that person becomes the liaison between the neighborhood watch participants and the program staff. All persons at the meeting are asked to write their name, address, and telephone number on a blank map of the block. Later, copies are distributed to all block watch members. Block captains subsequently make periodic contact with their neighbors, either individually or through block meetings, to provide information on the current status of the program and its effectiveness, to arrange for home security inspections or the marking of property, and to obtain current information on problems that residents believe should be addressed by the police and residents together.

Other programs in Detroit, San Diego, Minneapolis, Chicago, New York City, and Newark have been highlighted as useful examples of effective citizen involvement in crime prevention (Figgie International, 1983; Feins et al., 1983). A program in Hartford, Connecticut, has received special attention because of its use of community, law enforcement and environmental security strategies (Fowler & Mangione, 1982). Several features are common to these successful programs. They build strong support in the neighborhood, usually beginning with existing community organizations but also establishing new links between police and residents and among other neighborhood organizations, service groups, and city agencies. Attention is given to building an organizational structure that makes the best use of available resources in the community and police department. The programs employ a variety of methods to maintain citizen interest and commitment to crime prevention. To ensure that efforts

STRATEGIES

	Communication and Persuasion	Provision of Incentives and Reduction of Constraints
PROTECTIVE BEHAVIOR		
Private-minded Concerns (Self-Protection and Household Protection)	1	3
Public-minded Concerns (Neighborhood and Other Forms of Mutual Protection)	2	4

Figure 12.1. Strategies for promoting protective behavior.

are maintained, crime prevention may be linked to a broader agenda of community issues such as fire protection, adequate street lighting, housing rehabilitation, and safe roads.

Strategies for promoting citizen involvement in the prevention and control of crime

Figure 12.1 provides a conceptual framework for considering the strategies used to promote protective behavior, not only against crime but against other hazards as well. It is important to consider both "private-minded" actions (dealing with personal protection or household safety) as well as more "public-minded" actions, such as those involved in the promotion of neighborhood security. This public–private distinction can be applied to other kinds of protective behavior. For example, in discussing injury prevention, attention can be given to behaviors that lead to home accidents as well as to collective efforts to reduce traffic accidents by improving lighting or reducing visual barriers on neighborhood streets.

Communication and persuasion strategies

A major strategy employed to encourage crime prevention behavior has been the communication of crime prevention information. The goal is to persuade people to carry out recommended actions *voluntarily,* either as individuals or in concert with others. The communication vehicles include television, newspapers, radio, posters, brochures, and newsletters. The materials are distributed door to door, at community meetings, and via the mass media. In addition, more direct and personal forms of communication have been used with individuals or members of small groups. It is important to recognize that the audiences being addressed may respond to these forms of communications in terms of their own values, beliefs, and personal needs. Therefore, the information presented may not always be processed in accordance with the intent of the communicator.

The messages generally emphasize the relevance and effectiveness of particular crime prevention actions. Less attention is devoted to the nature and severity of the crime threat, perhaps on the assumption that the threat is already well recognized. This focus on action differs from other hazard reduction campaigns, such as natural hazard, disease, and safety campaigns, in which a concerted effort is usually made to convince people of the seriousness of a threat. Many community crime programs use materials provided by the National Crime Prevention Campaign (National Crime Prevention Council, 1984). Typical of publications that convey these messages are booklets–entitled, for example, "Protect Yourself" and "Protecting Your Neighborhood"–that present a variety of recommendations. The materials on self-protection involve actions to be taken in one's home, on the street, against rape, as a senior citizen against fraud, against arson, and as a small business owner. The recommendations include the use of proper locks, lights, and other security devices, means of responding to suspicious situations, recognizing and avoiding dangerous areas, traveling with someone rather than alone, and taking specific actions to ensure that one's home never appears unoccupied. In the booklet entitled "Protecting Your Neighborhood," the emphasis again is on a variety of actions, including joining one's neighbors in such activities as neighborhood watch, citizen patrols, or escort services. Whether the program materials focus on self-protection or collective or mutual protection, they often include specific examples of how others in designated locations have effectively carried out similar actions.

Mass media communication strategies

Use of the mass media to encourage crime prevention actions is currently reflected in the National Crime Prevention Campaign. This national media campaign is sponsored by the Crime Prevention Coalition in cooperation with the Advertising Council. The objectives of the campaign are to promote a sense of responsibility for crime prevention among citizens and to dispel unwarranted feelings of frustration and hopelessness regarding crime and criminal justice. The campaign encourages citizens to work with law enforcement agencies, to take specific actions to reduce the risk of victimization, and to improve the security of their households and neighborhoods through individual and cooperative efforts. The campaign generally does not focus explicitly on the likelihood or seriousness of the threat of crime, because public concern about crime is already quite evident.

The media campaign consists of public service advertisements (PSAs), which are disseminated by broadcast and print media at their own expense. The campaign symbol in these PSAs is a trenchcoated, hound dog cartoon character named McGruff, who urges citizens to "help take a bite out of crime." More than $50 million in broadcast time and print space was donated annually to the campaign by media outlets during the campaign's first two years of operation. About 1 million crime prevention booklets were distributed free of charge in the first two years in response to PSAs, and another 250,000 were sold through the Government Printing Office. In addition, the media campaign was tied to local community-based crime prevention efforts throughout the country.

In 1984, an evaluation of the first three years of the campaign was completed (O'Keefe & Mendelsohn, 1984). The focus of the evaluation was the degree to which the campaign promoted crime prevention competence among citizens, as determined by their awareness, attitudes, and behavior. The evaluation design included a national probability sample survey of 1,200 adults to determine overall citizen response to the campaign and a three-city panel survey of 426 adults (carried out before and two years after the campaign began) to assess changes in crime prevention competence as a function of exposure to the campaign.

The results indicate that the campaign received widespread public exposure. More than half of the adult population had seen or heard the public service crime prevention ads. In general, the response to the ads was very favorable. The findings suggest that the campaign had marked and consistent influences on citizen knowledge and attitudes regarding crime prevention. Respondents indicated they not only had obtained new information about prevention techniques but had been reminded of information they had forgotten. The confidence of persons exposed to the campaign in their ability to protect themselves increased considerably, as did their belief in the effectiveness of crime prevention efforts.

Most important, however, the campaign actually increased crime prevention behavior. About one-fourth of the respondents in the national probability sample who were exposed to the campaign said they had taken preventive actions as a result of the campaign. This represents approximately 30 million Americans. The actions taken most frequently were directed at improving household security and cooperating more often with neighbors – two of the principal campaign recommendations. Increased preventive activity was even more impressive in the panel sample. Before the campaign, panel members were asked how often they carried out 25 specific crime prevention actions. Seven of these actions were subsequently given particular emphasis in the campaign, including locking doors when out of the house, using time-controlled lights, reporting suspicious events to police, and joining with others to prevent crime. Two years later panelists who had seen or heard the crime prevention ads registered statistically significant increases in reported actions over persons who had not been exposed to the campaign with respect to six of the seven crime prevention activities recommended in the ads. There were no such increases in the 18 nonrecommended actions.

In summary, the National Crime Prevention Campaign influenced both private- and public-minded forms of crime prevention behavior (Figure 12.1, cells 1 and 2), serving as an effective mechanism of communication and persuasion. On the whole, the program had its greatest effect in promoting cooperative actions, but it also promoted individual crime deterrence and surveillance actions. These evaluation findings are consistent with the results of other studies that suggest that public information campaigns may have significant effects on public cognition, attitudes, and behaviors including those related to disease prevention and the promotion of health and personal well-being (Douglas, Westley, & Chafee, 1970; O'Keefe, 1971; Hanneman & McEwen, 1973; Mendelsohn, 1973; Salcedo, Read, Evans, & Kong, 1974; Schmeling & Wotring, 1980; Atkin, 1979; McAlister, Puska, Korkela, Pallonen, & Maccoby, 1980; Maccoby & Solomon, 1981).

The use of newsletters to transmit information about crime and crime prevention to citizens was examined in an exploratory study (Lavrakas, Rosenbaum, & Kaminski, 1983). Monthly newsletters were prepared in two versions: with and without information on local crime incidents. Both versions contained crime prevention tips for residents. The residents who received the newsletter with the crime incident listings were more likely to report taking crime prevention actions, were more likely to report being motivated by the newsletter, and were more likely to attribute responsibility for prevention crime to citizens rather than the police than were those who received the second newsletter. The crime information version of the newsletter was also rated more interesting and informative than the other, yet it did not appear to increase fear or feelings of personal vulnerability to crime. The use of similar newsletters in two other study sites did not reveal significant changes in citizen crime prevention attitudes or behavior, but the newsletters received a very positive response from citizens (Pate, Lavrakas, Wycoff, Skogan, & Sherman, 1984). Thus, newsletters that include information on crime prevention may be effective means of communicating with neighborhood residents without necessarily increasing the fear of crime.

Other communication strategies

Attention has been given to the use of more personal and direct forms of communication and persuasion. For example, a number of studies have demonstrated the effectiveness of small-group discussion in promoting behavior change (Lewin, 1947; Bennett, 1955; Bond, 1956; Brunner, 1959; Heinzelmann, 1959). Many of these small-group education efforts were aimed at promoting behavior and citizen participation in programs that address disease prevention and other risks, although none of the studies dealt directly with crime prevention. The evidence suggests that small-group discussion per se is not the key factor in behavior change. More important is that the individual's *decision* to change his or her behavior is made public in a small-group context and is seen to be supported by the group. However, the small-group context can provide an opportunity to explore and evaluate ways of carrying out recommended actions or behavior. The small-group setting also makes it possible to identify misunderstandings and to deal with other barriers to action that may not become apparent when feedback is not provided. Small-group meetings can provide an increased awareness of the need for action as well as greater understanding and support for the implementation of such actions.

Although small-group discussions require considerable resources and time, they can be very effective. For example, attendance at small-group block meetings to discuss crime prevention has been found to increase significantly both private- and public-minded forms of protective behavior (e.g., private anticrime actions, bystander helpfulness, and actions involving mutual protection) (Bickman et al., 1977; Cirel et al., 1977; Schneider & Schneider, 1978). In general, small-group approaches are more likely to be effective than mass media approaches in establishing real changes in behavior.

Person-to-person contact can also promote crime prevention behavior. This approach is particularly useful as a follow-up to encourage implementation of crime prevention recommendations. For example, in an evaluation of commercial security survey programs, it was found that compliance with recommendations was greatly enhanced through personal follow-up in which the visiting program representative answered questions from business people and encouraged further compliance (Cahn & Tien, 1983).

Communication content

The types of messages that inform citizens about crime prevention and attempt to persuade them to adopt appropriate behaviors also merit attention. In this context, consideration should be given to a model of individual decision making that has important implications for the promotion of protective behavior. The health belief model developed by Rosenstock (1960) has been found to be relevant to health behaviors as well as crime prevention actions (Becker & Maiman, 1975; Becker et al., 1977; Lavrakas et al., 1981; Skogan, 1981).

Mendelsohn and O'Keefe (1981) suggest that the health belief model provides a useful framework for the design of crime prevention communications. According to the model, responses to communications advocating crime prevention actions depend on beliefs concerning vulnerability to victimization, the perceived impact of victimization, and the likelihood that the advocated actions will reduce or eliminate the crime threat. Mendelsohn and colleagues propose the development of communications on behalf of crime prevention that address these beliefs and that present risk–benefit messages in forms that are realistic and meaningful.

The research evidence concerning the effects of specific messages on crime prevention behavior is not consistent or complete. For example, although moderate fear appeals are sometimes effective, messages that have a narrative, dramatic, or even humorous content, but do not capitalize on fear arousal – as in the National Crime Prevention Campaign – are effective nonetheless. Mendelsohn and O'Keefe (1981) conclude that communications exploiting high fear arousal are usually more persuasive than low-fear appeals with the following caveats. (a) Beyond a certain point, high-fear appeals are more likely to inhibit action, than to promote it; (b) high-fear communications must incorporate realistic solutions that can be easily pursued by audiences *plus* explicit directions and instructions for accomplishing such solutions; (c) high-fear appeals must have credible sources; (d) such appeals must be directed to recipients who are more used to *coping* with threats than avoiding them and; (e) persons who consider themselves highly vulnerable to crime cannot be frightened into taking actions other than avoidance.

It is helpful to keep in mind that citizen reactions to crime may also be influenced by evidence of physical and social disorganization (Lewis, Salem, & Szoc, 1980). These signs of disorder may include broken windows, litter, graffiti, boarded-up buildings, or abandoned cars. Other problems may include groups of loitering youths or adults and evidence of alcohol or drug abuse. All of these factors can convey a lack of control and contribute to feelings of insecurity, which may lead to subsequent increases in crime (Wilson & Kelling, 1982).

Although the perception of crime risk is influenced by victimization and by evidence of disorder, the degree of satisfaction with safety in one's neighborhood is affected to a greater extent by global assessments of the present or future quality of the neighborhood (Taub, Taylor, & Dunham, 1981). Thus, persons may tolerate fairly high levels of crime as long as they find other aspects of community life gratifying. However, when the residents' level of satisfaction is reduced because of physical deterioration or social change, crime is likely to become a major source of citizen dissatisfaction. This means that citizen response to crime can be understood only in the context of other aspects of community life. Therefore messages designed to motivate citizens to become involved in crime prevention may have to focus not only on crime but also on other factors affecting the quality of life in the neighborhood.

One other aspect of crime prevention messages concerns the receptivity of the audience. The concept of "teachable moments" is relevant here. Certain events may make a problem particularly salient, leaving persons especially interested in learning what should be done. In crime prevention programs, such teachable moments may exist immediately after persons learn about a burglary or other crime in their area. These events often generate a strong identification with the victim, making people more aware of their own vulnerability and therefore more receptive to crime prevention messages. Some police departments link their crime prevention efforts to such events. This approach appears relevant to most kinds of prevention programs for other hazards as well.

Incentives to encourage citizen involvement

To encourage both private- and public-minded forms of crime prevention behavior, the use of incentives should be considered (Figure 12.1, cells 3 and 4). The nature of such incentives varies, although many are financial. All are designed to provide a favorable cost–benefit perception when individuals consider specific actions. Among the incentives for taking actions that increase household security are insurance premium reductions, discounts for security hardware purchases, and reductions in the cost of hardware installation. A review of more than 200 programs offering premise security surveys found that 10% of the programs provided incentives such as these to encourage citizen participation (ITREC, 1977).

A financial incentive has been institutionalized throughout the country through the Crime Stoppers Program. This program provides rewards to citizens for information that leads to the arrest and indictment of offenders. Anonymity is guaranteed through a procedure in which people who call the police are assigned code numbers that enable them to collect rewards later without revealing their identity. If the information provided by the citizen leads to an arrest and indictment, the caller sets up a meeting to collect the reward from a citizen who is on the program's board of directors. The board member meets with the tipster in a public place, such as a parking lot or department store, and the reward is paid in cash in a plain white envelope. The board of directors raises reward funds for the program through auctions and other means and determines the amounts of specific rewards. All board members are civilians, and they often represent various sectors of the business community. In many areas, police select a crime of the week that carries a maximum reward of $1,000 and publicize it widely through local media. The crimes selected are usually those for which police have no significant leads. The Crime Stoppers Program was founded in 1976 in the Albuquerque Police Department, and since then more than 600 similar efforts have been established throughout the United States. Programs report increased arrests, increased closing of cases, and the recovery of large amounts of property and drugs. For example, these programs indicate that collectively they have solved 92,000 felony cases, recovered $562 million in stolen property and narcotics, and convicted more than 20,000 criminals. A national evaluation suggests that Crime Stoppers Programs do solve certain felony cases that were difficult to solve previously, and the programs can generally be viewed as cost effective (Rosenbaum, Lurigio, & Lavrakas, 1986).

In addition to such financial incentives, social incentives also encourage collective forms of citizen action. Programs offering these incentives emphasize that such actions benefit the neighborhood by improving the quality of life of all of the residents (Greenberg et al., 1985). Moreover, participation in community programs helps to integrate individuals into the community and alleviates the alienation many newcomers feel. Awards given by community organizations as well as by police and other municipal officials provide recognition and reinforcement of citizen volunteer efforts. As suggested earlier, citizen involvement in the prevention and control of crime can often be maintained when programs include social activities in which residents interact and come to know each other in informal neighborhood settings. Finally, linking crime prevention activities to other neighborhood problem-solving efforts can create a wider variety of incentives to encourage citizen participation.

Reduction of constraints on citizen involvement

Even when citizens are motivated to participate in crime prevention activities, they may find it difficult to act. Barriers to citizen involvement include the costs involved in taking certain actions, conflicting demands on the individual that limit the opportunity to carry out protective behavior, lack of knowledge about a program, and limited understanding of how to implement recommendations. For example, in one evaluation of a crime prevention program, it was found that lack of information about the program was the major reason for nonparticipation (Schneider, 1975). In addition, ambiguity regarding recommended crime prevention behaviors may inhibit citizen response. For example, citizens may be reluctant to report crimes if they are not clear about the kinds of events to report or the manner in which they should be reported. In order to encourage citizens to report crimes more effectively, programs should make citizens aware of the need for increased surveillance, improve their ability to recognize suspicious or criminal events, and increase their level of competence in providing good reports (Bickman et al., 1977). By making a concerted effort to address these potential barriers to citizen involvement, improvements can be made in both the quantity and quality of citizen crime reporting.

Titus (1984b) has pointed out that programs such as neighborhood watch often deal successfully with the factors identified by research as constraining citizen involvement in bystander situations (Latane & Darley, 1970). Thus, concern and a sense of responsibility to act are heightened by small-group meetings that familiarize residents with the magnitude of the crime problem, encourage them to get to know each other socially, and outline specific duties that are judged to be effective in dealing with crime (i.e., citizen surveillance and reporting). Program leaders can reduce ambiguity by teaching residents to recognize common suspicious incidents and by encouraging neighbors to become familiar with one another's faces and habits. Rewards for appropriate behavior are provided through recognition from the police and the community, from the social benefits of membership, and from evidence of progress being made in dealing with community security and other neighborhood problems.

An additional set of constraints on citizen involvement concern citizens' experiences in dealing with the criminal justice system. Crucial information leading to arrest and prosecution is frequently obtained from cooperative citizens. Yet the interests of these citizens are often virtually ignored. For many, the initial victimization is the beginning of an ordeal in which they feel they are victimized again by the criminal justice system (Herrington et al., 1982). Such experiences can make citizens reluctant to cooperate in the future. Recognition of this problem has led to a federal initiative to make the system more responsive to the needs and rights of victims and witnesses (President's Task Force on the Victims of Crime). Such changes can reduce the barriers to citizen cooperation and encourage meaningful forms of citizen involvement in the administration of justice.

The same problem applies to health care. Just as citizen willingness to cooperate with the criminal justice system is influenced by the actions of system personnel, so too the response of the health care system to its clients influences the extent to which citizens are willing to cooperate with health professionals both in taking steps to prevent illness and in following prescribed treatment regimens.

Conclusion

In considering both citizen crime prevention behavior and protective behavior in general, it is useful to view such actions as being influenced by opposing forces. Attention must be given to strengthening the forces that induce citizens to become aware of and respond to risks, as well as to eliminating the countervailing forces that inhibit citizen action. In some circumstances it may be necessary to consider both forces, whereas in others a better strategy may be to focus on increasing the incentives for citizens to respond or on removing the barriers to action. It is clear, however, that whatever strategies are selected, the approach should start with the public's own beliefs about the prevention and control of the hazard in question.

In general, although both private- and public-minded forms of protective behavior can be useful in preventing and controlling crime, collective citizen actions merit special consideration. The evidence suggests that such actions make participants less fearful and more optimistic about their neighborhood, and they also promote an increased sense of community. Because of the benefits that collective actions provide, it is worthwhile for programs to promote and reinforce such forms of behavior.

References

Atkin, C. K. (1979). "Research Evidence on Mass Mediated Health Communication Campaigns." In D. Mimmo (Ed.), *Communication Yearbook 3.* New Brunswick, NJ: International Communication Association.

Becker, M. H., Haefner, D. P., Karl, S. V., Kirscht, J. P., Maiman, L. A., and Rosenstock, I. M. (1977). "Selected Psychosocial Models and Correlates of Individual Health Related Behaviors." *Medical Care, 13:* 10–24.

Becker, M., and Maiman, L. (1975). "Sociobehavioral Determinants of Compliance with Health and Medical Care Recommendations." *Medical Care, 15*(5): 17–46.

Bennett, E. B. (1955). "Discussion, Decision, Commitment, and Consensus in Group Decision." *Human Relations, 3:* 251–73.

Bickman L., Lavrakas, P. J., Green, S. K., North-Walker, N., Edwards, J., Borkowski, S., Shane-DuBow, S., and Wuerth, J. (1977). *Citizen Crime Reporting Projects.* Washington, DC: U.S. Government Printing Office.

Bond, B. W. (1956). *Group Discussion-Decision: An Appraisal of Its Use in Health Education.* Minneapolis: Minnesota Department of Health.

Bureau of Justice Statistics. (1983). *Report to the Nation on Crime and Justice.* Washington, DC: U.S. Department of Justice.

Bureau of Justice Statistics. (1986). *Bureau of Justice Statistics Annual Report: Fiscal 1985.* Washington, DC: U.S. Department of Justice.

Brunner, E. (1959). *An Overview of Adult Education Research.* Chicago: Adult Education Association of the U.S.A.

Cahn, M. F., and Tien, J. M. (1983). "Systematic Evaluation of the Commercial Security Field Test" (Final Report). Cambridge, MA: Public Systems Evaluation.

Cirel, P., Evans, P., McGillis, D., and Whitcomb, D. (1977). *Community Crime Prevention: An Exemplary Project.* Washington, DC: U.S. Department of Justice.

Clarke, R. V. (1983). "Situational Crime Prevention: Its Theoretical Basis and Practical Scope." In M. Tonry and N. Morris (Eds.), *Crime and Justice: An Annual Review of Research,* Vol. 4, (pp. 225–56). University of Chicago Press.

Douglas, D. F., Westley, B. H., and Chafee, S. H. (1970). "An Information Campaign That Changed Community Attitudes." *Journalism Quarterly, 47:* 479–92.

Feins, J. D., Peterson, J., and Rovetch, E. L. (1983). *Partnership for Neighborhood Crime Prevention.* Washington, DC: U.S. Department of Justice.

Figgie International. (1983). *Reducing Crime in America, Successful Community Efforts.* Figgie Report, Part IV. Willoughby, OH: Figgie International.

Forst, B., Lucianovic, J., and Cox, S. J. (1978). *What Happens after Arrest?* Washington, DC: U.S. Government Printing Office.

Fowler, F. J., and Mangione, T. W. (1982). *Neighborhood Crime, Fear, and Social Control.* Washington, DC: U.S. Department of Justice.

Greenberg, S. W., Rohe, W. M., and Williams, J. R. (1985). *Informal Citizen Action and Crime Prevention at the Neighborhood Level.* Washington, DC: U.S. Government Printing Office.

Greenwood, P., and Petersilia, J. (1975). *The Criminal Investigation Process.* Santa Monica, CA: Rand.

Hanneman, G. J., and McEwen, W. J. (1973). "Televised Drug Abuse Appeals: A Content Analysis." *Journalism Quarterly 50:* 329–33.

Heinzelmann, F. (1959). "An Evaluation of Two Methods of Promoting Behavior Change in a Health Program Context" (Administrative Report). Washington, DC: U.S. Public Health Service.

Heinzelmann, F. (1981). "Crime Prevention and the Physical Environment." In D. Lewis (Ed.), *Reactions to Crime* (pp. 87–102). Beverly Hills, CA: Sage.

Heller, N. B., Stenzel, W. W., Gill, A. D., Kolde, R. A., and Schimerman, S. R. (1975). *Operation Identification Projects: Assessment of Effectiveness*. Washington, DC: U.S. Government Printing Office.

Herrington, L. H., Bobo, G., Carrington, F., Damos, J., Dolan, D. L., Eikenberry, K. O., Miller, R. J., Robertson, P., and Samenow, S. S. (1982). *President's Task Force on Victims of Crime*. Washington, DC: U.S. Government Printing Office.

International Training, Research and Evaluation Council (1977). *Crime Prevention Security Surveys*. Washington, DC: U.S. Government Printing Office.

Kelling, G., and Pate, T. (1981). *A Study of Foot Patrol: The Newark Experiment* (Research Bulletin No. 11). London: Home Office Research Unit.

Kelling, G., Pate, T., Dieckman, D., and Brown, C. (1974). *The Kansas City Preventive Patrol Experiment*. Washington, DC: Police Foundation.

Krug, R. E. (1984). "Community Against Crime: Two Federal Initiatives" (Final Report). Washington, DC: American Institute of Research.

Latane, B., and Darley, J. (1970). *The Non-responsive Bystander: Why Doesn't He Help?* New York: Appleton-Century-Crofts.

Lavrakas, P. J., Normoyle, J., Skogan, W. G., Herz, E. J., Salem, G., and Lewis, D. A. (1981). *Factors Related to Citizen Involvement in Personal, Household and Neighborhood Anti-Crime Measures*. Washington, DC: U.S. Government Printing Office.

Lavrakas, P. J., Rosenbaum, D. P., and Kaminski, F. (1983). "Transmitting Information about Crime and Crime Prevention to Citizens: The Evanston Newsletter Quasi-Experiment." *Journal of Police Science and Administration, 11:* 463–73.

Lewin, Kurt. (1947). "Group Decision and Social Change." In T. M. Newcomb and E. L. Hartley (Eds.), *Readings in Social Psychology*. New York: Holt.

Lewis, D., Salem, G., and Szoc, R. (1980). "Crime and the Urban Community" (Final Report). Evanston, IL: Northwestern University.

Maccoby, N., and Solomon, D. (1981). "The Stanford Community Studies in Health Promotion." In R. Rice and W. Paisley (Eds.) *Public Communication Campaigns*. Beverly Hills, CA: Sage.

McAlister, A., Puska, P., Korkela, K., Pallonen, U., and Maccoby, N. (1980). "Mass Communication and Community Organization for Public Health Education." *American Psychologist, 35:* 375–9.

Mendelsohn, H. (1973). "Some Reasons Why Information Campaigns Can Succeed." *Public Opinion Quarterly, 37:* 50–61.

Mendelsohn, H., and O'Keefe, G. J. (1981). *Public Communications and the Prevention of Crime: Evaluations and Strategies*. Denver, CO; University of Denver, Center for Mass Communications Research and Policy.

National Advisory Commission on Criminal Justice Standards and Goals. (1973). *Report on Community Crime Prevention*. Washington, DC: U.S. Government Printing Office.

National Crime Prevention Council (1984). "The National Crime Prevention Campaign." Washington, DC.

National Criminal Justice Information and Statistics Service. (1979). *The Cost of Negligence: Losses from Preventable Household Burglaries*. Washington, DC: U.S. Department of Justice.

National Institute of Justice. (1983). *Robbery in the United States: Analysis of Recent Trends and Patterns*. Washington, DC: U.S. Department of Justice.

National Institute of Justice. (1986). *Guardian Angels: An Assessment of Citizen Response to Crime*. Washington, DC: U.S. Department of Justice.

O'Keefe, M. T. (1971). "The Anti-Smoking Commercials: A Study of Television's Impact on Behavior." *Public Opinion Quarterly, 35:* 248–57.

O'Keefe, G., and Mendelsohn, H. (1984). *Taking a Bite Out of Crime: The Impact of a Mass Media Crime Prevention Campaign.* Washington, DC: U.S. Government Printing Office.

Pate, A., Lavrakas, P. J., Wycoff, M., Skogan, W. G., and Sherman, L. W. (1984). "Neighborhood Police Newsletters: Experiments in Newark and Houston" (Final Report). Washington, DC: Police Foundation.

Pennell, F. E. (1978). "Private vs. Collective Strategies for Dealing with Crime, Citizen Attitudes toward Crime and the Police in Urban Neighborhoods." *Journal of Voluntary Action Research, 1:* 59–74.

Percy, S. L. (1979). "Citizen Co-production of Community Safety." In R. Baker and F. Meyer (Eds.), *Evaluating Alternative Law-Enforcement Policies.* Lexington, MA: Lexington Books.

Podolefsky, A., and DuBow, F. (1982). *Strategies for Community Crime Prevention.* Springfield, IL: Thomas.

President's Commission on Law Enforcement and Administration of Justice. (1967). *The Challenge of Crime in a Free Society.* Washington, DC: U.S. Government Printing Office.

Roehl, J. A., and Cook, R. F. (1984). *Evaluation of the Urban Crime Prevention Program.* Washington, DC: U.S. Department of Justice, National Institute of Justice.

Rohe, W. M., and Greenberg, S. W. (1984). "Participation in Community Watch Programs." *Journal of Urban Affairs, 6:* 53–65.

Rosenbaum, D. P. (Ed.) (1986). *Community Crime Prevention: Does It Work?* Beverly Hills, CA: Sage.

Rosenbaum, D. P., Lurigio, A. J., and Lavrakas, P. J. (1986). "Crimestoppers: A National Evaluation of Program Operations and Effects" (Final Report). Evanston, IL: Northwestern University.

Rosenstock, I. (1960). "What Research in Motivation Suggests for Public Health." *American Journal of Public Health, 50:* 295–308.

Rosentraub, M. S., and Harlow, K. S. (1980). "The Co-production of Police Services." Arlington: University of Texas, Institute of Urban Studies.

Rubenstein, H., Murray, G., Montoyama, T., and Rouse, W. V. (1980). *The Link Between Crime and the Built Environment: The Current State of Knowledge.* Washington, DC: U.S. Department of Justice.

Salcedo, R., Read, H., Evans, J., and Kong, A. C. (1974). "A Successful Information Campaign on Pesticides." *Journalism Quarterly, 51:* 91–5.

Schmeling, D. G., and Wotring, C. E. (1980). "Making Anti-Drug-Abuse Advertising Work." *Journal of Advertising Research, 20:* 33–7.

Schneider, A. L. (1975). "An Evaluation of the Portland Neighborhood-Based Crime Prevention Program (Occasional Paper in Applied Policy Research). Eugene, OR: Institute of Policy Analysis.

Schneider, A. L., and Schneider, P. B. (1978). "Private and Public-Minded Citizen Responses to a Neighborhood-Based Crime Prevention Strategy" (Unpublished Report). Eugene, OR: Institute of Policy Analysis.

Seattle Law and Justice Planning Office. (1975). "Burglary Reduction Programs" (Final Report). Seattle, WA.

Skogan, W. G. (1981). "On Attitudes and Behavior." In D. A. Lewis (Ed.), *Reactions to Crime,* (pp. 19–46). Beverly Hills, CA: Sage.

Skogan, W. G., and Maxfield, M. G. (1981). *Coping with Crime: Individual and Neighborhood Reactions.* Beverly Hills, CA: Sage.

Spelman, W., and Brown, D. (1981). *Calling the Police: Citizen Reporting of Serious Crime.* Washington, DC: Police Executive Research Forum.

Taub, R., Taylor, D. G., and Dunham, J. D. (1981). "Neighborhoods and Safety." In D. Lewis (Ed.), *Reactions to Crime,* (pp. 103–22). Beverly Hills, CA: Sage.

Taylor, R., Gottfredson, S., and Brower, S. N. (1983). "Crime and Fear in the Urban Residential Environment: Physical, Social and Territorial Determinants" (Final Report). Baltimore, MD: Johns Hopkins University.

Titus, R. (1984a). "Residential Burglary and the Community Response." In R. V. G. Clarke (Ed.), *Coping with Burglary: Research Perspectives on Policy.* Boston: Kluwer-Nuhoff.

Titus, R. (1984b). Panel remarks at the Catherine Genovese Memorial Conference, Fordham University, Bronx, NY.

Wallis, A., and D. Ford (1980). *Crime Prevention Through Environmental Design: An Operational Handbook.* Washington, DC: U.S. Department of Justice.

Wilson, J. Q., and Kelling, G. L. (1982). "The Police and Neighborhood Safety: Broken Windows." *Atlantic Monthly, 127:* 29–38.

Yin, R. K. (1979). "What Is Citizen Crime Prevention?" In *How Well Does it Work? Review of Criminal Justice Evaluation* (pp. 107–34). Washington, DC: U.S. Government Printing Office.

Yin, R. K., Vogel, M. E., Chaiken, J. M., and Both, D. R. (1977). *Citizen Patrol Projects.* Washington, DC: U.S. Government Printing Office.

13   Injury prevention: limits to self-protective behavior

Leon S. Robertson

Introduction

Injury is generally underestimated as a health problem and overestimated as a behavioral problem. Injury ranks third as a cause of death per capita, but this statistic is somewhat misleading because of the large impact of injury on the young. Although heart disease and cancer kill more people in total, the median ages at death – 76 for cardiovascular disease and 68 for cancer – suggest that prevention of these deaths would add less to the preservation of life than the total deaths due to those causes would suggest. In contrast, the median age at death from motor vehicle injury is 27 and that from other unintentional injuries is 50. For homicide and suicide, it is 31 and 42, respectively. Injury is the leading cause of loss of productive years of life.

Injury accounts for about 150,000 deaths per year, some 65 million physician contacts, and 3.6 million hospitalizations. Injury is the leading cause of death and hospitalization among persons 1 to 44 years old (Baker, O'Neill, & Karpf, 1984).

Traditionally, injury was thought to be a behavioral problem, and little consideration was given to causes other than behavior. Trains were a major hazard in the nineteenth century, but some railroad companies delayed for up to 40 years the adoption of risk-reducing equipment – automatic couplers, braking systems, and signaling systems. One of their major arguments was that railroad worker behavior had to be changed to reduce risk (Adams, 1879; Robertson, 1983). Similarly, it was not until about 60 years after the invention of the automobile that the manufacturers were finally forced to adopt the simplest lifesaving technology, such as steering-wheel columns that absorb energy in a frontal crash rather than impale drivers. Virtually the entire emphasis during the preceding period was on preventing the behaviors that increased the probability of crashes (Eastman, 1984).

The field of injury control is currently evolving toward a public health view. Analogous to infectious disease, injury can be considered to be the result of a hazardous agent delivered to a susceptible host by an inanimate vehicle or an animate vector (Haddon, 1980). The agents and vehicles are well known. In most cases their injurious characteristics are more easily modified, technically if not politically, than the behavior of the injured or other persons involved.

The theme of this discussion is that the use of behavior-change strategies should be highly selective and based on scientific results at least as impeccable as those required to justify other forms of intervention. Before discussing the successes and failures of attempts to change behavior relevant to injury, a brief overview of strategies for the modification of agents and vehicles for injury control is in order.

Types of injury and agents and vehicles involved

The generic agent in all injury is energy in its various forms: mechanical, heat, electrical, ionizing, and chemical (Gibson, 1961). Injury occurs when energy is exchanged with the human organism at a rate and in an amount that is beyond the organism's resilience. Mechanical energy is the agent common to most motor-vehicle-related injuries, firearm wounds, and falls. Heat injures directly in the form of burns and indirectly by the depletion of oxygen and generation of toxic gases. Thus, fire-related injuries involve several forms of energy exchange. The lack of oxidation, an energy exchange necessary for life, is also the agent in drowning and choking. Injury classified as poisoning occurs primarily from alcohol, drugs, and carbon monoxide. Electrocution is relatively rare, and acute injury from ionizing radiation is very rare because elaborate measures are taken to shield the population from these forms of energy.

The concentration of energy in potentially injurious amounts is primarily the result of its relatively unregulated distribution for numerous uses ⸻ ⸻ ᵃl societies. Until recently the producers and distributors of of energy gave little or no consideration to the effect of ᵃergy concentrations on the population. Users of or others in ⸻ motor vehicles, guns, fire ignition sources such as matches ᵃs, and farm and industrial machinery were left to cope with ᵃoncentrations and their consequences.

ᴛechnical strategies for injury control

The lack of attention to the modification of energy and its vehicles cannot be attributed to a lack of basic knowledge about the processes involved.

The principles of the energy of moving objects have been known since Sir Isaac Newton published the *Principia* 300 years ago. Yet such energy accounts for more than three-quarters of fatal injuries (Baker et al., 1984).

A systematic array of technical strategies for injury control was developed by Haddon (1970), and several writers have suggested applications to specific forms of energy and vehicles (Baker & Dietz, 1979; Dietz & Baker, 1974; Feck, Baptiste, & Tate, 1977; Haddon, 1973,1975,1980; Robertson, 1981,1983). Some examples from that literature follow:

1. Prevent the creation of a hazard. Do not manufacture handguns, minibikes, motorcycles, or similar high-risk vehicles that are of little or no benefit to society.
2. Reduce the amount of hazard created. Restrict the maximum potential speed of motor vehicles and reduce the maximum horsepower of boat motors relative to the size of boats. Allow the sale of guns only to police or military units.
3. Prevent the release of a hazard that already exists. Increase the braking capabilities of vehicles. Keep guns locked up at supervised hunting and target-shooting ranges where they are not accessible to enraged adults or curious children. Increase the coefficient of friction of floors, bathtubs, sidewalks, and other surfaces, particularly those used by the elderly.
4. Modify the rate or spatial distribution of release of a hazard from its source. Use child restraints and seat belts in motor vehicles and other forms of transportation. Prohibit the manufacture, distribution, or use of any gun that can be fired more than once without reloading. Use sensors in dams and levees to release water at a controlled rate to avoid hazardous buildup. Use flame-retardant materials in homes, institutions, and transportation vehicles. Develop an additive to alcoholic beverages that would give them an offensive taste after a couple of drinks.
5. Separate, in time or space, a hazard and its potential victims. Separate pedestrian and bicycle paths from roads for motor vehicles. Evacuate populations from areas of approaching storms. Cook when children are not in the kitchen; use cooking units that children cannot reach; and use long handles or remote controls to manipulate heated materials. Transport hazardous chemicals only on routes set aside for that purpose at the time of transport.
6. Separate a hazard from its potential victims by a physical barrier. Use air bags in motor vehicles. Place energy-absorbing barriers between roads and rigid objects at roadsides. Use bulletproof vests in areas with a history of gun injury. Use insulated firewalls in buildings and transportation vehicles. Develop an additive for alcoholic beverages and other hazardous drugs that prevents absorption across the intestinal wall.
7. Modify relevant qualities of a hazard. Eliminate hard surfaces, pointed knobs, sharply edged sheet metal, and other characteristics of the interiors and exteriors of motor vehicles that will concentrate energy exchange in a collision. Require that the tension necessary to pull the trigger of a gun be increased beyond the strength of children. Do not allow objects that are of a size to lodge in children's throats to be sold for obvious uses

in children's environments. Prohibit the sale of cigarettes that will not self-extinguish when dropped on sheets, furniture, or carpets.

8. Make potential victims more resistent to a hazard. Provide blood-clotting factors to persons with hemophilia. Increase calcium intake to reduce the development of osteoporosis.
9. Begin to counter the damage already done by a hazard. Train the population to stop hemorrhages and to forego avoidable movement of persons with potential spinal cord damage. Increase the number of emergency roadside telephones and place emergency medic teams such that the time of response is minimized.
10. Stabilize, repair, and rehabilitate the object of damage. Provide surgery for broken bones and torn muscle and organs, burn centers, prosthetic devices for amputees, wheelchairs, special beds, and so on for the immobile. If necessary provide job training, psychological counseling, and other services.

The tactics mentioned under each strategy are merely illustrative. There is a much richer variety for each type of hazard, including environmental hazards that produce damage other than injury. The options are obviously not limited to those that can be accomplished by "self-protective behavior." Indeed, many can be implemented at the community or societal level without any modification of the behavior of those to be protected.

Public health strategies

Three broadly defined strategies are available to protect the public's health: (a) Persuade or condition those at risk to take action that would reduce the risk or increase protection; (b) require by law or administrative directive a change of behavior of those at risk; or (c) modify the agents, vehicles, or environment in order to reduce risk without requiring that individuals change their behavior (Robertson, 1975a). The first two involve self-protective behavior, but the third is the responsibility of those who control the distribution of energy in space and time. Behavioral scientists have paid much attention to the first, some to the second, and little to the third.

From the public health standpoint, no one strategy is inherently preferable to another. The issue is the extent to which the strategy can be employed to improve health to the maximum. Objections to strategies that involve coercion or the protection of people without their consent are based primarily on ideological arguments regarding personal freedom, but manufacturers and processors of hazardous products and health educators sometimes use the arguments as a justification for their actions. The fact that people are endangered without their consent and that few forms of "self-protection" are confined to a single individual is usually ignored in debates of these issues.

For example, seat belt use reduces risk not only for the user but also for others in the vehicle who can be injured by the movement of unrestrained bodies in a crash. The psychosocial and economic damage to families that must bury or care for a disabled motorcyclist who crashed without a helmet may have profound health consequences for family members.

Aside from the ideological arguments is the question of the effect of each approach on injuries. Research on injuries suggests that the favorable effects of organized persuasion or programs of behavior modification are very limited, and some efforts have actually been harmful. An important if not primary factor in compliance with recommended self-protection measures is the amount of effort involved. Although it is possible to persuade a majority of the population to take a single or occasional action, such as purchase a smoke detector or reduce the temperature of hot-water heaters, it is much more difficult to convince people to adopt frequently required behaviors, such as seat belt and child restraint use.

Education and persuasion

Motor vehicles account for almost a third of deaths from injury. Training people to operate vehicles has been the focus of education programs for decades. Early studies of courses offered in high schools found lower crash rates among those who had taken the courses than among those who had not. This was considered to be evidence of effectiveness (e.g., Allgaier, 1964). In the 1960s, that conclusion was challenged by studies that found no correlation between driver education and number of subsequent crashes when miles driven and school achievement were controlled statistically. These findings suggested that the courses were selected by those who would drive less often than others and that the course had no effect on number of crashes per mile driven (Conger, Miller, & Rainey, 1966; Mcquire & Kersh, 1969).

Two subsequent controlled experiments, in which high school students were assigned to (but did not voluntarily select) one or more courses or to a control group, found no effect of the course on number of crashes per miles driven (Ray, Weaver, Brink, & Stock, 1982; Shaoul, 1975). The former experiment included two experimental conditions, one the usual course and one a course designed by psychologists and educational experts. The specially designed curriculum failed to improve the students' crash records.

Shaoul (1975) found that students assigned to the course were licensed to drive earlier than other students, and the net effect of the course was that there were more crashes in the aggregate than among those who learned to drive by other means because of the earlier licensure of those in the course. Comparison of 27 U.S. states during a five-year period beginning in 1968 also revealed much greater licensure and a larger number of fatalities involving 16- to 17-year-old drivers in states in which a larger proportion of young people of that age completed high school driver education (Robertson & Zador, 1978). When funds for high school driver education were no longer available from the state in Connecticut, nine communities dropped the course. A comparison of these and nine communities of comparable size that retained the course with fees and local funds revealed a sharply reduced licensure and crash rate among 16- to 17-year-olds in the communities that dropped the course, with little change in the others (Robertson, 1980).

One searches in vain for an education or rehabilitation program aimed at driving behavior that can be shown in well-designed research to have reduced the number of crashes. The literature is vast and bleak (Council, Roper, & Sadof, 1975; Edwards & Ellis, 1976; Fuchs, 1980; Hill & Jamieson, 1978; Jones, 1973; Mulhern, 1977; Payne & Barmack, 1963). In at least one case, education-rehabilitation was substituted for license suspension in cases of driving while intoxicated, and the crash rate was worse in the rehabilitation group than in a control group that received the usual court treatment (Preusser, Ulmer, & Adams, 1976).

Although it is always difficult to explain why something does not have an expected effect, one suspects that most severe crashes occur because of factors that cannot be modified by a short course. With a quarter of the U.S. population functionally illiterate after 12 years of education, it is naive to expect fundamental change in attitudes and behaviors during a 36-hour course. Also, there is evidence from several studies that human beings, as a species, are substantially limited in their abilities to perceive and react to motion in the time necessary to avoid many collisions at even moderate driving speeds (Robertson, 1983). An important lesson to be learned from the high school driver education experience is that training people to do something hazardous may do no more than increase the number of people who engage in that hazardous activity.

A modest exception to the failure of education is the success of physicians in persuading their patients to use certain types of protection, most notably smoke detectors. In an experimental–control trial of brochures and physician counseling during a checkup, about half of the patients in the experimental group who did not have a smoke detector purchased one, and more than a third were observed to have used them correctly during a home visit. The control group exhibited no change in use (Miller, Reisinger, Blatter, & Wucher, 1982).

Less successful was a similar attempt by physicians to encourage the use of child restraints in road vehicles. Parents in the experimental group were counseled on the importance of restraint use and given a prescription for a restraint as well as a demonstration of its use by the physician. The control group received counseling on other matters. Observations during subsequent visits revealed substantial increases in the use of child restraints in the counseled group relative to the control group in the first two months but only a 9 to 12% increase 14 to 15 months after the counseling (Reisinger et al., 1981).

Attempts to educate parents in the use of child restraints without the involvement of the physician were unsuccessful. Mothers in the hospital with newborns were assigned to a control group that was not informed about child restraints or to one of three experimental groups: One was given literature on the importance of restraint use; the second was given literature, a discussion with a health educator trained in persuasive techniques, and watched a demonstration of restraint use; the third was given literature and a free restraint. Only the free-restraint group demonstrated higher use two to four months later in a follow-up visit to the hospital – 28% compared with 20 to 22% in the other groups (Reisinger & Williams, 1978).

Attempts to educate parents about 10 common household hazards had a similar result. Participants in a prepaid health service were assigned to experimental and control groups. The experimental group participated in a discussion with a health educator and received a booklet on the hazards. In a surprise home visit eight weeks after the counseling of the experimental group, no significant difference in the presence of the 10 hazards was found between experimental and control groups (Dershewitz & Williamson, 1977).

The mothers in the household hazard study claimed on the telephone to have reduced hazards substantially, but actual observation did not support the claims. Several chapters in this volume cite studies that claim success on the basis of interview data rather than observed behavior. This writer is skeptical of such claims.

In addition to the limited effect of counseling, one must consider the problem of whether physicians would actually offer counseling on a variety of protective actions. Although some physicians may have done so upon reading the results of the research mentioned, it is doubtful that there has been a widespread change in physician behavior in that regard. Any labor-intensive behavior-change program also involves changing the behavior of the educators and counselors, a factor seldom considered in the use of the approach.

Media campaigns

To reach a large audience, the mass media are often used, but seldom with adequate research as to their effect on behavior. A few studies suggest that the capacity of media advertising to change behavior is much lower than is commonly thought.

In one study, radio and television advertisements urging seat belt use were aired intensively in one community, moderately in a second community, and not at all in a third. No significant change in seat belt use that could be attributed to the campaigns occurred in the five weeks of the study (Fleischer, 1972).

A nine-month seat belt use campaign on one cable of a dual-cable television system used for marketing studies produced the same result. Observations of seat belt use were linked to the household by license tag numbers. Seat belt use was no more frequent in the households on the experimental cable than in those on the control cable or the community at large. The ads were shown 943 times and were directed by content to specific audiences, often during prime time, in contrast to most "public service" advertising (Robertson et al., 1974).

A mixture of ad campaigns and programs for civic groups, schools, and other community organizations had a small effect on behavior related to fire hazards. An eight-month campaign increased the hazard-related knowledge of 44% of surveyed community members, but only 13% claimed to have applied the knowledge, such as the importance of feeling a door for heat before opening it, during a fire, and there was no detectable reduction in fire-related injury relative to control communities (McLoughlin, Vince, Lee, & Crawford, 1982).

Conditioning

A form of persuasion based at least partly on the principles of conditioning of behavior developed by psychologists (also known as behavior modification) has been attempted for a few injury-related behaviors, with mixed results. This approach involves delivering a reward or punishment for a given behavior soon after the behavior is evoked. There is no doubt that captive subjects in the laboratory or other highly controlled settings, such as some work places, will respond to conditioning with a high rate of repetition of the behaviors. This has been demonstrated among small samples of children and parents with respect to "pedestrian skills" (Embry and Malfetti, no date; Yeaton & Bailey, 1978) and in several work places (Komaki, Barwick, & Scott, 1978; Rubinsky & Smith, 1973; Zohar, Cohen, & Azar, 1980).

The application of these techniques on a mass basis is much more difficult because the administration of rewards and punishments cannot be controlled adequately and the population may rebel and administer some punishments of its own. The buzzer–light and interlock systems intended to encourage seat belt use in cars caused such a reaction. Both systems were developed by Ford Motor Company as alternatives to increasing automatic protection and were allowed as such by the U.S. Department of Transportation after a visit by Ford executives with President Nixon (Nixon [conversation], 1982).

From January 1972 through the 1973 model year, most cars manufactured for sale in the United States were equipped with a buzzer and light that were activated when a certain weight was detected in the front seat without belts being extended or latched. Comparison of 1972 model year vehicles with and without the system revealed little if any effect of the system on observed seat belt use (Robertson & Haddon, 1974). The public's response was to knot the belts, making them permanently unusable, or to have the buzzer disconnected.

Installed in most 1974 cars, the interlock would not allow a car to start if the seat belts were not extended from the retractor or latched. Initially, seat belts were used by nearly 60% of the people observed, more than three times the percentage achieved with previous models (Robertson, 1975b), but within three years it had declined to nearly the same as that with other cars (Phillips, 1980). In addition to having the system disconnected, many car owners complained bitterly to their congressional representatives. The Congress quickly disallowed interlocks as an alternative to governmentally required crash protection.

Rewards for seat belt use in the form of prizes in shopping centers, parking lots in work places, and the like increase seat belt use during the period of the awards (e.g., Elman & Killebrew, 1978). Salaried workers respond more frequently to the incentives than hourly workers, but seat belt use diminishes when the incentive is removed (Geller, Davis, & Spicer, 1983).

Laws and administrative rules

Laws directed at individual behavior can be separated into those aimed at deterring behavior that increases risk, such as drunk driving, and laws requiring protective behavior, such as seat belt use. A proportion of the population will comply with a law simply because it is the law. Although most of the interest in law enforcement is focused on the effect of the probability of arrest and punishment, other factors such as augmentation of enforcement by persons other than authorities may be of equal or greater importance (Robertson, 1983).

Examples of laws augmented by community or family enforcement include minimum purchasing age for alcoholic beverages, minimum age for driving a car, driving curfews, and restrictions on the sale of handguns. Fatal crashes involving teenage drivers increased when the minimum age for the purchase of alcohol was lowered in several states (Williams, Rich, Zador, & Robertson, 1975) and decreased when the purchasing age was increased (Williams, Zador, Harris, & Karpf, 1983). In New Jersey, which does not allow licensure until age 17, sixteen-year-old drivers are in 75% fewer fatal crashes than would be expected from their rates in Connecticut, which allows licensure at age 16 (Williams, Karpf, & Zador, 1983). States, such as Pennsylvania, that prohibit driving during certain hours at night by drivers less than a certain age, specified in each state, have substantially fewer crashes than expected in those hours involving drivers of that age, with no offsetting crashes at other hours of the day (Pruesser, Williams, Zador, & Blomberg, 1984). Gun control laws that specify conditions for sale and registration are more effective than those aimed at possession in general or use in a felony in particular (Geisel, Roll, & Wettick, 1969). In these two cases, it is parents' control over the family car or enforced compliance by business establishments that most likely contributes to the effects of these laws.

If compliance is dependent solely on police enforcement, one obvious factor is observability of the behavior. Motorcycle helmet laws result in virtually 100% compliance (Robertson, 1976), whereas laws that prohibit less observable behavior, such as driving while intoxicated, are flagrantly violated. The effects of "drunk driving crackdowns" are temporary, and there is no evidence that severe punishment is a deterrent (Ross, 1982). Not only is alcohol concentration in the blood not observable to a police officer, resulting in an arrest rate of about 1 illegally impaired driver per 2,000 estimated on the road; arrests often result in plea bargaining and reduction to a less serious charge.

Like the use of motorcycle helmets, seat belt use can be observed while the vehicle is in use. Countries with laws requiring seat belt use have use rates varying from 50 to 80% (Robertson, 1978). Use rates in New York, the first state to require seat belt use, ranged from 45 to 60% in the first months after the law was in force (Insurance Institute for Highway Safety, 1985).

Restraint use by younger children has been required in all U.S. states, but the compliance with the law is low. In the first state to enact the law, restraint use in the targeted age group was only 29% in the third year of the law (Williams & Wells, 1981). More recent data from crashes following a period of intensified enforcement indicates about 40% use (Decker, Dewey, Hutcheson, & Schaffner, 1984). Apparently, the inconvenience of using the device and the objection of some children to being restrained contribute to widespread violation of the law, despite the observability of compliance.

With some notable exceptions, in general, laws directed at individual behavior are more effective than attempts at persuasion. In instances where a specific public group objects strongly to the law, it may be repealed. This was the case in more than half the states when motorcycle clubs led their members in demonstrations and lobbying forays in the state legislatures. Although these motorcyclists did not represent a majority of riders (Baker, 1980a), they were nevertheless successful in their lobbying. This experience with motorcycle helmets and the opposition to government involvement in "personal" safety issues that it represents may partly explain the lag in the adoption of seat belt laws in the United States in contrast to most of the other liberal democracies.

Individual and organizational limits

In choosing injury prevention strategies, one must be aware of the limitations of individuals in perceiving and reacting to hazards. Also, attempts to implement behavior change on a large scale are not likely to achieve the same effects that have been established scientifically on a small scale. The limits of human perceptual and motor functions may account for a larger proportion of injury related to kinetic energy than has been realized. These factors are particularly lethal when coupled with the psychological denial of vulnerability.

Among rested, sober, experienced drivers in a laboratory, half required 0.9 second or more to react to stimuli, such as red lights and sounds, that are commonly encountered in driving. Some took as long as 2 seconds (Johansson & Rumar, 1971). A motor vehicle driven at 30 miles per hour is moving 44 feet each second. In a majority of cases, a child pedestrian, bicyclist, or other vehicle darting in front of a vehicle within 35 feet will inevitably be struck at 30 miles per hour.

There is a widespread tendency to underestimate speed. In experiments with the speedometer masked, drivers traveling at 30 miles per hour or less underestimated their speeds by an average of 25% (Evans,

1970). If the speedometer, as currently designed, were monitored closely, reaction time to road hazards would increase because the driver's eyes would be off the road part of the time.

Adaptation has been demonstrated to result in an underestimation of speed by drivers decelerating from high speeds. Drivers with the speedometer masked were asked to slow to 40 miles per hour after various periods at 70 miles per hour. After 5 seconds at 70 miles per hour, the drivers slowed to an average of 44.5 miles per hour. Twenty miles of driving at 70 resulted in an average of 50.5 miles per hour thought to be 40, and that estimate increased to an average of 53.4 after an additional 20 miles at 70 miles per hour (Schmidt & Tiffin, 1969). Drivers in a simulated passing situation on a two-lane road underestimated the distance necessary to pass a vehicle in front of them by an average of 78% at 50 miles per hour (Gordon & Mast, 1970).

Apparently, drivers of cars and trucks have difficulty perceiving the approach of small vehicles and/or their speeds. In 39% of collisions involving motorcycles, the drivers of the larger vehicles are turning left across the path of the motorcyclist going straight. In only 4% of motorcycle crashes with cars and trucks is the motorcyclist turning left across the path of an oncoming car or truck (Griffin, 1974).

In other types of injury – falls, asphyxiation, burns – children and the elderly are disproportionately involved (Baker et al., 1984). At least some of these injuries are undoubtedly the result of limitations in ability to perceive or avoid the hazard in time.

Our understanding of other important behaviors that contribute to injury is limited. Alcohol and drug addiction is undoubtedly a factor, and the effectiveness of behavioral interventions in reducing the use of these substances on any sustained basis is very much in doubt (Robertson, 1983). Even less understood is the contribution of normal contingencies of life that result in anger, stress, preoccupation with matters other than the task at hand, and the like. It is clear that the person who is always calm and completely attentive does not exist.

There are many theories of why people fail to take precautions. Inability to perceive a risk, amount of effort required to take precautions against a risk, a plethora of distractions that increase risk but at the same time reduce self-protection are among the most obvious factors. Theories of rational decision making are prominent, but a more likely explanation is nonrational.

The voluntary use of protective equipment involves anticipating a hazard and admitting that one is vulnerable. As discussed by Cleary in Chapter 6 and by Slovic, Fischhoff, and Lichtenstein in Chapter 1, one factor in lack of protective behavior that has not been studied adequately is denial. This was illustrated in a survey of new-car buyers. Each buyer was asked whether her or his risk of being injured or killed in a crash was greater than, the same as, or less than persons "like yourself." More than 40% said "less than," compared with 6% who said "greater than" (Robertson, 1977). It would be useful to know the extent to which denial is related to protective behaviors. And if it is, would attempts to overcome the denial result in more protective behavior without harming the individual psychologically by increasing a sense of vulnerability?

Despite the evidence of human limits on perception of hazards, a few economists and psychologists continue to advocate a so-called risk compensation or risk equilibrium theory. The basic hypothesis is that people have a level of risk that they are willing to accept and that any change in risks will be offset by more risky behavior (Peltzman, 1975; Viscusi, 1979; Wilde, 1982). The empirical evidence cited in support of the theory consists of aggregated data and highly correlated predictor variables. When disaggregated data are examined, the theory does not predict injury outcomes (Robertson, 1984; Robertson & Keeve, 1983). In the best study of driver behavior after a reduction in risk, several behaviors were observed before and after enactment of a seat belt use law and compared with those behaviors in an area without such a law. Although driver seat belt use more than tripled after the law went in force, substantially reducing driver risk, there was no change in speed on curves (except a decrease in one case), running red lights, or following distances (Lund & Zador, 1984).

Neoclassical economists believe that a free market efficiently distributes not only commodities, but health and safety, according to consumer demand. They attempt to discredit any research that demonstrates the success of a government regulation, because a successful regulation suggests that the free market is not providing adequate safety. This assumes the existence not only of rational consumers, but also of rational producers.

The behavior of producers of hazardous products sometimes appears nonrational. The so-called head rests in cars are actually supposed to limit the motion of the head in a rear collision so as to limit damage to the neck. Engineers who tested the restraints in the 1960s uniformily concluded that a higher seat back, at least the height of a 95th percentile male, would be much more protective than an adjustable restraint (Severy, Brink, & Baird, 1968). Recent research has confirmed that prediction. Drivers of cars with the automatically protective high seat backs were found to have sustained 70% fewer neck injuries in rear-end collisions than drivers of cars with adjustable head restraints. Yet car manufacturers placed the adjustable restraints on 72% of their cars from 1969 through 1981. This was not for financial reasons. High seat backs cost an average of $28 less per vehicle than adjustable head restraints (Kahane, 1982). Corporate decisions regarding gas tanks that are easily punctured in crashes, failure to install automatically inflating air bags in severe crashes, and others that have an adverse effect on the public's health are worthy of further study (Robertson, 1983).

The strategies for hazard reduction that reduce risk automatically without altering the behavior of everyone who is in proximity of the hazard are attractive alternatives where they exist. Several were mentioned in the discussion of the 10 technical injury control strategies, and the list has been elaborated elsewhere (Robertson, 1983). Those of us in the behavioral sciences should be aware of these alternative approaches. Their implementation requires changes in the behavior of organizational executives in government and private enterprise, behavior that is largely neglected by behavioral scientists, particularly by those who focus on health behavior. Perhaps research on corporate behavior toward the public's health would contribute more to the public's health than the current, virtually exclusive focus on the individual's self-protective behavior.

Conclusion

Focusing on one behavior at a time leads one to ignore the magnitude of the problem of protecting health by behavior change and the issue of choosing approaches that will be the most effective in improving health. Educating a population of 225 million on the hazards of hundreds, possibly thousands, of products and behaviors is an impossible task. The research suggests some principles to follow in choosing the behaviors we will attempt to change and the means by which we will do so. Frequency of the required behavior, comfort and convenience, cost in time and effort are related, but logically distinct characteristics of behaviors that affect the probability of changing them (Baker, 1980b; Robertson, 1975a). We know it is far easier to influence a behavior that must be performed only once or occasionally than a behavior that must be performed frequently. Why, then, have we spent millions of dollars on seat belt use campaigns and virtually nothing to encourage the purchase of safer vehicles?

In places where behavior can be monitored, such as work sites, or when persuasion is highly personalized, such as in physicians' offices, persuasive approaches (including rewarding of seat belt use and other protective behaviors) can have some effect. For large population changes, however, laws requiring protective behaviors that are easily observable are far more effective. Augmentation of enforcement by the community also, apparently, contribute to the efficacy of laws, particularly laws regarding behavior not easily monitored by police. Ironically, general education in the skills required to deal with hazards and deterrence-type laws with severe punishment for violation are the most commonly advocated and used programs for injury control, and the least effective.

References

Adams, C. F. 1879. *Notes on Railroad Accidents*. New York: Putnam's.

Allgaier, E. 1964. Driver education reduces accidents and violations (mimeo). Washington, DC: American Automobile Association.

Baker, S. P. 1980a. On liberty, lobbies and the public good. *American Journal of Public Health 70:*573–4.

Baker, S. P. 1980b. Prevention of childhood injuries. *Medical Journal of Australia 1:*466–70.

Baker, S. P., and Dietz, P. E. 1979. Injury prevention. In *Healthy People: The Surgeon General's Report On Health Promotion and Disease Prevention, Background Papers*. Washington, DC: U.S. Department of Health, Education and Welfare.

Baker, S. P., O'Neill, B., and Karpf, R. 1984. *The Injury Fact Book*. Lexington, MA: Heath.

Conger, J. J., Miller, W. C., and Rainey, R. V. 1966. Effects of driver education: The role of motivation, intelligence, social class, and exposure. *Traffic Safety Research Review 10:*67–71.

Council, F. M., Roper, R. B., and Sadof, M. G. 1975. An evaluation of North Carolina's Multi-Vehicle Range Program in driver education. Chapel Hill: University of North Carolina Highway Safety Research Center.

Decker, M. D., Dewey, M. J., Hutcheson, R. H., and Schaffner, W. 1984. The use and efficacy of child restraint devices: The Tennessee experience, 1982 and 1983. *Journal of the American Medical Association 252:*2571–5.

Dershewitz, R. A., and Williamson, J. W. 1977. Prevention of childhood household injuries: A controlled clinical trial. *American Journal of Public Health 67:*1148–53.

Dietz, P. E., and Baker, S. P. 1974. Drowning: Epidemiology and prevention. *American Journal of Public Health 64:*303–12.

Eastman, J. W. 1984. *Styling versus Safety: The American Automobile Industry and The Development of Automobile Safety, 1900–1966*. New York: University Press of America.

Edwards, M. L., and Ellis, N. C. 1976. An evaluation of the Texas driver improvement training program. *Human Factors 18:*327–34.

Elman, D., and Killebrew, T. J. 1978. Incentives and seat belts: Changing a resistant behavior through extrinsic motivation. *Journal of Applied Social Psychology 8:*72–83.

Embry, D. D., and Malfetti, J. L. (no date). Reducing the risk of pedestrian accidents to preschoolers by parent training and symbolic modeling for children: An experimental analysis in the natural environment. New York: Safety Education Research Project, Columbia University.

Evans, L. 1970. Speed estimation from a moving automobile. *Ergonomics 13:*219–30.

Feck, G., Baptiste, M. S., and Tate, C. L., Jr. 1977. An epidemiologic study of burn injuries and strategies for prevention. Report prepared for the Centers for Disease Control by the New York Department of Health, Albany.

Fleischer, G. A. 1972. *An Experiment in the Use of Broadcast Media in Highway Safety.* Los Angeles: University of Southern California Department of Industrial and Systems Engineering.

Fuchs, C. 1980. Wisconsin driver improvement program: A treatment-control evaluation. *Journal of Safety Research 12:*107–14.

Geisel, M. S., Roll, R., and Wettick, R. S., Jr. 1969. The effectiveness of state and local regulation of handguns: A statistical analysis. *Duke Law Journal 1969:*647–76.

Geller, E. S., Davis, L., and Spicer, K. 1983. Industry-based incentives for promoting seat belt use: Differential impact on white-collar versus blue-collar employees. *Journal of Organizational Behavior Management 5:*17–29.

Gibson, J. J. 1961. The contribution of experimental psychology to the formulation of the problem of safety. In *Behavioral Approaches to Accident Research.* New York: Association for the Aid of Crippled Children.

Gordon, D. A., and Mast, T. M. 1970. Driver's judgment in overtaking and passing. *Human Factors 12:*341–6.

Griffin, L. I., III. 1974. *Motorcycle Accidents: Who, When, Where, and Why.* Chapel Hill: University of North Carolina Highway Safety Research Center.

Haddon, W., Jr. 1970. On the escape of tigers: An ecologic note. *Technology Review 72:*44.

Haddon, W., Jr. 1973. Exploring the options. In *The Conference, Research Directions toward the Reduction of Injury in the Very Young and Very Old.* Washington, DC: National Institute of Child Health and Human Development.

Haddon, W., Jr. 1975. Reducing the damage of motor vehicle use. *Technology Review 77:*53–9.

Haddon, W., Jr. 1980. Advances in epidemiology of injuries as a basis for public policy. *Public Health Reports 95:*411–21.

Hill, P. S., and Jamieson, B. D. 1978. Driving offenders and the defensive driving course: An archival study. *Journal of Psychology 98:*117–27.

Insurance Institute for Highway Safety. 1985. Early New York results show belt use varies from 43 to 80 percent. *Status Report 20*(3):1.

Johansson, G., and Rumar, K. 1971. Drivers' brake reaction times. *Human Factors 13:*23–7.

Jones, M. H. 1973. *California Training Evaluation Study.* Sacramento: California Department of Motor Vehicles.

Kahane, C. J. 1982. *An Evaluation of Head Restraints: Federal Motor Vehicle Safety Standard 202.* Washington, DC: National Highway Traffic Safety Administration.

Komaki, J., Barwick, K. D., and Scott, L. R. 1978. A behavioral approach to occupational safety: Pinpointing and reinforcing safe performance in a food manufacturing plant. *Journal of Applied Psychology 63:*434–45.

Lund, A. K., and Zador, P. L. 1984. Mandatory seat belt use and driver risk taking. *Risk Analysis 4:*41–53.

McGuire, F. L., and Kersh, R. C. 1969. *An Evaluation of Driver Education.* Berkley: University of California Press.

McLoughlin, E., Vince, C. J., Lee, A. M., and Crawford, J. D. 1982. Project burn prevention: Outcome and implications. *American Journal of Public Health 72:*241–51.

Miller, R. E., Reisinger, K. S., Blatter, M. M., and Wucher, W. 1982. Pediatric counseling and subsequent use of smoke detectors. *American Journal of Public Health 72:*392–3.

Mulhern, T. 1977. The National Safety Council's defensive driving course as an accident and violation countermeasure. Unpublished doctoral dissertation, Texas A & M University, College Station.

Nixon, President Richard M., part of a conversation with Lee Anthony Iacocca, Henry

Ford II, and John D. Ehrlichman in the Oval Office on April 27, 1971, between 11:08 and 11:43 A.M. (1982). *Automotive Litigation Reporter,* November 18, 1784–98.

Payne, D. E., and Barmack, J. E. 1963. An experimental field test of the Smith–Cummings–Sherman driver training system. *Traffic Safety Research Review* 7:10–14.

Peltzman, S. 1975. The effects of automobile safety regulation. *Journal of Political Economy 83:677.*

Phillips, B. M. 1980. *Safety Belt Use Among Drivers.* Springfield, VA: National Technical Information Service.

Preusser, D. F., Ulmer, R. G., and Adams, J. R. 1976. Driver record evaluation of a drinking driver rehabilitation program. *Journal of Safety Research 8:98–105.*

Preusser, D. F., Williams, A. F., Zador, P. L., and Blomberg, R. D. 1984. The effects of curfew laws on motor vehicle crashes. *Law and Politics 6:115–28.*

Ray, H. W., Weaver, J. K., Brink, J. R., and Stock, J. R. 1982. *Safe Performance Secondary School Education Curriculum.* Washington, DC: National Highway Traffic Safety Administration.

Reisinger, K. S., and Williams, A. F. 1978. Evaluation of programs designed to increase protection of infants in cars. *Pediatrics, 62:280–7.*

Reisinger, K. S., Williams, A. F., Wells, J. A. K., John, C. E., Roberts, T. R., and Podgainy, H. J. 1981. The effect of pediatricians' counseling on infant restraint use. *Pediatrics, 67:201–6.*

Robertson, L. S. 1975a. Behavioral research and strategies in public health: A demur. *Social Science and Medicine 9:165.*

Robertson, L. S. 1975b. Safety belt use in automobiles with starter-interlock and buzzer-light reminder systems. *American Journal of Public Health 65:1319–25.*

Robertson, L. S. 1976. An instance of effective legal regulation: Motor-cyclist helmet and daytime headlamp laws. *Law and Society Review 10:456–77.*

Robertson, L. S. 1977. Car crashes. Perceived vulnerability and willingness to pay for crash protection. *Journal of Community Health 3:136.*

Robertson, L. S. 1978. Automobile seat belt use in selected countries, states and provinces with and without laws requiring belt use. *Accident Analysis and Prevention 10:5–10.*

Robertson, L. S. 1980. Crash involvement of teenaged drivers when driver education is eliminated from high school. *American Journal of Public Health 70:599–603.*

Robertson, L. S. 1981. Environmental hazards to children: Assessment and options for amelioration. In *Better Health for Our Children: The Report of the Select Panel for Promotion of Child Health: Volume 4. Background Papers.* Washington, DC: U.S. Department of Health and Human Services.

Robertson, L. S. 1983. *Injuries: Causes, Control Strategies and Public Policy.* Lexington, MA: Heath.

Robertson, L. S. 1984. Automobile safety regulation: Rebuttal and new data. *American Journal of Public Health 74:1390.*

Robertson, L. S., and Haddon, W., Jr. 1974. The buzzer-light reminder system and safety belt use. *American Journal of Public Health 64:814–15.*

Robertson, L. S., and Keeve, J. P. 1983. Worker injuries: The effects of workers' compensation and OSHA inspections. *Journal of Health Politics, Policy and Law 8:581–97.*

Robertson, L. S., Kelley, A. B., O'Neill, B., Wixom, C. W., Eiswirth, R. S., and Haddon, W., Jr. 1974. A controlled study of the effect of television messages on safety belt use. *American Journal of Public Health 64:1071–80.*

Robertson, L. S., and Zador, P. L. 1978. Driver education and fatal crash involvement of teenaged drivers. *American Journal of Public Health 68:959–65.*

Ross, H. L. 1982. *Deterring the Drinking Driver: Legal Policy and Social Control.* Lexington, MA: Heath.

Rubinsky, S., and Smith, N. 1973. Safety training by accident simulation. *Journal of Applied Psychology* 57:68–73.

Schmidt, F., and Tiffin, J. 1969. Distortion of drivers' estimates of automobile speed as a function of speed adaptation. *Journal of Applied Psychology* 53:536–9.

Severy, D. M., Brink, H. M., and Baird, J. D. 1968. *Backrest and Head Restraint Design for Rear-End Collision Protection.* Detroit, MI: Society of Automotive Engineers.

Shaoul, J. 1975. *The Use of Accidents and Traffic Offenses as Criteria for Evaluating Courses in Driver Education.* Salford, England: University of Salford.

Stuart, R. B. 1974. Teaching facts about drugs: Pushing or preventing. *Journal of Educational Psychology* 66:189–201.

Viscusi, W. K. 1979. The impact of occupational safety and health regulation. *Bell Journal of Economics* 10:117.

Wilde, G. J. S. 1982. Critical issues in risk homeostasis theory. *Risk Analysis* 2:249–58.

Williams, A. F., Karpf, R. S., and Zador, P. F. 1983. Variations in minimum licensing age and fatal motor vehicle crashes. *American Journal of Public Health* 73:1401–3.

Williams, A. F., Rich, R. F., Zador, P. L., and Robertson, L. S. 1975. The legal minimum drinking age and fatal motor vehicle crashes. *Journal of Legal Studies* 4:219–39.

Williams, A. F., and Wells, J. A. K. 1981. The Tennessee Child Restraint Law in its third year. *American Journal of Public Health* 71:163.

Williams, A. F., Zador, P. L., Harris, S. S., and Karpf, R. S. 1983. The effect of raising the legal minimum drinking age on fatal crash involvement. *Journal of Legal Studies* 12:169–79.

Yeaton, W. H., and Bailey, J. S. 1978. Teaching pedestrian safety skills to young children: An analysis and one year follow-up. *Journal of Applied Behavioral Analysis* 11:315.

Zohar, D., Cohen, A., and Azar, N. 1980. Promoting increased use of ear protectors in noise through information feedback. *Human Factors* 22:69.

14 Perspectives on self-protective behaviors and work place hazards

Alexander Cohen

Introduction

Need for hazard control at work

Occupational disease and injury are preventable. Historically, efforts to improve work place conditions have been directed toward identifying and evaluating significant dangers in the expectation that, with knowledge of the hazards, someone would do something to reduce their impact. New regulatory legislation and other factors in the past decade have shifted this passive approach to hazard reduction to a more active one that emphasizes the development and application of relevant control technologies (Occupational Safety & Health Act, 1970; Department of Health & Human Services, 1980; Burton, Coleman, Coltharp, Hoover, & Vandervort, 1980; Sheehy, 1983). Although there were indications of a declining rate of occupational injuries and illness in the period from 1980 to 1983 (Office of Technology Assessment, 1985), later data for 1984 show an upturn (Occupational Health and Safety Letter, 1985). The composite figures taken from several reporting systems reveal the enormity of the problem. For example, the National Institute for Occupational Safety and Health (NIOSH), in collating the latest data from hospital emergency room cases, state workmen's compensation claims, Bureau of Labor Statistics reports, and National Safety Council surveys, estimates that at least 10 million people suffer traumatic injuries on the job each year (*Morbidity & Mortality Weekly Reports,* 1984). About 3 million of these injuries are severe, 70,000 resulting in some form of permanent impairment, and 10,000 are fatal. In terms of cost, the latest National Safety Council estimates indicate an annual $31.4 billion loss from work-related injuries, reflecting insurance and medical payments, wage losses, production losses, and administrative expenses covering the investigation of the accident and filing of reports and claims (National Safety Council, 1984).

Recognizing that these data do not include occupational illness and apply to a time period of decreased employment and reduced production makes this situation even less tolerable. Clearly, more intense corrective action is warranted.

Place of behavioral measures in work place hazard control programs

A plan of hazard prevention at the work site may consist of engineering or physical control approaches, monitoring systems, work practices, and use of personal protective equipment. Eliminating known dangers in industrial processes, production machinery, and job operations through technical or hardware solutions introduced at the design stage is most preferred. Substitution of less hazardous materials, the use of closed (containment) systems to cope with problems of toxic substances, and automating dangerous machine functions are examples of engineering methods that, in effect, remove hazards to which workers would be otherwise exposed. Monitoring systems can provide information about the processes or equipment under control. If there is a process control breakdown or malfunction, signals for corrective measures can be communicated, including worker alerts to take evasive action. Safe work practices are procedures that employees are expected to follow in order to reduce exposure to harmful agents in their work places and/or limit opportunity for injury. Personal protective equipment consists of devices worn by workers when other techniques for hazard control are inadequate or not feasible.

According to federal law (Occupational Safety & Health Act, 1970), employers are responsible for safe and healthful work conditions and for the control programs needed to them. Management, owing to cost and technical feasibility considerations, may forego engineering approaches, placing emphasis instead on safe work practices and the use of personal protective equipment. Unions react to such plans with disfavor. They are seen as shifting the burden of protection from the employer to the employee, because the latter's actions now determine the level of hazard control in the work place. Deferring to this point of view, current legislative directives require employers to draft an engineering or physical plan for hazard control, considering the other options as interim-type measures.

In actuality, workers' actions and behaviors can influence any and all elements of a work site hazard control system. Even the most innovative engineering controls are useless if the workers have not been trained to use them properly. Ventilation controls do not work if employees forget to turn them on or decide to turn them off. Monitoring systems that identify and signal potential hazards are of little help if employees choose to ignore them. Protective equipment does not protect workers who do not wear it or wear it improperly. Well-designed hazard control procedures for production, housekeeping, and maintenance functions can be beneficial only when employees follow them. In sum, behavioral factors are integral to any work site hazard protection program.

Adding further impetus to the study of behavioral factors and worker health is the growing popularity of health promotion programs. In broad terms, health promotion represents varied education and motivational efforts aimed at effecting behavioral and lifestyle changes that can enhance one's health and well-being (Parkinson, 1982). Programs accenting weight control, improved nutrition, smoking cessation, reduced alcohol consumption, physical fitness, and stress management are among the most popular health promotion offerings, cigarette smoking, alcohol consumption, and so on, being acknowledged as factors in the etiology of many chronic diseases and injuries. The work site has been recognized as an ideal site for implementing health promotion programs because it provides access to large populations and because support groups can be formed to assist employees in such efforts. Although the goals of health promotion programs transcend issues of work site hazard protection, their approaches and objectives can enhance occupational health and safety. The following offer three illustrations:

1. Reduction of drinking and smoking and greater physical fitness, as outcomes of health promotion programs, can lower the risk of certain job hazards for which drinking, smoking, and poor physical fitness pose added risks (e.g., smoking as a cofactor in the development of occupational respiratory disorders [Selikoff, Hammond, & Churg, 1968], drinking as a cause of work place accidents [Sleight & Cook, 1974], poor physical fitness heightening the risk of overexertion and musculoskeletal strains in lifting and carrying jobs [Rowe, 1971]).
2. The intent of health promotion programs to induce greater self-care can be easily translated into greater self-protection against work place hazards. Indeed, educational and motivational strategies for enhancing health-seeking behavior can include greater acceptance of personal protective equipment, greater adherence to safe work practices, and increased awareness of job hazards in order to increase one's margin of protection against occupational health and safety risks (Cohen, Smith, & Anger, 1979).
3. Major types of illness and injuries deemed to be influenced by behavioral factors, and therein the current targets of health promotion efforts, include several of the 10 leading work-related disorders, namely, cancer, lung disease, traumatic injury, cardiovascular disease, and psychological disorders (Millar & Myers, 1983; *Morbidity & Mortality Weekly Reports,*

1983). Hence, ideas for reducing behavioral risk factors in these cases have implications for health and safety problems both on and off the job.

Viewed in this manner, health promotion and hazard protection are clearly complementary.

Objectives of the chapter

Briefly stated, this chapter is concerned with behavioral options for enhancing hazard control at the work place. Its goal is to furnish ideas for promoting and maintaining self-protective actions among workers in order to increase the level of work place health and safety. Included here will be reports of field trials, case studies, and other observations to document techniques having particular merit. Although similar to a 1979 publication on the same topic by this author and two colleagues (Cohen et al., 1979), this version offers an amplified treatment of significant issues and includes updated material.

Nature of hazard control behaviors

Conard (1983) acknowledges eight broad classes of behavioral actions having work site hazard control implications. These are listed below along with some illustrative comments.

1. Proper use and operation of the hazard control systems in place, thus realizing their maximum protective benefits. Booth-type ventilation controls with spray mist arrestors represent one common solution to reducing exposure hazards in spray painting. These controls would have little effect without appropriate employee actions such as ensuring that the ventilation is engaged, that the applications are made within the capture range of the ventilation, and that the mist arrestors are not saturated.
2. Work habits in performing job tasks that could include acts unnecessarily increasing one's risk of illness or injury. Employees have many behavioral options under their control that can influence exposure to hazards. For example, Williams, Harris, Arp, Symons, & van Ert, (1980) noted that employee exposure to hazardous substances was frequently higher than necessary because they tended to spend much (needless) time close to exposure sources in the course of performing various tasks. Cohen and Jensen (1984) found in observing driver behaviors in forklift truck operations that the drivers frequently failed to signal or yield to co-workers at intersections, a factor implicated in accidents involving their equipment.
3. An increased awareness and recognition of work place hazards. Recognition of hazards is a necessary first step to their avoidance. Educational and informational techniques for this purpose may include the use of labels, information posters, safety pamphlets, pocket cards, and safety

data sheets, all of which may be coupled with regular training activities
in which the avoidance actions themselves are expected to be addressed.

4. Acceptance and use of personal protective equipment. The acceptance
    of personal protective devices and clothing to control occupational haz-
    ards is acknowledged to be problematic. Respirators and hearing protec-
    tors are the most well known personal protective devices and present
    particular difficulties in terms of effective fit, encumbrance, and general
    discomfort (Schulte, 1973; Swift, 1975; Pritchard, 1976).

5. Observance of housekeeping and maintenance measures to keep work
    areas clear of agents that could pose additional risks of illness or injury.
    Hopkins (1981) observed that failure to replace lids on trash containers
    of styrene-coated scraps in laminated plastics manufacturing processes
    increased the concentration of the toxic styrene material in the workers'
    environment. Frequent changing of disposable floor coverings to prevent
    an accumulation of styrene overspray in the forming areas of the same
    work sites was believed to be an important factor in reducing the expo-
    sure level.

6. Following good personal hygiene practices, such as regularly washing,
    showering, changing and laundering work clothes, and not eating in
    process and production areas. These measures are intended to nullify
    other modes of contact or retention of toxic materials that could amplify
    their hazard potential.

7. Proper responses to emergency situations. Employee behaviors are criti-
    cal if there is a chemical spill, fire, control equipment failure, explosion,
    or machine malfunction. They must be informed, trained, and rehearsed
    in procedures enabling them to cope effectively with the apparent
    danger.

8. Self-monitoring and early recognition of any signs or symptoms of hazard-
    ous exposures. Instructing workers in early symptom recognition can help
    to avoid more serious problems. In situations in which acute reactions can
    be expected, this is especially important. One NIOSH publication pre-
    scribing good work practices for fibrous glass lay-up and spray-up opera-
    tions encourages daily self-inspection of the skin for sensitization symp-
    toms and signs of dermatitis (NIOSH, 1978).

Given these different forms of behaviors having self-protective importance in the work setting, what means are available to effect them? This is
addressed in the remainder of the chapter.

Directive methods for shaping self-protective actions

Training and motivational ideas

Training remains the fundamental means of acquiring knowledge and
developing skills; motivation is needed to drive this process and to elicit
the behaviors that are the ultimate goal of training. This was a main point
in an earlier paper by the author (Cohen et al., 1979), which also included the following guidelines for hazard control training:

1. Informing workers of the need for learning job procedures accenting health and safety considerations and inviting their inputs in the instruction process is critical to its acceptance.
2. The actual behaviors to be learned must be clearly identified through demonstration, with conditions of practice fostering maximum carryover to the actual work situation.
3. Approaches to trainee motivation should include rewards that are contingent on the display of the desired behaviors, well-defined performance goals encompassing those acts, and knowledge of results or feedback to mark progress.

Although industrial training programs directed toward improving job performance and promoting safe work practices may incorporate some of these ideas, the training literature as a whole lacks critical attention to them (Goldstein, 1975; Cohen & Jensen, 1984). Most references deal with course descriptions, lesson plans, and programs in use by individual companies. Little concern is paid to defining training needs, examining how they can be best met through instruction, or evaluating a program once implemented. This situation may now be changing. A more deliberate and systematic process has emerged for determining both the critical behaviors that are to be the focus of a given health and safety training program and the means needed to ensure the adoption of those behaviors by the work force. The approach here involves the application of behavior management strategies that emphasize the targeting of specific behaviors for change and setting a course to alter them in a very direct manner (Frederickson, 1982). Although behavior management programs for hazard control behaviors vary in complexity, four key components are common:

1. *Assessment.* In selecting the behavioral targets, an analysis is first undertaken in which the work conditions or operations of concern and their related worker behaviors are observed. Particular attention is paid to worker actions that are seen as affecting exposure risk to a toxic chemical or influencing safety margins for other forms of hazards.
2. *Formulation of objectives.* The list of behaviors and job conditions is then prioritized, the important hazard conditions and related high-impact behaviors being ranked at the top of the list. This offers an initial basis for selecting the behavioral objectives for a training program, but final decisions also must take account of a number of practical matters. How difficult will it be for workers to make the indicated behavior changes? How much will the changes conflict with ongoing practices? Will management support the practices? How difficult will it be to maintain and monitor the changes once they are instituted? If one expects problems in effecting change, the number of behavior targets should be reduced to the few offering the greatest expected benefits.
3. *Behavior change methods.* The training and motivational methods used here are quite varied. Lectures, audio–visual presentations, and one-on-one instruction are all viable means. Opportunities for practice, contin-

gent reward schedules, and feedback to indicate progress in obtaining
the behavioral objectives are important.

4. *Evaluation.* Evaluation of the extent of behavior change is a basic feature of a behavior management program. Hence, provisions for observing the targeted worker actions before, during, and after the employees
   have been trained are made. The ultimate objective of the behavior
   management program is to change critical work behaviors in ways that
   reduce job accident and illness risk. Correlating the behavior changes
   against independent outcome measures reflecting health and safety can
   establish the credibility of the program.

Applications

The literature demonstrating successful applications of behavior manage-
ment approaches in occupational safety and health programs is growing
(Komaki, Barwick, & Scott, 1978; Sulzer-Azaroff & de Santamaria, 1980;
Zohar, 1980; Zohar, Cohen, & Azar, 1980; Hopkins, 1981; Komaki,
Collins, & Penn, 1982; Fellner & Sulzer-Azaroff, 1984). Examples of its
use are described in this section.

Hopkins (1981) adopted a behavior management strategy to institute
work practices for reducing worker exposure to styrene in the manufacture of laminated plastics products. Styrene is a polymerizing agent used
in such production and a known neurotoxin. Following the sequence
outlined earlier, an analysis was first made of the basic steps in the
manufacture of laminated plastics in order to identify the operations causing the highest styrene concentrations and the job routines and related
worker actions that could influence exposure levels. Observations taken
at several plant sites indicated that two operations, spraying and roll-out
work, yielded the greatest peak levels of styrene exposure as well as the
greatest total time of relatively high exposure. Consequently, these operations became the focus of a hazard control program including behavioral options for reducing exposure levels. Initial ideas were obtained
from additional work site observations using job task analyses and interviews with workers and management. A pilot effort undertaken at one
site suggested the value of certain procedural changes for limiting styrene
exposure and the kind of training and reinforcement efforts needed to
promote worker adoption. This pilot program identified 11 work procedures and 20 housekeeping practices as candidates for the hazard control
program. The work procedures encompassed such ideas as avoiding high-
exposure areas, taking better advantage of existing control measures, and
using proper personal protection. Specific examples are shown in Table
14.1. Table 14.2 lists examples of the 20 housekeeping practices and their
expected benefits in reducing unnecessary styrene exposure.

Table 14.1. *Classes of health-promoting (styrene-reducing) work procedures*

Procedure	Example
Using appropriate personal protection	Wear respirator when working inside spray booths
	Keep all skin below neck, including hands, covered
Avoid high-exposure areas	Stay out of spray booth except when spraying, setting up parts
	Keep head at least 12 inches away from un-cured resin applications on molds
	Maintain 6-foot separation between yourself and next spray gun operator
Exploit existing engineering controls	Activate booth exhaust ventilation before spraying
	Spray toward exhaust ventilation
	Stay upwind of the part being rolled out

Table 14.2. *Examples of housekeeping practices*

Practice	Benefit
All spray booth filters should be in place and properly seated	Without effective filtering, exhaust ventilation could be blocked or clogged with spray material
Floors in work areas should be covered with disposable material allowing frequent changing	Reduces overspray buildup as source of evaporating styrene
Waste cans of excess resin coating and trim scraps should be close to exhaust ventilation ports	Permits quick venting of any styrene evaporated from such material
Cured parts should be removed from work areas	Isolation of parts being cured keeps amount of evaporated styrene from adding to air in areas where people are working

The elements of a training and motivational plan to establish these work procedures and housekeeping measures followed the learning and motivation guidelines mentioned earlier. Specifically, videotape presentations of the practices were prepared, with input from workers helping to enhance detail and relevance. The tapes were used in a number of training sessions, none longer than 30 minutes to maintain audience attention. There was much trainer–worker interaction and worker practice and many on-the-job tests to certify worker knowledge and conformance with the work practices and housekeeping measures set forth. Frequent trainer feedback, praise, and monetary rewards for passing the certification tasks were used to motivate worker adoption of the prescribed behavioral actions. The monetary rewards varied from $5 to $25 depending on the number of performance tests passed.

The training plan was implemented at three plants representing a variety of laminated plastics product manufacture. Preparatory to the training, paid observers were given instruction in recognizing the behavioral actions comprising the specific work procedures and housekeeping measures slated for adoption. These observers were assigned to each plant (as part of the training group) and from remote positions would take samples of worker actions or inspect work areas to ascertain compliance. The sampling was done at random times during a data collection day, there being one to three data collection days per week.

To evaluate the intervention efforts described, worker behavior was observed, air samples were taken, and metabolic measures of worker styrene exposures were recorded before, during, and after training. The time period for pretraining data collection varied from 13 to 37 weeks to provide a stable baseline (presumably free of novelty effects introduced by the presence of the trainer-observers). The training period in each of the three work sites was spread over four to five weeks, with post-training extending for nearly 17 weeks.

The results of the program are shown in Tables 14.3 and 14.4. In terms of behavioral data, it is apparent that conformance with the specified work procedures is nearly complete, only 2 to 4% of observed acts failing to meet the practices as specified. With regard to housekeeping measures, a sharp improvement is noted relative to baseline observations, reaching 90% compliance in two plants and 95% in a third.

Comparisons of the baseline and post-training measures of breathing zone concentrations of styrene give evidence of reduced exposure, as does the decrease in the urinary mandelic acid levels, an indicator of actual body uptake of styrene.

Taken together these findings suggested that the training and motivation procedures were effective in altering the workers' job behaviors and that these changes had the desired effect of reducing styrene exposure. A critical question concerns the length of time the behavior changes, once effected, are sustained. Follow-up observations at two of the three participating plants two years later indicated that about two-thirds of the

Table 14.3. *Observed compliance with prescribed work practices and housekeeping measures during baseline, training, and post-training periods*

Plant	Baseline	Training	Post-training
Work practices (% nonconforming behaviors)			
A	30	9	4
B	34	8	4
D	35	7	2
Housekeeping (% complying observations)			
A	17	84	90
B	34	83	90
D	55	84	95

Table 14.4. *Percentage of reduction in exposure dose from baseline to post-training*

	Breathing zone samples (intermittent)[a]	Breathing zone samples (continuous)[b]	Mandelic acid in urine samples
A	33	36	26
B	62	65	55
D	56	80	31

[a]Refers to measures taken in select operations.
[b]Refers to measures taken during total work shift.

practices originally instituted were still being followed to a significant extent, despite no obvious encouragement or incentives by management (Hopkins, 1983). This durability was remarkable, though satisfaction with the results must be tempered by the fact that several of the practices showing the greatest decline were also those that had to be carried out most frequently. Effective means for maintaining these kinds of practices should be studied.

It could be argued that the training and motivational methods used by Hopkins (1981) were so elaborate and time-consuming that they are unlikely to be adopted voluntarily in industry. It is possible to devise less elaborate versions of these programs, however. As will be shown, the next example was simpler and still yielded a substantial positive outcome.

This example of the use of behavior management principles in hazard control differs from the previous one in that it focused on a single behavior change, namely, increasing worker use of ear protectors in excessively noisy work areas. As already noted, the problems of promoting worker acceptance and regular use of personal protective equipment can be difficult, and the promotion of earplug use is no exception. Discomfort, interference with hearing normal sounds, and hygienic considerations all loom as obstacles to worker compliance (Swift, 1975). Efforts to increase the usage of ear protectors have taken a variety of forms. Design and material changes in the devices have been introduced to relieve discomfort, and promotional campaigns, generally involving plant or department competition or informational compaigns aided by lectures and posters, have been mounted to make workers aware of hearing conservation needs.

Despite these efforts, the effectiveness of personal ear protection programs for noise control in industry is still regarded as uncertain, due in large measure to issues of worker acceptance. This second application involved an alternative behavioral management approach that took account of two major considerations. One was that noise conditions capable of causing permanent hearing loss with prolonged exposure almost invariably first induce a temporary threshold shift (TTS), following brief periods of exposure to the same noise (Kryter, 1970). In this regard, TTS is an early warning indicator of permanent hearing loss risk. The second was that by feeding back TTS measures to workers who wear and do not wear personal ear protectors in noisy environments, owing to the expected differences in the amount of TTS, it would be possible to demonstrate the benefits of the protectors and hence offer a strong incentive for their use. It has been well established in the research literature that immediate and specific knowledge of results can motivate behavior change and learning (Goldstein, 1975; Sulzer-Azaroff & de Santamaria, 1980; Komaki et al., 1982).

Zohar et al. (1980) used these ideas in a plan first tried out in a metal fabrication plant where workers in several departments were subject to excess noise levels (87 to 99 decibels, A-weighted [dBA]) throughout their work shift and were issued earplugs to control the hazard. Despite lectures, poster campaigns, and supervisory threats, few workers wore the ear protectors.

Two departments were chosen for study. One was to serve as an experimental or treatment group, whereas the other was to be used as a reference group for gauging the treatment effect. Baseline observations, collected at the outset for a period of one month, were made by the plant's assistant safety officer, who made unannounced tours of the work stations in both departments and noted the number of workers wearing earplugs out of the total number observed during each tour. After these baseline measures were made, lectures were presented to workers in both departments on aspects of hearing conservation in noise. The usual subject matter found in industrial hygiene guides was covered (Wyman, 1969). In addition, workers in the experimental group were given audiometric tests before and after their workdays. Such tests were given to four to six workers at one time, with differences between pre- and postworkday measurements being individually reported to them as evidence of noise-induced TTSs and reviewed in the light of whether they had or had not used the ear protectors. One copy of the audiogram was given to the workers, and a second copy was posted on a special bulletin board in the production hall of this department. Members of the study team helped the workers who gathered around the bulletin board at the start of the workday or during breaks to interpret the results. Differences in the amount of TTS when ear protectors were or were not worn were readily apparent, as was evidence of substantial permanent hearing loss among those workers with many years of service who never wore the protectors.

The treatment period lasted for one month and was immediately followed by a post-treatment observation period of five months. As before, the assistant safety officer made tours of the work stations to determine the number of workers wearing the protectors. The results are shown in Figure 14.1, which reports the percentage of users in both the experimental and control departments for the different phases of the demonstration. It is clear that, beginning in the treatment stage, a steady increase in ear protection use occurs in the treatment group and continues throughout the post-treatment, reaching an 85 to 90% level. In contrast, the control department shows no such increase (and actually shows a further decline due to management's ill-advised attempts to force use through punitive actions). The sustained effect of the treatment is especially notable and was believed attributable to several factors. The first was the potency of the feedback in providing sufficient motivation at the individual worker level to overcome the usual resistance to wearing ear protective devices. The second, at the department level, was the demonstrated acceptance of earplugs by a sufficiently large number of workers in a given group, in effect creating new norms and behavior standards favoring their use. A sign of this norm development was the fact that, despite an annual worker turnover rate of 65%, the trend toward increased usage of ear protectors continued to be seen in the experimental department following the feedback treatment. Even more dramatic, at the end of the follow-up period, only one-third of the workers in the experimental department had actually received the earlier feedback treatment, the remaining two-thirds having come into the department after the treatment stage. Yet the percentage of earplug use continued to rise through the period and leveled off at the 85 to 90% level. The practical significance of this finding is that

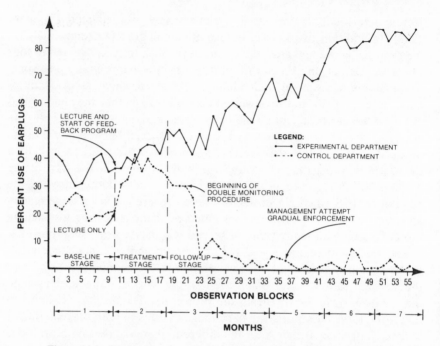

Figure 14.1. Percentage of workers observed to be wearing ear protectors in the experimental and control departments during the baseline, treatment (feedback), and follow-up stages of the study. Each plotted percentage point represents the average of three behavior sampling tours conducted on three consecutive days. Reproduced with permission from Zohar, Cohen, & Azar (1980).

the feedback procedure need not be perpetuated and applied to every new worker. Rather, it can be conducted for a limited time so as to effect the desired result in a majority of workers. Once this occurs, its effects seem to be sustained through the newly established norms for accepted work behaviors.

Zohar (1980), in Israel, extended this promotion work with ear protectors by offering token rewards to workers observed to be wearing such equipment that were later redeemable for monetary gifts. Trials in two plants found that ear protector use increased from baseline levels of 35 to 50% to nearly 90% with the introduction of the token rewards. This use level was maintained when observations were made nine months after the token-dispensing period had ended.

Zohar (1980) has proposed that the behavioral changes for hazard control as exemplified by the above experiences reflect a three-stage process involving (a) sufficiently potent reinforcers to effect the desired change in individual worker behavior for a sufficient number in the target group, (b) group adoption of new norms for accepted behaviors, and (c) modified management standards to maintain the new behaviors. Regarding the last stage, Zohar (1980) and others (Komaki et al., 1978) have noted that supervisors who become party to the development of behavioral safety plans can become committed to their success and through closer monitoring and prompting can lend further support to the goals of the program. That management commitment is a major determinant of the outcomes of safety and health activities is also evident in other contexts (A. Cohen, 1977; Cohen et al., 1979).

Non-directive approaches to fostering self-protective actions

In this writer's earlier review (Cohen et al., 1979), strategies for communicating information, incentive plans, and management-style factors were examined with regard to their potential for promoting worker self-protection. By changing attitudes, increasing knowledge, and heightening awareness, these approaches were expected to strengthen an individual's disposition or readiness to act in safe and healthful ways. This is in sharp contrast to the behavior management strategy, which focuses on specific self-protective behaviors. The coverage on communications dealt with source, content, transmission mode, and receiver elements underlying the audience's acceptance and understanding of presented material and conformity with its specified intent. Credible sources using face-to-face, two-way forms of communication with suitably arousing material intelligible to the target group were believed to be critical.

The incentive approach emphasized safety contests and awards for accident-free work to arouse increased worker and company interest in job safety. These efforts were most effective in providing an added spur to hazard control programs having well-established safety training, housekeeping, safety inspection, and reporting functions. Incentive plans, however, were no substitute for the latter kinds of program practices, and preoccupation with contests and awards was found in some instances to have problematic results (A. Cohen, 1977). Increased self-protection was also seen as a by-product of management style and leadership. Management actions expressive of a genuine commitment to job safety, the frequent interactions of managers with supervisors and workers on safety issues, plus a clear management concern for developing and conserving its personnel resource were patterns seen in companies having low injury rates.

The reader is referred to the earlier review (Cohen et al., 1979) for a general treatment of these nondirective approaches to fostering self-protection at the work place. To be presented here are additional ideas and refinements in two subject areas—namely, communication of information and management style—which are subjects of ongoing NIOSH work.

Communications and informational guidelines

The Occupational Safety and Health Act of 1970 stipulated, among other things, that employees be informed of any hazardous substances or agents in their work environment that are regulated by federal standards and the steps being taken to minimize such threats. Communications for this purpose have taken a variety of forms, the most common being material safety data sheets describing the hazardous properties of materials in use, special precautions and emergency procedures, and warning labels and posters presenting shorthand versions of such information. Lectures, films, and safety pamphlets may elaborate the exposure hazards and their control. The content, style, and mode of these communications directed to workers are frequently based only on concerns for technical accuracy and legal liability. The need to ensure the assimilation and comprehension of such information among the work force at risk is only now being addressed. This is evidenced in part by new directives from the Occupational Safety and Health Administration (1983) calling on employers to develop more comprehensive hazard communication plans. "Right to know" legislation is also pressuring employers to ensure greater worker awareness of work place substances and conditions that could potentially threaten their health and safety (Melville, 1981).

The delayed, insidious health threats posed by exposure to many industrial chemicals and physical agents present formidable obstacles to information efforts aimed at promoting worker understanding of the apparent risks and adherence to work procedures that can reduce them. A current NIOSH project is attempting to furnish guidelines for health risk communications to overcome such difficulties (Cohen, Colligan, & Berger, 1985). In a first stage, ideas for guidelines were extracted from the literature on persuasive communications, behavioral medicine, decision processes, and reading education. Additional inputs were obtained from an ad hoc panel of specialists in these areas plus management and union persons responsible for health education and training in their organizations. Some sample extracts are as follows:

1. Communicating statistics or risk data that refer specifically to the plant work force that is the target for a health information effort should induce a greater worker response than statistics referring to the industry as a whole.

2. Persons in the target audience for a health communications program should be represented in groups planning such efforts. This can alleviate concern over a "presenter" bias. Sources of messages must be trustworthy and authoritative.
3. Comparing the health risks of the work place conditions in question against those arising from other sources could enhance workers' appreciation of the danger and need for action.
4. Tryout and evaluation of ideas, not just expert intuition, is needed to determine which health risk communications are the most effective.
5. Messages informing workers about hazard risk and control options should be separate from those used to motivate worker compliance with protective work practices.
6. People's responses to health threats are highly dependent on their perceptions of personal vulnerability and beliefs about their ability to control outcomes. Hence, messages that provoke fear can provide motivation to act, but only if recommended actions are thought to be effective means of controlling the fear.
7. Methods of ascertaining workers' needs for information about job hazards could include (a) direct observations of their work behaviors to determine whether they deviate from safe practices and (b) verbal questioning of individual workers or groups to clarify their perceptions of risks and determine their appreciation of control measures. (That is, the problem may not be lack of knowledge but lack of motivation.)

These and other ideas have now been cast in the form of suggested guidelines. Two examples of guideline statements are presented below. A third is shown in Figure 14.2, which also contains the supporting material or rationale that will accompany all the guidelines.

Sample suggested guideline: Messages emphasizing potential dangers from work place conditions for motivational purposes must also emphasize actions that can be taken to control or otherwise minimize such threats. High fear arousal produced by messages containing strong, vivid descriptions of work place threats should be accompanied by equally explicit instructions or explanations of control measures known to offer effective protection.

Sample suggested guideline: Messages identifying the presence of agents or conditions exposing workers to health threats should be specific. Particular job operations, job locations, and exposure factors likely to present the greatest risk should be explicitly described and differentiated from those that pose little or no harm.

These guidelines deal with message content issues. Other guidelines concern background preparation (determining the reading level of the affected group, workers' present knowledge and perception of job risk), delivery factors (via respected peers, mailings to workers' homes), and evaluation.

The guidelines reflect much of the current thinking in the communication field regarding health beliefs. One of the critical ideas here is that the audience is not a passive receiver of messages supplied by some expert

GUIDELINE #6: <u>Sources of health hazard and risk data used in constructing the</u> <u>messages must be credible to the target group of exposed workers.</u> Expertise and <u>trustworthiness are critical to this perception.</u> Credible sources may include <u>Governmental agencies charged with protecting worker health and safety,</u> <u>recognized national and international bodies of health researchers and industrial</u> <u>hygienists.</u> Within the work establishment, credible sources may include health <u>and safety committees or company and union health professionals.</u> Local <u>conditions may dictate other forms of attribution or need for endorsements.</u>

Supporting Material

Research in the attitude change literature, in general, and that focussed on health risk issues, in particular, indicates that source credibility can be an important factor in shaping audience response to persuasive messages (McGuire, 1969, 1980; Eagly and Himmelfarb, 1968; Cialdini, et al., 1981). Experiments testing the effects of such factors as source knowledge, experience and/or objectivity towards the information were found to alter the opinions and learning of the audience. The thrust of these findings was that the sources perceived as having more expertise and less to gain from the audience being persuaded caused the most response shifts in the direction of the message's appeal. Information stemming from research scientists and health professionals in governmental programs directed to occupational health and safety concerns would appear to embody these elements through public confidence may not necessarily be high in government officials in general. The company as the composer or originator of material identifying hazards in working conditions can have difficulty in assuring credibility. As they are not a disinterested party to the intent of the message, their communications raise questions about full, factual disclosures. Health risk information representing joint communications from company management and worker interest groups may ease this doubt. For a detailed summary and analysis of source credibility factors in communicating information, see McGuire (1969; 1980). Health risk messages to workers could use issuances, directives, bulletins from the Occupational Safety and Health Administration, National Institute for Occupational Safety and Health, National Toxicology Program, the International Agency for Research on Cancer, the American Conference of Governmental Industrial Hygienists as the basis for defining particular hazards found in their work environs. Joint company/union composed literature referencing the above could serve this purpose within the work establishment.

Key References

Cialdini, R.B., Petty, R.E. and Cacioppo, J.T. Attitude and attitude change. In: Annual Review of Psychology 32, 1981.

Eagly, A.H. and Himmelfarb, S. Attitudes and opinion. In: Annual Review of Psychology 29: 517, 1978.

McGuire, W.J. Attitudes and Attitude Change. In Handbook of Social Psychology (Eds. G. Lindzey and E. Aronson) 2nd Edition, Addison-Wesley Publishing Co., Reading, Mass. 136, 1969.

McGuire, W.J. The communication-persuasion model and health risk labeling. In Product Labeling and Health Risks (Eds. L. Morris, M. Mazis, I. Barofsky) Banbury Rept. No. 6. Cold Spring Harbor Laboratory, Cold Spring Harbor, New York, 1980.

Figure 14.2. Reproduction of Guideline 6 showing format. Prescriptive statement, supporting material, and list of references followed this style in all of the guidelines.

health communicator. Rather, the audience is an active processor of such information, one that perceives and construes threats from its own frame of reference and copes with the danger consistent with its perception and understanding of the risk.

Because the suggested guidelines will require tryout and evaluation to assess their utility, companies will be asked to incorporate them, on a trial basis, in their health information programs for workers. It is envisioned that a company's usual communications plans will be revised in light of the guidelines, with before-and-after evaluations performed to determine the benefits obtained.

Worker participation

Worker participation in company operational planning and decision making has become recognized as a viable means of improving productivity, quality of products, and work motivation (H. Cohen, 1983). That this approach could be extended to hazard control functions seems plausible, especially in work places where safety risks and job accidents are already a concern. Because of their daily job experiences, workers should be intimately aware of many of the hazards connected with their work tasks and should be a rich source of corrective ideas. The adoption of solutions based on worker inputs would be especially effective in reinforcing worker commitment to risk reduction. This rationale was the basis for a NIOSH demonstration study in which an employee-based system of hazard recognition, reporting, and problem solving was tested in a community hospital (Lin & Cohen, 1983).

Data suggesting that health care workers are at high risk of developing illnesses and sustaining injuries were one of the factors supporting the choice of a hospital setting for the study (Patterson et al., 1985). The project methodology involved an initial employee hazard survey. Workers filled out forms indicating their perceptions of unsafe working conditions and procedures encountered in their everyday tasks and giving suggestions for eliminating the hazards. The intent of this survey was to furnish a learning exercise for the work force in hazard recognition and control and also to apprise the hospital management and safety staff of worker knowledge of such problems. The employee-based system was then set into operation. Its basic features included (a) locating hazard report forms at convenient points throughout the hospital complex and, through the activities of a special worker hazard identification group, which became part of the general hospital's safety committee, encouraging workers to fill out the forms; (b) arranging for quick processing and verification of all submitted forms by the hospital safety staff and prompt decisions on corrective actions; (c) providing feedback, at monthly intervals, to all managerial, safety committee, and individual employees regarding hazards detected, corrective actions suggested, corrective actions taken, and the status of corrective actions not yet taken. This feedback, the highlighting of select hazard reports and remedial measures in hospital newsletters, and contacts with worker members of the hospital safety committee were viewed as ways of drawing hospital-wide attention to the employee involvement in such efforts. The intent was to maintain and even increase worker involvement in the system.

Over a 12-month period of evaluation, the hazard reporting rate was one report for every three full-time hospital workers, indicating substantial employee involvement. Although the bulk of this response occurred at the outset of the program, the reporting rate suggested a stable level of participation ranging from 5 to 10 new reports being filed each month from a work force numbering nearly 1,000.

Comparisons of the hazards noted in worker reports and those detected through traditional injury/illness reports for the hospital work force suggested some merits and weaknesses in the participation approach. The overlap between the two sets of reports shown in Figure 14.3 indicated, for example, that the workers have the capability of identifying specific hazards. Where worker reports are particularly numerous, greater information about such hazards and ideas for control actions could provide the basis for preventing future mishaps. In several instances during this demonstration, accident risk factors identified in work reports were not acted on soon enough to prevent the occurrence of an injury soon thereafter.

Figure 14.3 also indicates that some hazards resulting in numerous illness/injury reports were not discernible to the workers. Needle puncture wounds and physical overexertion are particularly notable. Because these mishaps are inherent in routine procedures, their risks may be less obvious than those posed by fixed, physical features in one's work area. Their omission would indicate the need for more employee training in appreciating these kinds of hazards.

More than 80% of the employee suggestions for correcting reported hazards were in fact adopted during the 12-month monitoring phase of this demonstration. A comparison of the injury/illness rate during this period with the rate during the preceding 12-month period indicated a declining rate coincident with the introduction of most of the corrective measures.

The hospital management and the work force were sufficiently pleased with the outcomes of the worker participation project in hazard control to

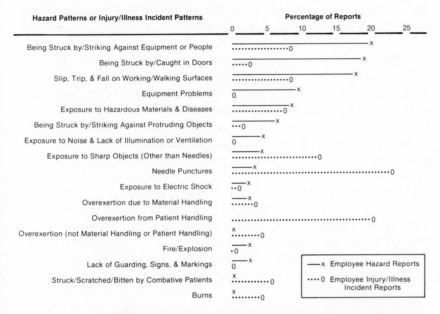

Figure 14.3. Comparison of employee hazard recognition reports and injury/illness incident reports classified by agent or nature of real or potential injuries.

adopt it on a permanent basis. One suggestion for improving the approach was to consider establishing "safety circles," akin to "quality circles," in which workers could participate in problem-solving with regard to certain hazards. Another was to provide them with specific training to improve hazard recognition skills.

Recommendations and other considerations

Earlier in this chapter, eight classes of self-protective behaviors were noted as having potential for reducing hazards at the work place. Acquisition of these behaviors through direct, focused instruction and reinforcement measures has now been described, as have less direct strategies involving attitudinal or dispositional changes. The directive measures, targeting specific behaviors as goals of training and using an array of established learning and contingent reward ideas to effect such changes, seem particularly potent. Proponents of these techniques regard them as a behavior management *technology*. As seen in the field applications, these procedures do require more than the typical training program, especially during the reinforcement and monitoring or evaluation phases of the activity. Still, a single element such as performance feedback would seem only a modest addition to an ordinary job training program and could yield positive results.

Communicating ideas and management-style factors in order to instill consciousness about self-protective needs and actions requires more careful consideration. The volume and variety of job health and safety information imported to workers can be enormous. Yet whether this information is understood and acted on by the intended audience remains questionable. Ideas for enhancing communications dealing with job health and safety risks need greater exposition, application, and evaluative study.

Management's expressed concerns and commitment to work place safety are important factors in marshaling worker interest in hazard control. Allowing workers to become participants in the process has the advantage of generating more information about job hazards than would be found by customary inspection and accident reporting procedures. Formalized roles for workers in a hazard control program, however, might necessitate special training.

Perhaps the best approach to fostering self-protection among workers would be a combination of both directive and nondirective strategies. As conceived, the communications and management-style factors would create a climate favoring safe and healthful worker actions, with the training and reinforcement effecting the emergence and establishment of those behaviors believed most critical.

The training, communication, and managerial approaches described in this chapter capitalize on scientific knowledge developed in different fields having relevance to behavioral safety issues. They stand in contrast to the more traditional formulations, which have been faddish, lacking a sound basis and empirical assessment of their utility in meeting specified health and safety objectives (Goldstein, 1975). The results from the demonstration and evaluation studies presented here auger well for the success of the newer methods. At the same time, the reservations expressed by Robertson in Chapter 13 about the efficacy of informational or educational techniques in getting people to take precautions cannot be understated. The literature contains numerous instances of the failure of mass media and public health instructional campaigns aimed at promoting self-protective actions. The conditions of the work place offer better prospects for realizing improvements in this regard. The worker population is localized and subject to control measures that can be closely monitored. Prescribed acts are repeated and can be regularly reinforced by an alert supervisory staff committed to the maintenance of good safety practices. Moreover, company policy may insist that compliance with safety measures be a condition of employment; hence, those not conforming can be terminated. In effect, the latter represents the equivalent of a law directed at individual worker behavior. Robertson notes that laws requiring observable behaviors are sometimes more effective than persuasive methods.

That there are limits to behavioral approaches to controlling work place hazards also has to be appreciated. Despite the elaborate training and reinforcement provisions of the Hopkins (1981) study mentioned earlier, one of the prescribed practices, the use of respirators, proved difficult to enforce. Evidently, the encumbrance and discomfort of this equipment outweighed the perceived benefits of its use as presented in the training. Similarly, Cohen and Jensen (1984), in using a behavior management strategy to modify the unsafe work practices of forklift truck operators, observed that two prescribed behaviors defied adoption. Later analyses showed that one required an unnatural kind of movement and the other meant exposure to a noxious odor. In such instances, other approaches to hazard control must be taken.

Before concluding, mention must be made of certain new industrial trends that have implications for worker self-protection. Both the work place and the work force in modern, well-developed nations such as the United States are changing. Among the most apparent technical changes are those associated with computer-driven automation in production processes and office operations (Ginzberg, 1982; Giuliano, 1982; Gunn, 1982). Robots on the shop floor and video display terminals in office environments are good examples. Changes in the composition and nature of the work force are reflected by current statistics: The percentage of white collar workers is increasing significantly, whereas the portion of the population engaged in blue-collar jobs is the same or decreasing (Giuliano, 1982). More women have entered the work force, and now assume jobs in mining, construction, and manufacturing that traditionally were held only by men. Also, the mandatory retirement age is being eliminated or set back so that more workers are now remaining employed into their later years. These developments may redefine as well as sharpen issues of worker self-protection against job hazards. The following are illustrative:

1. Although relieving workers from tasks that expose them to high risks of injury or illness, expected forms of worker–robot interaction may present other threats. Servicing and maintenance of robots by workers and the manual mode of robot operation may pose particular problems, given the fact that robot design and engineering are not optimal in terms of human capabilities and function (Salvendy, 1983).
2. White-collar jobs make more cognitive than physical demands on workers, and negative psychosocial factors in the work environment cre-

ate stress. Self-protective actions in this instance entail improving stress-coping skills, which are quite different from the types of behaviors previously addressed (Cooper & Marshall, 1976; Murphy, 1984).

3. Women engaged in work traditionally done by men may require additional self-protective measures. For example, the average woman may not have the strength or size to perform jobs that were originally the province of male workers.

4. Older workers might resist new work place training and other approaches aimed at encouraging self-protection.

These thoughts constitute a beginning agenda for considering future issues of worker safety behaviors.

References

Burton, D. J., Coleman, R. T., Coltharp, W. M., Hoover, J. R., and Vandervort, R. 1980. *Control Technology Assessment in the Secondary Nonferrous Smelting Industry.* DHHS (NIOSH) Publication NO. 80–143. National Institute for Occupational Safety and Health, Cincinnati, Ohio.

Cohen, A. 1977. Factors in successful occupational safety programs. *Journal of Safety Research 9* (4): 168–78.

Cohen, A., Colligan, M. J., and Berger, P. 1985. Psychology in health risk messages to workers. *Journal of Occupational Medicine 27* (8): 543–51.

Cohen, A., Smith, M. J., and Anger, W. K. 1979. Self-protective measures against workplace hazards. *Journal of Safety Research 11:* 121–31.

Cohen, H. H. 1983. Employee involvement: Its implications for work safety. *Professional Safety 28:* 30–35.

Cohen, H. H., and Jensen, R. C. 1984. Measuring the effectiveness of an industrial lift truck operator safety training program. *Journal of Safety Research 15:*125–135.

Conard, R. J. 1983. *Employee Work Practices.* NIOSH Contact Report 81-2905. National Institute for Occupational Safety and Health, Cincinnati, Ohio.

Cooper, C. L., and Marshall, J. 1976. Occupational sources of stress: A review of the literature relating to coronary heart disease and mental ill health. *Journal of Occupational Psychology 49:* 18–28.

Department of Health and Human Services. 1980. *Promoting Health/Preventing Disease: Objectives for the Nation.* U.S. Government Printing Office, Washington, D.C.

Fellner, D. J., and Sulzer-Azaroff, B. 1984. Increasing industrial safety practices and conditions through posted feedback. *Journal of Safety Research 15:* 7–21.

Frederickson, L. (Editor). 1982. *Handbook of Organizational Behavior Management.* New York: John Wiley.

Ginzberg, E. 1982. The mechanization of work. *Scientific American 247* (3): 66–76.

Giuliano, V. E. 1982. The mechanization of office work. *Scientific American 247* (3): 148–66.

Goldstein, I. L. 1975. Training. In *The Human Side of Accident Prevention,* B. L. Margolis and W. H. Kroes, eds., pp. 92–113. Thomas, Springfield, Illinois.

Gunn, T. G. 1982. The mechanization of design and manufacturing. *Scientific American 247* (3): 114–32.

Hopkins, B. L. 1981. *Behavioral Procedures for Reducing Worker Exposure to Carcinogens.* NIOSH Contact Report 210-77-0042. University of Kansas, Lawrence.

Hopkins, B. L. 1983. *An Investigation of the Durability of Behavioral Procedures for Reducing Workers' Exposures to a Suspect Carcinogen.* University of Kansas, Lawrence.

Komaki, J., Barwick, K. D., and Scott, L. R. 1978. A behavioral approach to occupational safety: Pinpointing and reinforcing safe performance in a food manufacturing plant. *Journal of Applied Psychology 63:* 434–45.

Komaki, J., Collins, R. L., and Penn, P. 1982. The role of performance antecedents and consequences in work motivation. *Journal of Applied Psychology 67:* 334–40.

Kryter, K. D. 1970. *Effects of Noise on Man,* Chapters 5 and 6. Academic Press, New York.

Lin, L. J., and Cohen, H. H. 1983. *Development and Evaluation of an Employee Hazard Reporting and Management Information System in a Hospital.* NIOSH Contract Report 210-81-3102. National Institute of Occupational Safety and Health, Morgantown, West Virginia.

Melville, M. 1981. Risks on the job: The worker's right to know. *Environment 23* (9): 12–20.

Millar, J. D., and Myers, M. L. 1983. Occupational safety and health: Progress toward the 1990 objectives for the nation. *Public Health Reports 98:* 324–36.

Morbidity and Mortality Weekly Reports. 1983. *32:* 24–26.

Morbidity and Mortality Weekly Reports. 1984. *33:* 213–15.

Murphy, L. 1984. Occupational stress management: A review and appraisal. *Journal of Occupational Psychology 57:* 1–15.

National Institute for Occupational Safety and Health. 1978. *Good Practices for Employees: Fiberglass Layup and Spray Up.* HEW (NIOSH) Publication 76-158, Cincinnati, Ohio.

National Safety Council. 1984. *Accident Facts,* p. 24, Chicago.

Occupational Health and Safety Letter, November 22, 1985.

Occupational Safety and Health Act of 1970, Public Law 19-596. 91st Congress. U.S. Government Printing Office, Washington, D.C.

Occupational Safety and Health Administration. 1983. Hazard communication. *Federal Register 48* (228): 53280–348.

Office of Technology Assessment. 1985. *Preventing Illness and Injury in the Workplace.* OTA-H-256, Washington, D.C.

Parkinson, R. 1982. *Managing Health Promotion in the Workplace.* Mayfield, Palo Alto, California.

Patterson, W. B., Craven, D. E., Schwartz, D. A., Nardell, E. A., Kasmer, J., and Noble, J. 1985. Occupational hazards to hospital personnel. *Annals of Internal Medicine 102:* 658–80.

Pritchard, J. 1976. *A Guide to Industrial Respirator Protection.* Technical Report (NIOSH) 76-189. National Institute for Occupational Safety and Health, Cincinnati, Ohio.

Rowe, L. 1971. Low back pain: Updated position. *Journal of Occupational Medicine 13:* 476–8.

Salvendy, G. 1983. Review and appraisal of human aspects in planning robotic systems. *Behavioral Information and Technology 2:* 263–87.

Schulte, H. F. 1973. Personal protective devices. In *The Industrial Environment: Its Evaluation and Control.* National Institute for Safety and Health, Cincinnati, Ohio.

Selikoff, I. J., Hammond, E. C., and Churg, J. 1968. Asbestos exposure, smoking and neoplasia. *Journal of the American Medical Association 204:* 106–12.

Sheehy, J. W. 1983. *Occupational Health Control Technology for the Primary Aluminum Industry.* DHHS (NIOSH) Publication 83-115. National Institute of Occupational Safety and Health, Cincinnati, Ohio.

Sleight, R. B., and Cook, K. G. 1974. *Problems in Occupational Safety and Health: A Critical Review of Select Worker Physical and Psychological Factors.* HEW (NIOSH) Publication 75-124. National Institute of Occupational Safety and Health, Cincinnati, Ohio.

Sulzer-Azaroff, B. and de Santamaria, C. M. 1980. Industrial safety and hazard reduction through performance feedback. *Journal of Applied Behavioral Analysis 13:* 287–95.

Swift, R. L. 1975. Personal hearing protective devices. In *Industrial Noise and Hearing Conservation,* J. B. Olishifski and E. R. Harford, eds. National Safety Council, Chicago, pp. 526–49.

Williams, T., Harris, R., Arp, E., Symons, M., and van Ert, M. D. 1980. Worker exposure to chemical agents in the manufacture of rubber tires and tube: Particulates. *American Industrial Hygiene Association Journal 41:* 204–11.

Wyman, C. W. 1969. *Industrial Hearing Conservation: Administration and Human Relations Aspects of Getting Employees to Wear Hearing Protectors.* National Research Council, Chicago.

Zohar, D. 1980. Promoting the use of personal protective equipment by behavior modification techniques. *Journal of Safety Research 12:* 78–84.

Zohar, D., Cohen, A., and Azar, N. 1980. Promoting increased use of ear protectors through information feedback. *Human Factors 22:* 69–79.

Part III

Conclusion

15   Cross-hazard consistencies:
conclusions about self-protective behavior

Neil D. Weinstein

Introduction

A number of general conclusions about self-protective behavior can be distilled from the concepts, programs, and empirical findings described in the preceding chapters. The conclusions do not amount to a complete theory of risk behavior. As Cleary suggests in Chapter 6, no manageable theory could incorporate all the specific features that give different hazards and settings their uniqueness. Nevertheless, there are many cross-hazard consistencies, enough to provide a realistic starting point for the design of prevention programs and for the development of more detailed theories to fit particular situations.

The view of individuals as decision makers striving to weigh the potential costs of taking a precaution against the benefits that may be received is the basis for the most widespread model of self-protective behavior. This perspective is recognized, explicitly or implicitly, in every chapter in this volume (see, especially, Slovic, Fischhoff, & Lichtenstein, Chapter 1). The individual's beliefs about the likelihood and the severity of harm, the efficacy of a precaution, and the cost of acting are the central variables in such risk–benefit decision making. Evidence from investigations of health behavior, crime prevention, and natural hazards preparedness demonstrates clearly that these variables do make a difference.

How, then, do we explain people's failures to adopt precautions that could reduce their risk? Why do so few individuals use automobile seat belts, purchase flood insurance, or adopt low-fat diets? There are four major types of answers to such questions. These answers add other aspects of human nature to our original decision-making model and lead us to a more complex but more accurate picture of preventive behavior.

The first category of answers admits that perceived costs and benefits are important but proposes that people's actions are governed disproportionately by short-term outcomes (e.g., Rogers, Chapter 4). According to this model of human behavior, people are seldom willing to accept costs in the present in order to prevent future harm, especially since, even if they take no action, future harm is only a possibility. Using a seat belt requires that we expend energy each time we enter an automobile, so that, perhaps, we will prevent an injury at some future time. People do not often act in this farsighted manner. Their behavior is governed more strongly by short-term consequences.

The second category of answers emphasizes the difficulty of the decision-making task and our limited cognitive abilities. It stresses the problems we have in making decisions about uncertain risks and uncertain precautions (Kahneman, Slovic, & Tversky, 1982; Nisbett & Ross, 1980; Slovic et al., Chapter 1). Often, people may misunderstand the warnings and the value of the protective measures available and end up making the wrong decision. They may treat low probabilities as if they were zero probabilities, give exaggerated emphasis to outcomes that are certain, and alter their decision when the problem is phrased in terms of lives saved rather than lives lost. Furthermore, most risk situations are complicated. Dependable information about risks and benefits is often unavailable, even to experts. At present, for example, it is not at all clear whether a low-salt diet will really benefit people who do not already suffer from hypertension. Thus, people may fail to act because their analysis of the situation is faulty or because they are unable to decide what to do. They strive to be rational, but the difficulty of obtaining and processing information leads them astray.

Rather than protection motivation, the third group of answers emphasizes the role of social models and explicit social pressures in shaping behavior (McAlister, Chapter 2). Adolescents start to smoke because their peers have begun to smoke, not because they think smoking is safe or because they like cigarettes. No adequate explanation of risk behavior can ignore such issues as social pressures, maintenance of self-esteem, role expectations, and cultural values (Crawford, Chapter 5). One reason for the powerful influence of modeling and imitation on protective behavior is the difficulty people have in deciding what precautions to take. Instead of taking the trouble to gather and analyze relevant information, people often imitate their neighbors, assuming that if the neighbors have, for example, installed a burglar alarm, the risk and value must justify the expense.

The fourth category of answers discussed in the introduction to this book focuses on situations in which the public is quite right in its refusal to act. Prevention advocates often overestimate the value of their recommendations, aiming unrealistically for zero risk. People cannot possibly protect themselves against all the hazards in their lives; they must set priorities. When a physician tells us to wear a sunscreen from April to October in order to reduce the risk of skin cancer (a measure recently advocated by a university researcher), no one needs a sophisticated theory to explain why the public does not comply. People who rationally consider the costs and benefits of various courses of action may conclude that a precaution is simply not worthwhile. Rational decision makers may also fail to change their behavior in situations where experts think change is called for because they doubt their ability to do so (McAlister, Chapter 2). Few cigarette smokers deny the value of stopping, but they feel that they are unable to quit.

With this brief summary of the major forces governing hazard behavior in mind, let us return to the questions posed in the introduction to this book. In the next section we shall explore some of the issues they raise and try to formulate some preliminary answers to the questions themselves.

Some basic questions about protective behavior

Under what conditions are educational approaches unlinked to fear arousal or to positive incentives worthwhile?

Information about risks that draws people's attention and is presented clearly and simply does encourage protective behavior. But the effects are likely to be small when the risk is uncertain or far in the future, or when the precaution requires repeated or difficult action (Rogers, Chapter 4; Robertson, Chapter 13).

Appeals to fear can capture the attention of the audience and also provide information about hazards. They increase the salience of the risk, making it less likely that the threat will be forgotten. Research has found that the effectiveness of fear arousal increases with the strength of the fear appeal (Boster & Mongeau, 1984; Sutton, 1982). There is little evidence that strong fear appeals produce immobilizing anxiety. Nevertheless, the fear produced in prevention campaigns is usually weak and short-lived, incapable of sustaining self-protective behavior.

Most attempts to encourage preventive behavior involve quite low levels of fear because the probability of harm is low or because the threat is located in some unknown future time. (An exception is the level of fear aroused when immediate evacuation during a natural disaster is required). As Averill (Chapter 3) points out, the unpleasant sensations of fear will be weak or absent in such situations, and fear reduction (as distinct from risk reduction) will not be an important motivator of behavior change.

Nevertheless, a different kind of hazard issue is becoming more common, one in which fear levels are very high even though the magnitude of the risk appears to be relatively low. For example, the public seems to be disproportionately concerned, even terrified, about radioactive emissions or toxic substances like asbestos and dioxin. (Slovic et al., Chapter 1, discuss some reasons for the differences in the perceptions of the public and experts concerning risk.) In such situations the problem is the opposite of that implicit in most of this volume. Rather than needing to increase concern in order to encourage protective action, public officials feel obliged to decrease apprehension in order to facilitate communication about risk and to reduce the public's perception that costly protective measures are necessary. The problems of communication and behavior change in high-fear situations have received relatively little attention from social scientists.

Positive incentives – gifts, lotteries, payments – can produce rapid and substantial behavior change if the rewards are large enough, but the changes almost always disappear as soon as the incentives are withdrawn. The problems of observing and promptly rewarding appropriate behavior make incentive strategies difficult to implement except in restricted settings like schools and work places (Cohen, Chapter 14).

Can information about low-probability, high-cost risks be presented in a way that leads people to act?

High-probability risks usually receive sufficient attention unless they are thought to be very far in the future. This volume tends to ignore high-probability hazards because people take precautions against such hazards without special encouragement. In contrast, low-probability, high-cost risks, the implicit focus of most of the research in this book, pose problems. They are hypothetical – that is, people rarely have personal experience with such risks – and protective action is unattractive because it requires a current outlay of money or effort for a questionable future benefit. Below a minimum perceived probability, people may treat risks as zero no matter what the potential cost. Slovic et al. (Chapter 1) discuss the issue of communicating about risk in more detail. One suggestion is to increase the perceived probability of a risk by presenting the risk on a lifetime basis rather than in terms of the probability per year or per exposure. The superiority of this approach has not yet been demonstrated in actual prevention programs.

Is there a consistent tendency to deny or underestimate risk?

Empirical research (Robertson, 1977; Weinstein, 1980; Zakay, 1983) shows that people tend to claim that negative events are less likely to happen to them than to their peers (and that positive events are more likely to happen to them). This unrealistic optimism appears to have several sources (Weinstein, 1984, in press). One is the belief, especially regarding many illnesses, that if the problem has not occurred by a particular age, it is never going to occur. For example, college students mistakenly believe that diabetes is a childhood disease. If they have no signs of it, they think they are not susceptible. Furthermore, whenever a risk is thought to be preventable, such as drug addiction, people tend to believe that they will be more effective than others in avoiding the risk. Surprisingly, no relation has been found between the severity of a threat (e.g., whether or not it is life threatening) and the amount of optimism shown. People do not claim that they are less likely than others to get cancer, apparently because they see this threat as largely uncontrollable.

Are appeals to motives like status, well-being, and financial savings more effective than appeals to self-protection?

The literature suggests that the satisfaction derived from reducing one's risk of experiencing a low-probability, high-cost hazard is not a strong motivator for most people. A gain in status, a feeling of strength and fitness, and financial savings are rewards that are not hypothetical. They can be experienced now. For this reason they can serve as powerful supplements or alternatives to protection motivation in prevention campaigns. In addition, McAlister (Chapter 2) describes how people can be encouraged to reward themselves ("self-reinforcement") for adopting a precaution. Even in self-reinforcement, however, the goal is to translate the appropriate behavior into enhanced self-esteem, not to rely on a direct sense of satisfaction for having adopted the precaution. Whether or not a person gains much self-approval for taking a precaution is linked to relatively deep seated values about individual responsibility and self-improvement that are discussed by Crawford in Chapter 5.

Are people such prisoners of their past experiences that they will not act until they themselves have become victims?

Personal contact with a hazard is a powerful experience. It makes the hazard threat much more salient. If an individual actually experiences harm, any doubts about his or her susceptibility to the hazard are eliminated. Future warnings will bring to mind a real experience, not a hypothetical problem. Nevertheless, the consequences of personal experience are not straightforward. Heart attack victims usually stop smoking (Burling, Singleton, Bigelow, Baile, & Gottlieb, 1984), but the extent to which this change in behavior is due to the attack or to increased pressure from relatives and physicians is difficult to determine. People who have lived through a severe hurricane are more likely to evacuate the next time, but people who experience a mild hurricane are less likely to evacuate (Mileti & Sorensen, Chapter 9). Finally, the data show that drivers who are seriously injured in an automobile accident are *not* more likely to wear seat belts than those who have not been in an accident (Robertson, 1975; Runyan, 1983). Despite these variations, it seems that personal experiences generally incline people to adopt protective behavior. Nevertheless, direct experience is not necessarily a prerequisite for action; people can have a vivid sense of a hazard and be convinced of their vulnerability without having previously experienced harm, even in the case of low-probability, future-oriented threats. Moreover, even personal experience must usually be supplemented with social pressure or other forms of reinforcement if the protective behaviors it triggers are to be sustained.

How important are social pressure and imitation in the adoption of new precautions?

The desire to be accepted and admired is one of the strongest human motives. Prevention programs that include interpersonal contact are usually more effective than programs that provide no opportunity for social influence. Several successful programs in which the staff was carefully selected to maximize social influence are described by McAlister (Chapter 2) and Rogers (Chapter 4). Not only do people act in order to receive praise and avoid blame; they use the behavior of others as a source of information, particularly in ambiguous situations. As mentioned earlier, most hazard situations are highly ambiguous. Information may be unavailable, the relevance of warnings to one's own specific circumstances may be unknown, and the effectiveness of the proposed precaution may be uncertain. In such cases people frequently follow their neighbors, assuming (often incorrectly) that the neighbors have made a careful study of the situation and have chosen the most appropriate response.

*Should more emphasis be placed on group and community
approaches to hazard response and less effort given to the delivery
of risk information to individuals?*

Educating people about hazards and precautions by the dissemination of information through impersonal channels, including such routes as television, newspapers, and mailed brochures, is the method relied on by most risk reduction programs (e.g., Sorensen & Mileti, Chapter 10). It is an inexpensive way of reaching many people, and it requires relatively little planning and expertise. However, it is not a very effective approach unless the threat is strong and the precaution is simple and effective. Often educational campaigns are hardly noticed. The sponsors forget that the public is bombarded with recommendations to buy products, support charities, take precautions, support candidates, and invest their limited time and resources in a thousand different ways. Many of the recipients of the flood plain information brochures described in the introduction to this book could not remember ever having seen them.

Community- and group-oriented approaches have several advantages (Greenberg, Chapter 11; Heinzelmann, Chapter 12). The presence of other people provides an opportunity for social influence: praise or admiration for people who adopt a recommended action and criticism for those who do not act. Groups that deal with community problems are also sources of friendships and recreation. By providing satisfaction unrelated to the hazard itself, group and community programs keep their members committed and thus help to sustain protective behaviors. Furthermore, although few individuals are likely to have had personal experience with a low-probability hazard, it is much more likely that there will be someone in a group who has experienced a problem and can provide the rest of the group with vicarious experience.

We must recognize, however, that few hazards are serious enough to justify the formation of special groups. (Many groups are formed to deal with specific *existing* problems—the long-term effects of a heart attack, alcoholism—but few people are concerned enough with *preventing* a problem to join a special group. (The threat of crime leads people to join organized prevention activities, but this is an exception.) A more feasible means of gaining the advantages of the group or community approach is to link the prevention program to an existing organization—civic, religious, ethnic, professional—that may decide to work on a given problem in addition to its preexisting concerns (Greenberg, Chapter 11; Heinzelmann, Chapter 12). Even community crime prevention programs are more successful and longer lasting if they are part of the agenda of an ongoing organization.

Still, not all prevention programs can be run by community groups. If a hazard operates at the individual level (e.g., home safety or a lifestyle-related health threat), there is no particular need for a group to address the problem. Only individual action is required. The group approach is more likely to be suitable for crime prevention and for natural hazards preparedness (threats in the shared environment) and less appropriate for most health and home safety issues. Nevertheless, part of the power of the group approach is retained if a prevention program uses face-to-face contact to alert people to a risk and to advocate a recommended action. The effective use of individual change agents is described by Rogers (Chapter 4) and Heinzelmann (Chapter 12).

Is individual behavior so difficult to change that we should stop trying to get people to protect themselves and instead attempt to reduce the riskiness of the environment in which they live and work?

This is the question posed by Robertson (Chapter 13), and there are enough examples of unsuccessful prevention programs to make us consider it very carefully. Unsophisticated educational programs are unlikely to lead to the adoption of any but the easiest one-shot precautions. Programs that sustain protective behavior require careful presentation of risk information, using approaches discussed by Cohen (Chapter 14) and by Slovic and colleagues (Chapter 1). Even so, only limited effects should be expected unless a precaution provides additional sources of satisfaction – feelings of fitness and attractiveness, praise from important others, financial advantages, fear reduction, or self-reinforcement. Most of the safety programs described by Robertson do not provide these additional reinforcements. Buckling a seat belt, for example, is usually a solitary action, and seldom provides opportunities for social approval or disapproval. People *will* change their behavior, but not readily. Unless we are prepared to make the effort required to develop appropriate informational materials and to provide sources of reinforcement for taking a recommended action (or punishment for not acting), we should realize that our success will be limited and should emphasize other ways of reducing risk.

The answers given to the preceding questions are the author's and do not necessarily represent the views of the other contributors. They are generalizations that cannot reflect all the idiosyncracies of specific situations.

The conclusions may need modification, and no one should translate them into an actual prevention program without reading the chapters on which they are based. Nevertheless, the fact that they rest on the accumulated knowledge in several hazard fields gives some assurance that they represent robust findings and can serve, as claimed earlier, as a solid starting point for further efforts to understand and encourage protective behavior.

Future directions

We know a great deal about why people take precautions and how to encourage self-protective behavior. Yet this knowledge is seldom displayed in actual prevention programs. In practice, the work of risk assessors – those who measure the concentration of a pollutant, a factory's sound level, or a dam's strength – is much closer to the state of the art than the work of those who design programs to persuade the public to reduce their risk. We have the information *now* to be more effective in encouraging the adoption of precautions.

Discussions among the contributors to this book produced a number of suggestions for correcting common weaknesses in prevention programs. Prevention programs should automatically consider the possibility of collective or group-oriented strategies and, if these are not feasible, an approach that provides opportunities for face-to-face communication. Even the relatively simple step of providing information in a group setting, where group members have an opportunity to discuss the problem, restate the warnings in their own words, and relate the problem to their own experiences, may be better than disseminating warnings directly to individuals.

It is amazing how few information programs tailor their communications to their intended audience. They ignore such basic issues as the norms and values of the audience, its beliefs about the hazard and the precaution, its reading level, and its financial resources. The safety message guidelines being developed by the National Institute for Occupational Safety and Health (Cohen, Chapter 14) suggest several ways in which the audience can be taken into account.

Programs ought to pay more attention to the problem of maintaining an intended behavior and accept the responsibility for providing regular feedback to the public about the success of precautions in reducing vulnerability. Most interventions are not based on a careful consideration of the constraints that individuals face – a spouse who does not cooperate with a low-fat diet, the discomfort of protective clothing in a chemical factory – and how the intervention might help to eliminate these constraints.

Prevention efforts will also benefit from increased attention to evaluation. The naive assumption that people will simply follow "good advice" and take whatever precautions are recommended is still strong and makes it difficult to generate funds for evaluation efforts. We have surprisingly little information about the consequences of most safety, natural hazard preparedness, and crime prevention programs.

Discussions among the contributors also raised many questions for future research. For example, can we identify a limited number of dimensions that can be used to classify hazards? Such dimensions would reflect the ease or difficulty of encouraging the adoption of precautions and the types of intervention strategies that will be most effective. Hazard dimensions that influence risk *perceptions* are described by Slovic et al. (Chapter 1), and this work should be extended to questions of risk *behavior*. The chapters in this volume have already suggested several important features: the likelihood and severity of risk and the number of times a precaution has to be repeated. But such characteristics as the speed of onset of a hazard, whether the hazard is visible to the eye, and others may be equally significant.

The contributors raised a number of other questions: What norms and values have the greatest influence on protective behavior? How are they distributed among population groups? Who are the early adopters of preventive innovations? How influential are the media, our major source of information about hazards, compared with interpersonal contacts (Rogers, Chapter 4)? What specific forms of media messages convey warnings most effectively?

Our ability to detect even small hazards, such as low levels of naturally occurring radiation and earthquake fault lines that have been inactive for hundreds of years, makes us aware of many more risks and makes it more difficult to reach a state where the risk will seem to have been eliminated. Can people learn to live with so many sources of risk? Must feelings of helplessness ("everything causes cancer") develop? How can we communicate information about hazards when levels of fear are high? Does the psychological stress produced by risk information sometimes cause more harm than the hazard itself? When do people fail to act as decision makers and instead deny the existence of a problem or engage in superstitious behavior?

These are a few of the intriguing and challenging questions that require further research. They illustrate clearly the links between the study of self-protective behavior and some important social problems, and they show the potential contribution of this work to our general understanding of human behavior. All these questions will be easier to answer if researchers dealing with different hazards communicate with one another. There are too many shared issues to allow the barriers that have divided one type of hazard research from another to remain. If this volume has shown the value of looking across hazards, the benefits to be gained by thinking in terms of "self-protective behavior" rather than narrower concepts like health behavior and hazards preparedness, then it has achieved its aim.

References

Boster, F. J., & Mongeau, P. 1984. Fear-arousing messages. In *Communication Yearbook 8*, ed. R. N. Bostrom, pp. 330–75. Beverly Hills, CA: Sage.

Burling, T. A., Singleton, E. G., Bigelow, G. E., Baile, W. F., & Gottlieb, S. H. 1984. Smoking following myocardial infarction: A critical review of the literature. *Health Psychology 3:* 83–96.

Kahneman, D., Slovic, P., & Tversky, A. 1982. *Judgment Under Uncertainty: Heuristics and Biases.* Cambridge University Press.

Nisbett, R., & Ross, L. 1980. *Human Inference: Strategies and Shortcomings of Social Judgment.* Englewood Cliffs, NJ: Prentice Hall.

Robertson, L. 1975. Factors associated with safety belt use in 1974 starter interlock equipped cars. *Journal of Health and Social Behavior 16:* 173–7.

Robertson, L. 1977. Car crashes: Perceived vulnerability and willingness to pay. *Journal of Community Health 3:* 136–41.

Runyan, C. W. 1983. Public health policy making: The role of epidemiologic data in decisions about motor vehicle safety. Unpublished doctoral dissertation. Chapel Hill, NC: University of North Carolina.

Sutton, S. R. 1982. Fear-arousing communications: A critical review of theory and research. In *Social Psychology and Behavioral Medicine,* ed. J. R. Eiser, pp. 303–37. New York: Wiley.

Weinstein, N. D. 1980. Unrealistic optimism about future life events. *Journal of Personality and Social Psychology 39:* 806–20.

Weinstein, N. D. in press. Unrealistic optimism about susceptibility to health problems: Conclusions from a community-wide sample. *Journal of Behavioral Medicine.*

Weinstein, N. D. 1984. Why it won't happen to me: Perceptions of risk factors and illness susceptibility. *Health Psychology 3:* 431–57.

Zakay, D. 1983. The relationship between the probability assessor and the outcomes of an event as a determiner of subjective probability. *Acta Psychologica 53:* 271–80.

Index

337